DATE			

Northwestern University
STUDIES IN *Phenomenology &*
Existential Philosophy

Phenomenology and the Social Sciences

Edited by

Phenomenology and the Social Sciences

VOLUME 1

MAURICE NATANSON

NORTHWESTERN UNIVERSITY PRESS

EVANSTON   1973

Copyright © 1973 by Northwestern University Press
All rights reserved
Library of Congress Catalog Number: 72–91001
ISBN 0–8101–0400–8 (Vol. 1)
ISBN 0–8101–0402–4 (Vols. 1 and 2 as a set)
Printed in the United States of America

Maurice Natanson is Professor of Philosophy
and Fellow of Cowell College, University of
California, Santa Cruz.

In memory of
Alfred Schutz

Contents

Preface

A DISTINCTION CAN BE MADE between fixed and mobile anthologies. The former are built out of published essays, work already done. The editor's task is to locate what is available and sort out those pieces he thinks will form a significant whole. The editor of a fixed anthology can face plenty of troubles, but they are of a different kind from those with which the editor of a mobile collection is afflicted. The latter book is based on hope but willed on confidence, for the editor makes a promise to his potential contributor and receives a promise in return. Some risks are obvious, but there is also an underlying danger that is worth at least a passing remark. That danger, as I see it, is that the individual contributors may come through in a satisfying and even heartening way, and yet their performance may still not add up to the patterned unity envisaged by the editor. On the one side, then, we have the relative security of what is set; on the other, the potential hazard of what is envisaged. The present collection is based on an act of faith.

The idea of this anthology is to explore the relationships between phenomenology and the social sciences. Almost all the chapters were written expressly for this venture. I attempted to bring together social scientists as well as philosophers who are either centrally concerned with the problems of phenomenology or who are interested in exploring the intersection of their disciplines with phenomenological philosophy. Some of the contributors are expert phenomenologists, others are quite knowledgeable about certain aspects of the tradition, and still others are exploring its grounds from some distance. I have tried to avoid the kind of professional homogeneity which makes for an insulated conversation between fellow phenomenologists. I have also sought to keep this anthology from being an arena where philosophers lecture to social scientists. By design, the majority of the contributors are social scientists. Finally, I have invited authors to participate who are critical of as well as sympathetic to phenomenology. The result is not a testimonial to orthodox phenomenology but a center for divergent interpretation and debate. To further the ideal of critical variegation, the efforts of two contributors in each field (and three in a few instances) have been enlisted.

The term "phenomenology" is understood here as centered on the thought of Edmund Husserl. However, the essayists were free to interpret phenomenology broadly enough to include such related thinkers as Scheler, Heidegger, Sartre, Merleau-Ponty, and Schutz. The contributors to some sections were encouraged to touch on problems involved in the writings of Hegel, Marx, and Weber. Clearly, the issues faced by a writer in sociology or psychology (fields in which there is a considerable phenomenological literature) are different from those confronted by someone working in economics or linguistics (where relatively little work in phenomenology has been done). Occasionally, an essayist will turn to a conceptual position or movement—linguistic analysis or praxeology, for example—which cannot be counted in the phenomenological camp but which offers a bridge between differing orientations. Invitations to contribute, then, were tendered on the principle of flexibility. That openness extended to the question of the length of individual essays. Each author was given a handsome amount of space in which to present his ideas, yet left free to model his essay along the lines he deemed appropriate to the interior demands of his subject. As the reader will quickly discover, some authors found what was appropriate for them in fairly modestly proportioned essays; others went far beyond the initial boundaries and composed small monographs. The general spatial imbalance of the results is not a defect, in my judgment, but part of our achievement.

I said that almost all of the essays were commissioned for this book. There is one exception and one partial exception. The latter is an essay which I discovered fairly late in the course of putting together this work but which had not been published before. Since the essay was so close to the needs and spirit of the anthology, I decided to include it. The former involves a longer explanation. Originally, two essays were planned for the section on anthropology. The second author withdrew when it was far too late to seek a replacement. In his place, it was decided to include the one "fixed" piece we have, the essay by Merleau-Ponty. No apology is needed for that choice, but the reader may wonder about it and deserves an explanation. Although Merleau-Ponty's essay is not narrowly focused on anthropology, its larger theme is philosophical anthropology. Besides, it offers what I regard as a splendid overview of the problems of the entire anthology. The missing author will probably not disturb the reader as much as his absence irritates the editor. I continue to hope that charitable thoughts toward him will eventually come to me.

This work is published at a time when interest in phenomenology is in the ascendancy, especially in the English-speaking world. One effect of what I take to be the mobile character of this collection is that it will, in its total impact, help to generate further serious discussion and understanding between social scientists and philosophers about fundamental questions of the theory and application of phenomenological principles. These volumes are addressed to university students and their teachers as well as to others outside the academy who, if not eager, are at least genuinely willing to listen carefully to the voice of a new, different, often difficult, but, I think, ultimately rewarding philosophy. There are not absolute conclusions presented here but rather explorative efforts, *essays*.

For myself, however, this work is a kind of conclusion: it is the termination of about five years of labor. Within the microcosm created out of a joint effort of this kind, I and some of the contributors have shared some minor and some major crises (including the untimely death of one of our authors, Professor Friedmann), observed the passing of academic seasons of teaching and sabbaticals, pursued each other through the international mails (the company of our foreign contributors adding varying perspectives to the whole), and emerged, I believe, with some sense of mutual accomplishment and respect. That, at least, is my own feeling.

In a work of this magnitude, the list of individuals who deserve recognition for help is large. I trust that my listing will not sound like a roll call or a receiving line. I do offer my thanks to everyone who has aided in the preparation of this work. In particular, I wish to acknowledge those correspondents who were kind enough to answer questions which I raised about possible contributors: Aron Gurwitsch, Herbert Spiegelberg, Josef L. Kunz, James M. Edie, E. R. Leach, Clifford Geertz, and John W. Chapman among them. Bob Scholte offered a number of extremely helpful suggestions. Joan Hodgson provided bibliographical assistance. Secretarial aid came from Charlotte Cassidy, Phyllis Halpin, and Helen Smith. The director, editors, and staff of Northwestern University Press have given very substantial assistance. I am indebted to them for their understanding and patience. Finally, I wish to pay tribute to Lois Natanson, my teacher in matters of style, for her incorruptible sense of language.

INTRODUCTION

Phenomenology and the Social Sciences

Maurice Natanson

The Nature of Phenomenology

IN 1945 MAURICE MERLEAU-PONTY began his *Phenomenology of Perception* with the question, "What is phenomenology?" And he went on to say: "It may seem strange that this question has still to be asked half a century after the first works of Husserl. The fact remains that it has by no means been answered." [1] A quarter of a century after these remarks, it is possible to suggest that, although Merleau-Ponty's question is still unanswered in any definitive or completely satisfactory way, it has been absorbed into a more philosophically sophisticated pattern of questioning than existed in the forties in social-scientific circles, especially in the English-speaking world. With philosophers, too, there has been developing in recent years a greater sensitivity to the meaning of Husserl's work, a willingness to listen in a new way to the nuances of a phenomenological interpretation of man's involvement in the experiential world. The surface reasons for the change from a large silence regarding phenomenology to the considerable interest in it which now prevails are readily available: the acceleration of translations and commentaries, the continued interest in existential thought and its connections with phenomenology, the convergence recognized by a number of philosophers between phenomenology and certain forms of linguistic philosophy, the

1. Maurice Merleau-Ponty, *Phenomenology of Perception*, trans. Colin Smith (New York: Humanities Press, 1962), p. vii.

[3]

lively concern of students for the insights of phenomenological philosophy, and the recognition in some quarters that each substantial philosophy faculty should be stocked with at least one exotic specimen. In the social sciences as well there has been a noticeable advance, as evidenced by a number of anthologies which give major attention to phenomenologically oriented studies, by symposia at professional meetings, and by a general recognition that phenomenology today represents a distinctive voice in the conversation of social scientists. The deeper reasons for the heightened attention being given to phenomenology have less to do with changes in the academic or the publishing scene than with the nature of philosophical reasoning. Merleau-Ponty's question still needs to be asked but, even more, to be interrogated itself.

To ask what phenomenology is can mean either to inquire into Husserl's philosophical motives or to turn directly to his work and attempt to discern its immanent character and implications. The former leads to a history of Husserl's intellectual career, the latter to a systematic analysis of his philosophy. Obviously, the two are intertwined profoundly, but it is possible to explore them in contrapuntal fashion. As a discipline concerned with the description and analysis of phenomena, phenomenology has always maintained a structural stance with respect to its subject matter; that is, phenomenology is concerned with the essential form of what it investigates rather than with contingent content. Phenomenology's business is with the architecture of phenomena, not the steel and cement of buildings. Accordingly, we may say that one of the prime characteristics of Husserl's thought is its insistence on formal aspects of phenomena. But that statement needs immediate correction, lest it be interpreted as meaning a logic barren of the concreteness of experience. To the contrary, Husserl's logic is one bound to the immediacy of all experience insofar as phenomena are understood as givens in their immediate and irreducible presentative force. Most simply, Husserl is after the formal qualities of the concrete reality which human beings recognize as their experience, but form here means the essential immanent in the particular: the truth of the given. The history of Husserl's development as a philosopher supports the thesis that throughout his life he was, at various levels, searching for an architectonic of thought (and, as we shall see, of consciousness altogether) which would express and uncover the specificity of the world. If the term "logic" be understood in its philosophic sense as a grounding discipline for all reflection, then phenomenology as a logic treats the genesis and development of phenomena from their most primordial roots in prereflective consciousness to their most reflectively sophisticated exemplification in science. If this logic has its delineated objects and its proper methods, why is it necessary to reraise Merleau-Ponty's question?

There are three aspects of phenomenology which may help us to understand the vitality of the question, What is phenomenology? First, the reader coming fresh to Husserl is bombarded with a variety of different phenomenological emphases: the search for essence, the emphasis on the intentionality of consciousness, the methodology of phenomenological reduction, the repudiation of psychologism, the turn to transcendental questions, the radical thematization of the natural attitude, and the celebration of the life-world. How can Husserl be chasing so many hares in one hunt? If we ask what phenomenology is in a searching, genuinely attentive manner, then we may begin to recognize that we can understand essence only by comprehending the status of intentional objects, that intentional objects are rendered available for inspection and analysis by way of reduction, that so long as we restrict ourselves to the psychological origin and actuality of thinking we can never attend to structural features of phenomena, that opening up the phenomenological field is, ultimately, to inquire into the conditions, a priori, for the possibility of there being a field at all, that the mundane world of our daily, taken-for-granted activities itself harbors the most complex philosophic commitments, and that the naïve life we live as common-sense men possesses an infinitely rich logic upon which the whole of reality is founded. In short, all the phenomenological themes listed (and the listing, of course, is not exhaustive) are related to one another in integral fashion. In fact, no one of them can be understood without the others being understood. But, more decisively, the meaning of each of the elements is not static. It is not the rules of chess which Husserl is describing, so that one could say that, unless the moves of all the pieces are grasped, the game cannot be truly understood. Rather, phenomenology is an unfolding dynamic, each thematic element of which shares and matures in the development of the whole. When the interested reader asks, "What is phenomenology?," he wants as straightforward a definition as possible. When Merleau-Ponty raises the question, he is expressing phenomenology's own effort to elucidate its problems. In one sense, then, we certainly know what phenomenology is; in another sense we are refusing to settle for textbook instructions. The stress on the initiative of the phenomenologist, the individual doing philosophical work, leads to our second point.

Phenomenology is a science of "beginnings." The genuine beginner is an adept, not a novice. To begin, in this sense, is to start from the primordial grounds of evidence, from oneself as the center (not the sum) of philosophical experience. Such self-centeredness is the opposite of philosophic *hubris;* it is a confession of humility: the admission that, unless the inquirer has turned to himself in full awareness of his life, he cannot claim to have sought, let alone found, the truth. Philosophy, for Husserl, is inextricably bound to the philosopher in the sense that each inquirer must assess his experience and dare not assume that the traditional problems he has inherited either in the academy or in daily life are properly posed and suitably open to analysis. To *begin* philosophically is to find in a scrupulously self-honest manner a point of genuine access to the problems of philosophy. That manner is itself phenomenologically examined and interpreted. Thus the beginning in philosophizing is not so much a threshold to as the locus of phenomenological work. Husserl writes:

Philosophy, as it moves towards its realization, is not a relatively incomplete science improving as it goes naturally forward. There lies embedded in its meaning as philosophy a radicalism in the matter of foundations, an absolute freedom from all presuppositions, a securing for itself an absolute basis: the totality of presuppositions that can be "taken for granted." But that too must itself be first clarified through corresponding reflections, and the absolutely binding quality of its requirements laid bare. That these reflections become more and more interwoven as thought advances, and lead eventually to a whole science, to a science of Beginnings, a "first" philosophy; that all philosophical disciplines, the very foundations of all sciences whatsoever, spring from its matrix—all this must needs have remained implicit since the radicalism was lacking without which philosophy generally could not be, could not even make a start. The true philosophical beginning must have been irretrievably lost in beginning with presuppositions of a positive kind. Lacking as did the traditional schemes of philosophy the enthusiasm of a first beginning, they also lacked what is first and most important: a specifically philosophical groundwork acquired through original self-activity, and therewith that firmness of basis, that genuineness of root, which alone makes real philosophy possible. The author's convictions on such lines have become increasingly self-evident as his work progressed. If he has been obliged, on practical grounds, to lower the ideal of the philosopher to that of a downright beginner, he has at least in his old age reached for himself the complete certainty that he should thus call himself a beginner. He could almost hope, were Methuselah's span of days allotted him, to be still able to become a philosopher.[2]

In its very nature, phenomenology is self-questioning, and the phenomenologist is, at every stage in his inquiry, raising the question, What is the rigorous and fundamentally warranted way into the characterization of the phenomena? And to pose that question is, in effect, to be asking about phenomenology itself. The genuine beginner is, then, the most sophisticated of all thinkers; for, beyond honoring the Socratic injunction, he is unwilling to admit as taken for granted that which impinges most heavily on his outlook as a man in the world: the root assumption that, though we may be ignorant of philosophic truth, we are, after all, beings in a real world in which philosophic doubt emerges as something worth bothering about. The true beginner does not deny the reality of the world, nor does he place artificial strictures on what honest men accept on faith as the evident character of everyday life; but he does attempt something even more harrowing: the beginner worthy of a science of beginnings attempts to reconstruct his world in the face of a continuing effort to search out the constitutive elements of his own procedure. The phenomenologist, as beginner, will not surrender the question of his own activity.

The problem of beginnings leads necessarily to a third aspect of the nature of Merleau-Ponty's question, that of the point of access of the phenomenologist to phenomenology and of the novice to phenomenology. The difficulty for the uninitiated seems to be his worry that unless he becomes a phenomenologist he

2. Edmund Husserl, *Ideas: General Introduction to Pure Phenomenology*, trans. W. R. Boyce Gibson (New York: Macmillan, 1931), p. 28.

cannot understand phenomenology, yet how can he become a phenomenologist without first having a satisfactory answer to the question, What is phenomenology? If you have to have the answer before you can really understand the question, then what is the point of raising it? Expressed differently, How is the phenomenologist possible? What seems to be a paradox *is* in fact a paradox, though it is meaningful only at a certain level of sophistication. We must distinguish between the rough and fair sense of the would-be phenomenologist's question and that raised by the phenomenologist. The former reduces to this: one learns what phenomenology is step by step, through reading, discussion, and reflection. There is neither a mystery nor a metaphysical puzzle at issue here. The elements of the discipline Husserl inaugurated are not esoteric signs, nor is a talisman of some occult order needed for gaining entrance to the community of phenomenologists. What is needed is rather simple: to learn what is meant by the natural attitude, to practice *epochē*, to attempt descriptions of presentations without prejudicing the results by taking for granted the history, causality, intersubjectivity, and value we ordinarily associate with our experience, and to examine with absolute care the fabric of the world of daily life so that we may grasp its source and its direction.

To suggest that such procedures are "rather simple" may seem like an insult to the serious reader who has struggled with phenomenology. I mean no harm. What I am concerned with showing is that there is no mysterious entrance requirement in first encountering the language and the practice of phenomenology. The serious difficulties begin once one has already read and even comprehended a good deal of Husserl. It is only when the reader has gained some proficiency in approaching and posing phenomenological problems that he can see the distinctively phenomenological difficulties in moving from the reduced sphere to communication in the natural attitude. Language, so deeply affected by and affecting the natural attitude of man in daily life, *is* profoundly problematic as an instrument for reporting faithfully and relaying in trustworthy fashion the characterizations of the phenomenologist seeking to bracket the presuppositions of language. There *is* a legitimate sense in which it is necessary to say that one must become a phenomenologist in order to comprehend phenomenology. The point I would stress, however, is that such a statement must be restricted to its proper level. It cannot be used as a bludgeon to warn off readers interested in studying phenomenology. At the level of Merleau-Ponty's work, let us say, the paradox of the phenomenologist explaining himself to the nonphenomenologist achieves proper statement. Merleau-Ponty's question becomes, in fact, the emblem of phenomenological self-scrutiny.

PHENOMENOLOGY AND THE NATURAL ATTITUDE

PHENOMENOLOGY as a radical philosophical quest arises within the world of ordinary day-to-day activity, yet it is evident that the critique of daily life is a problematic part of what men take for granted in mundane existence. It is not clear that philosophy is "part" of the world at all or that its problems are "in" the experiential world of daily life. The words we have placed in quotation marks are too spatially inflected to give us an accurate account of what it would mean to take philosophical work as a continuous facet of mundane reality. In place of space words we need the vocabulary of a radicalized imagination through which the world and its parts are seen in their constitutive becoming, as features of what is possible for consciousness reflectively concerned with its antecedent, prepredicative condition. The world is already there at any moment that we happen to or choose to think about it, point to it, or gamble on its reliability. What Husserl terms the "natural attitude" is an essential dimension of all possible experiencing in and of the social world. It is an inescapable term of any phenomenological discourse which seeks to interpret man as a social being, and so we must try to be as clear as possible about what phenomenologists mean by it. Husserl's own characterization of the natural attitude (or natural standpoint) may serve as a point of departure for our discussion:

> I find continually present and standing over against me the one spatio-temporal fact-world to which I myself belong, as do all other men found in it and related in the same way to it. This "fact-world," as the word already tells us, I find to *be out there*, and also *take it just as it gives itself to me as something that exists out there*. All doubting and rejecting of the data of the natural world leaves standing the *general thesis of the natural standpoint*. "The" world is as fact-world always there; at the most it is at odd points

"other" than I supposed, this or that under such names as "illusion," "hallucination," and the like, must be struck *out of it,* so to speak; but the "it" remains ever, in the sense of the general thesis, a world that has its being out there.[3]

Within the field of our activities in everyday life certain philosophical matters remain outside the scope of reflection: that there *is* a world accessible to all men; that this world is real; that it is essentially the same for all normal men; that it continues to be itself through the flow of historical time; that the sector of the world we perceive is a reliable clue to those portions we do not now perceive and may never come to know. Problems, puzzles, impasses, and even minor aggravations of day-to-day existence manifest themselves (and are expected to continue to do so) against the backdrop of the continuous texture of everydayness. The problem may be severe and worrisome; the reality within which it turns up to nettle us is taken for granted. To say that such matters are not reflected on means only that they are the grounds on which mundane reflection operates. When man in the natural attitude does think about the basic philosophic contours of his reality, one of two things may be going on: first, he may entertain the idea of the oddness of reality, in the sense in which an employee of the postal service may occasionally ponder the strangeness of mail being delivered at all, of there being a postal system. Such thinking is not so much scattered or fragmented as it is a kind of skimming of reality, for there is no urge or reason to penetrate the momentary insight and explore its underlying implications. Occasional surface reflection in this context is a mode of epistemological dilettantism.

There is a second kind of naïve philosophical musing within the natural attitude which centers on particular problems: the snares of communication, the phenomenon of generational transformation, the deceits of language, or the ephemeral character of life itself. To speak of problems here means that the individual who is "philosophizing" has been led to his reflections by something exploding within his immediate world, whether it be a dramatic failure in trying to express something of great importance in conversation, feeling the impact of suddenly

3. *Ibid.,* p. 106.

finding himself regarded as part of the Establishment, finding out that language can trap him despite his devotion to her, or being hurled into the uncanniness of another's death. In both kinds of reflection, the reflector—man himself—is supported by the familiarity of *the world* turned strange, turned sour, or psychologically decomposed. For Husserl, it is "the world" which hides the more subtle features of philosophical concern, and it is man's believing in "the world" which persists, a granite of common sense which is impervious to anything less than truly radical philosophical analysis.

It would be misleading to separate what we have referred to as "the world" from our believing in it. In fact, the natural attitude reflects a unity of the two. Within the world I act as though its elements, however puzzling they may be, are at least discernible *as* facets of mundane reality. The turn in reflection to an examination of the natural attitude may utilize examples or situations within daily life as a starting point, but they should not be confused with phenomenological analysis. Very often, writers not only in philosophy but in other disciplines will commence the analysis of a theme or will approach a problem by turning to their own concrete situation in space and time at the moment of their reflections. The device is common enough in both literature and science and has the advantage of picking up the reader in the most direct way. It is not necessary to be an expert on the nature of space to follow the author's simple description of where he is writing, nor must the reader have special knowledge about the phenomenological theory of "horizon" in order to be led by the author from what is immediately at hand to the hills beyond. Two examples of what I have in mind can be cited, the first from a social scientist, the second from a philosopher. Kenneth E. Boulding begins his *The Image* this way:

As I sit at my desk, I know where I am. I see before me a window; beyond that some trees; beyond that the red roofs of the campus of Stanford University; beyond them the trees and the roof tops which mark the town of Palo Alto; beyond them the bare golden hills of the Hamilton Range. I know, however, more than I see. Behind me, although I am not looking in that direction, I know there is a window, and beyond that the little campus of the Center for the Advanced Study in the Behavioral Sciences; beyond that the Coast Range; beyond that the Pacific Ocean. . . .[4]

And here is how Alfred Schutz opens his *Reflections on the Problem of Relevance:*

> Having decided to jot down some thoughts on the matter of relevance, I have arranged my writing materials on a table in the garden of my summer house. Starting the first strokes of my pen, I have in my visual field this white sheet of paper, my writing hand, the ink marks forming one line of characters after the other on the white background. Before me is the table with its green surface on which several objects are placed—my pencil, two books, and other things. Further on are the tree and lawn of my garden, the lake with boats, the mountain, and the clouds in the background. I need only turn my head to see the house with its porch, the windows of my room, etc. I hear the buzzing of a motorboat, the voices of the children in the neighbor's yard, the calling of the bird. . . .[5]

In both cases the author is interested in inspecting the matrix of the individual's perceptual world, but he begins with the essential placement of the individual—his here-and-now being. For Boulding, the outlines of being situated in the world of everyday life are sufficient for orienting the reader to his subsequent theme. In Schutz, the effort is to explore in philosophic detail as well as phenomenological depth the nature of the preliminary elements introduced: the meaning of "here" and the ways in which one is motivated to attend to what is not only "there" but what is in the far reaches of what typically concerns man in the natural attitude. The bare recognition of being present in the world is presupposed by the two authors, the first for purposes of establishing an orientation to his topic, the second for distinctively philosophical ends: to achieve a radical stance in terms of which the natural attitude itself can be thematized.

There are, then, at least two senses of being "in" the natural attitude. On the one hand, man naïvely lives his everydayness,

4. Kenneth E. Boulding, *The Image: Knowledge in Life and Society* (Ann Arbor: University of Michigan Press, 1961), p. 3.

5. Alfred Schutz, *Reflections on the Problem of Relevance*, edited, annotated, and with an introduction by Richard M. Zaner (New Haven: Yale University Press, 1970), p. 1.

does his chores, goes to work, enjoys his leisure, dreams his pleasures, and suffers his disappointments. At this level, there is no self-conscious awareness *that* all of this is going on. On the other hand, the individual may indeed think about his being in the business world, at his desk, on the phone, dictating, maneuvering. The second level of awareness involves a separation of a circumscribed activity from its larger relationship to the economy in general, world trade, etc. However, both levels share the same essential identification with the natural attitude, for they build upon what Husserl calls the "general thesis" of the natural attitude: the prereflective believing-in the reality of both the delineated problem and its larger background. It would be proper to speak of an "unconscious" belief as characterizing the natural attitude if only that term had not already been appropriated by psychoanalysis. It may still serve its function, though it might be more prudent to name the mode of belief at issue here a "primordial" intending. Husserl is careful to distinguish between believing in this sense and judging:

> The General Thesis according to which the real world about me is at all times known not merely in a general way as something apprehended, but as a fact-world *that has its being out there,* does *not* consist of course *in an act proper,* in an articulated judgment *about* existence. It is and remains something all the time the standpoint is adopted, that is, it endures persistently during the whole course of our life of natural endeavour.[6]

Believing-in the world, in this phenomenological sense, is the root, I would say, of man's social being. It is the predominant expression of what Santayana called our "animal faith." Indeed, it is above everything else a shared truth: *we* have our grounding in the natural attitude. It is that intersubjective aspect of believing-in which phenomenology seeks to explain. If the causal and psychological history of belief is set aside for present purposes, then believing-in may be approached directly. An illustration of the we-implicated nature of believing-in may be of aid at this point.

Imagine that you are about to board a railroad train for a major trip. As you wait for the arrival of the train on the platform, you look toward the distal section of the track on which the train is to come. Other passengers are there with you, but

6. Husserl, *Ideas,* p. 107.

your attention is riveted on the track, and, secondarily, you are aware also of your luggage nearby. Your ticket is in your jacket pocket, along with your passport, wallet, and some letters. At the first sign of the approaching train, you lean over to bring your suitcases closer to you, your arms and hands tense a bit in anticipation of picking up your things, and at the same time your arm grazes the slight bulge in your jacket, where your ticket is secreted. The voices and bodily movements of the others who are waiting are resonant with your own activities. You and they stand poised now as the train comes to its stop. Together you raise your baggage and move toward the coaches. Mingling with the crowd, you walk toward the guard who waits to check your ticket; and, as you make your way forward, your neighbor's handbag touches yours, the steam from the engine plays about your feet, the giant pull toy rests its weight, and you pause to ascend the coach steps as a workman with a lantern walks on adjacent tracks.

The chief consideration in our example is its intrinsic selectivity, that is, its picking out from a welter of possible attractions certain items of interest and concentration: the railroad station rather than the city which includes it, the platform, tracks, and train pertinent to travel to Knoxville rather than Chicago, and waiting for the express rather than the local. From a terrifyingly large set of possibilities and options, in our example you attend to sectors and pieces of what is available for attention. More than that, you hold on to each experienced bit of the scene with the immanent acknowledgment that it belongs not only to you but to all who wish to concern themselves with any aspect of the scene, those who have business with it: travelers, railroad employees, vendors, or anyone who happens to find himself for whatever reason in this patch of the world at the time. In looking down the tracks, the individual is taking for granted the physical, objective character of the equipment used by the railroad; he assumes that the metal used for the tracks was made by workmen who knew what they were doing, that officials of some kind must have checked and approved the material and workmanship involved, that other equally reliable workmen set the track in place in established and accepted ways, that periodic checks are made by still other individuals to make sure that the track remains in safe working order. Still further, the glance down the track believingly assumes that the same track is there for all of us, that anyone taking a look will see the same thing, even though vision varies among persons and there are all of the obvious differences among us all. Despite everything, what I see and what you see are the same object, the same basic state of affairs involving the parallel tracks going down the line. In perceiving the track, I perceive it as there for us (that is, for anyone choosing to look in the same direction), a "we" of perceptual experience which lies below the threshold of ordinary self-reflective consciousness but which is potentially explicable if we search out the elements which comprise the taken-for-granted in everyday life.

So, too, with the more subtle intendings in our illustration. Anticipating the train's arrival is, I am suggesting, a *social* phenomenon in the deepest sense because the object anticipated is or will be there for the crowd on the platform just as for me. "For me" turns out, in this context, to carry with it a hidden legend which says, "In anticipating the phenomenon, you help to constitute it." Thus the full reality of the platform scene is alive with the perception of *our* situation as persons who are aware of one another more or less, selectors of facets of the total reality within which the scene exists, encouragers of a mutual support in appreciating the unity of objects and events as they are perceived by common-sense men. Of course, all of this falls away if we insist on a psychological account of what the individual members of the crowd are in fact thinking and perceiving as they stand waiting for the train. It is important to recognize that the phenomenological description of the scene does not produce or presuppose anything like a "group mind" or some transcendent entity of coalescing images. Quite to the contrary, it is to the scene in its direct givenness that we turn, a givenness whose structural features interest us. When you look down the track a second or a third time, you are not only seeing the same object but are *returning to* the same object. Within the illustrative context we have followed, it is taken for granted that we may turn again and again to what is given, find it essentially the same, and count on its leading us toward horizonal continuities: the platform, the tracks, the signal tower in the distance, the bridge at the very end of the railroad yard, etc. And in assuming that *we* can return again and again to the same experiential element of what is given, the sociality of intention is assured; for regardless of whether in fact, in terms of the psychoneurological aspect of perception, returning to the same object is possible, the individual believes that he does, that he can, return and that his fellow men are endowed equally with the gift of repetition. As we shall see, the belief in the possibility of return to the same object in perception is, in the language of Alfred Schutz, a way of typifying the world. Such typification is vital to the natural attitude and constitutes a major theme for a phenomenology of the social world.

Phenomenology and Typification

Before abandoning the railroad station, we may point to one further aspect of its character—its typicality. I may never have been in Pennsylvania Station before, but I recognize it as an exemplar of a certain type; I may never have traveled on the Orient Express, but I perceive the engine and cars as members of a general class; I may never have had the occasion to ask directions in the Austerlitz Station, but I know how one goes about seeking information in foreign countries. If I can't find anyone who understands English, I know what to do in order to locate such a person. Both the object of my perception and the modes of perception are grounded in a typifying consciousness. Typification is the blood of daily life. Alfred Schutz writes:

> The factual world of our experience . . . is experienced from the outset as a typical one. Objects are experienced as trees, animals, and the like, and more specifically as oaks, firs, maples, or rattlesnakes, sparrows, dogs. This table I am now perceiving is characterized as something recognized, as something foreknown and, nevertheless, novel. What is newly experienced is already known in the sense that it recalls similar or equal things formerly perceived. But what has been grasped once in its typicality carries with it a horizon of possible experience with corresponding references to familiarity, that is, a series of typical characteristics still not actually experienced but expected to be potentially experienced. If we see a dog, that is, if we recognize an object as being an animal and more precisely as a dog, we anticipate a certain behavior on the part of this dog, a typical (not individual) way of eating, of running, of playing, of jumping, and so on. Actually we do not see his teeth, but having experienced before what a

dog's teeth typically look like, we may expect that the teeth of the dog before us will show the same typical features though with individual modifications. In other words, what has been experienced in the actual perception of one object is apperceptively transferred to any other similar object, perceived merely as to its type.[7]

The social dimension of daily existence—its "we" character —amounts to a sharing of typified constructs and interpretations. That sharing is in turn possible because the specificity of my or your perception of an object is irrelevant to the way in which it is understood or handled for ordinary purposes. The tableware I use in a cafeteria may be more or less aesthetically exciting or noteworthy; but for the purpose of cutting meat and picking it up, any one of the dozens of knives and forks in the box will do. If an old food stain still adheres to one of the spoons, I may set it aside in favor of a clean one; but then, *any* clean one will do. Moreover, I typically assume that the same rough sets of discriminations hold good for you as well. An individual who holds up the cafeteria line by rummaging endlessly among the silver will eventually be asked to move on. If he persists, he may be considered eccentric; and if he tells us that, in the hundreds of soup spoons, one was intended for him alone, we may think him deranged. A child may insist on one ice-cream cone rather than another, but adults ordinarily settle for what is offered.

Throughout, the consideration of the problem of typicality suggests a delimitation on what interests and concerns men in daily life, a motivational curb, a pragmatic motif of sorts. If I am purchasing silver for my home, I may be very involved in inspecting each piece, looking for imperfections or for subtle variances in design and workmanship. In picking up an inexpensive paperback at the bookstore, I may ignore minor smudges or a shaky binding. My inspection of a first edition of *Finnegan's Wake* is a completely different matter. Yet in all of these instances, I recognize the objects as exemplars of their types or classes and treat them, more or less, as substitutable for

7. Alfred Schutz, *Collected Papers*, Vol. I: *The Problem of Social Reality*, edited, with an introduction, by Maurice Natanson and with a preface by H. L. Van Breda (The Hague: Martinus Nijhoff, 1962), pp. 281–82.

each other. And even in cases when the object is exceedingly rare and valuable—the British Guiana "One-Penny Magenta" of the stamp collectors—how I perceive it depends on the typifications I have made not only of the individual phenomenon but of the realm within which it has its value: A magnificent philatelic treasure! or A bit of paper some nuts are willing to pay thousands of dollars for! At both extremes there is nevertheless the recognition that, for stamp collectors, certain items are worth a fortune. Quite apart from the causal conditions which may explain why an individual has a given interest, there is the selective operation through which "any this" is taken as more interesting to a person than "any that." The collector typifies his fellows, expects that any connoisseur will take an interest in a remarkable find, and has no doubt that, for anyone interested in X's, this X will arouse comment. The range of interest must of course be specified. The professional breeder of bulldogs may not take the slightest interest in the family pet of an acquaintance. It is an acknowledged fact among dog-fanciers that anyone you meet knows someone who owns a bulldog. But if that dog has papers, has won best in his class at Madison Square Garden, and is a great grandson of Fearnought-Dreadnought, the breeder will want to have a look for himself. In a way, the limits of typification are themselves typically constituted.

Implicit in the discussion of typification so far has been the assumption that the same phenomenon can be considered again and again in experience and that returning to it means that we may well abandon it for a time and go on to other matters. Also, there is the related assumption that each time I attend to some item of experience I can go on from that consideration to others, to consider other items, and to appreciate the relationships among all items so considered. The typical in this sense is not only what is taken to be generalizable for all men but representable and continuous with the flow of experience outward to typified expectation and typified recall. The fundament of typification for Husserl includes two related idealizations of a logical order, called "and so forth" and "one can always again." These are such odd locutions that we might do well to pause for a moment before going on. "And so forth" is a translation of *und so weiter,* and "one can always again" is English for *man kann immer wieder.* Schutz adapts the terminology by speaking of "and so forth and so on" and "I-can-do-it-again." [8] The first idealization is inspired by mathematics. Husserl writes:

> One can, for example, always have another set, which is excluded from a given set, and join it to the latter by addition: Given any cardinal number, a, one can always form an $a + 1$; and in this manner, starting from 1, form the "infinite" series of cardinal numbers. In the theory of forms of analytic senses, we have none but reiterational laws; in all of them infinity—"always again," "and so forth"—is involved. [9]

We might reduce the terminology to its typificational minimum by substituting "continuity" for "and so forth" and "repetition" for "one can always again," remembering that these are shorthand expressions for the more complex but awkward terminology. What do the idealizations mean?

In the logic of experience, once we see its constitutive dimension, the individual moves from one topic or event to another, related, or thought to be related, to it. The projected relationship may be deeply grounded in history or in nature or may merely be imagined or fancied by the perceiver, but the assumption of continuity between a given phenomenon and its related phenomena undergirds the movement of thought and experience. How does such undergirding operate? The railroad example may serve again. As I anticipate boarding and traveling on my train, I also plan on arriving at an intermediate point where I must change trains. Although I have never before been in Washington, D.C., I know that it is at Union Station that I must make my change. The envisaged series of steps I must take in order to make my connection is present in my mind in typified form: disembarking, getting my possessions off the racks and back on to *a* platform, lugging them to still another platform in all likelihood, perhaps arranging for a porter to carry them if I discover that the distance from platform to platform is great, checking to see whether my new train is waiting, when it can be boarded, *and so forth*. The *et cetera* is a cardinal component of continuity,

8. Alfred Schutz, *Collected Papers*, Vol. II: *Studies in Social Theory*, edited, with an introduction, by Arvid Brodersen (The Hague: Martinus Nijhoff, 1964), p. 285.

9. Edmund Husserl, *Formal and Transcendental Logic*, trans. Dorion Cairns (The Hague: Martinus Nijhoff, 1969), p. 189.

for it points to the open horizon of probabilities which I, as a typical passenger, expect to encounter. Moreover, each element of the continuity has its own open horizon, the details of which are triggered into relief if something unexpected turns up or if one of the possibilities I entertained is given a different slant because of new circumstances. Having disembarked at Union Station, I may find that a wildcat strike has started that morning on the Southern Railroad. For the time being, no trains are running. I may then decide to change my plans and call or wire ahead to let my friends know that they can expect me by plane or bus or that I have resolved to call off my visit. If I choose to rent a car and drive the rest of the way myself, I may have to convince the rent-a-car people that my Swiss driver's license is good in the States, that my personal check is reliable, that my expired credit card still has value, *and so forth.* Any one of these possibilities may lead to an unanticipated but intense inquiry into some facet of my life. In a pinch, a long-distance call may have to be made to my bank to verify my solvency or my identity, but it is taken for granted that such inquiries will proceed in traditional and familiar ways, that the man at the bank will understand what the car agent wants to know, and that, in the end, some resolution of the problem at hand will be possible.

Repetition is related to continuity. Husserl says that "one can always again" is the subjective correlate of "and so forth." [10] The range of application of the idealization of repetition is equal to all possible acts of awareness, reflection, and ratiocination. Whatever continuity brings to the attention of consciousness involves the location and relocation of constituent elements, of identities, which can be grasped, remembered, and imagined or anticipated because the typical or idealized character of their being remains essentially constant. Schutz presents two extremely important and, I believe, helpful illustrations of the idealization of repetition. The first involves the projecting of social action:

> All projects of my forthcoming acts are based upon my knowledge at hand at the time of projecting. To this knowledge belongs my experience of previously performed acts which are typically similar to the projected one. Consequently all projecting involves a particular idealization, called by Husserl the idealization of "I-can-

10. *Ibid.,* p. 188.

do-it-again," i.e., the assumption that I may under typically similar circumstances act in a way typically similar to that in which I acted before in order to bring about a typically similar state of affairs. It is clear that this idealization involves a construction of a specific kind. My knowledge at hand at the time of projecting must, strictly speaking, be different from my knowledge at hand after having performed the projected act, if for no other reason than because I "grew older" and at least the experiences I had while carrying out my project have modified my biographical circumstances and enlarged my stock of experience. Thus, the "repeated" action will be something else than a mere re-performance.[11]

If reading *The Brothers Karamazov* is a repeatable experience, it is because the ideal meaning of the book, its essential themes and interior life, and its dramatic vivacity are never bound to a time-and-place reading. To be sure, I can always turn over the pages of the novel, read it once again in ordinary terms. But the ideality pointed to in repetition goes beyond "mere reperformance"; it signifies the phenomenological realm of essence.

The second illustration of repetition which Schutz offers concerns the placement of the human being as the center of a system of coordinates in which the individual's body defines what is "here" (*hic*) for him in contradistinction to what is "there" (*illic*). Schutz writes:

> By an act of locomotion there came out of my reach what was formerly "world within my reach." The shifting of the center O of my system of coordinates has turned my former world in the *hic* into a world now in the *illic*. But under the idealization of the "I can do it again" I assume that I can retransform the actual *illic* into a new *hic*. My past world within my reach has under this idealization the character of a world which can be brought back again within my reach. Thus, for instance, my past manipulatory area continues to function in my present as a potential manipulatory area in the mode of *illic* and has now the character of a specific chance of restoration.[12]

In addition to what is given directly as "there" at some moment in actual life, there is also the unstated, prereflective, or at

---

11. Schutz, *Collected Papers*, I, 20–21.
12. *Ibid.*, pp. 224–25. Cf. Edmund Husserl, *Cartesian Meditations: An Introduction to Phenomenology*, trans. Dorion Cairns (The Hague: Martinus Nijhoff, 1960), pp. 116 ff.

least tacit recognition that, were I to move from here to there, I would have a new here from which a part of the scene would still be there. Every here as well as every there is repeatable in essential terms. But, more than that, it is assumed that the principle of transformation of perspectives holds good for all men at all times. When the change takes place, moreover, the "there" which has become "here" is the same "there" I now regard as I look back to where I was. I am inclined to suggest that there is only one "here" and but one "there," if we take the meaning of being typically located in the world, rather than where one is geographically, as the index to social placement. In this sense, two bodies can occupy the same "here" at the same time, though for each of them the other is "there"—*the same "there."*

The idealizations of continuity and repetition are fundamental examples of the a priori status of typification in the social world. That experience is possible is, in part, assured by "the individual's" being able to comprehend and return to the *same* element of experience within a horizon of related possible elements. To accept such a prioris, there is no need to deny the facticity of experience or the force of history. The individual is not isolated from the context of society, nor is he free to choose what he wishes to epistemologically, if freedom be interpreted to mean some simple fiat of the will divorced from society. The perspective of phenomenology has quite another orientation: it looks at the social world as a vast achievement of man, and it regards daily life as the complex ground for that achievement. Hence, the quest for typification has a strong realistic motive. *Given* the enmeshment of the individual in the routines of everyday life, how is routine existence itself to be understood? The turn to the a priori follows the drama of actuality and is not an artificial device the philosopher puts together so that what he finds in social life will measure up to his prearranged specifications. Rather than hold that the philosopher or the phenomenologist is primarily responsible for establishing such a prioris, we may with justification say that common-sense men are the first to rely on typification. All—though that is no small achievement—the phenomenologist does is to elucidate and bring to a coherent order that which daily life takes for granted. In this sense, phenomenology is the conceptual conscience of the quotidian.

PHENOMENOLOGICAL METHOD

IT SHOULD BE CLEAR from what has been said so far that the different strands which make up phenomenology retain their identity and do not merge into a timid eclecticism in the face of their mutual tensions as well as sympathies. Even if we think of phenomenology in terms of Husserl, there are several kinds of phenomenology explicit in his work. In fact, it has been said that Husserl thought of "phenomenology" as a proper name for whatever he was doing at the time. A number of schemes have been devised and offered as outlines of the major periods and turning points in Husserl's thought, from his early reflections on mathematics to his last years, devoted to the crisis of Western man.[13] Although distinguishing the Husserl of the *Logical Investigations* from the Husserl of *Ideas* is essential for understanding his developing thought, it does not help us here in trying to gather up the various philosophical aspects of his thought and viewing them under the guise of phenomenological attitude and method rather than the history of phenomenolgy. The interesting fact is that Husserl, his followers, and significant sectors of his philosophical audience today may be said to represent dimensions of philosophical thought which vary radically and which are far from being held in mutual esteem by the full spectrum of thinkers involved. In Husserl we may distinguish between the logician, the descriptivist, the philosopher of intentionality, the transcendental-phenomenological idealist, and the defender of an ultimate rationalism. In his immediate circle of disciples, Husserl was followed in his transcendental phase by only a few. Those who joined the Husserl of Göttingen could not always follow the Husserl of Freiburg. And among the larger readership for his work, we find philosophers who have great respect for Husserl the logician but are quite distant from phenomenological philosophy.[14] So, too, there are those who respect Husserl but are wary of what existentialists have made of

13. See Herbert Spiegelberg, *The Phenomenological Movement: A Historical Introduction*, 2 vols. (The Hague: Martinus Nijhoff, 1960), I, 74–75.
14. See, e.g., Gustav Bergmann, *Logic and Reality* (Madison: University of Wisconsin Press, 1964), Chap. X, "The Ontology of Edmund Husserl."

his ideas. In sum, it would seem that divergent strains in phenomenology threaten to burst the allegiance of resonance which holds them together. Despite appearances, I think that there is a unity in both Husserl's thought and in phenomenology in general which gives it a philosophical momentum and preserves it from doctrinal fragmentation.

It is in the concept of method that the unity of phenomenology will be found. It has been suggested that phenomenological method can be distinguished from the larger philosophical framework of Husserl's later writings and utilized as an organon by philosophers of all philosophical positions, without its taking on imperialistic proportions.[15] If we expand the scope of phenomenology to include other major representatives of phenomenologically oriented philosophy (in a generic sense), such as Brentano, Heidegger, Sartre, and Merleau-Ponty, we may center on the problem of method in a different way: by elucidating basic procedures held in common despite variations in the way they have been conceived and, even more important, deployed. In a discussion of "The Essentials of the Phenomenological Method," Herbert Spiegelberg summarizes the steps he finds to be fundamental in the practice of phenomenology:

1. investigating particular phenomena;
2. investigating general essences;
3. apprehending essential relationships among essences;
4. watching modes of appearing;
5. watching the constitution of phenomena in consciousness;
6. suspending belief in the existence of the phenomena;
7. interpreting the meaning of phenomena.

The first three steps have been accepted, at least implicitly, and practiced by all those who have aligned themselves with the Phenomenological Movement; the later ones only by a smaller group.[16]

What is common to these procedures and what constitutes the impulse of phenomenological method is a way of posing questions

15. See Marvin Farber, *The Foundation of Phenomenology: Edmund Husserl and the Quest for a Rigorous Science of Philosophy* (Cambridge, Mass.: Harvard University Press, 1943), pp. 569 ff., and Farber's *The Aims of Phenomenology: The Motives, Methods, and Impact of Husserl's Thought* (New York: Harper & Row, 1966), Chap. III.
16. Spiegelberg, *The Phenomenological Movement*, II, 659.

and searching for answers. First, there is the recognition that phenomena are immediately given states of affairs rather than empirical posits. Second, it is agreed that attending to the phenomena in both descriptive and analytic terms is the proper task of the investigator. Third, it is accepted that essences are the prime source of philosophical knowledge. Inevitably, a turn to the phenomena (to "the things themselves," in Husserl's words) is an affirmation of the realm of essence as well as an acknowledgment of the distinctive role of phenomenological intuition in the appreciation of essence. Method has at its center the initial recognition of essential intuition as the necessary condition for locating the experiential world that philosophers seek to understand.

The affirmation of essence leaves open the question of the philosophical framework within which intuition operates. The epistemological and ontological issues related to a doctrine of essence which tries to describe and analyze experience remain unresolved. It is here that different interpretations of phenomenology appear. Thus, what is at issue in maintaining the primacy of phenomenological method is not the epistemology proper to fulfilling a rigorous and comprehensive view of experience but the root agreement that any proper epistemology must be built on and *through* the disciplined investigation of phenomena taken in their essential givenness and elaborated in terms of a reflective consciousness. It would be misleading to suggest that the quite different versions of phenomenology which have appeared in the works of Scheler, Heidegger, and Schutz are variants of one method. It is clear that phenomenology appears in the writings of these authors in many ways, for differing purposes, and, sometimes, with ulterior motives.[17] Here it is a question of how phenomenological method has brought some of these thinkers to articulate their problems and programs of inquiry. Nor is it the case that a phenomenologist always does phenomenological work in all of his books or even in all parts of a single book. The emphasis on the commonality of method must be understood correctly: for the phenomenologist, the experienced world is thematized as experience-of, the necessary conditions for "experience-of" are inspected and elucidated, and the

17. See, e.g., Martin Heidegger's Preface to William J. Richardson, *Heidegger: Through Phenomenology to Thought,* 2d ed. (The Hague: Martinus Nijhoff, 1967).

activity of consciousness in relation to its thematizable possibilities is explored. In these terms, serious disagreements within the phenomenological fold may be given due emphasis without dismissing their underlying interconnection and indebtedness to phenomenological method. As Ricoeur has suggested, ". . . in a broad sense phenomenology is both the sum of Husserl's work and the heresies issuing from it." [18]

The specific application of phenomenological method to some of the problems of the social sciences can be seen most explicitly and systematically in the work of two thinkers who have not only pursued actual inquiry in the subject but have discussed the methodological problems involved in phenomenology of the social sciences: Alfred Schutz and Maurice Merleau-Ponty. In turning to their thought, we must restrict ourselves to a severe condensation of their contributions to both methodology and original inquiry related to our present theme. Since we have already introduced some of Schutz's ideas in the discussion of typification, we may turn first to his position.

Although he touches on transcendental phenomenology at certain points in his work,[19] Schutz was chiefly concerned with what he called a phenomenology of the natural attitude carried on at the level of phenomenological psychology. In virtue of what might be called the principle of phenomenological isomorphism, it is possible to find for every distinction located at the psychological level of analysis a transcendental counterpart, "for Husserl himself," Schutz writes, "has established once and for all the principle that analyses made in the reduced sphere are valid also for the realm of the natural attitude." [20] All descriptions made at the psychological level have constitutive roots in transcendental subjectivity, though it does not follow that the phenomenological-transcendental reduction must be employed to make out the eidetic contours of the social world. It is a matter of what one wishes to achieve. Typologies of the kind Schutz offers of the recipes and routines of mundane life do not demand transcendental phenomenology for their expression and efficacy as in-

18. Paul Ricoeur, *Husserl: An Analysis of His Phenomenology*, trans. Edward G. Ballard and Lester E. Embree (Evanston, Ill.: Northwestern University Press, 1967), p. 4.
19. See Alfred Schutz, *The Phenomenology of the Social World*, trans. George Walsh and Frederick Lehnert, with an introduction by George Walsh (Evanston, Ill.: Northwestern University Press, 1967), pp. 43–44.
20. Schutz, *Collected Papers*, I, 149.

formative studies of the natural attitude. However, a full examination of the time structure of the worlds of predecessors, contemporaries, consociates, and successors, as Schutz has developed this theme, does demand transcendental phenomenology if such notions as "anticipation" and "recollection" are to be elucidated in any fundamental way. In a certain sense, there is a pragmatic motive which dictates the practical direction of any philosophical piece of inquiry. What is it we wish to do, to learn, to come to terms with in our study of a given problem? The level of phenomenological work we settle for is a function, in part, of what we are after. With full respect for transcendental phenomenology, Schutz used to say that he had undertaken a more humble task: the phenomenology of the natural attitude. As he well knew, the implications of such a task were enormously demanding and intricate.

There is another aspect of the transcendental to be considered. It is one thing, Schutz held, to pursue the transcendental dimension of phenomenology as a search for the ultimate roots of the constitution of meaning; it is something else to commit oneself to the transcendental as the creative source of intersubjectivity and the social world. There are certain considerations which weigh against empowering the transcendental with a kind of generating force. Husserl, so Schutz believes, had not succeeded in resolving the problem of a phenomenological proof of other selves, nor did he work out his theory of empathy and its connection with understanding in the social world. Beyond that, Schutz maintained that the ultimate foundation of the social lies in a "we-relationship" which is the ground for any phenomenological inquiry and which cannot be constituted by any transcendental source. Indeed, it is in the very concept of "constitution" that much of the trouble lies in trying to understand the possibilities and self-imposed limits of phenomenological philosophy. There is a deeply embedded ambiguity in Husserl's conception of constitution which must be confronted. Schutz writes:

> At the beginning of phenomenology, constitution meant clarification of the sense-structure of conscious life, inquiry into sediments in respect of their history, tracing back all *cogitata* to intentional operations of the on-going conscious life. These discoveries of phenomenology are of lasting value; their validity has, up to now, been unaffected by any critique, and they are of the greatest im-

portance for the foundation of the positive sciences, especially of the social world. For it remains true that whatever is exhibited under the reduction retains its validity after return to the natural attitude of the life-world. But unobtrusively, and almost unaware, it seems to me, the idea of constitution has changed from a clarification of sense-structure, from an explication of the sense of being, into the foundation of the structure of being; it has changed from explication into creation. . . .[21]

In these terms phenomenological method, at all levels of application, can concern itself only with the genesis of meaning, not the establishment of being. The recalcitrant ground for the reconstruction of meaning is the social reality men share in everyday life. Accordingly, Schutz concludes ". . . that the empirical sciences will find their true foundation not in transcendental phenomenology, but in the constitutive phenomenology of the natural attitude." [22]

For Merleau-Ponty, phenomenological method is a process of reconciliation rather than an instrument for restricted descriptive-analytic purposes. What needs reconciling are, at first approximation, the objective world and its subjective interpretation, or, more carefully and subtly understood, the need for reconciliation is based on an effort to reconceive the fullness of the experiential world so that its apparent "exterior" is grasped in integral continuity with its human signification. What we referred to earlier as the principle of phenomenological isomorphism is tacitly invoked by Merleau-Ponty in order to get beneath the surface distinctions of "object" and "subject," of "thing" and "meaning," which have isolated science from philosophy and given nightmares to social scientists trying to remain open to the subjective while retaining their empirical conscience. Phenomenological method as the art of reconciliation tries to bring us back to the unity that always existed between the perceiver and the perceived. Merleau-Ponty writes:

Husserl's great merit is that from the time he reached philosophical maturity, and increasingly so as he pursued his efforts, he made use of his "intuition of essences," "morphological essences," and "phenomenological experience" to mark out a realm and an atti-

---

21. Alfred Schutz, *Collected Papers*, Vol. III: *Studies in Phenomenological Philosophy*, edited by I. Schutz, with an introduction by Aron Gurwitsch (The Hague: Martinus Nijhoff, 1966), p. 83.
22. Schutz, *Collected Papers*, I, 149.

tude of inquiry where philosophy and effective knowledge could meet. We know that he began by affirming, and continued to maintain, a rigorous distinction between the two. Nevertheless, it seems to us that his idea of a psycho-phenomenological parallelism (or as we may say in generalizing, his thesis of a parallelism between positive knowledge and philosophy such that there is for each affirmation of one a corresponding affirmation of the other) leads him in truth to the idea of *reciprocal envelopment*. As far as the social is concerned then, the problem is to know how it can be both a "thing" to be acquainted with without prejudices, and a "signification" which the societies we acquaint ourselves with only provide an occasion for—how, that is, the social can exist both in itself and in us.[23]

The idea of "reciprocal envelopment" tells us more about Merleau-Ponty's view of phenomenological method than it does about Husserl's. The reciprocity involved functions at several levels. There is, for Merleau-Ponty, a primordial bond between the knower and what he knows, between science and philosophy, and between the formal constructions both social scientists and philosophers utilize and the lived experience whose "interior" is the intersubjective intentionality phenomenologists seek to express. What has traditionally been discussed as the fragmentation or at least the separation of the various disciplines—symbolized by Merleau-Ponty's essay title "The Philosopher and Sociology"— has been given a new placement here. The problem is no longer how social scientists can speak to one another or even how social scientists and philosophers can achieve genuine understanding of each other's language and efforts but rather how we can regain the autonomy of the social world, which holds within it both the secret of its nature and the possibility of generating an authentic inquiry into its own being. The presence of philosophy within social reality is first announced in the social scientist's efforts to bring to clarity the basic terms of his own discourse: the meaning of "fact," "event," "cause," "law," and "theory." What the psychologist or sociologist settles for initially in framing his definitions, postulates, and rules of procedure in setting up his system of explanation is paid in philosophical currency. The payment may be explicit or implicit; there may be more or less clarity

23. Maurice Merleau-Ponty, *Signs*, trans. with an introduction, by Richard C. McCleary (Evanston, Ill.: Northwestern University Press, 1964). p. 102.

about philosophical commitments; the social scientist may wince at or greet epistemological questions. Whatever the case, welcome or unwanted, philosophy is flesh of the social scientist's flesh, bone of every theorist's bone. Instead of the man of knowledge continuing to labor under agronomy's image and speaking of "fields," it is time that he reaffirmed the *universe* he interprets. Merleau-Ponty writes:

> . . . philosophy is not defined by a peculiar domain of its own. Like sociology, it only speaks about the world, men, and mind. It is distinguished by a certain *mode* of consciousness we have of others, of nature, or of ourselves. It is nature and man in the present, not "flattened out" (Hegel) in a derivative objectivity but such as they are presented in our present cognitive and active commerce with them. Philosophy is nature in us, the others in us, and we in them. Accordingly, we must not simply say that philosophy is compatible with sociology, but that it is necessary to it as a constant reminder of its tasks; and that each time the sociologist returns to the living sources of his knowledge, to what operates within him as a means of understanding the forms of culture most remote from him, he practices philosophy spontaneously. Philosophy is not a particular body of knowledge; it is the vigilance which does not let us forget the source of all knowledge.[24]

Here phenomenological method becomes translated into the fundamental task of philosophy itself, and the idea of reciprocal envelopment is extended to embrace the whole of social science. The social for Merleau-Ponty becomes the way in which the situational historicity of the individual is lived in both concreteness and universality. If phenomenological method in Schutz's interpretation becomes a way of fulfilling the demands of a constitutive phenomenology of the natural attitude, in Merleau-Ponty's elaboration it is transformed into a philosophy in which the living present reveals its historical as well as structural reciprocity. Both thinkers return us to the problem of method in a new sense, for in reinterpreting Husserl they have renewed the vitality of phenomenology.

24. *Ibid.*, p. 110. Cf. Claude Lévi-Strauss, *The Scope of Anthropology,* trans. Sherry Ortner Paul and Robert A. Paul (London: Jonathan Cape, 1967), pp. 42–44.

THE USES OF PHENOMENOLOGY

IN ADDITION TO there being different interpretations of phenomenological method, there are diverse conceptions of the meaning of its application. Part of the problem in understanding the utility of phenomenology stems from ambiguities in the larger relationship between philosophy and the social sciences; another part arises from more subtle complexities in the very concept of "application." Both parts will receive some consideration here.

It is not necessary to recount the history of the general study of philosophy of the social sciences to remember the mixed character of their relationship. There has been both amity and enmity and, just as often, a combination of the two. The attraction is not hard to appreciate: the disciplines concerned with man as a social being and with the reality he confronts and participates in as a human being involved with fellow men need some conceptual matrix in terms of which they can order their principles and methodology. Philosophy provides a fundamental perspective in terms of which the pieces of the work of the social scientist can be put together into a coherent unity. Quite apart from what his philosophical orientation may be, the philosopher is concerned with what has traditionally been called analysis and synthesis, with clarification of the epistemological and axiological concepts which the social scientist draws upon, and with trying to give some patterned sense to what otherwise might remain piecemeal endeavor. It is hard to oppose order, and it is even harder to refuse to follow one's argument to its final limits. Yet the need and even the desire for philosophical aid carries with it, not infrequently, a hostility for what is not "science," that is, a profound suspicion of theories which move outside the circle of scientific analysis in order to provide its rationale. Perhaps the sense of discipline-dependency is resented. In any case, the suspicion is there, sometimes in blatant form, more often dissembled.[25] It takes on its strongest cast when the philosophy involved is not in

25. In his essay "Phenomenology and the Sciences of Man," reprinted below, Merleau-Ponty writes: "If one took a plebiscite among psychologists to find out what they think of phenomenologists, the result would be, without doubt, humiliating to the phenomenologists" (p. 50).

the empirical or naturalistic tradition. It would be wrong to assume that the social scientist's suspicions are uniformly unfounded and that his reluctance to follow the philosopher is always to be attributed to prejudice and ignorance. Indeed, the same skepticism which serves the scientist in his own work has value in his appraisal of philosophy. He is right to be suspicious, but he is wrong to mistake rigorous doubt for genuine criticism of philosophy. The time is past when philosophical systems can be imposed arbitrarily on the subject matter of the sciences, though it is not true, in my judgment, that a strong case can be made for showing that such impositions were really ever intended by such philosophers as, let us say, Kant and Hegel. But even assuming that the charge of a priori imposition is right to some degree, at least in some instances, it is clear that the temper of modern science will not allow such interference. Yet for some social scientists, phenomenology carries with it the specter of a vicious apriorism. That fear leads us to turn from the general nature of philosophy of the social sciences to the more restricted theme of the phenomenology of the social sciences.

Despite the many expositions of Husserl's thought available today, there are still deeply grounded questions, reservations, and suspicions about its utility. Many social scientists are unconvinced that reliable, intersubjectively warranted knowledge can be attained through the method of what they take to be, if not a solipsistic, at least a deeply introspective philosophy. There is also an unwillingness to recognize the intuition of essences as anything more than another version of private, idiosyncratic, and insulated theorizing. The phenomenologist, in these terms, is a person who asks, "What is the essence of man, of society, of the state?" and proceeds to list dark properties, tricked out in transcendental garb, or else presents a series of generalizations which may be a priori true but are empty of any empirical content or consequence—phenomenological banalities. This attitude reminds me of a comment I remember reading in one of the journals some years ago. All the followers of Husserl have ever done, the author wrote, is to flex their phenomenological muscles. That, at least, sets the problem for us.

Phenomenology cannot present its method or its results in empirically verifiable terms because it does not accept empiricism as an adequate philosophy of the experiential world. Moreover, the phenomena at issue are either presupposed in empirical philosophy or unavailable to its procedures. So, for example, the phenomenologist is deeply interested in the logic of prepredicative experience, in passive syntheses of meaning, in the covert no less than the overt aspect of action, and in the many facets of intentionality which are involved in tracing out the sedimentation of meaning. Empiricism begins where phenomenology leaves off—that is why it is pointless to ask the phenomenologist for some sort of equivalent for empirical verification.

One example must suffice for showing the way in which empiricism presupposes the phenomenological domain. Let us suppose that we are teaching someone to play chess. We begin by explaining the idea of the game and by recounting the moves of the different pieces. The king, we say, can move one square in any direction, though he is forbidden, of course, to move into check. What would happen, then, in a game where only two pieces are left on the board—the two kings? It would be a draw. How can you be certain? If you understand the rules which govern the move of a king and the prohibition of moving into check, then you must see that it is impossible for either king ever to be in a position to capture his opponent's king. Now suppose our pupil is obstinate and insists on trying out all of this on the board. He places the kings in various positions and moves them about, searching for a position in which victory is possible. Is it a question of how long it will take him to realize that a draw is inevitable (setting aside surrealistic encounters in which, given the king-versus-king game, one of the players decides to resign!), or is it not rather a question of what "to realize" means in this context? It might be suggested that realizing here amounts to no more than following a rule. But is the rule comprehended or is it merely followed, in the way in which a high-school student makes a proof in geometry when he knows what he is supposed to do but does not really understand what he is doing? At issue in any teaching and learning is the capacity to see that something is the case; indeed, the primordial demand is the seeing of something. Before we can confirm, we must be directed toward, we must intend, some object. Just as the Law of Identity is fundamental to logic, so it is necessary, in transposed form, in the realm of experience. The phenomenologist is, above all, concerned with the way in which unities of meaning are intended, the genesis of identity and difference, and the formation of a coherent reality in which direct apprehension is the basis for the scientific as well as the mundane world. Empiricism offers no access to these problems; they cannot even be formulated in empirical terms.

If phenomenology moves in a different philosophical direction from empiricism, it does not challenge the legitimacy of empirical work in the sciences. It would be a disastrous misinterpretation of Husserl to think that he sought to replace empirical science with phenomenological science. No such replacement is conceivable because phenomenology and empirical science operate at qualitatively different levels. They relate to but do not contradict each other. At the same time, it is necessary to understand that the relationship between the scientific and the phenomenological is an intimate one, for the phenomenologist, as we have seen, is concerned with the unity of philosophy and knowledge, with the reconstruction of experience in its integrity. In these terms, Husserl maintains that phenomenology can provide a foundation for the conceptual vocabulary and grammar of such a discipline as psychology. But phenomenology is not to be confused with psychology. Husserl writes:

> . . . I may state from the outset most emphatically, in the face of prevailing and far-spreading misinterpretations, *that the pure phenomenology . . . is not psychology*, and that it is not accidental delimitations and considerations of terminology, but grounds *of principle*, which forbid its being counted as psychology.[26]

Properly understood, phenomenology and empirical sciences are coworkers in a many-leveled realm, asking different questions but not always heeding each other's voices.[27] In the end, however, phenomenology claims to be a grounding discipline for psychology because it investigates those questions which transcend empirical science: questions of the philosophical roots of the familiar, everyday world which includes us all.

Whatever the relationship between philosophy and the social sciences, it is assumed that *some* kind of application of the one to the other is possible. Let us grant the fact that philosophers and scientists may squabble about the merit of work in philosophy of the social sciences or even dispute the value of the entire enter-

---

26. Husserl, *Ideas*, p. 42.
27. In the next chapter Merleau-Ponty points out that the blame is not one-sided: "Most of the time phenomenologists have not understood what might be basically convergent with their own inspiration in contemporary psychology" (p. 49).

prise. Still, both sides have accepted the concept of "application" itself; the quarrel is over how good an application has been offered or whether a valid application can be made at all. "Application" itself is not the subject of controversy. I believe that philosophers as well as social scientists have tended to take for granted the meaning of application and in doing so have kept themselves at distance from one of the most fundamental problems of knowledge. In another context I hope to present a more detailed analysis of the issue than can be managed here, but I do wish to touch upon at least a few of the pertinent problems. First, a few essentials: I do not think that philosophers deal with matters of fact; they distinguish matters of fact from other classifications and probe the meaning of "matters of fact" in contradistinction to doing the work of the biologist or the demographer. The history of philosophy would seem to demand some serious qualification to the divorce between philosopher and scientist. There is no doubt that philosophers have been involved quite deeply in work which cuts across artificial boundaries; more important, it would be a mistake to think of Aristotle or Descartes as compartmentalized philosophers when they were concerned with a distinctively scientific problem. Not only were science and philosophy integral in many respects when these men lived, but the problems they investigated remain intertwined. The issue is not one of increased specialization but of regaining an appreciation of the essential unity of philosophy and science which was at the basis of the intersection and overlapping of their spheres of operation. Thus, I interpret the closeness of philosophy and science in both ancient and modern philosophy to be, perhaps paradoxically, a supporting reason for suggesting that philosophy and science have distinctively different work to do. My suggestion falls within the province of philosophical analysis rather than the history of science.

As a first step in clarifying the concept of application, let us say that the model of "applied mathematics" will not help. We are not speaking of a movement from theory, in the sense of a formal body of postulates and rules, to application in the actual world. To the contrary, in phenomenological terms the very opposite is the case: the phenomenologist is concerned with possibility, not actuality. More positively put, philosophical application may be said to move within an orbit which is defined by the continuity between the inquirer and the object of his inquiry. The inquirer theorizes in a priori terms, just as the object of his analysis is not reality but *irreality*. As Schutz expresses it, "phenomenological description does not refer to existence and real experience of existence. Its aim is the investigation of the apodictically posited frame of possibilities within which the empirical realities occur." [28] It would appear, then, that phenomenology moves in a circle: its method and its object are continuous because they constitute the circumference of one mode of pure reflection. If that were so, phenomenology would never be able to get beyond its own intendings. In the simplest terms, what the phenomenologist thinks and what he thinks about would be identical, and tagging the object would merely be one more act of intending it. Of course, all circles are not vicious, and it is important not to relinquish a position because of a geometric slur. Still, if we accept the circularity of phenomenology, we in turn are bound to the thesis that all the intentionality in the phenomenologist's world will never touch, literally come into touch with, a single piece of the real, joy-possible, and death-turned world within which each of us finds himself locked. The logical conclusion of this line of argument is that no application of phenomenology to social science is possible in principle because a discipline concerned with irreality cannot converge with one which deals with fact. The impasse is an artificial one, but it needs further analysis.

There will be a separation of intentionality from reality only if there is first an acceptance of a split between consciousness and being. We are the inheritors of Descartes's metaphysical fission. But the point of phenomenology is to show that the separation was a false one to begin with and that philosophy can heal itself by reapproaching both consciousness and world in integral fashion. At least one part of the healing process involves the recognition that the truth of intentionality brings the inquirer face to face with the naïve world he took for granted in the natural attitude. In the orientation of daily life, we settle for the typical, that is, for the real as it is typically intended. At that level there is no call to arms for the cause of uniqueness. When the unique does arise as a mundane reality, the individual longs for it in its familiar form. The child I mourn for is irreplaceable and

28. Schutz, *Collected Papers*, III, 45.

irreducible to the typification of "a child," yet my sorrowing leads me back to what *my* child did as *a* child. It is through the screen of intention that the individual and the concrete are viewed. How do the unique and my intending of the unique come together? Let us at least say that comprehending the sorrow of a friend is a genuine possibility in human experience. In such comprehension, a friend may comfort us by showing that he does know what this death has meant. Limited to *his* grasp of my world and rooted in his own reality, he does manage to come into touch with a singular event: uniqueness is grasped in the frame of a necessarily typified and typifying alter ego.

The concept of application, to the extent that we have explored it here, is ambiguous in a productive sense. There are some things in philosophy which are not clear, and it is wrong to try to wring clarity out of them in haste. Rather, the uncertainty we are dealing with here may be treated as a philosophical enigma to meditate on and appropriate in a more leisurely manner as philosophers come to appreciate the obdurate nature of their own activity. Some clues have been given, however, in the search for the meaning of application. What appears to be the insularity of phenomenological philosophy is in reality a refusal of Cartesian dualism; what seems to be a qualitative difference between the typical and the unique is comprehensible as a continuity in the structure of mundane existence; and what started as a study of the distance between intentionality and the real world turns out to be an experiential density whose locus is the natural attitude. In fine, the problems of a phenomenology of the social sciences lead us back to that immediate world of experience in which the typifications of daily life find their grounding and rationale in the abstractive power of intentional consciousness. In moving from the abstraction of formal knowledge to the immediacy of the life-world, phenomenology becomes less a particular doctrine than it does the impulse of all radical philosophy, for, as Merleau-Ponty suggests:

> Philosophy is indeed, and always, a break with objectivism and a return from *constructa* to lived experience, from the world to ourselves. It is just that this indispensable and characteristic step no longer transports it into the rarefied atmosphere of introspection or into a realm numerically distinct from that of science. It no longer makes philosophy the rival of scientific knowledge, now

that we have recognized that the "interior" it brings us back to is not a "private life" but an intersubjectivity that gradually connects us ever closer to the whole of history.[29]

PHENOMENOLOGY AND THE LIFE-WORLD

HUSSERL'S CONCEPTION of the life-world—the immediately experienced reality of man as a mundane being—contains within it a number of different though related themes. First, there is the distinction between the character of naïvely lived experience (man in the natural attitude) and the scientific interpretation of that experience. Historically, there has come to be a replacement of man's self-understanding in mundane life by a fundamental abstraction out of recognizable experience into a mathematical-physical formalism whose roots go back directly to Galileo. Second, the meaning of "subjectivity" has been obscured and degraded by the philosophical attitude underlying much of the positivistic and naturalistic interpretation of the social world. Not only has "subjectivity" been made synonymous with the purely psychological sense of individual attitude, it has been made an object for behavioral investigation, the assumption being that the main consideration in the analysis of the subjective is what the observer can make of it. Third, the role of philosophy in reclaiming the domain of the life-world has undergone a pernicious transformation in our time: philosophy, in fact, has lost its position as the discipline committed to wisdom and has instead settled for becoming the spokesman for a world view in which objectivism replaces lived experience and the methodology of the natural sciences becomes the sole claimant to a veridical account of human experience. Finally, with the turn from the truth of subjectivity to the objectivity of a naturalistic view of man a double void appears. On the one side, if a genuine philosophy of the subjective is abandoned, there arises in its place an irrationalism, affectivity unbound, which heralds an attack against philosophy itself; on the other side, the price paid for accepting the logic of the natural sciences as unquestionably the proper instrument for the study of man is the avoidance of the richness of everyday life—its wealth of subtly structured typifications, its remarkable prepredicative organization, and its

29. Merleau-Ponty, *Signs*, p. 112.

history of sedimented meanings which brings to the present the intonations of human continuity.

Not infrequently in discussions of this kind it is said that what was alive and consequential for Husserl in the first third of this century has passed into the antiquarian's domain. The great debate concerning the *Geisteswissenschaften* versus the *Naturwissenschaften* has long since found burial; the positions of "naturalism" and "positivism" which Husserl criticized have been thoroughly reformulated by contemporary thinkers; and the "behaviorism" so strongly attacked by phenomenology is a curiosity of the history of psychology. To these sorts of criticisms, an over-all rejoinder is necessary. The prime consideration in trying to understand any major thinker is that his greatness consists in getting at issues which transcend what has been done in the past six months in learned journals: being current is not identical with being profound. Furthermore, it is easy enough to dismiss a philosopher by insisting that the questions he answers are not those you are interested in raising. Finally, it is necessary to ask whether it indeed *is* the case that the problems at issue in Husserl's time have been abandoned because they have been resolved and whether the philosophical issues involved in behaviorism have evaporated. In the end, it might be suggested that, far from Husserl's ideas being out of date, phenomenology has become the most contemporary of philosophies because it is most faithful to the oldest tradition. For the social scientist, Husserl's message is a simple but devastating one: "Know thyself." The voice of the Delphic oracle is here turned to the scientist in his everyday activity, in the midst of his talking with fellow men, in his hotel room at the convention, in the stream of shoppers, in the center of typicality.

The question must be posed unequivocally: Is there a philosophical problem of intersubjectivity for the sociologist who submits his paper to a professional journal? Is the world of editors, referees, and critics a *social* world? Or is it the case that some segment of social reality turns problematic when the sociologist switches on his desk lamp? Husserl writes:

> Considering ourselves in particular as the scientists that we here factually find ourselves to be, what corresponds to our particular manner of being as scientists is our present functioning in the manner of scientific thinking, putting questions and answering them theoretically in relation to nature or the world of the spirit;

and [the latter are] at first nothing other than the one or the other aspect of the life-world which, in advance, is already valid, which we experience or are otherwise conscious of either prescientifically or scientifically. Cofunctioning here are the other scientists who, united with us in a community of theory, acquire and have the same truths or, in the communalization of accomplishing acts, are united with us in a critical transaction aimed at critical agreement. On the other hand, we can be for others, and they for us, mere objects; rather than being together in the unity of immediate, driving, common theoretical interest, we can get to know one another observingly, taking note of others' acts of thought, acts of experiencing, and possibly other acts as objective facts, without critically assenting to them. Naturally, all these things are the most obvious of the obvious. Must one speak about them, and with so much ado? In life certainly not. But not as a philosopher either? Is this not the opening-up of a realm, indeed an infinite realm, of always ready and available but never questioned ontic validities? Are they not *constant presuppositions* of scientific and, at the highest level, philosophical thinking? [30]

It is in the unquestioned givenness of the life-world for its denizens, including those whose business it is, in professional terms, to analyze problems of the social world, that phenomenology finds the ground of the social scientist's activity. The nature of "role," "status," "position," and "class" may be troublesome for the sociologist, but the world in which his questioning begins includes real men, a shared public world, and languages which permit men to converse with one another in more or less efficacious ways. It is the task of a phenomenology of the social sciences to explore the history of the life-world, to uncover the sedimentation of meaning which accompanies the dialectic of the constitution of sociality, and to trace out the relationships between the constructs of man in daily life and those employed by the social scientist. Ultimately, the phenomenologist is concerned with displaying and illuminating the derivation of scientific abstraction from typification in the mundane sphere. The life-world is held to be the matrix from which all abstractive activity is generated.

From a different standpoint, the importance of the life-world

---

30. Edmund Husserl, *The Crisis of European Sciences and Transcendental Phenomenology: An Introduction to Phenomenological Philosophy*, trans., with an introduction, by David Carr (Evanston, Ill.: Northwestern University Press, 1970), p. 110.

for phenomenology of the social sciences is related to the "crisis of European sciences" which gives part of the title to Husserl's last work. The crisis has many facets. In one way, the acceptance of a formal account of man's social being in place of a rigorous examination of the immediate experiential world he inhabits permits the substitution of what is empirically observable for the way in which the social world is perceived and interpreted by those who constitute the everyday world. The ensuing distance between what is intended by common-sense men and the constructions offered by the social scientists leads to a loss of philosophical coherence: man can no longer recognize himself in the accounts which certain of his fellow men offer of him. In another way, the crisis of which Husserl speaks is the product of a loss of confidence in human reason, a sense that science no longer offers men a productive understanding of human existence, and the feeling that below the conceptual systems of the social scientist there is an inviting swell of passion and sentience which can sweep away the edifice of knowledge. In historical terms, of course, Husserl was thinking out his philosophy of crisis during the convulsion of Nazism and the torment of the years which led to its rise. Taken in this context, the refusal of and retreat from reason amounted to a negation of the meaning of coherence and order in the life-world and a repudiation of any philosophical as well as scientific effort to comprehend mundanity. The sundering of reason from experience, of philosophy from life, is nihilism, for what is denied is the validity of inquiry itself, of consciousness coming into self-responsible clarity. The crisis of Western man consists in the denial of reason and the affirmation of conceptual fragmentation.

But the crisis goes even deeper. Supported by a kind of nominalism of the spirit, those who deny the centrality of reason in historicopolitical terms also abandon the mission of philosophy in its classical form. Nihilists are the "know-nothings" of philosophy, the suicides of Delphi. The kind of nominalism I am speaking of here is one which manifests itself less in programmatic utterances than it does in a refusal to recognize the possible legitimacy of eternal truth, of essential knowledge, and of universal science. In place of the ideal of what Husserl called "rigorous science," primordial apodicticity, there is proclaimed the superiority and even the desirability of patchwork analysis, limited questions posed in restricted ways, in order to achieve partial results. Circumscription is elevated into a new ideal. No indictment of science is intended here, for the problem is not the adequacy of concrete procedures and results in the various sciences but the philosophical nature of the scientific enterprise. Husserl raises his voice in warning against the abandonment by philosophers no less than scientists of their common heritage and ultimate responsibility: the justification and celebration of reason. In Aron Gurwitsch's formulation:

> The crisis of the Western sciences does not concern their technical validity. What is in question is the meaning of the sciences in a philosophical sense and, no less important, their human significance. They familiarize us with facts and their concatenations, with the conditions under which certain facts occur. In a world in which there are merely facts and in which man himself appears as nothing but a most complex fact, there is no room for the norms and ideas of reason. They become unintelligible. Science, it seems, has nothing to say regarding things that matter most for human existence. Hence the growing skepticism, if not hostility, with regard to the sciences extends to reason itself, whose paramount manifestations and creations the sciences are. Losing faith in reason, Western man loses faith in himself.[31]

Philosophy, in these terms, is the discipline of all disciplines, for it calls man back to his own justification. For Husserl, it was the privileged task of phenomenology to remind philosophy of its inner meaning and to return the philosopher to his proper business. Although it may seem a brazen claim to say with Husserl that phenomenology seeks the redemption of philosophy, it is, in truth, the voice of humility which speaks. Husserl is convinced that, amidst the destruction of our time, phenomenology alone can recall man to his philosophical senses, introduce him again to the meaning of philosophy.

The importance of phenomenology for the social sciences is no less forcefully expressed in Husserl's characterization of the sickness of Western man. To the extent to which philosophy is excluded from social-scientific inquiry or relegated to a marginal position, self-reflection becomes impossible and the social scientist cuts himself off from a purview of his own activities. More

31. Aron Gurwitsch, *Studies in Phenomenology and Psychology* (Evanston, Ill.: Northwestern University Press, 1966), p. 400.

and more, social science retreats from any attempt to comprehend man in the actual context of his immediate experience, his life-world. An element of the absurd enters the scene of the sociologist's performance: once the teleological bond between action and justification is severed, the activity of the investigator is reduced to conceptual rubble. It is rather like Camus's image of the man in the glass telephone booth. We see his gesturing, his mouth opening and closing, his facial animation, but we hear nothing. Perhaps, we might say, what appears to be a delightful conversation is an anguished effort to communicate, what seems to be a diversion is business routine; we may be witnessing the act of an informer or a placer of anonymous calls. Cut off from the unity of the conversation as given to both parties, all we have to go on is the surface scene: the jaw working up and down, one hand waving about, sudden thrusts of the head back in what we assume is laughter. Without the reality of the person at the other end of the line and without the microcosm they share, within which the conversation occurs, the phenomenon of the telephone booth would be splintered into absurd bits: the physics of the mandibles, the mechanics of head motion, the calculus of a flickering tongue. In Husserl's image, knowledge divorced from its telos results in the shattering of reason and the deformation of the life-world. The social scientist cut off from his own philosophical roots finds himself a stranger to the life-world.

The return of phenomenology to the life-world completes the circuit of our discussion, for in raising the theme of the crisis of Western man Husserl has sought, in a new way, to present an approach to the meaning of his own philosophy. The subtitle of his last work is "An Introduction to Phenomenological Philosophy." After a long lifetime of phenomenological labor, in which all of his books may be said to bear the same subtitle as *The Crisis*, Husserl still asks himself and his reader, "What is phenomenology?" It should be evident that the force of the question leads us to reconsider the nature of all theoretical inquiry. The many themes we have examined—the natural attitude, typification, method, and the uses of phenomenology—are philosophical adumbrations of one reality, the realm of man seeking his own truth in the truth of philosophy. Phenomenology insists on reraising the question of its own meaning because it knows that initial presuppositions are decisive in all theoretical work. Moreover, self-scrutiny is itself philosophical analysis. Husserl sought for an ultimate foundation on which the edifice of all certain knowledge of the whole of man's experience could be founded. The social sciences are part of that unitary pattern. Taken together, phenomenology and social science are ways of honoring philosophy by reaffirming the privileged station of reason.

PART I

Phenomenology
and Anthropology

Phenomenology and the Sciences of Man

Maurice Merleau-Ponty

INTRODUCTION

IN CONSIDERING THE RELATIONS between phenomenology and the sciences of man, I do not think that I am approaching a mere scholastic problem which would be raised only by certain theses or opinions of a special philosophical school. Since its beginning, phenomenology has been attempting to solve a problem which is not the problem of a sect but, perhaps, the problem of our time. Since 1900 it has concerned us all, and it still concerns us all today. Husserl's philosophical endeavor is basically directed toward the simultaneous solution of a crisis in philosophy, a crisis in the sciences of man, and a crisis in science as such which we have not yet passed through.

The crisis in science is attested by the many studies devoted to the value of science from 1900 to 1905 in France (Poincaré, Duhem, LeRoy, and others). It was to be expected that Husserl, coming to philosophy from scientific disciplines (he began as a mathematician and his first work was a *Philosophy of Arithmetic*), should take very seriously this questioning of dogmatism

Translated by John Wild from students' lecture notes, which had been reviewed by Merleau-Ponty; in 1961 these were circulated in mimeographed form under the title "Les Sciences de l'homme et la phénoménologie" in the "Cours de Sorbonne" series. This translation is reprinted from Maurice Merleau-Ponty, *The Primacy of Perception and Other Essays*, edited by James M. Edie (Evanston, Ill.: Northwestern University Press, 1964). Minor editorial changes have been made in the reprinted text, and information in some of the footnotes has been updated.

concerning the foundations of geometry and physics. His desire to work out a new foundation for the sciences certainly weighed heavily in his decision to pursue a radical investigation in philosophy.

The sciences of man (psychology, sociology, history) also found themselves in a crisis situation. To the extent that it was really advancing, research in these fields was tending to show that all opinion, and in particular all philosophy, was the result of external psychological, social, and historical conditions working in combination. Psychology was tending toward "psychologism," as Husserl called it, sociology toward "sociologism," and history toward "historicism." But in the process they were undermining their own foundations. If, indeed, the guiding thoughts and principles of the mind at each moment are only the result of external causes which act upon it, then the reasons for my affirmation are not the true reasons for this affirmation. They are not so much reasons as causes working from the outside. Hence the postulates of the psychologist, the sociologist, and the historian are stricken with doubt by the results of their own researches.

So far as philosophy is concerned, under these conditions it loses any possible justification. How can one pretend as a philosopher that one is holding truths, even eternal truths, as long as it is clear that the different philosophies, when placed in the psychological, social, and historical frame where they belong, are only the expression of external causes? In order to practice philosophy, in order to distinguish between the true and the false, it is necessary for the philosopher to express not merely certain natural or historical conditions external to him but also a direct and internal contact of the mind with itself, an "intrinsic" truth which seems impossible so long as research in the field of the human sciences shows that at each moment this mind is externally conditioned.

The crisis of science in general, of the sciences of man, and of philosophy leads to an irrationalism. Reason itself appears to be the contingent product of certain external conditions. From the beginning of his career, Husserl recognized that the problem was to give a new account of how all three—philosophy, science, and the sciences of man—might be possible. It was necessary once again to think them through to their foundations. He saw that these different disciplines had entered into a state of permanent crisis which would never be overcome unless one could show, by a new account of their mutual relations and their methods of knowing, not only how each alone might be possible but how all three might exist together. It must be shown that science is possible, that the sciences of man are possible, and that philosophy also is possible. The conflict between systematic philosophy and the advancing knowledge of science must cease.

Husserl raised this problem at the beginning of the century, and he raised it again at the end of his life in 1936 in the last work he partially published: *Die Krisis der europäischen Wissenschaften.*[1] This book is made up of lectures delivered at Belgrade during the last years of his life. The role of the philosopher is here defined in a very striking manner. The philosopher is, he says, "working in the service of humanity," meaning that the philosopher is professionally bound to the task of defining and clarifying the conditions which make humanity possible—that is, the participation of all men in a common truth.

The problem that we shall deal with is not a problem of the history of philosophy in a narrow sense. This would be a question of knowing just what phenomenologists have thought or think of psychology, and just what psychologists have thought or think of Husserl, Scheler, and Heidegger. It would be necessary to present the views of phenomenologists on psychology exactly as they have expressed them and, on the other side, the reactions of the psychologists to these phenomenological theses exactly as found in their writings. Such an enterprise would lead to very confusing results, for there have perhaps never been writers who were further from understanding one another. Most of the time phenomenologists have not understood what might be basically convergent with their own inspiration in contemporary psychology. We shall soon find an example of this in Husserl's criticisms of Gestalt psychology. And on their side the psychologists have been very deficient in their understanding of the phenomenologists.

1. First published in 1939 in Belgrade in Volume I of the journal *Philosophia,* this work has now been published as Volume VI in the *Husserliana* series, *Die Krisis der europäischen Wissenschaften und die transzendentale Phänomenologie: Eine Einleitung in die phänomenologische Philosophie,* ed. Walter Biemel, 2d ed. (The Hague: Martinus Nijhoff, 1962). English translation by David Carr, *The Crisis of European Sciences and Transcendental Phenomenology: An Introduction to Phenomenological Philosophy* (Evanston, Ill.: Northwestern University Press, 1970).

For example, they almost constantly fall into the error of supposing that phenomenology wishes to lead them back to a psychology of introspection. Misunderstandings are so very frequent on both sides that we could never finish sorting them out.

We may grant that our question is indeed a historical question, but only on the condition that we understand by the "history of philosophy" a dialectical history. This means that we shall not develop the ideas of the phenomenologists merely according to the texts but according to their intentions. It is a question here not of an empirical history, which limits itself to the gathering of facts on the one hand and texts on the other, but rather of an "intentional history," as Husserl called it, which in a given assemblage of texts and works tries to discover their legitimate sense. We shall not restrain ourselves from explaining the phenomenological texts by considerations which are not found there in writing. It will even happen sometimes that certain discoveries of the psychologists will help us in interpreting them. Similarly psychology will not be interpreted merely from its express declarations. If one took a plebiscite among psychologists to find out what they think of phenomenologists, the result would be, without doubt, humiliating to the phenomenologists. But we shall seek to discover whether there is anything in the spontaneous development of psychology that is in convergence with the insights of phenomenology correctly understood. We shall not, therefore, restrict our attentions to psychologists who, rightly or wrongly, make some claim to phenomenological knowledge. Rather we shall consider the modern development of psychology and the conditions under which it has occurred. It is in the problems and difficulties it has encountered that we shall find both an influence of phenomenology and a harmony of two parallel investigations into common problems of the time.

In a broad sense our study will be historical. But the perspective on this history will be established by us and by the problems with which we are concerned. Our basic intention is, therefore, just as much systematic as it is historical. At the end, we shall attempt to reinterpret both the meaning of philosophical activity and the conditions underlying a psychology that is truly rigorous.

The history of philosophy can never be the simple transcription of what the philosophers have said or written. If this were the case, we would have to replace the historical manuals of philosophy with the complete works of all the philosophers. As a matter of fact, as soon as one approaches two texts and opposes to them a third, one begins to interpret and to distinguish what is really proper to the thought of Descartes, let us say, and, on the contrary, what is only accidental. Thus in Cartesianism, as it is defined by the texts, one begins to see an intention that the historian has taken the initiative in singling out, and this choice evidently depends on his own way of encountering the problems of philosophy. The history of philosophy cannot be separated from philosophy. There is, of course, a difference between re-flection on texts and the purely arbitrary. But in interpreting these texts, we do not exceed the ordinary rights of the historian if we distinguish what our author has said from what we think he should have said. Let us now say only that the questions we pose to psychology and phenomenology are ours and that they have never been raised in the same words by the authors them-selves.

[1] THE PROBLEM OF THE SCIENCES OF MAN ACCORDING TO HUSSERL

1. *The problem of psychology and the problems of Husserl*

LET US first of all ask how Husserl, the founder of phe-nomenology in the modern sense, understood the sciences of man and their relation to his own research. We need to consider this, of course, not only at the beginning of his thought and in his earlier works but in the development of his philosophy and especially during the last ten years of his life.[2] In commenting on the last works of Husserl we shall indicate briefly how they are related to the investigations of Scheler and Heidegger, to which they are very near and yet from which they are at the same time very far.

Then we shall have to speak of the psychologists and so-ciologists who have expressly recognized their debt to phenom-enology. Many are the psychologists who have done so—for example, Koffka, one of the three principal members of the school of Berlin, and Jaspers, who before becoming a philosopher pub-

2. Some of the works of this period have already been published, and the rest are in the process of being published, in the *Husserliana* series by the Husserl Archives of Louvain under the direction of H. L. Van Breda.

lished a general psychopathology. In this work he recognized expressly, by the very terms he used, the phenomenological origin of his conceptions. Binswanger, the Swiss psychologist and psychiatrist, explicitly states that his works have come forth under the simultaneous or successive influence of both Husserl and Heidegger.

Among us Minkowski has often spoken of the role played by Husserl and also by Heidegger in the formation of his thought. Last year at the Philosophical Institute he gave two lectures on phenomenology and existential analysis which have since been published in the journal *Evolution psychiatrique*.

But we shall not limit ourselves to those authors who have explicitly recognized a debt to phenomenology. We also wish to deal with a diffuse influence that was not always intended by Husserl or recognized by those who experienced it. All that was done in Germany from 1915 to 1920 under the direct or indirect influence of phenomenology was by no means accomplished exclusively in the courses of Husserl.

This diffuse influence was transported to the United States by Koffka, Köhler, Wertheimer, and Goldstein, and the same current is found to be at work there in the revision of behaviorism carried out by American psychologists.

Psychoanalysis, though in many respects it represents a very different mode of thought, has felt these phenomenological tendencies in its recent development. Nothing in the writings of Freud reveals the least knowledge of, or the least sympathy with, the phenomenological literature. But the exigencies of his own problems led him to a dynamic conception of psychoanalysis and elicited from Freud himself a revision of the theoretical framework which he had first used. One can see the joining of these two currents in a psychologist like Lewin, who was strongly influenced by phenomenology.

There will not be sufficient time to complete what we propose to do even concerning psychology. We must pass over the development of sociology, history, and linguistics, though it would be possible and useful to attempt this—perhaps as the subject matter for another course of lectures.

The man who philosophizes believes wrongly that when he thinks and affirms he is only expressing the mute contact of his thought with his thought. He is wrong to proceed as if he were not linked with the surrounding circumstances, for as soon as one considers him from the outside, as the historian of philosophy already does, he appears to be conditioned by physiological, psychological, sociological, and historical causes. His thought appears therefore as a product with no intrinsic value, and what seems to him the pure adequation of his thought, appears to the external critic as a residual phenomenon or a mere result. From the standpoint of a psychologist, a sociologist, or a historian one could therefore conceive of a critique which would consist simply in relating the thought which is considered to its exterior conditioning. Instead of discussing the problems of philosophy by plunging into them, one would do much better to discredit philosophy in general by revealing the historical, social, and physiological conditions on which it depends.

But this process has the inconvenience of turning against the very person who employs it. If "psychologism" says to us that the philosopher and his thinking are only the marionettes either of psychological mechanisms or of an external history, one can always answer that the same holds true of *it,* and thus discredit this criticism. Thus if it is consistent, psychologism becomes a radical skepticism which is skeptical with respect to itself.

"Sociologism" is open to the same consequence. By showing that all our thinking is the expression of a social situation whose limitations prevent it from being *true,* one falls into the danger of proving too much, since sociologism also will bear no true meaning in itself. This can lead to political irrationalism and to political action without criteria. It was against these dangers, as we have seen, that Husserl decided to return to the task of philosopher: to restore certitude and the distinction of the true from the false.

His originality at this point was that he did not oppose psychologism and historicism by simply reaffirming the contrary position which he himself calls "logicism." This attitude admits that beyond the chain of psychological and social causes there is a special sphere, the place of thought in the strict sense of the term, where the philosopher may get in touch with an intrinsic truth. Elevating the sphere of thought in this way brings forth the return of psychologism and sociologism as soon as one perceives that philosophical thinking actually is not without roots.

From the beginning to the end of his career, Husserl tried to discover a way between logicism and psychologism. By a truly radical reflection, which reveals the prejudices established in us by the external environment, he attempts to transform this automatic conditioning into a conscious conditioning. But he never denies that it exists and that it is constantly at work. He notes in a striking way that even philosophy descends into the flux of our experience and that it must itself flow on (*sich einströmen*). Even the thought which pretends to ignore the temporal flux or to dominate it takes place in this flux and descends into it as soon as it is constituted. The philosopher, in so far as he is a philosopher, ought not to think like the external man, the psychophysical subject who is *in* time, *in* space, *in* society, as an object is in a container. From the mere fact that he desires not only to exist but to exist with an understanding of what he does, it follows that he must suspend the affirmations which are implied in the given facts of his life. But to suspend them is not to deny them and even less to deny the link which binds us to the physical, social, and cultural world. It is on the contrary to *see* this link, to become conscious of it. It is "the phenomenological reduction" alone which reveals this ceaseless and implicit affirmation, this "setting of the world [*thèse du monde*]" which is presupposed at every moment of our thought.

What is peculiar to the philosopher is certainly that he considers his own life, so far as it is individual, temporal, and conditioned, as one possible life among many others. But then, by taking account of what it is actually, he may grasp what it might be, considering his own empirical personality as only one possibility in a much larger universe which needs to be explored. But this effort never permanently disregards our links with the physical and human world. We consider these spontaneous theses *ohne mitzumachen*—that is, without ourselves carrying them out at the very same moment. But this is the condition of all thought which claims to be true, and at the end of his career Husserl admitted that the first result of reflection is to bring us back into the presence of the world as we lived it before our reflection began (*Lebenswelt*).

The phenomenological reduction of the link, which is indeed a schism established by life between our thought and our physical and social situation, never leads us in any way to negate time or to pass beyond it into a realm of pure logic or pure thought. One never gets beyond time. Husserl says only that there are many ways of living time. On the one hand, there is the passive way, in which one is inside time and submits to it—being in time

(*Innerzeitigkeit*). On the other hand, one can take over this time and live it through for oneself. But in either case one is temporal and never gets beyond time. Philosophy has been traditionally regarded as the science of eternal truths. If we are to be exact, we should, rather, follow Husserl in the last years of his life and call it the science of the all-temporal, that which holds throughout all time, instead of a truth which would absolutely escape from the temporal order. This is a deepening of temporality. There is no passing beyond it.

Logic is not wrong in considering the laws of our thinking as universally valid. But we need to ask why they are universal and to see how Husserl justifies this. Logicism maintains that when I am concerned with a recognized law and affirm it unconditionally, I am communicating through the center of my being with a pre-personal thought. It founds the universality of logic, therefore, on an absolute right that is derived from its capacity to express the internal structure of the world as it is for a universal thinker. Even in his earliest works, Husserl's procedure of justification is very different. In the first part of the *Logical Investigations* he says that the laws of our thought are for us laws of being, not because we communicate with a pre-personal thought but rather because they are for us absolutely coextensive with everything that we can affirm.

If we wished to suppose other laws of a superhuman thought, either divine or angelic, then in order to find any meaning in these new principles, we would have to bring them under ours, so that to us they would be as nothing. We cannot conceive of them truly as thinkers, except in so far as they conform to the laws of our thought. An angel who would think in accordance with laws radically different from those governing human thought and who would thus cast doubt on these—this angel cannot be thought by me. Hence the universality of thought is not founded on any communication with a universal thinker, the center of all spirits, but simply on the fact that my thinking belongs to me. In order to be sure that a certain thought is a rule for all men and for all being, it is sufficient if I find that it concerns something truly essential, something which cannot be separated from me even in thought.

It is relevant to note here that Husserl goes so far as to say that even God could not have an experience of the world which would not present itself in the manner of our experience as a series of always incomplete profiles.[3] This leads us, therefore, to a phenomenological positivism which refuses to found rationality, the agreement of minds, and universal logic on any right that is prior to fact. The universal value of our thinking has no justifiable foundation in anything independent of the facts. It is founded, rather, on a central and fundamental fact that I myself discover by reflection: the nonsense of anything that violates a principle of thought, such as the law of contradiction or other laws, for naturally the question remains open as to whether we may not arrive at a better formulation of the principles of true logic.

Husserl, therefore, never agreed with a certain philosophical tradition in holding that philosophy could be a system of definitive results never requiring reexamination with the advance of experience. For him philosophy is essentially progressive. As he says in his last years, it is an *infinite meditation;* and one of his better students, Eugen Fink, says that we are here involved in a "situation of dialogue." This means that as long as the philosopher remains within the realms of fact which limit his vision, he will never become a thinker who is universal in all respects. He is always situated and always individuated; this is why he is in need of dialogue. The surest way of breaking through these limits is to enter into communication with other situations—that is, other philosophers or other men. As Husserl stated in his last years, the last subjectivity, philosophical, ultimate, radical subjectivity, which philosophers call *transcendental,* is an *intersubjectivity.*

It is also stated in a passage of the "Nachwort" to the *Ideas* [4] that "philosophy is an idea." Husserl used the word "idea" here in the Kantian sense of a limiting concept to designate a thinking which we cannot properly think through, or totalize, which we envisage only on the horizon of our efforts as the limit of a certain number of thought operations which we are able to perform.

3. The idea of God is used here, as Husserl said in another place, not to introduce a theological affirmation, but as a philosophical index to place the situation of man in better relief.

4. Husserl's "Nachwort zu meinen *Ideen*" was originally prepared as an "Author's Preface to the English Edition," i.e., to the translation by W. R. Boyce Gibson, *Ideas: General Introduction to Pure Phenomenology* (New York: Humanities Press, 1931), pp. 11–33. The "Nachwort" was also published at the same time in German (see below, n. 8), and further references in the text are to the German edition.

"It is an idea which is realizable only in the style of a relative, provisional validity, and in a historical process without end, but which, under certain conditions, is also effectively realizable." [5]

We see, therefore, that what Husserl opposed to the crisis resulting from psychologism and sociologism is not the mere reaffirmation of the old philosophical dogmatism of eternal truths. The philosophical task to which he devoted himself was, rather, the establishment of an integral philosophy which would be compatible with the development of all the different investigations on the conditioning of man. During the whole career of Husserl, therefore, the struggle is on two fronts. On the one hand it is a struggle against psychologism and historicism, in so far as they reduce the life of man to a mere result of external conditions acting on him and see the philosophizing person as entirely determined from the outside, lacking any contact with his own thought and therefore destined to skepticism. But on the other hand, it is also a struggle against logicism, in so far as this is attempting to arrange for us an access to the truth lacking any contact with contingent experience. Husserl is seeking to reaffirm rationality at the level of experience, without sacrificing the vast variety that it includes and accepting all the processes of conditioning which psychology, sociology, and history reveal. It is a question of finding a method which will enable us to think at the same time of the externality which is the principle of the sciences of man and of the internality which is the condition of philosophy, of the contingencies without which there is no situation as well as of the rational certainty without which there is no knowledge.

In short, this enterprise is fairly close to that of Hegel, as is suggested by Husserl's use of the word "phenomenology." In Hegel's sense this is logic of content. Instead of a logical organization of the facts coming from a form that is superimposed upon them, the very content of these facts is supposed to order itself spontaneously in a way that is thinkable. A phenomenology, therefore, has a double purpose. It will gather together all the concrete experiences of man which are found in history—not only those of knowledge but also those of life and of civilization. But at the same time it must discover in this unrolling of facts a

5. Cf. *Ideas*, p. 28.

spontaneous order, a meaning, an intrinsic truth, an orientation of such a kind that the different events do not appear as a mere succession. For a conception of this kind one comes to the spirit only by "the spirit of the phenomenon"—that is, the visible spirit before us, not just the internal spirit which we grasp by reflection or by the *cogito*. This spirit is not only in us but spread far and wide in the events of history and in the human milieu. If it is true that Husserl sought by the study of phenomena to find the roots of reason in our experience, we should not be surprised that his phenomenology ended with the theory of a "reason hidden in history."

Only, with Hegel, phenomenology is merely a preface to logic, so that, at least according to certain interpreters, it is only the introduction to a philosophy which belongs to another order. But if it finally turns out to be a logic which is ruling over the development of the phenomena, the philosopher is doing just what Hegel warns against in his introduction to *The Phenomenology of Mind*. "He is putting himself in the place of consciousness itself, in making up his experiences." With Husserl, on the other hand, it is logic itself which becomes phenomenological. That is, he will not wish to give any other foundation to the affirmations of logic than our actual experience of truth.

For a philosopher of this kind, who desires to be integral, there is no question—as many of us, and above all many psychologists, have believed—of sacrificing science and in particular the science of psychology. On the contrary, Husserl thinks that the reform of psychology for which he is striving will lead to a new development then being retarded, in the psychologism of his time, by an inadequacy of methodological conceptions. In the *Ideas* he speaks of certain criticisms which implied that his investigations had been meant to replace psychological research. "I have protested against this conception," he says, "without any success, it seems." The explanations that

I have added have not been understood, and have been rejected without careful examination. Instead of answering the simple sense of my demonstration, this criticism of psychological methods has merely been dismissed. It never questioned the value of modern psychology. It never rejected the experimental work of eminent men. It pointed out certain radical weaknesses in method, in the literal sense of this word. In correcting them, psychology must be elevated, in my opinion, to a higher level of scientific certitude, and must vastly enlarge its field of work. I shall add a few words elsewhere on the way in which psychology has been very inadequately defended against these supposed attacks of mine.[6]

Husserl, therefore, is not opposed to a scientific psychology. He simply believes that the existence and development of such a psychology raise certain philosophical problems, the solutions of which are relevant to psychology itself if it is to advance. In the light of the situation at the time when Husserl was writing, the problem was this: there seemed to be a conflict between the needs of philosophy, considered as pure rational interiority, and the needs of a psychology considered as the science of the external determination of human conduct.

How, then, does Husserl face this difficulty? He must find a way of knowing which is neither deductive nor purely empirical. This knowledge must not be purely conceptual in detaching itself from facts. Nevertheless it must be philosophical, or at least it must not make the existence of a philosophizing subject impossible. It is essential that our life should not be reduced exclusively to psychological events and that in and through these events there should be revealed a meaning which is irreducible to these particularities. This emergence of truth in and through the psychological event is what Husserl called *Wesensschau,* the intuition of essences.

In defending Husserl against the false interpretations that are so common, we must emphasize the concrete and familiar nature of this *Wesensschau.* It is a grasping of universal meanings in and through my contingent experience, which is not at all, as Husserl sees it, a peculiar, mystical operation that transports us beyond empirical facts. Thanks to its dual character, at the same time universal and concrete, this *Wesensschau* is capable of renewing and of developing psychology. For anyone who considers them from the outside, the experiences we live through, our *Erlebnisse,* as Husserl calls them, can certainly be socially and physically determined. Nevertheless there is a way of taking them through which they acquire a meaning that is universal, intersubjective, and absolute. But in pursuing this way, I must

6. *Ideen zu einer reinen Phänomenologie und phänomenologische Philosophie* (Halle: Niemeyer, 1928), p. 2. The translation in the text is based on Paul Ricoeur's translation, *Idées directrices pour une phénoménologie* (Paris: Gallimard, 1950), p. 4. Cf. *Ideas,* trans. Gibson, pp. 41–42.

not limit myself to living through the experience; I must grasp its sense, and this is the function of "eidetic intuition."

It is indeed a fact, a simple fact determined by external conditions, that I am going to such and such a concert today and that I am hearing the Ninth Symphony. But I am able to discover inside this experience, as I live it through, something which is independent of the factual conditions which have brought forth my decision. The Ninth Symphony is not enclosed within the time during which I am listening. It appears in the different performances of different orchestras. It is a cultural object which is brought forth under the baton of this director and through the playing of these violinists. But it cannot be reduced to any single performance that one gives of it. Hence if I succeed in bringing out of my experience all that it implies, in thematizing what I have lived through at this time, I come to something which is neither singular nor contingent—namely, the Ninth Symphony in its essence. This orientation of consciousness toward certain "intentional objects," which are open to an "eidetic" analysis, is what Husserl calls *intentionality*.

One can say that, by its antecedent conditions, my consciousness is bound to the contingent events which act on me. But in so far as it envisages certain terminations, in so far as it has a "teleology," in so far as it is concerned with certain cultural entities which are not divided by their different manifestations at different moments of my life or in different minds, it is open to a different kind of analysis. According to Husserl, the seeing of essences, or *Wesensschau*, is nothing but the clarification of the sense, or essence, toward which our consciousness is directed. He says in the *Ideas* that we should give neither a mystical nor even a Platonic meaning to the word *Wesensschau*. It does not involve the use of a super-sensible faculty absolutely strange to our experience and exercised only under exceptional conditions. *Wesensschau* is constant, he says, even in a life that conforms most closely to the natural attitude.

The insight into essences rests simply on the fact that in our experience we can distinguish *the fact that* we are living through something from *what it is* we are living through in this fact. It is by this vision that Husserl tries to find a way between psychologism and logicism and to bring forth a reform of psychology. In so far as the essence is to be grasped through a lived experience, it is concrete knowledge. But in so far as I grasp something through this experience which is more than a contingent fact, an intelligible structure that imposes itself on me whenever I think of the intentional object in question, I gain another kind of knowledge. I am then not enclosed in the particularity of my individual life, and I attain an insight which holds for all men.

I get beyond my singularity not in so far as my consciousness is merely a series of facts or events but in so far as these events have a sense. The intuition of essences is simply a regaining of this sense, which is not thematized in our spontaneous, unreflective experience.

[2] HUSSERL'S CONCEPTION OF AN EIDETIC PSYCHOLOGY

1. *The problem of eidetic psychology up to the* Ideas

IF ONE examines the *Philosophie der Arithmetik*,[7] the first work of Husserl, one must take account of the fact that at this moment the author had just left mathematics for philosophy. Having found the logicist conceptions of mathematics insufficient, he now proposed to found arithmetical operations on psychological acts, and he defined phenomenology as "descriptive psychology." Later on he renounced this conception because it led to psychologism, and interpreted basic notions of our thought —numbers, for example—as simple attributes of a psychological nature. In brief, he perceived at the beginning of his philosophical career that it was necessary to return to consciousness. One must look for the sense of mathematical concepts in the life of consciousness on which they rest.

But he did not understand this consciousness, to which he was returning as a philosopher, in the right way. He was opposing it to the world as one region to another. Later on he saw that this consciousness, on which the operations of logic are founded, is not merely a part of being but the source from which all being can receive its sense and its value of being for us. It is, in fact, the correlate of all being, whatever it may be. Mathematical being, for example, is an intentional correlate of consciousness, and so is the external world. Consciousness is, therefore, co-

---

7. *Philosophie der Arithmetik: Logische und psychologische Untersuchungen* (Halle: Pfeffer, 1891). Now published in *Husserliana XII*, ed. Lothar Eley (The Hague: Martinus Nijhoff, 1970).

extensive with all being of which we can gain any knowledge. Nothing can have the value of being for us if it does not offer its sense to consciousness. The notion of consciousness is now generalized. It is no longer one being among others. It is, rather, the theater of all being and of the transcendental positing of any object.

One is here confronted with a philosophy that seems close to idealism. The formulae of the *Philosophie der Arithmetik* were insufficient because they were too psychological. On the other hand, the later formulae were too Platonic, in the vague and historically controversial sense that one ordinarily gives to this word. It is always between the Scylla of psychologism and the Charybdis of logicism that Husserl steers his course. Let us now define the position he took at the moment when he published the *Ideas*. The famous reduction, which gives us access to phenomenology, is not a mere return to the psychological subject. But even less does it turn our thought away from existence toward essences which would transcend it. This reduction is the decision not to suppress but to place in suspense, or out of action, all the spontaneous affirmations in which I live, not to deny them but rather to understand them and to make them explicit.

By his theory of the "phenomenological reduction" Husserl broke absolutely with every remnant of psychologism in his thought as well as with every remnant of Platonism in his early works. The philosophical *I* is going to withdraw from every condition of fact, as well as from every way of perceiving and understanding them, in order to leave nothing unnoticed. And the task of philosophy will then be to explain, with a complete lucidity, how both the manifestations of the external world and the realizations of the incarnate self are possible. Every intentional object refers to consciousness but to a consciousness which is not the incarnate individual that I am as a man, living at a certain moment of time and in a certain position in space. When I carry out the phenomenological reduction, I do not bring back information concerning an external world to a self that is regarded as a part of being, nor do I substitute an internal for an external perception. I attempt rather to reveal and to make explicit in me that pure source of all the meanings which constitute the world around me and my empirical self.

At this stage of his thinking what, then, was Husserl's view of the situation of psychology in relation to phenomenology?

Psychology, he said, is a science of fact. It is the science of man in the world, facing different situations and responding to them by different types of behavior. Hence it is certainly not to be confused with transcendental, phenomenological philosophy, which, as we have just explained, is a universal reflection that attempts to make explicit and to clarify conceptually all the intentional objects that my consciousness can envisage.

But precisely because it has its own proper region, psychology is not in the position of philosophy. The thesis of psychologism is precisely this: that psychology can take the place of philosophy. But this is impossible because psychology, together with common sense and the different sciences, shares in those convictions concerning being which need to be clarified by philosophy. All of us live in the natural attitude—that is, in the conviction that we are a part of the world and subject to its action on us, which we passively receive from the outside. Psychology accepts this realistic postulate from common sense, and sets up its problems from this point of view. The psychologist tries to see how man works out his responses to certain situations and stimuli, and to discover the laws which rigorously bind together such and such a group of stimuli with such and such a reaction. As Husserl saw it, this is perfectly legitimate, but it simply does not take the place of philosophy. We must not give an ontological value—that is, an ultimate weight—to this way of thinking, for it is naïve and unreflective.

If we actually reflect on our situation, we will find that the subject, thus situated in the world and submitting to its influences, is at the same time he who thinks the world. No world whatsoever is conceivable that is not thought by someone. Hence while it is true that the empirical subject is a part of the world, it is also true that the world is no more than an intentional object for the transcendental subject. Husserl defended this Copernican revolution, as Kant called it, which defined philosophy by its opposition to psychology up to the very end.

He consistently maintained that even a psychology which, like Gestalt psychology, recognizes that consciousness is unified and autonomous, that it is not made up of elements like an external thing, and that it is, rather, a whole whose parts have no separable existence is radically incapable of replacing philosophy. For even though the Gestaltists conceive of consciousness as a totality which cannot be dissolved into its elements, they nevertheless conceive of it as a natural totality existing in things. My consciousness, they would say, is a form more integrated than this lamp, but it is nevertheless only a form. As Husserl sees it, the very fact that one uses the same term "Gestalt" to designate the unity of consciousness and that of the lamp justifies the conclusion that Gestalt psychology naturalizes consciousness. It defines consciousness as other objects can be defined, and does not see that it is the subject for every possible object.

In his philosophical rigor, Husserl excludes both Gestalt psychology and that of nineteenth-century atomism and places them almost on the same level. Notice what he writes about this in his "Nachwort" to the *Ideas:* "Both atomistic psychology and Gestalt psychology remain in the same sense basically psychological naturalisms which, from their use of the expression 'internal sense,' can also be called sensualisms." [8] There is no difference here, in principle, between "atomistically" accumulating psychic data like grains of sand and considering them as parts of totalities held together by some empirical or a priori necessity, but nevertheless made up of such parts. There is no essential difference between saying with the associationists, "Consciousness is a sum of sensations and images," and with the Gestaltists, "Consciousness is a totality in which the elements have only an inseparable existence." So long as one does not radically reform the notion of totality so as to think of consciousness as a totality with no equivalent at all among the things of nature, one is still trapped in naturalism and psychologism.

Husserl maintained this up to the very end. He never thought that psychology would be able to take the place of philosophy, even a highly refined psychology having nothing to do with any atomism or with any reduction to elements of any kind. But he held something even more than this. Not only will psychology never take the place of philosophy, but as psychology it necessarily involves a deformation of consciousness.

As a matter of fact, it shares in the natural attitude which indeed enables it to consider man, but only as a part of the world. When a psychologist speaks of consciousness, the mode of being he attributes to it does not differ radically from that of things. Consciousness is an object to be studied, and the psychologist

---

8. "Nachwort zu meinen *Ideen* . . . ," *Jahrbuch für Philosophie und phänomenologische Forschung,* XI (1930), 565; cf. *Ideas,* p. 24.

sees it among other things as an event in this system of the world. To arrive at a conception which will do justice to the radical originality of consciousness, we need an analysis of a very different type, which will find in our experience the meaning, or the essence, of every possible psyche. We will never really find out what consciousness is unless we grasp this internal meaning in ourselves and gain an eidetic intuition of it.

Consciousness is accessible only to intentional analysis and not to mere factual observation. The psychologist always tends to make consciousness into just such an object of observation. But all the factual truths to which psychology has access can be applied to the concrete subject only after a philosophical correction. Psychology, like physics and the other sciences of nature, uses the method of induction, which starts from facts and then assembles them. But it is very evident that this induction will remain blind if we do not know in some other way, and indeed from the inside of consciousness itself, what this induction is dealing with.

In order to understand truly what has been discovered about man, we must, therefore, combine induction with the reflective knowledge that we can obtain from ourselves as conscious subjects. This is what Husserl called *eidetic psychology*—that is, a reflective effort by which we clarify the fundamental notions which psychology uses constantly, through a contact with our own experience. According to Husserl, empirical psychology must be preceded by an eidetic psychology. The knowledge of facts belongs to psychology. But the definition of the notions which will enable us to understand these facts belongs to phenomenology.

We may take certain concepts, like image and perception, from common usage and then apply them without careful attention in interpreting psychological facts. But in so far as we have not given a coherent and adequate sense to these notions by reflecting on our experiences and perceptions, we will not know what they mean and what the facts concerning image and perception really show.

In general, Husserl thinks neither that psychology will be replaced by philosophy nor that philosophy will be replaced by psychology. It is essential that each should maintain its autonomy. To psychology is allotted the investigation of facts, and the relations of these facts. But the ultimate meaning of these facts and relations will be worked out only by an eidetic phenomenology which focuses the essence of perception, of image, and of consciousness itself.

2. *An illustration from the earlier works of Sartre*

The first works of Sartre on imagination and emotion illustrate very well Husserl's conception as it was presented in the middle period of his career.

At the end of his essay on the imagination,[9] Sartre shows that in so far as we have not reflected on what an image is, all the experimental investigations that we can make remain a dead letter. Of course they give us results that are ultimately quantitative in character. But we do not know what these results mean or what it is that has been measured. For example, one sees under what conditions the image is presented. One finds that in our conscious life it corresponds to states of low tension and that it appears almost instantaneously without definite contours. One speaks of clear images, and shows that they are not, as is often believed, complete pictures of the objects they represent but only schematic outlines. One shows again that the image is never altogether self-sufficient in our conscious life and that it serves only to resume a certain project of thought or to carry symbolic references to certain objects.

All this is true. But it does not enable us to understand what the image is, how it enters into relation with a thought that uses it, and what the predominance of imaginary life means for a given subject. As long as we regard the image as a little frozen picture in consciousness, it is impossible for us to understand how this image-thing can enter into any real relation with active thought. It remains simply a sensible thing, veiled or suppressed or less complete. This conception of the image, which has no scientific value, introduces fixed elements into psychological analysis which do not belong there but which are derived rather from prescientific common sense. The same thing can also happen in a phenomenological clarification. One often does not understand what it is to imagine something and what purpose this may serve. What is the sense of imagining attitudes and be-

9. Jean-Paul Sartre, *L'Imagination* (Paris: Alcan, 1936); English translation by Forrest Williams, *Imagination: A Psychological Critique* (Ann Arbor: University of Michigan Press, 1962).

havior? What does an act of imagining mean in the life of man?

To answer these questions we need an analysis which would show us that, in principle, the image is not something observable, though it pretends to be—that it is, in short, essentially deceptive. We all believe that images are observable like the things we sense. But when we try to observe them, we find that this is impossible and that, as Alain says, we cannot count the columns of the Pantheon in our images of it. The image is, therefore, a claim to the presence of the imagined object which is unfounded. It is an absence of the object which tries to pass as its presence. It calls up an object, as one speaks of calling up a spirit. The thinking self is referring to such and such a real object existing in the world, with the pretense of making it appear here and now just where I am. As Sartre says, there are not two Peters, one who is real and in West Africa and another Peter in my consciousness. In reality, there is my reference to the real Peter, with the pretense that I am making him appear here in my mental equipment. This kind of incorporation of something absent in present data is carried out naturally with the aid of certain perceptual elements which serve as analogues of the absent object. This is sufficient to show that in reality the image is not a content in my consciousness but rather an operation of my whole consciousness. To perceive oneself as imagining is to set up a certain kind of relation with the absent thing.

Understood in this way, the image can be compared to a whole series of other phenomena. For example, one can compare the awareness of a mental image of the Pantheon with an awareness of certain photographic images. Thus there is no essential difference between my awareness of the absent Pantheon and that which I have of a photograph under my eyes. When the object is totally absent without a representative, I make use of certain elements in my present perception which are analogous. To imagine is always to make something absent appear in the present, to give a magical quasi presence to an object that is not there. On this basis one may then investigate how the subject achieves this incantation of an absent visage in the present data of his perceptions. One will see that he must impress them with a physiognomy or a structure of some kind that he then projects actively by his motor-affective attitude. Such an eidetic analysis of the image will make possible experimental approaches which are no longer blind, because they will know something of what they are talking about and will understand the connection of the image with our motor-affective life.

In the same way, before we have worked out an eidetic psychology of emotion and before we have asked ourselves what it is to be emotionally moved, we may raise the problem of emotion in a very confused way, because we see it through a number of prejudices and prenotions which artificially separate the facts. Common sense, for example, will say of emotion that it involves two separate orders of fact, "corporeal manifestations" on the one hand and "representations" on the other. The question was raised in this way at the time of William James. One school then maintained that emotion must be understood from the standpoint of representations, while another defended the standpoint of corporeal facts.

Hence psychology held that a great victory had been won on the day when James reversed the traditional order in saying "I am sorry because I weep" instead of "I weep because I am sorry." Psychology still indulged in this type of speculation even after the coming of phenomenology and proposals to work out meaningful clarifications of emotion. But this does not involve any opposing of concepts to facts. It is a question, rather, of replacing habitual concepts, to which we pay no careful attention, by concepts which are consciously clarified and are therefore far less likely to remove us from experience as it is lived.

In connection with emotion, eidetic reflection will ask: after all, what is it to be moved; what is the meaning of emotion? Can one conceive of a consciousness which is incapable of emotion, and if not, why not? One will understand emotion as a total act of consciousness, as a mode of our relation to the entire world, and one will seek to determine its sense.

In earlier times psychology noted vaguely that emotion was both a "psychic" and a "physical" state and sought to determine which was the cause of the other. Phenomenology will remain neutral before this issue, and without assuming that emotion is either psychical or physical it will simply ask what emotion means and toward what it is tending.

Many psychologists have sketched out research of this kind. It will be a constant thesis of the following lectures that one does not have to be specially tutored by Husserl to discover psychological developments that are moving in a phenomenological direction. Janet, for example, raised the question of emotion in a very new way when he tried to find out what was the meaning of a given emotion. In a passage in *De l'angoisse à l'extase* [10] he brought up the case of a young girl who came to consult him but refused to answer his questions. She ended by falling into a nervous crisis which naturally made it impossible for her to do this. The emotion, the nervous breakdown, and the anger had a sense. They were a way of avoiding the interrogatory situation which the girl had instinctively accepted in coming to see Janet but which she had not really decided to undertake.

In the same way Freud considered emotion as an action or realization which is symbolic. In one of his formulae, clearly showing the relation between his whole enterprise and that of the phenomenologists, he also maintained that "psychic facts have a sense" which must be deciphered. He tried to place them in the total life of the subject, the dynamics of his behavior, and thus to show what they mean.

According to Sartre, for example, emotion is the modification of our relation to the world when we abandon an ordered way of acting which takes account of causality, and change over to an immediate, magical, and fictitious transformation of the situation. Thus a man in a fit of anger will stop trying to untie the knot of a string or a shoelace and will suddenly tear it apart, which does not resolve the problem of the knot but simply suppresses it. An orderly way of relating to the object and the world is replaced by an irrational way in which everything happens as if the unconditional will of the subject were able to reach its result by merely projecting itself into the object without any employment of means. This is an example of what Husserl calls an eidetic analysis. One gathers together the lived facts involving emotion and tries to subsume them under one essential meaning in order to find the same conduct in all of them. [11]

Thus we may say, in using a formula of Husserl, that the relation of psychology to phenomenology is analogous to that of physics to geometry. In relation to methodological questions, psychology refers to phenomenology. For example, to know what an emotion is and how to approach it by way of the body or the

---

10. Pierre Janet, *De l'angoisse à l'extase* (Paris: Alcan, 1926–28).

11. This kind of investigation of essence is at the same time an analysis of existence in the modern sense of the word, or at least leads toward this, since the essence of an experience is always a certain modality of our relation to the world.

spirit, or in a neutral phenomenological way, we need a clarification of the internal meaning of the phenomenon, which phenomenology can furnish. This does not mean that the work of the phenomenologist replaces that of the psychologist, any more than that of the geometer replaces that of the physicist. Geometry and mathematics in general were necessary preconditions for the development of a physics. But this does not mean that they can take its place.

In another passage Husserl says that the relation between empirical and eidetic psychology is the same as that between sociology and statistics. This means that statistics is necessary to sociology but does not coincide with it. We must get into contact with the social phenomenon, and understand it in its own proper frame, in order to find a social meaning in statistical facts. In the same way it is necessary to get into contact with the psyche by phenomenological reflection in order to understand the results of the empirical investigations of psychology.

In conclusion, Husserl believed that he saw in the psychological investigations of his time many uncertainties which are connected with the desire to use scientific techniques. Psychology rightly seeks to gain a factual knowledge which one obtains only through contact with a number of different instances of the phenomenon studied, not previously imaginable by us and therefore to be found only in experience. But the psychologist believes that it is sufficient merely to note down these facts in order to understand them. The result is that he examines them in a state of relative blindness and that in interpreting them he uses confused concepts taken from our prescientific experience.

From time to time, for example, the psychologist uses the concept of man, if only to mark off animal from human psychology. But what, more exactly, is the meaning of this notion of man? Since it is drawn from our common sense, perhaps it needs to be revised. Perhaps it is too broad, so that certain beings we commonly call men do not really merit the name in terms of a strict analysis. In any case, this needs to be examined. Or perhaps, on the contrary, our notion of man is too narrow. If we were to examine the chimpanzee more carefully, we might discover that there is no justifiable reason for excluding him from the class of animals known as men. Our present concept of man is not at all scientific. It is vague, confused, and in need of psychological clarification.

Phenomenological analysis is a clarifying effort of this kind. It is seeking to identify with rigor, and to link together in an intelligible way, the attitudes and traits that may justifiably be called human. One may say that "psychology will of course be able to define man, but only at the end of its inquiry." Still, this is not certain, since the investigation will be concerned with facts. Will it reveal merely certain characteristics which belong to the collection of individuals that one ordinarily calls "man," or will it show that these characteristics do not belong to all, or that they also belong to other individuals not usually called human? Such a factual investigation will never enable us to decide whether the collection of traits obtained in this way deserves to constitute a definition. Are they essential or only accidental? Sooner or later this investigation of the essence with which an eidetic psychology is concerned should be undertaken. But it will never come to anything so long as the traits accepted for empirical investigation are chosen only because of their frequent occurrence and have no power to reveal the essence that must be understood.

3. Difficulties involved in a subordination of psychology: the interconnections of psychology and phenomenology

To this conception of an eidetic psychology two kinds of objection can be made and, as a matter of fact, have been made. First, we may easily go astray, since this kind of psychology rests on a misunderstanding. The second objection goes much further. It was seen by Husserl himself, and led him to alter his ideas and to develop his doctrines beyond the stage of the *Ideas*.

The first objection maintains that an eidetic psychology would be merely a return to introspection and would therefore lead to all the difficulties from which psychology attempted to escape when it decided to become a science.

On this point no confusion is possible. For Husserl the discovery of the essence, or the meaning, of a process certainly involves a power of reflection, the ability to find the sense of what is lived through by oneself or by another. At the period of the *Ideas* he thought that reflective consciousness can arrive at an evidence concerning itself which is absolutely final and that in it what appears and what is are not distinct. In this sense Husserl held that consciousness, or *cogito,* is incomparable with external things. These external things appear in successive experiences through different perspectives, or *Abschattungen*. If consciousness were external to itself there would be no certitude nor science concerning it. In this sense, it is true to say that for Husserl, as for all the Cartesians, the existence of consciousness is inseparable from the consciousness of existing and that consequently the consciousness I need to know is the subject that I am. It is also clear, finally, that Husserl wishes to use this proximity of myself to myself, and more generally of man to man, in defining the *cogito* and reflection. In order that knowledge may be possible, I must not be cut off from myself and from the other.

But this does not mean that the internal relation of myself to myself and to the other is already scientific knowledge and that reflective psychology is introspective. This introspection is supposed to consist in the presence of data internal to the subject, which he observes and which are revealed to him by the mere fact that they are "in him." This is an internal perception, the noting of an event with which I coincide. But reflection is not at all the noting of a fact. It is, rather, an attempt to understand. It is not the passive attitude of a subject who watches himself live but rather the active effort of a subject who grasps the meaning of his experience. Husserl was so far from making internal perception into a principle that he granted a greater certitude, in certain respects, to external perception than to internal observation. *Reflection on the meaning or the essence of what we live through is neutral to the distinction between internal and external experience.*

It is rather a question of explaining what these phrases mean. In particular, nothing prevents my phenomenological reflection from having a bearing, for example, on another person, since I perceive him and his modes of behavior. Nothing prevents the clarification of the intentions or meanings or ways of acting from referring not only to my own conduct but to that of another whom I witness. Nothing prevents me from explaining the meaning of the lived experience of another person, in so far as I have access to it, by perception. According to Husserl, "Pure internal psychology, the authentic psychology of intentionality, is, in the last analysis, a psychology of pure intersubjectivity." This pure internal psychology is not restricted to the subject in himself. It grasps just as well the relations of different subjects to each other —i.e., intersubjectivity.

Internal observation is related to the empirical self. But Husserlian reflection is related to a transcendental subject which is prepersonal, and neutral with respect to the distinction between the empirical self and the other. In fact, in the *Cartesian Meditations*, he uses the notion of conduct, *Gebaren*, to introduce his discussion of the perceiving of another. Behavioristic psychology, therefore, offers no difficulties for an eidetic method. Eidetic insight applies just as well to the experience of another, because my experience and his are interrelated in my dealings with him (by "intentional transgression," as the *Cartesian Meditations* say). In a very early article of 1910 Husserl also said that the intersubjective determination of individual psychisms is possible.

Of this first objection, then, let us retain only the notions which Husserl left unclarified, at the time of the *Ideas*, concerning the relation between radical reflection—founded on the fact that I am no stranger to myself (Heidegger would say that I am not hidden from myself)—and that other awareness of myself which is not immediate and is capable of error as well as truth. This leads us now to the second objection, which is more interesting, since it penetrates to the heart of the matter. It will lead us to complete what we have said up to this point, just as it led Husserl himself to deepen his thought. Is it not true that an eidetic psychology, reflectively determining the basic categories of psychic life by reflecting on my experience of myself and the other, reduces psychology, in the narrower sense, to a very restricted role? Is it not, then, limited to a mere study of details?

In his earlier works Husserl went so far as to say at certain points that the relation of psychology to philosophy is almost that of content to form. It is philosophy that knows what space is. It is from psychology, on the other hand, that I gain some information concerning the perception of space through certain visual and tactual contents of experience. If one clings to formulae of this kind, everything essential seems to be furnished by phenomenology, or philosophic insight. Nothing more is left to psychology than to study certain empirical curiosities within the frames that are furnished by phenomenology.

In other texts Husserl wrote as if psychology ought to concern itself with causal relations, laws of fact through which the phenomena actually belonging to the province of philosophy are manifested. Psychology studies a consciousness which is introduced into the body and naturalized. It should concern itself only with those conditions of existence, or of the temporal order, in which certain aspects of the phenomenon, or essence, appear. But the description and comprehension of the phenomenon itself fall to phenomenology. Since the order of essences has its own certainties, these transcendental relations can never be denied by the order of psychological genesis which is concerned only with a special application. Is this really all that Husserl thought about the question? After all, the notion of *Wesensschau* was developed to found an activity of consciousness which would be concrete as well as philosophical, both linked to my experience as well as capable of universality. Does the conception of noetic insight, such as Husserl had developed it up to this point, correspond to these two conditions?

This question was not resolved in a satisfactory manner at the period of the *Ideas,* the work on which I have been so far commenting. But in the later works we can see a further effort to resolve it.

At the beginning of his career Husserl considered all questions concerning psychological genesis as secondary. They could in no case prevail against the philosophical problems concerning essence. But as his thought matured, he gave a meaning to genesis which was very different and much more positive—to such a degree, indeed, that in the *Cartesian Meditations* he speaks of a phenomenology of genesis.

If in Husserl's view the knowledge of facts is impossible without some insight into essence and is always helped by this, it follows that all sound knowledge of facts must include, at least implicitly, some insight into essences, and that Husserl must admit, as he does in effect, that those psychologists who have been preoccupied with facts have nevertheless been able to find out something concerning essences. The division of labor between eidetic and empirical psychology turns out to be extremely difficult, since as soon as one engages in even the most experimental type of psychological research, in so far as he says anything sound and true, some insight into essence is implied by his work.

Husserl himself pointed out an analogy between what has happened in physics and what has happened in psychology. The physicists who created physics, in the modern sense of the word, had an insight into what a physical thing is. Galileo, for example, of whom Husserl often spoke, was certainly not a phenomenologist. He was not even a philosopher in any strict sense of the word. Nevertheless when he decided to study falling bodies, a certain intuition of what a physical body is was implied in this experimental investigation. Spatial determination, for example, was regarded as altogether fundamental. And when, after Galileo, other physicists added to our knowledge of nature, one can say that each of them contributed to the development of *an eidetic of physical things*. Husserl was not interested in making the knowledge of essences an exclusive privilege of phenomenologists. These are implied in all experimental research, and they appear there whether one is looking for them or not and whether one wants them or not.

But more needs to be said. It is not only true that a knowledge of facts always implies a knowledge of essences, but in addition to the factual link between the two psychologies, we are going to see that there is a much closer connection. In order to make this more precise, let us turn for a moment to the nature of the *Wesensschau*. We must remember that for Husserl this has the nature of a finding (constatation). He often speaks of an "eidetic constatation." We must also remember that he never envisaged an a priori, in the sense of a deductive psychology. He says in the *Ideas* that there is no "mathematics of phenomena," no "geometry of the lived." [12] Why not? Because eidetic, or phenomenological, psychology, in distinction from mathematics, is a science which is essentially descriptive. The multiplicities with which geometry is concerned are "mathematical multiplicities," which can be exhaustively defined—that is, by a system of axioms. But in phenomenology there is no question of defining the objects of psychology by any system of axioms which would enable us to construct these different psychical realities.

This is because the essences we may discover, when we force ourselves to think about lived experiences, are not, in Husserl's terms, "exact essences" capable of an univocal determination. They are, rather, "morphological essences," which are inexact by nature. Husserl says in the *Ideas* that if one were to dream of a phenomenological psychology which would be deductive, he

12. Cf. *Ideas*, trans. Gibson, pp. 67, 185.

would fall into the same sort of difficulty as a geometer who, for example, might dream of giving a rigorous geometrical definition of terms such as "jagged," "notched like a lentil," or "like a sunshade." [13]

There is no geometric definition of these forms, and it is equally impossible to give any constructive definition of the different realities with which psychology is concerned. It is through experience alone that they can be known, and not otherwise. From the very beginning, therefore, it has been necessary to maintain a close relation between eidetic intuition and that which we do, in fact, experience.

Husserl often says that to see an essence one must begin by having a perception, which serves as the base, or point of departure, for a *Wesensschau* but not as the source of its validity. The relation between perception and *Wesensschau* is one of founding (*Fundierung*); perception, that is, serves as the ground, or pedestal, on which an insight into essence is formed. Thus insight into essence is an intellectual taking over, a making explicit and clarifying of something concretely experienced; and a recognition that it comes after something else, from which it starts, is essential to its nature. It also knows itself to be retrospective. The idea that it succeeds a more direct contact with the thing itself is enclosed within its very meaning.

One sees already in Husserl the idea of a double envelopment. It is true that reflective thought, which determines the meaning or essence, ends by possessing its object and enveloping it. But it is also true that essential insight always understands the concrete perception of experience as something here and now which precedes and therefore envelops it. In Husserl's words, the essence presupposes "an important part of intuition" bearing on the individual. It presupposes that an individual has appeared and that one has had a view of it. It also presupposes the *Sichtlichkeit*, the visibility of this individual. Or, to put it in another way, it is no insight into an essence if one's reflection cannot turn to a corresponding individual, if one cannot work out "a sense of examples" to illustrate his insight.

What, then, exactly is the relation between this sense of examples and what is called induction? It is in working out an answer to this question that we may be able to understand the

13. Cf. *ibid.*, p. 208.

relation between phenomenological and empirical, or inductive, psychology.

We must here recall the profound remarks of Husserl on induction in general. These were basically opposed to the theory of induction which held sway at the end of the nineteenth century, essentially that of Mill. According to this theory induction is a process by which, in considering a group of facts, we discover a common character and set it apart by abstraction, regarding it as essential to the group of facts from which we started. Or again, induction is an operation which enables us to find the cause of a phenomenon among its various antecedents, by discarding those which are neither constant nor unconditioned. According to Husserl, induction is not, and never has been, this. His remarks here anticipate those of Brunschwicg in his *L'Expérience humaine et la causalité physique*.

Let us return to the example of Galileo and the fundamental induction which, we may say, created modern physics. How does Galileo proceed? Does he consider different examples of falling bodies and then, by a method of agreement, following the theory of John Stuart Mill, abstract what is common to these examples? As a matter of fact, he proceeds in a totally different manner. The conception of the fall of bodies which guides his experiment is not found in the facts. He forms it actively; he constructs it. He freely conceives the pure case of a freely falling body, of which there is no given example in our human experience. Then, having constructed this idea, he verifies it by showing how the confused empirical facts, which never represent the free fall in its pure state, can then be understood through the introduction of additional conditions (friction, resistance, etc. . . .), which explain the difference between the facts and the pure concept. On the basis of the free fall, therefore, one constructs the fall of a body on an inclined plane.

Husserl says in the first volume of the *Logical Investigations* that the physicists proceed by *"idealisierende Fiktionen cum fundamento in re"*—that is, by idealizing fictions which are nevertheless founded on the facts. Let it be, he says, the law of Newton. Basically it makes no assertion about the existence of gravitating masses. It is another one of those idealizing fictions by which one purely conceives of what a gravitating mass would be. Then one determines what properties it would have, on the supposition that it exists. According to Husserl, Newton's law says nothing at all about existence. It refers only to what would belong to a gravitating mass as such.[14]

The method actually used by physicists, therefore, is not the chimerical induction of Mill, which is never practiced in the sciences. It is rather *a reading of the essence.* Through certain impure and imperfect phenomena, such as the fall of a body on an inclined plane, I read off the free fall of the body, which is theoretically conceived, or forged, by the intellect. That which gives its probable value to the induction and which finally shows that it is truly founded on things is not the number of facts invoked to justify it. No! It is rather the intrinsic clarity which these ideas shed on the phenomena we seek to understand. Just as Brunschwicg will show, in his *L'Expérience humaine et la causalité physique,* that one experiment will suffice to establish a law—that Davy, for example, established the existence of potassium by only one experiment of electrolysis—so Husserl maintained that induction is not founded on the collection of a vast number of cases. It is, rather, a process of intellectual analysis whose verification consists in the total, or at least sufficient, clarity which the group of concepts worked out in this way brings to the given phenomena. Thus laws are not basically live realities which would have a *force* and could rule over the facts. One should say, rather, in the language of Malebranche, that they are a light and not a force.

Let us now compare induction, understood in this way, with the phenomenological *Wesensschau.* This intuition of essences, like induction, as we have seen, is based on facts. The difference is that *Wesensschau* is based on the *imaginary "free variation" of certain facts.* In order to grasp an essence, we consider a concrete experience, and then we make it change in our thought, trying to imagine it as effectively modified in all respects. *That which remains invariable* through these changes is the essence of the phenomena in question.

For example, if we are seeking to form an idea of, or to understand the essence of, a spatial figure, such as this lamp, we must first perceive it. Then we will imagine all the aspects contained in this figure as changed. That which cannot be varied without

14. "Prolegomena zur reinen Logik," *Logische Untersuchungen,* 2 vols. (Halle: Niemeyer, 1913), I, 150; cf. English translation by J. N. Findlay, "Prolegomena to Pure Logic," *Logical Investigations,* 2 vols. (New York: Humanities Press, 1970), I, 106.

the object itself disappearing is the essence. Suppose that we wish to form the idea of melody. We recall a tune which we have learned to sing, and suppose that all the notes and all the relations between the notes are changed. That which remains invariable and without which there would be no more melody is the essence we are seeking. In the same way, if we are trying to conceive the essence of a "social process," we will represent to ourselves a social process in which we have participated or concerning which we have some historical understanding. That which does not vary through all conceivable variations will be the essence. Even when one thinks in terms of the pure essence, one always thinks of the visible—the fact. But in the case of *Wesensschau*, the individual fact is neither grasped nor assumed as a reality, which is shown by the fact that we subject it to an imaginary variation.

We are thus led to the following conclusion: If eidetic psychology is a reading of the invariable structure of our experience based on examples, the empirical psychology which uses induction is also a reading of the essential structure of a multiplicity of cases. But the cases here are real and not imaginary. After closer examination, the only difference which we find between inductive procedure—so far as it is justifiable and moves toward what is truly essential—and the procedure of eidetic psychology is that the latter applies imaginary variation to its examples, while the former refers to effective variations in considering the different cases that are *actually realized.*

If we reflect further, we may see that the relation between the two is even closer. For when you make an induction on the basis of facts which are very large in number, you do not examine every possible, individual case. For example, when you establish the law of a physical phenomenon, you are not going to verify the law by every possible value of each variable. You will limit yourself to a finite number of experiments, and you will then single out one relation that you consider to be always true, even for the intermediate values between those that you have verified. This is called "interpolating," and it requires the use of that free variation of which Husserl spoke—at least in the intervals between the values effectively verified. In a certain number of decisive experiments you perceive certain relations, and you imagine the rest in function of these relations which are actually perceived in a finite number of cases. You link together the different examples effectively perceived by an imaginary variation which will lead from one to the other.

Let us now turn to an example from psychology, not physics: the important and interesting notion, now widely used, of behavioral lability or instability. How does one arrive at a notion of this sort? One says that a type of behavior is labile either when it is reproduced without any change under very different conditions—that is, when it is not flexible—or when it changes or disappears in a way that is wholly unpredictable. One calls an attitude labile both when it is too rigid and when it is not rigid enough. In using this notion, one therefore identifies the two extreme cases—excessive fixity on the one hand and too frequent change on the other. How is this possible? How does one arrive inductively at such a psychological notion? It is certainly not by any comparison of the given characters of psychological facts. One could compare the relevant psychological facts as much as one wishes without finding anything held in common. What is there in common between a stereotyped mode of conduct and one that is ever ready to disappear? Nothing, certainly, that is given with the facts. The notion of lability is constructed.

Goldstein introduced it with reference to what he called centered or non-centered behavior. The common element in extremely automatic behavior, on the one hand, and ephemeral behavior, on the other, is that neither of them is centered in the whole conduct of the individual. The lack of centering is the meaning held in common by modes of behavior which are absolutely episodic and others which are invariable and monotonous. In both of them we see that the connection between the situation and the response is wholly external, so that the situation does not guide the response. The construction of a concept of this kind is very close to Husserl's *Wesensschau*. This is doubtless why he says so often that everyone performs the *Wesensschau*. "The intuition of essences does not involve any more difficulties or 'mystical' secrets than perception." [15]

This *Wesensschau* is not the exclusive possession of the phenomenologists. As a matter of fact, Husserl says in the *Ideas* that "everyone is constantly seeing ideas or essences, and every-

---

15. "Philosophie als strenge Wissenschaft," *Logos*, I (1910), 289; cf. English translation by Quentin Lauer, "Philosophy as Rigorous Science," in Quentin Lauer, ed. and trans., *Edmund Husserl: Phenomenology and the Crisis of Philosophy* (New York: Harper & Row, 1965), p. 110.

one uses them in the operations of thought, in spite of the widespread opposition put forth in the name of points of view in the theory of knowledge." [16] The empiricist theory of induction is one of these points of view (in the pejorative sense of this phrase), a vague opinion without rigor, which prevents us from seeing ourselves when we practice the *Wesensschau,* especially in making inductions.

In presenting the matter as I have, I am pushing Husserl further than he wished to go himself. He never expressly recognized the fundamental homogeneity of these two modes of knowledge, the inductive and the essential. He never admitted that in the last analysis they were indiscernible and simply differed in degree. Nevertheless his notion of an experienced essence, or an eidetic experience, contains in germ the consequence that I have just drawn from it. But it is a question here not so much of a consequence as of an inevitable dialectic of the concept of essence. It follows on principle from Husserl's point of departure and from what he proposed to do—namely, to show that this knowledge of essences is altogether experiential, that it does not involve any kind of supersensible faculty, and that in the last analysis the essence is just as contingent as the fact. It also follows inversely, from Husserl's point of departure and from the problem we have formulated in the preceding lectures, that any knowledge of fact always involves an a priori understanding of essence.

Instead of clearly recognizing the homogeneity of the two modes of knowledge, Husserl was content to insist, as he did very often, on the parallelism between psychology and phenomenology. "As a matter of principle," he said, psychology in its whole development is parallel to phenomenology. Of course, one might just as well say that phenomenology is always parallel to psychology and that every significant proposition of empirical psychology anticipates a phenomenological truth. As a matter of fact, Husserl did say that "every empirical discovery as well as every eidetic discovery made on the one side must correspond to a parallel discovery on the other." [17] This means that for every assertion of experimental psychology a corresponding eidetic assertion can be found.

16. *Idées directrices,* p. 74; cf. *Ideen,* p. 49, *Ideas,* p. 89.
17. "Nachwort zu meinen *Ideen,*" p. 556; cf. *Ideas,* p. 15.

We are here very far from the idea of an eidetic psychology which by reflection alone would give us the principles of any possible psychological process and which would pass from the particular case of a real mental activity to that of other men as well. We are far from the idea of a philosophical psychology which would determine not the real but the whole range of the possibly human. It is human reality which now emerges as *the locus of the Wesensschau*. It is in becoming conscious of myself as I am that I am able to see essences, and in this context the real and the possible are not distinct.

Husserl even came to say that "intentional psychology already carries the transcendent within itself." [18] This really means that there cannot be any basic discord between the point of view of psychology and that of phenomenology. It is always the same subject, man, that is being approached in one way or the other. Our image of man may be acquired with all the presuppositions of an empirical psychology, which takes him as situated within the chains of worldly causality. But this empirical psychology, if it really pays attention to what it is describing, will always end by making room for a different perspective which sees man not as a mere part of the world but as the bearer of reflection. Thus the interpenetration of psychology and phenomenology—their reciprocal envelopment—is clearly indicated in these texts as well as in those I have previously cited.

Certain formulae of Sartre, therefore, in the last chapter of his small book, *L'Imagination*, where he tries to define the thought of Husserl, definitely stand in need of correction. Sartre writes here as if phenomenological, or eidetic, psychology ought to come *first* and ought to rule over all the fundamental questions. Then after we have learned something about all possible psychic processes in general, experience may show us the actual facts. But in the basic intention of Husserl, the relation of these two approaches is not merely one of simple succession, as if one could see essences without any factual experience or could come to the facts without implying, in his very approach, a certain vision of essence. Sartre writes:

18. Based on the French translation by Gabrielle Peiffer and Emmanuel Levinas, *Méditations cartésiennes* (Paris: Armand Colin, 1931), p. 126. Cf. the English translation by Dorion Cairns, *Cartesian Meditations: An Introduction to Phenomenology* (New York: Humanities Press, 1964), p. 147.

After one has determined the various conditions that a psychic state must necessarily possess if it is to be an image, then only may we pass from the certain to the probable, and ask of experience what it can teach us about the images which are actually present in a contemporary human consciousness.[19]

What is perhaps the most important aspect of Husserl's whole project is lacking in this statement.

As a matter of fact, Sartre himself does not follow the rule that he here lays down. Although he presents empirical psychology as the servant of phenomenology, he says, nevertheless, that he embarks on the study of emotion "without waiting for the phenomenology of emotion to be completed." [20] This means that basically experimental studies, like those of Janet, Lewin, and the psychoanalysts, must already reveal to us, at least in a confused way, the essence of that with which they are concerned. However it may be with his formulations, Sartre actually understands the relation between psychology and phenomenology in the way which I have just now tried to explain.

When he departs from this, he is led to artificial distinctions For example, his book L'Imaginaire [21] follows this simple plan: Part I, "The Certain"; Part II, "The Probable." In the first part he gives a phenomenological analysis of the essence of the image. In the second, he turns to the data of experience with the understanding that what has been acquired in the first part is unshakable and certain, while what is now coming is only probable. But when one reads the work carefully, one finds that certain results of the first part are actually called in question in the second. At the beginning of his book, for example, Sartre shows that the image is defined by its deception and by the fact that it is unobservable and empty. When I try to imagine the Pantheon, I believe that I see it. But if I try to count the pillars, I find that I cannot do so, which means that basically I do not see anything at all. The initial phenomenological analysis determines the essence of the image as a false presence, as a nothing which tries to present itself as a something.

19. L'Imagination, p. 143; English translation, p. 131.
20. Esquisse d'une théorie des émotions (Paris: Hermann, 1939), p. 17. Cf. the English translation by Philip Mairet, Sketch for a Theory of the Emotions (London: Methuen, 1962), p. 29.
21. Sartre, L'Imaginaire (Paris: Gallimard, 1940); English translation by Bernard Frechtman, Psychology of the Imagination (New York: Philosophical Library, 1948).

But in the second part of the book this fundamental definition of the image is placed in question when the author analyzes certain states where a clear distinction between the perceived and the imaginary cannot be made. If the image were nothing but what was first said—empty and absent—we would never confuse it with a perception, and illusions would be hard to understand. Thus in so far as Sartre raises the question of illusions in the second part, he necessarily suggests the possibility of a situation anterior to the clear distinction between perception and imagination which was made at the start. He does this, and with good reason. But this means that it is impossible to understand the image by an examination of the pure possibility of an image in general and by a definition which we would then merely apply to the analogous empirical examples.

These remarks have a certain importance because they will enable us to reply to a certain objection often made against phenomenologists—namely, that they represent a new type of scholasticism. This means that phenomenological research remains purely verbal. In this view, eidetic intuition would consist in reflecting on the meaning of certain words in use, like the word "image" or the word "emotion," and then in developing this meaning with the firm conviction of reaching the things themselves. This complaint is not well founded if one refers to what Husserl actually intended. But there are certain formulae of Max Scheler which merit this reproach. For example, Scheler says that the intuition of essences is absolutely indubitable for a rather simple reason: because, by definition, experience can never contradict such an intuition. If experience should show me an image which does not correspond to what I have determined to be the essence, then of course, by definition, this is not an image. In the same way I may lay down a certain idea of social process. Then if I find a so-called process in everyday history or in the past which does not possess the essential characteristics I have focused, I have the right to say that it is not a social process. Here we are certainly close to scholasticism. If one had followed this principle in practice, the whole of phenomenology would be an instrument for developing the definitions of words.

But Husserl never thought in this way, and he was fully aware of the danger. Since his early article on "Philosophie als strenge Wissenschaft," he maintained that there was nothing in common between intuition, as he understood it, and a scholastic process which "pretends to draw a real knowledge of things from the analytic judgment that one can make on the meanings of words." [22] Husserl was, therefore, well aware of the danger of self-deception in proceeding by "eidetic intuition." It is possible for me to believe that I am seeing an essence when, in fact, it is not an essence at all but merely a concept rooted in language, a prejudice whose apparent coherence reduces merely to the fact that I have become used to it through habit. The best way of guarding against this danger would be to admit that, though a knowledge of facts is never sufficient for grasping an essence and though the construction of "idealizing fictions" is always necessary, I can never be sure that my vision of an essence is anything more than a prejudice rooted in language—if it does not enable me to hold together all the facts which are known and which may be brought into relation with it. Failing this, it may not be an essence at all but only a prejudice. I believe that the logic of things ought to have led Husserl to admit a very close relation between induction, as he understood it, and *Wesensschau*, and consequently a final homogeneity among the different psychologies, whether they be inductive or phenomenological. I have already said that Husserl never explicitly stated this. But at least he was well aware of the necessity of defending phenomenology against verbalism. Also, after he renounced the dogmatic solution of an "apodictic evidence" which would enable us from the very start to transcend language, he was obliged, as we shall see, to reconsider the imaginary "variation" of anthropological experience as the way toward eidetic intuition.

Husserl consistently rejected the different psychologies which developed in his time, including Gestalt psychology, which had been created by writers familiar with his teaching and influenced by him. In his "Nachwort," Husserl declared that it makes no difference in principle whether one conceives of consciousness as a totality or as a sum of psychic atoms, since even this totality of the Gestaltists is just another thing and therefore not a consciousness.

In his *Principles of Gestalt Psychology*, Koffka replied to this criticism in an interesting way. "A theory like mine," he said, "seems to imply an extreme psychologism, the idea that all logical relations and subsistents can be explained by existing rela-

22. "Philosophie als strenge Wissenschaft," p. 305; cf. "Philosophy as Rigorous Science," p. 95.

tions in the domain of psychology or physiology." Gestalt theory admits that all structures of consciousness finally depend on physiological processes of the same form ("isomorphic") as their causal foundation. This would seem to imply a position of extreme psychologism, since the whole order of meanings would seem to rest on the order of natural events. But Koffka is saying here that in a psychology like his there is a new way of describing consciousness which avoids the opposed difficulties of both psychologism and logicism. The description of "psychic process" in terms of structure should give basic satisfaction to philosophy in vindicating the order of meanings.

Koffka developed this idea in the following words:

> This view [of psychologism], which had gained ground at the turn of the century, was violently attacked by some of our best philosophers, notably Edmund Husserl, who claimed to have refuted it once and for all. But his arguments rested on the assumption, implicit or explicit, in all "psychologistic" theories, that psychological relations are merely factual or external. A "psychologism" based on this assumption has indeed been refuted by Husserl and other philosophers. But this refutation does not affect our psychologism —if our theory can rightly be given this name—since in our theory psychological and physiological, or rather psychophysical, processes are organized according to intrinsic or internal relations. This point can only be alluded to. It means that in our theory psychology and logic, existence and subsistence, even, to some extent, reality and truth, no longer belong to entirely different realms or universes of discourse between which no intelligible relationship exists. It is here, if anywhere, that psychology will have to prove the integrative function that we assigned to it in the first chapter.[23]

These remarks of Koffka go very far. Husserl's constant objection to Gestalt theory, as to all psychology, is that it fails to understand the radical and absolute originality of consciousness, which it reduces either to psychological atoms, as the older psychologists did, or to "total" structures which are nevertheless dependent on the natural order of events. But following certain suggestions of Husserl which we have cited above, we may give the following reply: If the notion of Gestalt helps us to under-

---

23. Kurt Koffka, *Principles of Gestalt Psychology* (New York: Harcourt, Brace, 1935), pp. 570–71.

stand many facts and is fruitful in the empirical order, it must have some phenomenological truth and must have something to contribute to phenomenology. We do not have to take over the physiological hypotheses of the Gestaltists, their cerebral explanations of conscious structures. We should directly consider what they say of consciousness and of the patterns of conduct. We may then see that they are calling our attention at this level, not to events that are completely external to each other, but to an internal organization which makes the notions of value and meaning come to life. This is enough to show that the Gestalt theory is not merely a new variety of psychologism. It is rather a way of showing that conscious phenomena are both temporal (for they happen in time and occur at a definite moment) and yet at the same time internally significant, so that they can support a certain kind of knowledge and truth.

In other words, I believe that to give weight to his eidetic intuition and to distinguish it sharply from verbal concepts, Husserl was really seeking, largely unknown to himself, a notion like that of the Gestaltists—the notion of an order of meaning which does not result from the application of spiritual activity to an external matter. It is, rather, a spontaneous organization beyond the distinction between activity and passivity, of which the visible patterns of experience are the symbol. In Gestalt psychology everything bears a meaning. There is no psychic phenomenon which is not oriented toward a certain significance. It is really a psychology founded on the idea of intentionality. But this sense, which inhabits all psychic phenomena, is not produced by a pure activity of the spirit. It is, rather, an earthy and aboriginal sense, which constitutes itself by an organization of the so-called elements.

This, perhaps, might have been the occasion for Husserl to recognize a certain truth in the "integrating psychology" of Koffka. By entering into the region of facts and clarifying some of them, it has at the same time glimpsed certain essential, philosophical truths without knowing or willing this—just as Galileo, who had no intention of working out an eidetic of the *res extensa,* actually did, in his experimental work, lay the foundations for this eidetic.

[3] THE SCIENCES OF MAN ACCORDING TO HUSSERL

IN HUSSERL'S THINKING concerning linguistics and history, we observe a development of the way in which he focused the problem, which is quite similar to what happened to his conception of psychology and which, in fact, sheds light upon the latter. In what follows, our aim will not be to repeat everything that Husserl said about linguistics and history but rather to apply his thoughts on these subjects to the clarification of psychology.

1. *Linguistics*

At the beginning of his studies, like the grammarians of the seventeenth and eighteenth centuries, he proposed to phenomenology the task of establishing a universal grammar by an apprehension of the essence of language. Just as we need an eidetic psychology which will determine the essences of the different regions of psychic activity, so also we need an eidetic of language which will enumerate and describe those "forms of meaning" without which no language is possible. The grammarian will never be able really to engage in the study of languages without going through this eidetic. We speak German, Husserl says, and when we embark on the study of a foreign language, we tend to understand this language from a German point of view. We conceive of its grammar and its categories in relation to those of the German language.

But if we wish to gain a truly adequate understanding of a foreign mode of speech, we must not proceed in this way. First of all, we must perform a reduction on all the presuppositions of our native tongue, in order to isolate the fundamental articulations of language itself, without which no language is possible. It is only on the basis of this universal grammar that we will be able to think through the different languages in their specificity, by reconstructing their inner patterns. We must study, Husserl says, such basic forms as categorical propositions with their primitive specifications, complex conjunctive and disjunctive propositions, and the ways of expressing universality, particularity, and singularity. It is only by keeping these fundamental operations in view that we will be able to ask how the German language, the Chinese, etc., express "the" proposition of existence, "the" categorical proposition, "the" hypothetical premise, "the" plural, and "the" different modalities of the possible.

Husserl goes on to say:

> We cannot evade the question as to whether the grammarian will be content with his own personal and prescientific views, or with the confused empirical representations provided by a particular historical grammar, like Latin, of the forms of signification. Is he following such feeble guides? Or does he have in view the pure system of linguistic patterns in a scientifically determined and theoretically coherent form—that is to say, in the form of our theory of patterns of signification? [24]

The eidetic of language should therefore be established at the very beginning. The empirical study of language should come afterward, directing itself to the relevant facts, clarifying them, and then reconstructing them in the light of the essences already determined.

At the beginning of his career, Husserl thought that we could bypass our mother tongue in reflecting on language as such, thus penetrating to the essences which belong necessarily to any possible language. After this, we might then understand our own peculiar ways of speaking as special cases of this universal language. This mode of approach is interesting, because it involves a dogmatic conception of the *Wesensschau*. With respect to such a conception the following question at once arises: Do we have at our disposal the means of detaching ourselves from the historical roots of the language we speak, so that we can penetrate directly to the essence of language in general?

To arrive at this universal, rational grammar, is it sufficient merely to reflect on the language which we already speak and possess, or is it essential that we should first make contact with other languages? Is language an instrument that we may directly objectivize and dominate by the *Wesensschau*, which will give us a reliable knowledge of its necessary and universal structure? Or is it not true, rather, that we gain access to the

---

24. "Untersuchung der Unterschied der selbstständigen und unselbstständigen Bedeutungen und die Idee der reinen Grammatik," *Logische Untersuchungen*, II, 339. Cf. Fourth Investigation, "The Distinction between Independent and Nonindependent Meanings and the Idea of Pure Grammar," *Logical Investigations*, II, 526.

universal structure of language only by first learning other languages and by coexisting with them?

Can we order the universal functions of language in a table of canonical forms that any language must possess to be a language? Or is it not true, rather, that we gain access to what different languages have in common only by grasping something of their total power of expression, without being able to make certain forms of one correspond to forms of the other, without seeing them all in the light of one single, universal language?

This question is exactly parallel to the one which we raised in our consideration of psychology. When Husserl laid it down that all empirical research must be preceded by an eidetic intuition of what an image is, what a perception is or in general by the apprehension of a pure essence, we raised the question of whether we could arrive at such conceptions without recourse to the facts. And since Husserl himself conceived of his eidetic intuition as an *experience,* a constatation, we then raised further questions concerning the relation between this contact with the facts, which is realized in science, and the sovereign insight which enables us to grasp essences through the facts in which they are incarnate.

At the beginning of his investigations, Husserl seems to absorb all facts into a universe of thought which determines every psychological possibility, as it should be determined, before any serious reference to empirical psychology. But here, as elsewhere, Husserl was not able, and finally did not wish, to defend a *dualism* between the experimental (scientific) knowledge of facts and philosophical reflection.

As his thought developed, his conception of the relation between language and reflection changed profoundly. At the beginning, there is a way of thought which detaches itself from concrete language and constructs a table of all linguistic possibilities. But as he advanced, our reflection on language appeared to him less and less an operation by which we may bypass concrete languages to arrive at a pure, universal essence, of which each empirical mode of speech is only a possible instance. This reflection becomes less and less a sovereign thinking, owing nothing to the facts. The a priori of language (what one finds by reflecting on it) is less and less a "general and rational grammar."

In an issue of the *Revue internationale de philosophie* devoted to Husserl, H. J. Pos [25] showed that, according to the last conceptions of Husserl, reflecting on language no longer means to depart from it in order to arrive at a thought which will completely envelop and possess it. To reflect on language is, rather, to recover an experience which is anterior to the objectivizing of language and certainly anterior to the scientific observation of it. In this experience the subject, who speaks and writes, passes beyond language only by exercising it and by taking it over.

According to Pos, there is a fundamental difference between the philosopher, or the phenomenologist, who reflects on language and the scholar who knows language objectively, according to the documents which are there before him. The phenomenologist tries to recover an awareness of what a speaking subject really is. He is certainly not in the attitude of a learned observer who is confronting something external to him. This observer, for example, may be considering the state of the French language at the time when I am speaking and may be showing how this is explained by some preceding state. He is thus relating the present to the past. But the speaking subject is not concerned with the past. Most of those who are presently speaking French know nothing of etymology or of the linguistic past which has made possible the language they are speaking. And the linguists themselves admit that this is explained not by its historical origins but rather by actual usage. The speaking subject is turned toward the future. Language for him is above all a means of expression and of communicating to others his intentions, which are also turned toward the future.

The observer also has a strong tendency to analyze into a series of processes which he regards as relatively independent of one another. He will show how such and such a French turn of phrase goes back to a certain origin and how other parts of the French system go back to other origins. He may even show, as a result of such analysis, how the unity of a given language breaks down. Thus there is no precise moment in history when Latin ceases and French begins. There is no such moment at which one can reasonably say: here is the frontier between Latin and French. There is no rigorous procedure which will

25. H. J. Pos, "Phénoménologie et linguistique," *Revue internationale de philosophie*, I (1939), 354–65.

enable us to determine the exact beginning of a linguistic reality. It has no precise spatial and temporal limits.

Similarly if we look within a given language, we find different dialects which are compatible with its unity but whose limits are extremely vague. If one defines Provençal by a certain number of words, turns of phrase, forms of expression, etc., there is no moment when all these are in use equally and at once, no determinate place where Provençal as a whole is perfectly realized. Between the regions where it is dominant and those where it does not prevail there are always zones of transition.

This led Vendryes [26] to say that a language can never be identified as a reality. It is, rather, "an ideal which never succeeds in being realized." We may say that it is in the air *between* the speaking subjects but never fully realized in any of them. From the point of view of the observer, therefore, there is reason for doubting the reality of different languages. And as we have seen, Vendryes conceded some truth to the idea that there is only one single language, since there is no way of finding the precise limit where one passes to another.

But for the subject who is actually speaking, who is no longer an *observer* confronting language as an *object,* his language is undoubtedly a distinct reality. There are regions where he can make himself understood and others where he cannot. For him it means something to be speaking French. The circumstances may be more or less precise, more or less rigorous, more or less complex, depending on the culture of the speaker. But for him there is always a moment, a boundary, beyond which he no longer understands and is no longer understood.

These two points of view are different. And according to Pos, the most distinctive idea in Husserl's thought about language at the end of his life is that the chief task of linguistic philosophy, or phenomenology, is to regain an awareness of the speaking subject. He moved far from the old text of the *Logical Investigations,* to which I have just referred. There is no longer any question of making us leap beyond language into a universe of thought in which it would be included as a particular sector. Reflection on language now consists not in returning to a transcendental subject, disengaged from all actual linguistic

26. Joseph Vendryes, *Le Langage: Introduction linguistique à l'histoire* (Paris: Renaissance du Livre, 1921); English translation by Paul Radin, *Language: A Linguistic Introduction to History* (New York: Knopf, 1925).

situations, but to a speaking subject who has no access to any truth nor to any thought with a claim to universality except through the practice of his language in a definite linguistic situation.

Husserl's change of mind on this point is linked with the maturing of his whole philosophy. In our thinking we do not find in particular phenomena, such as language, a consciousness which can dispose, in an explicit fashion, of all that is necessary to constitute itself. We must, rather, become aware of this paradox—that we never free ourselves from the particular except by taking over a situation that is all at once, and inseparably, both limitation and access to the universal. There is no longer any question of constructing a logic of language, a universal grammar, but rather of finding a logic already incorporated in the word. Husserl was saying of language what he also said of other sectors of his philosophy, that the most profound reflection consists in rediscovering a basic faith, or opinion (*Urglaube, Urdoxa*)—that is, a reason which is already incorporated in sensible phenomena. It seemed to him that to reflect on language is to clarify the activity of the speaking subject, to find a reason already incorporated in these means of expression, this language which I know because I am it.

This is why, in his last unedited writings, Husserl found a much deeper significance in the problem of language. In *Formal and Transcendental Logic,* published during his lifetime, he already expressly indicated that to speak is not at all *to translate a thought into words.* It is rather *to see a certain object* by the word.

> The intention of signifying [*Meinung*] is not found outside the words, or at their side. It is rather the case that, in speaking, I constantly achieve an internal fusion of the intention with the words. This intention, we may say, animates the words, and as a result all the words, and indeed each word, incarnate an intention; and once incarnated, they bear this in themselves as their meaning.[27]

The relation of language to thought is here comparable to that of the body to consciousness, a problem with which Husserl

27. *Formale und transzendentale Logik* (Halle: Niemeyer, 1929), p. 20; cf. English translation by Dorion Cairns, *Formal and Transcendental Logic* (The Hague: Martinus Nijhoff, 1969), § 3, p. 22.

was always preoccupied. At the beginning of his career, he insisted on the fact that this relation was purely external. When I reflect on consciousness, I find it pure. But when I think about man—that is, consciousness linked to a body—I must perform what he called an "apperception." This means that I must seize this consciousness not as it truly is in itself but only as it is causally linked to a certain object which I call "the body." Thus according to this first conception, my relation to another person consists only in conceiving, or "apperceiving," back of the body-object a thinker who is not mixed with this body and is not altered by being joined to it. But as Husserl's thought matured—for example, in the *Cartesian Meditations*, written much later—his conception of the relation of one person to another and of consciousness to the body became much more profound.

In the *Cartesian Meditations* the experience of the other is like something taught me by the spontaneity of my body. It is as if my body learns what my consciousness cannot, for this body takes the actions of the other into account, realizes a sort of coupling with them, or an "intentional transgression," without which I would never gain the notion of the other as other. Thus the body is not only an object to which my consciousness finds itself externally linked. For me it is the only way of knowing that there are other animated bodies, which also means that its own link with my consciousness is more internal and essential.

The same is true of language. Consciousness of language is no longer the separated foundation of a language, which is secondary to it and derived. To know what language is, it is necessary first of all to speak. It no longer suffices to reflect on the languages lying before us in historical documents of the past. It is necessary to take them over, to live with them, to speak them. It is only by making contact with this speaking subject that I can get a sense of what other languages are and can move around in them.

This explains why it is that finally, in the unpublished texts of Husserl—that on *The Origin of Geometry*,[28] for example—he admitted that the problem of language is fundamental, if one wishes to gain any true clarity on the existence of ideas and

---

28. Since published. See "Die Frage nach dem Ursprung der Geometrie als intentional-historisches Problem," *Revue internationale de philosophie*, I (1939), 203–25; English translation by David Carr, "The Origin of Geometry," in *The Crisis of European Sciences*, Appendix VI, pp. 353–78.

cultural objects in the actual world. We must recognize that what we call "ideas" are carried into the world of existence by their instruments of expression—books, museums, musical scores, writings. If we wish to understand how the phenomenon of "ideal existence" is possible for a number of subjects, who do not live at the same time, to participate in the same ideas, we must first understand how the thoughts of one single subject are incorporated in the cultural instruments which convey them outside and make them accessible to others.

> I do not wish to elaborate here on the problem of the origin of language in its ideal existence, as founded on external expression and on the public document, although I am perfectly clear that a radical clarification of the mode of being of ideal complexes finds here its last condition.[29]

We are far from the initial position of the *Logical Investigations*, where the existence of a given, particular language was founded on ideal existence, a universal grammar, the essence of language. Here the possibility of an ideal existence and of communication between particular subjects is finally founded on the act of speaking as it is realized in writing or in the spoken word. There is no longer any question of starting with a universal language which would furnish the invariable plan of any possible mode of speech, and of then proceeding to the analysis of particular languages. It is exactly the reverse. The language which is present, actual, and effective becomes the model for understanding other possible modes of speech. It is in our experience of the speaking subject that we must find the germ of universality which will enable us to understand other languages.

There is no doubt, I believe, that Husserl was here approaching certain insights of contemporary linguistics, especially that of Saussure. This return to the speaking subject, which Husserl called the phenomenology of language, is required not only for philosophic thought but for linguistics itself, as Saussure conceived of it. To deal with given languages objectively is not enough. We must study the subject who is actually speaking. To the linguistic of language we must add the linguistic of the word. This convergence of the thought of Husserl and Saussure is relevant to what I was saying above concerning the relation be-

29. *Ibid.*, p. 210; cf. English translation, p. 358.

tween psychology and phenomenology—namely, that there is agreement, not opposition, between the immanent development of the sciences of man and that of phenomenology. This agreement promises us a solution of problems concerning the relation between these sciences and philosophy. As his thinking developed, Husserl was led to link more and more what he had at first sharply separated—the possible and the actual, essence and existence. This movement corresponds to the evolution of the human sciences, in so far as they are tending to free themselves from those scientistic and positivistic postulates which perhaps favored their beginnings but which are now retarding their further development.

2. *History*

Here again, at the beginning Husserl affirmed the necessity of an eidetic of history, an a priori science which would determine the real meaning of a number of concepts historians use blindly and without careful examination. One cannot learn what a "social process" or a "religion" is simply by doing empirical history and by being a historian. It is certainly clear that, in so far as these historians have not clarified the sense of the words they are using, they themselves do not know what it is they are talking about. If it aims to show that historical work must define the categories, or essences, implied in it, this remark is sound.

Take, for example, Durkheim's famous investigation of totemism in his *Formes élémentaires de la vie religieuse*. He asked himself how one should understand the phenomenon of the sacred as it is found in Australian totemism. Having shown that, in the tribes considered, the experience of the sacred occurs at moments devoted to totemic celebrations and at annual reunions when social bonds are strongest, he thought he could draw the conclusion that in general the sacred is an expression of the social. Since the sacred is an essential element in religion, he also concluded that religion in general is the social.

It is of course true that definitions are free and that Durkheim had the right to call the social, and the sacred, religious. But in giving the title *Elementary Forms of the Religious Life* to his book, he implied something more. He meant to say that the phenomena studied by him (Australian totemism) are *elementary*—that is, they reveal the elements, or the essence, of religion in such a way that every particular religion must be considered as a variation on this theme. With respect to a postulate of this kind, the demands of Husserl seem to be justified. Even if this study of the sacred in Australian totemism were itself incontestable, the question of whether the sacred is the "elementary," or essential, religious phenomenon would still be left open. There are many religious phenomena which are more rich and more varied than Australian totemism. Must we believe that they are mere superstructures based on the sacred as it is experienced by these tribes? This cannot be postulated, and it is precisely the object of Husserl's questions to obtain such a clarification. What is a religion, or what is the essence of religion? If it really is the sacred, then Durkheim may draw his universal conclusion. But if the sacred is only a lateral, or derived, phenomenon, always present but never having the same sense in different religions, then Durkheim's investigations do not authorize the general conclusion he wished to draw from them.

There is, therefore, something well founded in this idea of Husserl that contact with the facts is not enough to determine, for example, whether we ought to distinguish between "religion as an idea and religion as a cultural form." History shows cultural forms to which we give the name "religion," but from the variety, confusion, and incoherence of these phenomena, as they are given, should we conclude that they can still be analyzed? Or should we wait for another possible experience that would be not only religious but also pure religion? This question cannot be answered by a mere examination of the facts. It requires reflection on the essence of religion, as well as a phenomenology of history. In the same way history shows us that Egyptian art is such and such, that Greek art is this and that. But on this basis one cannot come to any legitimate conclusion concerning the universal forms of all possible art. We must begin by reflecting on what art is, on what it can be—which is again a determination of essence. History also shows us a number of juridical systems. But according to Husserl the investigation of relevant historical facts in which just law is manifested remains "confused," unless one has determined what just law is, in principle, by a reflection that is not of the empirical order.

Husserl first said, in brief, that history is unable to judge an idea. It is true that there are historians who write as if the ideas are being judged by the facts. The reciting of events or the analysis of institutions seems by itself to show that a certain ideal pattern, such as religion or monarchy, either is or is not coherent, either depends or does not depend on a chance coincidence. But in reality, Husserl said, the history which sets up values and judges arrives at these values not in the facts but in an ideal sphere. It involves a latent phenomenology which is not expressed and which is, therefore, probably incorrect. In his first conception the hierarchy is very clear. There is a reflection on historical possibilities which is autonomous and independent of any knowledge of historical facts.

The conception of historicity which Husserl constructed at the beginning of his career resulted directly from this principle. He found among his contemporaries certain philosophers who were concerned to remain in close touch with the present. They accepted the *Weltanschauung* conception of Dilthey. According to them, philosophy is not a type of knowledge which develops with absolute certainty outside time. At each moment it should be, rather, a conscious grasp of what is sound in the scientific results already acquired as well as a synthesis of these, which must be provisional, approximative, and only probable. In his article "Philosophie als strenge Wissenschaft" Husserl took a stand against the position of these philosophers. He did this in a manner which was decisive but also carefully shaded.

He began by declaring that Dilthey and the *Weltanschauung* philosophy were certainly responding to a *legitimate need*—that of deciding in a single lifetime to live in the light of reflection and to arrive in this way at effective, practical conclusions. This philosophy, he said, has a firm grasp of the truth that we have an end in the finite, since our lives are limited and we have to govern them. It would be nonsense to deny these responsibilities. In a unique life there must be a method of constant approximation rather than practical, apodictic certainties. Morality would lose its meaning if it were emptied of its essential finitude. Moral man must arrive at judgments and, in any case, at acts which imply judgments. Similarly it is necessary for him to orient himself in the world and at each moment to have a conception of the world, even though scientific philosophy, which is certain and rigorous, is not yet fully developed.

Only, Husserl adds, this practical necessity of answering problems of existence is not a sufficient justification for the conception of philosophy as a *Weltanschauung* that is merely probable. A truly rigorous philosophy would give an answer to the problems of the time. It would construct the idea of our time, and would think this time through just as well as, or even better than, the others. As a consequence, precisely in being *philosophia perennis*, it would be the philosophy of the present. If under the pretext that this philosophy is not yet on hand, one turns from it and abandons it for the sake of a *Weltanschauung*, one weakens true philosophy and postpones the solution of the problems posed. Therefore we should not look to wisdom but to philosophy, not to a mere view of the world (*Weltanschauung*) but to the science of the world (*Weltwissenschaft*). So Husserl decided against these philosophers of *Weltanschauung*, who are able to struggle but never to gain a decisive solution. According to him, they "place their end in the finite. They wish to have their system, and then enough time to live in accordance with it." [30]

Husserl, therefore, recognized that the problems posed by the present are legitimate, and he never said that philosophy ought to abandon them. But he thought that it could not arrive at these problems of life except by the way of an absolute knowledge. If *de jure* philosophical research is not remote from the present, at least *de facto* it is, and since it requires much time and all our human powers, it should become in itself a way of existing and not a mere preparation for life, as it was for Dilthey. Thus Husserl never denied that the philosopher experiences the need of thinking through and of judging his time, in so far as he has to live an individual life. But he did not want to sacrifice the least element of philosophical rigor to present exigencies. Hence he conceded, as a consequence he had not wished but had to accept, that philosophers should not have any deeply motivated opinion on present affairs, if at this price they could contribute to the founding of a truly rigorous philosophy which eventually would be a total philosophy and, therefore, also a philosophy of the present.

We must here remember that even at the beginning Husserl never chose eternity as against time. He never said that philosophical existence was absolute. He said only that, since philosophy demands an unlimited effort, if we wish it to be truly rigorous and truly a philosophy, we must sell neither it nor our powers to our time. As a matter of fact, Husserl knew that

30. "Philosophie als strenge Wissenschaft," p. 338; cf. "Philosophy as Rigorous Science," p. 143 (see note 15, above).

philosophy had eaten up the whole of his life, and he never complained. But he never thought that philosophy was the whole of life.

Afterward he perceived that philosophical activity cannot be defined as reflection concerned with essences, as opposed to practical activity concerned with existence. In order to see things more clearly than he had been able to see them in the past, what was of primary importance now seemed to him to be historicity. When one reflects and thinks things through to the very end, one will not necessarily arrive at eternal truths. By the purest thought one will, rather, discover an intelligible becoming of ideas, a "generation of meaning" (*Sinngenesis*). In the last analysis, cultural realities are of such a nature that we cannot reflect on them without discovering in the sense of these notions a "sedimented history." It may be the theorem of Pythagoras; it may be the more modern conceptions of geometry in the nineteenth century. When we reflect on these ideas it may seem to us, at our first view, that we have arrived at invariable elements, always the same in all thinking for all men who have lived or ever will live.

But after regarding them more carefully, we preceive that Euclidean geometry includes ideas, of course, but ideas that have a date. Nineteenth-century geometry takes them over but defines them otherwise and finally considers Euclidean space as a special case of one that is more general. This means that in spite of its apparent lucidity and its air of eternity, Euclidean space was not self-evident. Until the time of the non-Euclidean geometries, it was not entirely penetrated by the spirit but included a certain coefficient of contingency. It was, after all, a cultural formation which included finite and "naïve" elements linked to a certain temporal state of knowledge. Hence while it did not have to be destroyed or discounted by what came after, it had to be at least completed, elaborated, and sublimated by later geometric conceptions. Thus when we reflect even on geometric notions, we discover a historical becoming. As Plato said long ago, we discover that the ideas are not at rest.

If this is true, where, then—if we may speak in this way—is the place of philosophy? It is evidently not in the event; nor is it in the eternal. It is in a history which is not the sum of these events placed end to end, since they force each other out of existence. But this history is thinkable, comprehensible. It offers us an order, a sense to which I do not have to submit but which I can place in perspective. Husserl called this an "intentional history." Others have called it "dialectic." This is why we find terms in the later writings of Husserl that he would not have thought of employing at the beginning, such as "the European sciences." He came to see an essential value in the historical development of European philosophy and science which must be continued. Certain notions cannot be attained except by a series of successive steps and by a sedimentation of meaning which makes it impossible for the new sense to appear before its time and apart from certain factual conditions. Of course, this knowledge is universal, and there is no question of restricting it to those who have brought it forth or of limiting it to European forms of existence. In order to surmount the crisis it is going through, it must be rendered universal in fact, as it is in right. Certainly nothing was more foreign to Husserl than a European chauvinism. For him European knowledge would maintain its value only by becoming capable of understanding what is not itself.

What is new in the later writings is that to think philosophically, to be a philosopher, is no longer to leap from existence to essence, to depart from facticity in order to join the idea. To think philosophically, to be a philosopher—in relation to the past, for example—is to understand this past through the internal link between it and us. Comprehension thus becomes a coexistence in history, which extends not only to our contemporaries but also to Plato, to what is back of us, and to what is before us and far distant. Philosophy is the taking over of cultural operations begun before our time and pursued in many different ways, which we now "reanimate" and "reactivate" from the standpoint of our present. Philosophy lives from this power of *interesting* ourselves in everything that has been and is attempted in the order of knowledge and of life, and of finding a sharable sense in it, as if all things were present to us through our present. The true place of philosophy is not time, in the sense of discontinuous time, nor is it the eternal. It is rather the "living present" (*lebendige Gegenwart*)—that is, the present in which the whole past, everything foreign, and the whole of the thinkable future are reanimated.

So far as historical investigations are concerned, we can now see that at the end of his life Husserl came to have a very different idea of them from that which he had at the beginning. He now saw in historical and ethnographic facts a value, a significance, a power of teaching that he had not seen before.

He admitted from the beginning that history can teach something to the philosopher; it can lead him to the objective spirit (*Gemeingeist*).[31] He had already indicated that a historian who criticizes a phenomenon—like "Christianity" or "monarchy," for example—showing that these are nothing but names given to series of incoherent facts lacking any essential unity, is already beginning a work of reflection and doing philosophy without knowing it. All criticism, he said, is the inverse side of a positive affirmation. Consequently, every historical criticism involves a systematic intuition which must be brought into the light. Hence he was prepared to grant, at this early stage of his career, that there was a confused intuition of essence in concrete historical research. Later on he conceded more explicitly that contact with historical or ethnological facts is not only suggestive but even indispensable for any true apprehension of the possible.

It is important to note the extraordinary interest aroused in Husserl by his reading of Lévy-Bruhl's *Primitive Mythology* [*Mythologie primitive*], which seems rather remote from his ordinary concerns. What interested him here was the contact with an alien culture, or the impulse given by this contact to what we may call his philosophical imagination. Before this, Husserl had maintained that a mere imaginative variation of the facts would enable us to conceive of every possible experience we might have. In a letter to Lévy-Bruhl which has been preserved, he seems to admit that the facts go beyond what we imagine and that this point bears a real significance. It is as if the imagination, left to itself, is unable to represent the possibilities of existence which are realized in different cultures.

> It is a task of the highest importance, which may be actually achieved, to feel our way into a humanity whose life is enclosed in a vital, social tradition, and to understand it in this unified social life. This is the basis of the world which is no mere representation [*Weltvorstellung*] but rather the world that actually is *for it* [*sondern die für sie wirklich seiende Welt ist*].[32]

31. *Ibid.*, p. 328; cf. English translation, p. 129.
32. The letter is in the Husserl Archives at Louvain.

Husserl was struck by the contact which Lévy-Bruhl had established, through his book, with the actual experience of primitive man. Having made this contact with the author's aid, he now saw that it is perhaps not possible for us, who live in certain historical traditions, to conceive of the historical possibility of these primitive men by a mere variation of our imagination. For these primitives are nonhistorical (*Geschichtlos*). There are certain "stagnant" societies, as they are sometimes called, in which our conception of history is simply absent. Life for them is only a present which is constantly renewed and simply succeeds itself. How is it possible for a German, born in the nineteenth century in a milieu (*Umwelt*) which is not fixed but in a world which has a national past to be realized and a future partly realized, to know this by mere imagination? If one is born into a culture which is structured by historical time, by an ancient past that has now arrived and a future becoming past, how will he represent "a life that is only a flowing present" (*strö-mende Gegenwart*)?

He will have to reconstitute the lived experience and the actual milieu of the primitive man. The merit of Lévy-Bruhl's work is that it revived this milieu, the environment of the primitive man. Civilizations like ours grant that men of the past had a future in view and that all these futures have come to a present in which they are sedimented. We now have the impression that we also are oriented toward a future which will take over what is good as well as what is bad in our present and, through this, in the life of our predecessors, perhaps giving them a sense which they did not have before or, on the contrary, remaining faithful to them. Whether we consider our lives as a rupture with the past or as a continuation of it, there is always an internal relation between that which has been, that which is, and that which will be. This is precisely that historicity (*Geschichtlichkeit*) which does not exist in stagnant, or frozen, societies.

We must have an experience which is organized in such a way as to express the whole environment (*Umwelt*) of these primitive men. There must be a joining of effort between anthropology as a mere inventory of actual facts and phenomenology as a mere thinking through of possible societies. It is essential that this abstract phenomenology should come into contact with the facts, that it should work out, as Lévy-Bruhl did, a way of animating and of organizing these facts which might convey them to the reader as they are lived by those who are actually caught up in this context.

With respect to this intentional analysis of different cultural formations, "historical relativism has its incontestable justification as an anthropological fact" (*der historische Relativismus sein zweifelloser Recht behält—als anthropologische Tatsache*). But while anthropology, together with the other positive sciences, may have the first word in the gaining of scientific knowledge, it does not have the last. Historical relativism is now no longer dominated at one stroke by a mode of thought which would have all the keys of history and would be in a position to classify all possible histories before any factual inquiry. On the contrary, the thinker who wishes to dominate history in this way must learn from the facts and must enter into them.

In order to grasp the essential structures of a human community, one must himself take into account, and relive, the whole milieu (*Umwelt*) of this society. Historical knowledge is a coexistence with the meanings of a people and not merely the solitary reflection of a historian. The eidetic of history cannot dispense with factual investigation. In the eyes of Husserl, philosophy, as a coherent thought which leads to a classification of facts according to their value and truth, continues to have its final importance. But it must begin by understanding the lived experiences.

At this point phenomenology, in Husserl's sense, rejoins phenomenology in the Hegelian sense, which consists in following man through his experiences without substituting oneself for him but rather working through them in such a way as to reveal their sense. The term "phenomenology" ends by bringing out into the open everything that is implicitly contained at the start. It was not by accident that Husserl made this choice.

CONCLUSION
FROM HUSSERL TO HIS SUCCESSORS

THE DEVELOPMENT OF Husserl's thought, which I have tried to trace, is not a mere change of mind, a hesitation, or a zigzag. His problem, as defined in the first lecture, was to find a way between psychology and philosophy—a mode of thinking, in short, which would be neither eternal and without root in the present nor a mere event destined to be replaced by another event tomorrow, and consequently deprived of any intrinsic value. Husserl began like all philosophers; that is, he tried to achieve a radical reflection. He tried to reflect on this power of thought which he was, and this radical reflection finally discovered, behind itself, the unreflected as the condition of its possibility, without which it would have no sense.

Reflection is historicity—on the one hand the possession of myself and on the other my insertion into a history. These two elements are not antagonistic to each other. In so far as thought matures, they become correlative. It belongs to the nature of my reflection to gain possession of myself and in consequence to free myself from determination by external conditions. But in reflecting in this way, and just because I am doing it with the purpose of escaping external temporality, I at once discover a temporality and a historicity that I am. My reflection is taken over from preceding reflections and from a movement of existence which offers itself to me. But, Husserl said, it always involves a certain degree of naïveté. It never lifts itself out of time.

For example, the relation between philosophy and the history of philosophy is reciprocal. The philosopher understands the history of philosophy by his own thoughts, and yet at the same time he understands himself in relation to the history of philosophy to which he has access as a spectacle. In short, he understands himself by the history of philosophy, and he understands this history by himself. "A relative clarification of the one side sheds some light on the other, which in its turn reflects back on the first," Husserl said in the last volume he prepared for publication. There is no doubt that he would have said of history in general just what he said here of the history of philosophy. As a result, we can say that the problem with which we were concerned at the beginning—must we be for fact or for essence, for time or eternity, for the positive science of man or philosophy?—was bypassed in the later thought of Husserl. Here he no longer considers essence as separated from fact, eternity from time, or philosophic thought from history.

It is at first rather surprising to find that in this effort to link philosophy with time and history, Husserl went much further than his successors, Max Scheler and Heidegger. They tried much more quickly than he to incorporate irrational elements, in the traditional sense of this phrase, into philosophy. They attempted to work out an analysis not only of consciousness, the privileged domain for Husserl, but of what Scheler called "the logic of the heart" and what Heidegger called "being in the world." One would therefore expect that they would be more ready to bring philosophy down into the sphere of "facticity," as Heidegger referred to it. But in fact, when they seek to define philosophical knowledge, we find them adopting dogmatic formulae which remind us of certain earlier statements of Husserl. They seem to see no difficulties in assuming an unconditional philosophic intuition.

For example, when Scheler defines intuition of essence in his famous book on ethics,[33] he says that we know an essence without the slightest intervention of physical, physiological, psychological, or historical factors arising from our individuality. He maintains that, in seeing the "unities of ideal meaning," there is no need to pay any attention to these factors of particularity. They have no influence on our vision of what we take to be an essence which is, in fact, truly an essence. Husserl would have replied that an affirmation of this kind is "naïve." If I were to consider ten years afterward what had been for me ten years before an insight into essence, I would perceive that I had not been in the presence of the *things themselves* and that a number of momentary factors, such as my ruling prejudices and my particular way of existing, had entered into this so-called evidence.

In *Formal and Transcendental Logic* Husserl made it clear that every insight into essence includes "a certain degree of naïveté"—that is to say, unconsciousness. He seemed to be much more conscious, much more rigorous than Scheler, and his effort to link essence with existence is finally much more mindful of the truth than Scheler's uncritical affirmation. Scheler expresses the curious juxtaposition of a philosophy which on the one hand seeks "alogical essences" and on the other hand conceives of itself as having an unconditioned power of arriving at the truth.

This comment also applies to Heidegger, who devotes himself to the description of being in the world. One might expect, therefore, that the philosopher who finds himself thrown into the

33. *Formalism in Ethics and Nonformal Ethics of Values*, translated by Roger L. Funk and Manfred S. Frings (Evanston, Ill.: Northwestern University Press, 1973).

world might also find some difficulty in arriving at an adequate state of knowledge. But Heidegger defines the attitude of the philosopher without recognizing any restriction on the absolute power of philosophical thought. For example, at the beginning of *Sein und Zeit*,[34] he says that the task of philosophy is to explore the natural concept of the world, independently of science, by the primordial experience we have of it. To determine the structure of this natural world, he adds, it is not at all necessary to have any recourse to ethnology or to psychology. These disciplines presuppose a philosophical knowledge of the natural world, and one can never find the principle which will enable us to order psychological or ethnographical facts by making inductions from these facts. In order to do this, the spirit itself must first possess the principle.

We have already found this antithesis of philosophy and psychology and this same reassertion of the priority of philosophy in Husserl. But we have seen how, as his thought matured, this relation of priority gave way to one of interdependence and reciprocity. In the point which concerns us, Scheler and Heidegger remained fixed in their thesis of a pure and simple opposition between philosophy and the sciences of man or, as Heidegger put it, between the ontological and the ontic. For Husserl, as we have seen, this opposition was only a point of departure, which later became a problem, and finally a hidden connection between the two kinds of research. Husserl, who defined philosophy as the suspension of our affirmation of the world, recognized the actual being of the philosopher in the world much more clearly than Heidegger, who devoted himself to the study of being in the world.

It will not be possible for us here to reflect at length on this paradox. If we were to subject it to a close examination, we would perhaps find nothing unexpected in it. A certain form of immediate dogmatism, or rationalism, is not only reconcilable but deeply allied with irrationalism. The most effective defenders of reason in practice and even in theory are not those who abstractly make the strongest claims for it. And inversely it is quite in order that a philosopher like Husserl, who was particularly sensitive on the subject of rationality, should be more capable, precisely to

34. 3d ed. (Halle: Niemeyer, 1931), p. 45; English translation by John MacQuarrie and Edward Robinson, *Being and Time* (New York: Harper & Row, 1962), p. 71.

this degree, of recognizing the link between reason and existence. This is because, for him, rationality is no phantom. He bears it within himself and practices it.

But let us now return to our problem. Phenomenologists, above all Husserl, have always felt that psychology was concerned with a very distinctive type of knowledge. It is not inductive in the sense which this word carries with empiricists. But neither is it reflective in the traditional philosophical sense—that is, a return to the a priori which would determine the form of all human experience. One may say indeed that psychological knowledge is reflection but that it is at the same time an experience. According to the phenomenologist (Husserl), it is a "material a priori." Psychological reflection is a "constatation" (a finding). Its task is to discover the meaning of behavior through an effective contact with my own behavior and that of others. Phenomenological psychology is therefore a search for the essence, or meaning, but not apart from the facts. Finally this essence is accessible only in and through the individual situation in which it appears. When pushed to the limit, eidetic psychology becomes analytic-existential.

Let us now turn to the psychologists. With reference to them I propose to show that, while the phenomenologists have been working out their reflections in the ways I have just indicated, the psychologists have also been led to redefine psychological knowledge in an analogous manner. This has been due in part to the direct influence of phenomenologies, in part to a diffuse influence of which they were not conscious, and above all to the pressure of the concrete problems with which they had to deal. I propose to show in the following lectures that psychology, as we have seen it developing during the last twenty-five or thirty years, is certainly not inductive in the empiricist sense of the term. But, of course, neither is it a priori in the sense of a reflection which owes nothing to the contact of the psychologist himself with the facts and with the situation he is trying to clarify. Psychology is tending, rather, to rely on a disciplined reading of the phenomena which arise both in me and outside of me, and on a resulting grasp of the meaning of human behavior. If this agreement is confirmed, it should enable us to relate philosophy to psychology in such a way as to make the existence of the one compatible with that of the other.

Phenomenological Method and the Anthropological Science of the Cultural Life-World

David Bidney

PHENOMENOLOGY AND PHILOSOPHICAL ANTHROPOLOGY IN HISTORICAL PERSPECTIVE

THE TERM PHENOMENOLOGY refers back to the distinction introduced by Kant between *phenomena,* which are the appearances of reality in consciousness, and *noumena,* which are the things-in-themselves, independent of consciousness. The term *phenomenology* was first utilized by Hegel in his *Phenomenology of Mind* in 1807. According to Hegel, phenomena reveal the nature of reality or absolute Being dialectically in the course of history. Historical, cultural phenomena are always relative to, and a function of, consciousness, but human consciousness itself develops in time as an expression of Absolute Mind or Spirit. Hegel's *Phenomenology of Mind* is an empirical, historical study of the spiritual or mental evolution of mankind as revealed in its culture history. This evolution of thought and culture is, however, interpreted ontologically as the self-revelation through human consciousness of the absolute subject or spirit immanent in nature. There is said to be a universal Mind at work in the world (*Weltgeist*), which manifests itself historically and phenomenally in collective human consciousness and social thought through determinate dialectical stages of development. Phenomenology, for Hegel, is the description and analysis of this development or evolution of human thought, which is culture (*Bildung*) from the perspective of individual consciousness but is self-revelation from the perspective of Absolute Mind. Hegel's phe-

[109]

nomenology is a record of the spiritual anthropology of man derived from a comparative study of the history of human culture. It is also a spiritual theodicy and philosophy of history which, like that of Vico, recognizes an immanent providence in human history which directs the development of human thought and culture. All the stages in the development of human culture are moments in the self-revelation of Absolute Mind as well as in the evolution of self-consciousness and freedom of expression of the human spirit.

Hegel's phenomenology may be said to be an ontological phenomenology as well as a philosophy of culture history. The phenomena of culture history reveal or make manifest the nature of the absolute, unconditioned noumenal reality which is Absolute Mind or Spirit. Cultural phenomena are objectifications in space and time of the eternal Mind, of which they are the modes of expression. Human cultural anthropology in historical perspective is the spiritual odyssey of man in history.

In the so-called Copernican revolution of Kant, man's transcendental ego is made the measure of all things. Kant's Critiques are critical anthropological treatises which investigate the a priori mental conditions of the whole of human culture, including natural science, ethics, religion, and art. The human mind is said to be limited to the study of the phenomena of experience as constituted by the categories of the understanding and the regulative ideas of pure and practical reason. The possibility of metaphysical knowledge of things-in-themselves as they exist, independent of the human mind, is denied on principle. In making the human mind the measure of all things, Kant, in effect, reduced the reality of nature to culture. All the phenomena of experience are anthropocentric, subjective, cultural phenomena; man lives in a phenomenal world of his own construction, while accepting on faith the possibility of a noumenal, metaphysical world independent of his consciousness. In denying that things-in-themselves can be the object of empirical, scientific knowledge, Kant was responsible for the alleged antithesis of science and metaphysics or ontology—a thesis which he shares with the later positivism of Auguste Comte. All human experience is cultural experience mediated by the mind of man in his own image. If the "Copernican revolution" means that perspective which views cosmic nature from a nonanthropocentric point of view, then Kant's philosophy may be said to be counterrevolutionary. For

Kant, the phenomena given in human experience are human constructs which conceal rather than reveal the objective reality to which they refer.

Nevertheless, Kant's sanity and common sense prevailed, in spite of his philosophical anthropology. He differentiates sharply between man's experience of nature and human moral and aesthetic culture. No matter how man constructs the phenomena of nature, nature remains the sphere of necessity and natural law; nature is that to which man has to conform and adapt, even though the human understanding prescribes laws to nature. By contrast, moral culture is an expression of human freedom and practical reason and is self-regulating. In moral culture, the maxim "Thou canst because thou oughtest" holds good, but in the sphere of nature and natural science man is confronted with an order of phenomena which is not dependent on human will.

Thus man may be said to live in two worlds: the world of nature, of which he is a part and to whose laws he is subject, and the human world of moral and aesthetic culture, which is an expression of his free will and ideal creativity. Man cannot change the order of nature; he can only understand it. But man can change the order of his historic cultural world because he himself has created it and brought it into existence. In this respect, it would appear, Kant is in fundamental agreement with Rousseau that human freedom is the source of the social, moral, and political order of culture and that it is subject to change through human will and effort.

Kant himself did not develop the historical implications of his theory of social culture. His single essay on history follows the Leibnizian model and suggests the possibility of a divine providence immanent in universal human history—a theory which, he thought, still required its Newton to develop and verify. In fact, this was precisely the thesis of Vico in his *New Science,* of which Kant apparently was ignorant. It is also the thesis of Hegel's *Phenomenology of Mind.*

The Neo-Kantian philosopher Wilhelm Dilthey proposed a Critique of Historical Reason to supplement Kant's Critiques of Pure and Practical Reason. Dilthey, however, never succeeded in bringing his project to life. Instead he continued to follow the essentially Kantian dualistic model in his philosophy of culture. He differentiates sharply between the sphere of natural science (*Naturwissenschaft*) and that of the humanities or human sciences (*Geisteswissenschaften*). In natural science one employs the method of observation and causal explanation of natural phenomena. In the human sciences one deals with life-forms and *Weltanschauungen,* which can be described and understood (*verstehen*) through actual lived experience but which cannot be explained by reference to natural law.

Heinrich Rickert criticized Dilthey's use of the term *Geisteswissenschaft* and suggested instead that the term *Kulturwissenschaft* be used to connote all those products of human activity not given by nature. He agreed that the cultural sciences require a subjective, "ideographic" approach and insight into the symbolism involved in each cultural instance. Rickert and Dilthey agreed with Kant that cultural, social phenomena are not subject to natural laws as are the phenomena of nature (nomothetic).

It should be noted in this connection that Auguste Comte did envisage a natural science of society, which he termed, for the first time, *sociology.* The evolutionary sociology and anthropology or ethnology of the late nineteenth and early twentieth centuries continued to follow the naturalistic, positivistic thesis of Comte in their quest for natural laws of society and culture history. The American anthropologist, A. L. Kroeber, adopted an eclectic approach by contrasting the nomothetic science of culture with the ideographic history of culture, both of which he thought to be compatible alternative approaches to the study of culture. Kroeber admitted, however, that ethnologists, though they have been most successful in providing historical patterns of culture, have not succeeded so far in discovering the elusive cultural laws.[1]

Ernst Cassirer follows Dilthey's Neo-Kantian historical idealism rather closely. Cassirer maintains that man cannot know himself as a substance or thing-in-itself apart from symbolic representations. He proposes to substitute the historic symbolic forms of culture for the categories of Kant. All human experience is said to be organized by the a priori symbolic forms which make culture possible. Man is said to be an *animal symbolicum* rather than an *animal rationale.* The various types of symbolic forms manifested or expressed in myth, language, art, and science are thought to be "organs of reality." The symbolic forms of human culture are creative, constitutive expressions of the human mind,

1. See David Bidney, *Theoretical Anthropology* (New York: Schocken Books, 1967), Appendix.

not of Absolute Mind, as in Hegel's *Phenomenology*. It becomes the task of the philosophical anthropologist to provide a phenomenological analysis and description of the various forms of symbolism revealed historically in the course of the evolution of the langauge and culture of mankind. In agreement with Hegel and Comte, Cassirer maintains that self-knowledge can be obtained only through an intuitive analysis of man's historic cultural achievements.

For Cassirer, all reality as known is ultimately cultural or symbolic reality, created by the human mind or spirit itself in the course of its evolutionary development. Man is said to live in a symbolic universe of his own creation. The symbol takes the place of Kant's "forms of intuition" and "categories of understanding." The symbol is the constitutive organ or instrument of reality as man knows it. The human world, the world as known by man, is a historic cultural world. More consistently than Kant, the Neo-Kantian Cassirer tends to reduce the concept of nature to that of culture, thereby reducing ontology or metaphysics to culturology or cultural anthropology.

In effect, Cassirer has transformed the Kantian Critique of Pure Reason and his Critique of Practical Reason into a Critique of Cultural Reason in his *Philosophy of Symbolic Forms*. The ultimate ontologic entity is human spirit or *Geist,* which is the source of all phenomenal, symbolic forms revealed objectively in culture history. Cassirer's philosophy may be characterized as a humanistic, spiritual, phenomenological anthropology which makes man the measure of all things. The Kantian dualism of nature and culture is superseded by the monism of symbolic, cultural idealism or spiritualism. Like Hegel, Cassirer combines a phenomenological analysis of culture history with ontologic idealism or spiritualism. The basic difference between Hegel and Cassirer concerns the nature of the *Geist* or spirit involved; in Hegel it is the Absolute Mind, of which the human mind is a mode of thought; in Cassirer it is man's transcendental ego or spirit, without reference to any metaphysical absolute spirit. Ultimately, Cassirer's philosophical anthropology has no place for metaphysical religion.

For Cassirer, as for Dilthey and Rickert, the method of cultural understanding is essentially phenomenological. It involves intuition and description of symbolic forms of consciousness as given historically in the course of human experience. Each mode or form of symbolism is qualitatively distinct from other modes and hence must not be reduced to, or explained in terms of, other modes. The symbolism of language is not that of art; the symbolism of myth is not that of science. In spite of his idealistic cultural monism, which reduces nature to culture, Cassirer, like other Neo-Kantian philosophers, retains the dualism of natural science and the humanities. Only in the sphere of natural science does one attempt causal explanations in terms of natural law. In the study of culture history and the arts, which are direct expressions of human creativity and freedom, one employs phenomenological analysis and description to achieve direct understanding. As Cassirer wrote in his *Essay on Man:*

> Human culture taken as a whole may be described as the process of man's progressive self-liberation. Language, art, religion, science are various phases of this process. In all of them man discovers and proves a new power—the power to build up a world of his own, an "ideal" world.[2]

> But the reality of history is not a uniform sequence of events but the inner life of man. This life can be described and interpreted after it has been lived; it cannot be anticipated in an abstract general formula, and it cannot be reduced to a rigid scheme of three or five acts.[3]

Cassirer's basic humanistic thesis that culture is the historic process of man's conscious self-liberation is the antithesis of the naturalistic culturological view that culture is an autonomous natural process, subject to its own laws. Cassirer's ultimate ontologic postulate, like that of Ortega y Gasset and Sartre, is that life or existence is prior to its essence and that human life creates itself progressively through its symbolic cultural forms. The notion of fate or destiny, whether put forth in science or myth, is not applicable in the philosophy of culture.

Phenomenology as Philosophical and Scientific Method: Husserl

As a special movement in the philosophical thought of the twentieth century, phenomenology owes its rise to the work

2. Ernst Cassirer, *An Essay on Man* (New Haven: Yale University Press, 1944), p. 228.
3. *Ibid.,* p. 201.

of Edmund Husserl. His *Logical Investigations* (1900) and *Ideas: General Introduction to Pure Phenomenology* (1913) initiated phenomenological philosophy. Husserl's "pure phenomenology" may be viewed as a special synthesis of Cartesian and Kantian thought. His *Cartesian Meditations,* which he also considered to be an "introduction to phenomenology," reveals the strong influence of both Kant and Descartes. Just as Descartes had felt that there was need for a new philosophy of science and scientific methodology at the beginning of the seventeenth century, so Husserl proclaimed the need for a new philosophical method to provide a foundation for the sciences. Like Descartes, too, Husserl began with mathematics, which served as a model of scientific, necessary truth. His objective was to revive the notion of "philosophy as a rigorous science."

In his "Philosophy as Rigorous Science" Husserl expressed his opposition to Dilthey's view that the function of philosophy is to formulate *Weltanschauungen,* or philosophies of life, which will give order and meaning to human life. The trouble, he felt, with this view of philosophy is that it ultimately leads to historical relativism and skepticism. If philosophy is held to be a historical construction of the human spirit, it is relevant only to the historical social conditions which produced it. "The 'idea' of *Weltanschauung* is consequently a different one for each time, a fact that can be seen without difficulty from the preceding analysis of its concept. The 'idea' of science, on the contrary, is a supratemporal one, and here that means limited by no relatedness to the spirit of one time." [4] By contrast, Husserl thought it possible to formulate a rigorous science of philosophy, one that would establish all knowledge on the firm foundations of immediate experience. What our age needs most, he insisted, is a radical philosophy of science which will affirm confidence in human reason and intuition through analysis of the true beginnings or origins of human experience. It is not a question of merely renewing philosophy but of approaching each problem anew, without prejudice or presupposition. In this sense, "philosophy is essentially a science of true beginnings or origins." [5]

Husserl's quest for a rigorous science of philosophy to be

---

4. Edmund Husserl, "Philosophy as Rigorous Science," in Quentin Lauer, ed. and trans., *Edmund Husserl: Phenomenology and the Crisis of Philosophy* (New York: Harper & Row, 1965), pp. 135–36.
5. *Ibid.,* p. 146.

established through the phenomenological method is reminiscent of Descartes's proposal for the unity of scientific and philosophical method in his *Discourse on Method.* In opposition to the duality of methods proposed by the Neo-Kantian philosophers, one for the natural sciences and one for the cultural sciences, Husserl proposes a single scientific method for both the natural and cultural sciences. The problem to be discussed, then, is whether Husserl succeeded where Descartes had failed and whether the new scientific and philosophical revolution proclaimed in the name of phenomenology has achieved its goal.

PHENOMENOLOGY AND THE CRITIQUE OF CONSCIOUSNESS: INTENTIONALITY AND MEANING

ALTHOUGH PHENOMENOLOGICAL METHOD is said to be unitary, Husserl distinguishes the function and objective of philosophy from that of the natural and social sciences. In the manner of Kant, Husserl regards the task of philosophy to be that of providing a critique, not of reason, but of consciousness in general with a view to understanding how an autonomous philosophy and science are possible. Descartes had maintained that his famous proposition *Cogito ergo sum* demonstrates that the first indubitable truth is the existence of the ego as a *res cogitans,* a thinking thing. But Descartes had not bothered to examine carefully what is involved in thinking—what the elements of thinking are, and what human consciousness of thinking is. Husserl would agree that the existence of consciousness is inseparable from the consciousness of existing as the subject of consciousness. What needs further clarification is what it means to be conscious, what makes consciousness possible as an activity of the subject. The first step in phenomenological philosophy is reflection on the meaning or essence of the experience of consciousness. "Phenomenological positivism" begins with the facts of experience and is followed by reflection, intuition, and description of the phenomena of consciousness. Husserl sought by the study of the phenomena of consciousness to find the roots of reason in our human experience. So understood, phenomenology as a philosophy is the science of the sciences, providing the principles which validate, a priori, all the sciences.

The concept of the "intentionality of consciousness" is the

foundation of phenomenological philosophy. Going back to Scholastic philosophy, Franz Brentano had maintained in his *Psychologie vom empirischen Standpunkt* (1924) that the difference between physical and mental or psychical phenomena is to be found in the fact that mental phenomena refer to, and are directed toward, an object which they intend. Husserl adopted Brentano's notion of intentionality and refined it.

Husserl distinguished the act of knowing (*noesis*) from the object (*noema*), whether existent or imaginary. To be conscious is to experience an act of knowing in which the subject is aware of an object. A conscious act is an act of awareness in which the subject is presented with an object.

Husserl distinguishes further between perception and intuition. One may perceive and be conscious of the fact *that* one perceives an object without understanding its essence, *what* it is, its principle of being and identity. Intuition of the essence of an object is the source of meaning and intelligibility of the particular phenomena. Eidetic intuiting (*Wesensschau*) is insight into essences through the experience of exemplifying particulars. Such particulars may be given in either perception or imagination. Intuition is intrinsic to the exercise of understanding and is not to be thought of as involving some faculty independent of reason. Intellectual reflection is not mere passive introspection of facts or mental events but involves the active effort of a subject who grasps and understands the objective meaning of his experience.

For Husserl the knowledge of facts of perception is impossible without insight into, or intuition of, the objective essence of a given phenomenon. That is why Husserl is opposed to Mill's theory of induction, which supposed that induction is a process by which the mind abstracts what is common to a group of facts as given in experience. Induction is, he maintains, based on intellectual intuition and analysis of essence discovered in the phenomena. What remains invariable through all the conceivable changes in the experience of a given phenomenon is its essence. Induction is a condition of intuition of essences but does not itself directly yield any knowledge of essences.

The problem of essence in Husserl can be rendered intelligible by reference to the distinction between subjective and objective essence as employed in the writings of Descartes and Spinoza. For Spinoza, every thing or mode has a formal or subjective essence and an objective essence. Every idea or object of experience has an objective essence in the sense that it is that form which differentiates one kind of object from another. The objective essence is always an attribute of an idea or phenomenal object as conceived through intuition by a given mind or subject. By contrast, the formal or subjective essence is that principle of being which pertains to an entity-in-itself, that which gives it its actuality or existence independent of the perceiver. This usage of "subjective" and "objective" is the opposite of that found in post-Kantian philosophy, where "subjective essence" refers to the experience of a subject. In Husserl's phenomenology, an "objective essence" is the essence of an object of experience and hence approximates closely to the meaning of the term in Scholastic as well as Cartesian and Spinozistic philosophy. Husserl is concerned only with objective essences of noemata or objects of knowledge and does not refer to subjective or formal essences, which have no place in his idealistic philosophy.

The task of phenomenological philosophy is to examine and make explicit all the intentional objects of human consciousness. Transcendental phenomenology is not concerned with the truth or validity of any particular *Weltanschauung* or any particular science but rather with the conditions immanent in experience which make any scientific knowledge possible. As the critique of consciousness, phenomenological philosophy is essentially philosophical anthropology, since it seeks in human consciousness the source of "objective" reality and meaning. *Consciousness is transcendental to the order of nature in that it is not part of the order of nature but rather that which is the source of the meaning and intelligibility of nature.* The affinity to Kant's *Critique of Pure Reason* is obvious.

THE PHENOMENOLOGICAL EPOCHĒ AND TRANSCENDENTAL REDUCTION

DESCARTES, IN HIS *Meditations on First Philosophy*, had maintained that the proposition *Cogito ergo sum* is true and valid regardless of skepticism concerning the very existence of the world. The existence of the ego, as the subject of thought, is the first principle of cognition. Descartes believed, however, that unless he could demonstrate the existence of God, the first cause and origin of all existence and reality, he would not be able to demonstrate the existence of the world and resolve his skepticism. He began, therefore, with the idea of the most perfect Being in his consciousness and convinced himself that the idea or objective essence of God derives from an existential Being which has a formal or subjective essence independent of his thought and therefore that such a Being actually exists. If such a Being exists, then it follows that such a Being will not deceive man into believing in the existence of the world, if it is not really the case. Ultimately, Descartes's belief in the existence of the world depends on his religious and moral faith in the truth of the existence of a most perfect Being.

Husserl does not follow Descartes in passing from the existence of the ego and its consciousness to the positing of a metaphysical Being who guarantees the validity of belief in the existence of nature. Instead he follows Kant's and Fichte's transcendental idealism by seeking to establish the transcendental ego as the basis or ground of all knowledge and belief, including that of the existence of the world. Since there is no object or objective essence apart from consciousness, one must turn to consciousness and intuition of essences as the source of our human knowledge of reality. In the last analysis, Husserl is committed to the idealistic thesis that consciousness is constitutive of reality and existence as the human mind knows it objectively.

By happy coincidence, Husserl himself delivered a lecture on "Phenomenology and Anthropology" in Berlin in 1931,[6] which clarifies his conception of the relation of essence to existence. In this lecture Husserl is critical of the philosophical anthropology derived from Dilthey's *Lebensphilosophie.* His main criticism is that the followers of Dilthey look

> to human existence as the sole basis for the reconstruction of phenomenological philosophy. Thus, the old contrasts which have always agitated philosophy recur in a modern guise. The subjectivistic tendency which characterized our period of history from the very beginning develops in two opposite directions: one is anthropologistic (or psychologistic), the other, transcendentalistic. While everyone feels that philosophy needs to be subjectively

6. First published under the title "Phänomenologie und Anthropologie" in *Philosophy and Phenomenological Research*, Vol. II (1941); reprinted in Roderick M. Chisholm, ed., *Realism and the Background of Phenomenology* (Glencoe, Ill.: Free Press. 1960).

grounded, one party claims that this must, of course, be done by psychology; the other demands a science of transcendental subjectivity, a science of a completely new kind, without which psychology and the other sciences cannot be grounded philosophically.[7]

Husserl's criticism comes down to the argument that to ground phenomenology on human existence is to reduce it to psychologism or anthropologism. The only realistic alternative which avoids this reduction is a rigorous science of transcendental phenomenology.

According to Husserl's interpretation of the history of the idea of philosophy, we must contrast pre-Cartesian and post-Cartesian philosophy. In the pre-Cartesian philosophy from the Greeks onward, the vision of philosophy as pure theory predominated. Philosophical cognition required the grasping of the essential form, "the pure *Ratio* of the world down to all its regional spheres of existence." Philosophical cognition provided a universal ontology or metaphysics of the actually existing world and hence a metaphysical foundation for the natural sciences. It is the aim of classical, pre-Cartesian philosophy to be "the science of the sum total of reality."

By contrast, Husserl maintains that "all modern philosophy originates in the Cartesian *Meditations*." The Cartesian revolution, as it may be called, is marked by a tendency toward subjectivism in contrast to the objectivism of previous philosophy. Descartes questioned the certitude of existence implicit in the experience of the world and felt obligated to impose a universal epochē on the belief in the existence of the world. The only absolute, unconditional certitude which remains is the proposition *Cogito ergo sum*. The Cartesian ego suffers from "transcendental solitude"; it is the ego who doubts the existence of the world.

In the epochē and "phenomenological reduction" of Husserl, the epochē or suspension is not, as it was for Descartes, a temporary one but is rather "a permanent, deliberate abstention from belief in the existence of the world, an abstention which I, as a phenomenologist, am bound to observe permanently." [8] What was for Descartes a mere temporary expedient became for Husserl a

7. *Ibid.*, pp. 129–30.
8. *Ibid.*, p. 135.

permanent attitude toward the world. The existential world is reduced through "the phenomenological reduction" to a "mere phenomenon" of the transcendental consciousness, possessing only phenomenal validity. "This 'world' with phenomenal validity is obviously inseparable from transcendentally reduced consciousness." [9] The phenomenological epochē involves not merely a temporary suspension of belief in the existence of the world but a permanent bracketing and abstention from belief in the existence of the world independent of consciousness. The Cartesian epochē was a temporary, fictional, "as if" attitude; the Husserlian epochē or attitude is not fictional but is rather a deliberate renunciation of the naïve universal belief in the existence of the world which permeates all the natural sciences.

Husserl reassures us that nothing is really lost by the phenomenological reduction and that much is gained through the disclosure of a vast new field of research. The world of ordinary experience still continues to exist for our human consciousness, and men continue to act pragmatically "as if" the world actually exists independently of human consciousness. Only the philosopher now recognizes that *belief in the existence of the world is a phenomenon of consciousness itself,* which has to be explained and validated like any other phenomenon of experience. In Husserl's words:

> The existence of this world is self-evident for me because it is self-evident only in my own experience and consciousness. This consciousness is the source of the meaning of the world and of any worldly objective facts. But, thanks to the transcendental epochē, I perceive that whatever is in the world, including my existence as a human being, exists for me only as the content of a certain experiential apperception in the mode of certitude of existence. . . . In this apperception the world and the human being are first constituted as existing. . . . As transcendental ego I am thus the absolutely responsible subject of whatever has existential validity for me. Aware of myself as this ego, thanks to the transcendental reduction, I stand now above all worldly existence, above my own human life and existence as man. . . . In this absolute attitude, I know the world itself and know it now, for the first time, for it was and had to be by its very essence: a transcendental phenomenon. [10]

9. *Ibid.*
10. *Ibid.*, p. 138.

The point Husserl is making is one that Descartes, in his naturalistic naïveté, would never have made. Husserl is maintaining that the belief in the existence of the world is itself a function or derivative of human transcendental consciousness. Adopting the attitude of natural science, Descartes believed that existence is a metaphysical fact presupposed by all experience of the world. Husserl, on the other hand, adopting the phenomenological attitude, regards existence as a datum of experience which has to be justified and validated. So-called self-evidence is itself a subjective fact of experience relative to human consciousness. One must investigate the genesis and ground of this existential belief and not assume naïvely that this belief is "caused" by some transcendent object which is the source of experience. The transcendental ego is, Husserl maintains, the absolute basis and source of whatever has existential validity for me, the subject.

The ontologic significance of the phenomenological reduction now becomes apparent. The first task of phenomenological philosophy is to perform the transcendental reduction of existence to phenomenal essence. The transcendental reduction *must* be performed in order to demonstrate that the transcendental ego is the source of all meaning and belief in the existence of the world, including belief in my existence as a man or human being. Husserl's phenomenological philosophy as rigorous science is dedicated to the proposition that existence of the world and of man in the world is a function, and is derivative, of the experience and intuition of objective essence. In principle, therefore, phenomenological philosophy is a philosophy of ultimate rationalism and idealism which affirms the primacy of human consciousness and of the transcendental subject of experience. "I must not forget," Husserl reminds us, "that nothing that I could ever conceive as existent lies outside the universal scope of the possible and actual consciousness of myself, the ego." [11] This is why he concludes that "the entire existing world is transcendentally relative." Thus, contrary to Dilthey and so-called phenomenological existentialists, such as Sartre, Husserl would not reduce the task of philosophy to that of constructing a *Lebensphilosophie*, or philosophical anthropology of human existence. As Husserl envisions it, the *task of philosophy is to provide a critique of human consciousness, and the first step in this direction is to*

11. *Ibid.*, p. 139.

perform the transcendental reduction of the phenomena of existence to those of objective essence. By contrast, so-called phenomenological existentialists attempt to derive essence from existence and to assert the primacy of existence over essence. This latter thesis, Husserl claims, leads to irrationalism and voluntarism and is the antithesis of the rationalism with which philosophy has traditionally been associated. Husserl proposes to restore the Platonic and Cartesian vision of philosophy as universal science through a radical philosophy of science based on the primacy of the transcendental ego and of intentional consciousness.

PHENOMENOLOGY AND THE PRINCIPLE OF ALL PRINCIPLES:
ANTIREDUCTIONISM OF PHENOMENA

HUSSERL'S PURE, transcendental phenomenology posits that absolute, unconditioned intuition of essences is actually possible and is to be recognized as a fact of radical experience. As opposed to the positivistic empiricism of Hume and Comte, he would not limit immediate experience to sense perception. Intuition as an activity of knowing or comprehending the essence of phenomena and their essential relations to one another is also accepted and recognized as a fact of experience. Husserl, like James, whom he read, is a radical empiricist who would not limit empiricism to the perception of atomic sense data.

Husserl attacked psychologism and historicism on the ground that they undermine recognition of, and faith in, absolute scientific cognition. Psychologism tends to reduce epistemology to psychology by positing psychological determinism and the conditioning of perception and logical inference. Similarly, historicism, in the mode of social and cultural determinism and relativism, tends to reduce epistemology to the relativistic phenomena of society and culture. As noted, Husserl was opposed to Dilthey's philosophical *Weltanschauungen* and *Lebensphilosophie* on the ground that these are relative to, and conditioned by, historic conditions of society and culture and hence are incompatible with the possibility of an absolute science of philosophy or pure phenomenology.

Thus we have the apparent paradox that Husserl advocated the phenomenological, transcendental reduction of existence and existential facts in the interest of pure phenomenology but was opposed to phenomenal reductionism of the objects of particular sciences. The two attitudes are, however, quite compatible. The phenomenological reduction and epochē are advocated in the interest of a rational critique of transcendental consciousness, but phenomenal reduction is opposed because it undermines the very possibility of objective empirical knowledge of the phenomena of any particular science. Phenomenal reduction threatens the autonomy of scientific intuition, but the phenomenological reduction is necessary in the pursuit of a universal science of philosophy. If one grants the autonomy of intuition as a source of absolute knowledge of ideal essences, it follows that one must also grant the autonomy of intuition in the particular fields of science, each of which has its own type of phenomena. Thus, phenomenological philosophy is related to all the natural and social sciences because phenomenology identifies the eidetic objects of each of the sciences through its intuition of essences. Each science then proceeds with the empirical, factual determination of the correlations among its own phenomenal data, but it can do so only if the eidetic identity of its own phenomena is recognized. The claim to recognition of any particular science always rests on phenomenological analysis and intuition of the essential reality of its phenomena and their irreducibility to the phenomena of another science.

Thus Husserl formulates as "the principle of all principles" the proposition that

> Every type of first-hand intuiting forms a legitimate source of knowledge; whatever presents itself to us by "intuition" at first hand, in its authentic reality, as it were (*sozusagen in seiner leibhaften Wirklichkeit*), is to be accepted simply for the thing as which it presents itself, yet merely within the limits within which it presents itself.[12]

The principle of principles in phenomenology is the autonomy of intuition of essences and their irreducibility to any other kind of phenomenon. This principle is correlated with that of radical

---

12. Edmund Husserl, *Ideas: General Introduction to Pure Phenomenology*, trans. W. R. Boyce Gibson (New York: Humanities Press, 1931), § 24. The translation used here is that given in Herbert Spiegelberg's *The Phenomenological Movement: A Historical Introduction*, 2 vols., 2d ed. (The Hague: Martinus Nijhoff, 1965), I, 128.

empiricism, which states that "in respect of all assertions relating to the facts of nature we must look for the experiences upon which they are grounded." [13] The claims of anthropology to be recognized as a distinct science rest upon this principle.

PHENOMENOLOGY AS RADICAL EMPIRICISM: JAMES AND HUSSERL

A PHILOSOPHY BASED on radical empiricism asserts that everything real must be experienceable and that every kind of thing experienced must somewhere be real. However, William James, who made this statement and who coined the term "radical empiricism," continued to contrast empiricism and rationalism as if they were opposites. "Rationalism," he observes,

> tends to emphasize universals and to make wholes prior to parts in the order of logic as well as in that of being. Empiricism, on the contrary, lays the explanatory stress upon the part, the element, the individual, and treats the whole as a collection and the universal as an abstraction. My description of things, accordingly, starts with the parts and makes of the whole a being of the second order.[14]

The distinctive feature of James's radical empiricism is his thesis that "the relations that connect experiences must themselves be experienced relations, and any kind of relation experienced must be accounted as 'real' as anything else in the system." [15] For example, change itself is one of the things immediately experienced as one sort of conjunct relation. James's generalized conclusion is that "the parts of experience hold together from next to next by relations that are themselves parts of experience. The directly apprehended universe needs, in short, no extraneous, transempirical, connective support, but possesses in its own right a concatenated or continuous structure." [16] It is because he felt that relations between the phenomena of experience are themselves given empirically that James maintained that there is no need for a transcendental ego to perform the work

13. *Ideas*, § 24, trans. Gibson.
14. William James, *Essays in Radical Empiricism* (New York: Longmans, Green, 1922), pp. 41–42.
15. *Ibid.*, p. 42.
16. *Ibid.*, p. xii.

of relating phenomena, and he even questioned the existence of consciousness as a separate reality.[17]

Husserl, as we have seen, adds intellectual intuition of essences as essential to the act of experiencing or knowing. In Husserl's phenomenological philosophy, rationalism and empiricism coalesce and are not contrasted as opposites, as they are in James. The intuition of essences is considered as much a fact of experience as are the perception of sense data and relations among them. Husserl thus opens up the realm of essences as an integral part of experience, whereas James excludes essences from immediate experience on the ground that they are abstractions and constructs derived from experience, not direct objects of experience. From the perspective of phenomenology, James's empiricism is not radical enough.

RADICAL EMPIRICISM AND THE *Lebenswelt*

RADICAL EMPIRICISM, as discussed by James and Husserl, tends to presuppose the experience of the phenomena of nature as "given" to a subject of experience. In his *The Varieties of Religious Experience,* James extended radical empiricism to include cultural phenomena as well. In effect, James was engaged in a phenomenological study of what it means to have a religious experience, as witnessed by the subjects undergoing the experience. James appreciated the uniqueness of the religious experience and opposed its reduction to any other mode of psychological experience. The essence of the religious experience was made known through analysis of the meaning of the experience for the subjects and analysis of the evidence for their acceptance of a transcendent Being who communicated with them. In *The Idea of the Holy,* Rudolf Otto continued this type of phenomenological analysis. The essential attitude of phenomenological analysis is its correlation of the subject and object of experience with a view to ascertaining what the experience means to the subjects and how it affects their lives. In the study of religious experience, the essence of the religious experience is correlated with the existence of the subjects so as to give the sense of a living experience. In radical empiricism, experience of the

17. *Ibid.,* Chap. 1.

essence of a cultural phenomenon is combined with experience of subjective existence to yield the meaning of the phenomenon in the life of the subject.

We noted earlier that Husserl was opposed to the historicism of Dilthey on the ground that *Weltanschauungen* are relative to the historic conditions of society and culture and hence are incompatible with the objective of a rigorous phenomenological science of philosophy. It is significant to note, however, that Dilthey himself appreciated the new insights provided by Husserl's intentional logic and epistemology.[18] The whole concept of intentional experience as discussed in Husserl's *Logical Investigations* provided Dilthey with a philosophical framework for his historical and comparative studies in the history of philosophical ideas. As far as method is concerned, there is no incompatibility between Dilthey and Husserl. Phenomenology as an epistemology and logic of science based on radical empiricism is directly relevant to the natural and anthropological sciences, provided one recognizes that essence is immanent in existence.

Here it is necessary to distinguish both pure phenomenology, as an idealistic philosophy, and meta-anthropology from the empirical sciences, which involve reference to objects and things existing independently of human consciousness. The realistic concept of formal essence, as that without which an entity can neither be nor be conceived, can be supplemented with the concept of objective essence known by intellectual intuition. Phenomenological analysis may then be applied to the data of historical culture as well as to the data of the experience of nature. In the writings published during his lifetime, Husserl did not resolve the problem of the relation of pure phenomenology to the natural and cultural sciences, and especially to history. In the manner of Descartes, he continued to contrast the science of essences, which deals with timeless, necessary truths, and the contingencies of history and historical existence. The possibility of a critique of historical consciousness did not occur to him.

In his posthumously published work, *The Crisis of European Sciences and Transcendental Phenomenology,* Husserl introduced the concept of the *Lebenswelt,* which prepared the way for an eventual reconciliation of phenomenology and the historical, cultural sciences. The *Lebenswelt* is literally the world of human

18. See Spiegelberg, *The Phenomenological Movement,* I, 123.

existence, the world as it is experienced by man living in society in a given ecological environment. The *Lebenswelt* is the world of immediate experience as given to unreflecting consciousness; it is the world of common sense and common experience. As such, it is a prescientific world, since it is logically and historically prior to critical reflection and abstraction. It is the world which scientific thought reflects upon and modifies but which it presupposes as given in all its analyses. So understood, the *Lebenswelt* is a precultural world as given in immediate experience, unmediated by the cultural symbolism of the philosopher and scientist. In order for modern civilized man to comprehend this naïve world of immediate experience, he must suspend his philosophical and theoretical attitude, divest himself of intellectual intuition. In effect, *he must practice the phenomenological epochē in reverse.* Instead of bracketing or suspending all beliefs in existence to attain intuition of the essence, he must suspend intuition of essence in order to retain consciousness of the existence of his world and its horizons. Thus Husserl now speaks of "the epochē of objective science":

> Clearly required before everything else is the epochē in respect to all objective sciences. This means not merely an abstraction from them, such as an imaginary transformation, in thought, of present human existence, such that no science appeared in the picture. What is meant is rather an epochē of all participation in the cognitions of the objective sciences, an epochē of any critical position-taking which is interested in their truth or falsity, even any position on their guiding idea of an objective knowledge of the world. In short, we carry out an epochē in regard to all objective theoretical interests, all aims and activities belonging to us as objective scientists or even simply as [ordinary] people desirous of [this kind of] knowledge.[19]

The *Lebenswelt* may be understood as the human world posited as existing by man and constituting the intentional field of his action. It is the world as relative to man, the kind of world he shares with other human beings. It is the world as naturally selected by man in virtue of his interests in a given ecological environment. The *Lebenswelt* comprises not only the naturally

19. Edmund Husserl, *The Crisis of European Sciences and Transcendental Phenomenology*, trans. David Carr (Evanston, Ill.: Northwestern University Press, 1970), p. 135.

selected environment but also the social and cultural world of human society. The sociocultural life-world is a historic achievement of man in a given ecological environment and varies with time and place for different societies. Husserl is explicit on this point: "Among the objects of the life-world we also find human beings, with all their human action and concern, works and suffering, living in common in the world-horizon in their particular social interrelations and knowing themselves to be such." [20] He now recognizes that historians in particular are concerned with the reconstruction of the changing, surrounding life-worlds of the peoples and periods with which they deal. His reading of the writings of Lévy-Bruhl, especially the latter's *Primitive Mythology*, led him to the discovery that ethnologists, or cultural anthropologists, reconstitute the lived experience and life-world of primitive man.[21] Evolutionary ethnology may be said to be concerned with the historic continuity of man's cultural life-worlds.

The new science of the *Lebenswelt* which Husserl now envisages involves the description and intentional analysis of the human life-world as a phenomenon of human consciousness. The task of a scientific phenomenological philosophy is ultimately the construction of a meta-anthropology to investigate the genesis of the life-world in human consciousness, how it is constituted, and its a priori structure in the human subject. The prerequisite for this new science is that the philosopher should practice a radical "transcendental epochē" which would suspend "the natural attitude of life."

The natural attitude takes the existence of the life-world for granted or as given. In a scientific study of the life-world, one seeks to understand *how* it is given and how it is constituted in human consciousness so as to have meaning and ontic validity. In order to examine the life-world as a phenomenon and to intuit its essence, the phenomenologist must perform the transcendental epochē or reduction which Husserl originally advocated in his *Ideas* with reference to pure phenomenology. But in the earlier work, *Ideas,* Husserl had advocated the epochē of existential beliefs concerning the objects of experience in the interests of a phenomenological science of pure essences. In the *Crisis* he

20. *Ibid.,* p. 146.
21. See Maurice Merleau-Ponty, "Phenomenology and the Sciences of Man," above, pp. 102–4.

refers to this earlier transcendental epochē as the "Cartesian way," since, in principle, it follows Descartes in suspending belief in the existence of the world.[22] In the later work he calls for the transcendental reduction of the natural attitude toward the life-world, not toward the objective existence of nature as such. As noted, in order to experience the life-world, there must first be an epochē of the theoretical, objective attitude of natural science. Second, we must perform an epochē of the natural attitude to obtain an intuition of the essence of the life-world as a phenomenon of consciousness. The science of the life-world is not the science of pure phenomenology, as envisaged in *Ideas*. One may distinguish the phenomenological philosophy of the life-world —the meta-anthropology—from the empirical comparative studies of the historian and cultural anthropologist. Phenomenological philosophy, like natural, objective science, presupposes experience of the life-world and builds its constructs upon its foundations. The existence of the life-world is not proved but is taken for granted as the basis for any possible experience and for any possible scientific theory.

Husserl contrasts two kinds of facts and two kinds of worlds.[23] There are the facts of the life-world and the facts of objective science. The facts of the life-world are historic, practical, and relative to the experiences of given subjects and their cultural worlds. The facts of objective science are universal, cross-cultural, and valid for all mankind. The two worlds are related as ground and superstructure. To illustrate this point Husserl notes:

> But when we are thrown into an alien social sphere, that of the Negroes in the Congo, Chinese peasants, etc., we discover that their truths, the facts that for them are fixed, generally verified or verifiable, are by no means the same as ours. But if we set up the goal of a truth about the objects which is unconditionally valid for all subjects, beginning with that on which normal Europeans, normal Hindus, Chinese, etc., agree in spite of all relativity—be- beginning, that is, with what makes objects of the life-world, common to all, identifiable for them and for us (even though conceptions of them may differ), such as spatial shape, motion, sense- quality and the like—then we are on the way to objective science. When we set up this objectivity as a goal (the goal of a "truth in itself"), we make a set of hypotheses through which the pure

22. *Crisis*, p. 155.
23. *Ibid.*, p. 132.

life-world is surpassed. We have precluded *this* [type of] "surpassing" through the first epochē (that which concerns the objective sciences), and now we have the embarrassment of wondering what else can be undertaken scientifically, as something that can be established once and for all and for everyone.[24]

Husserl's answer is that phenomenological philosophy may undertake the science of the life-world itself as constituted by the human transcendental consciousness.

History and the Meaning of Man

THE BASIC MEANING of a proposition or an idea is the object which it intends. Intentionality, however, can have two kinds of reference, historic and nonhistoric objects. In ordinary perception, the meaning is the empirical object or phenomenon which is indicated in the present experience. But meaning or intentionality when directed toward a goal is historic meaning and is oriented toward the future. One may then speak of the history of ideas to indicate their regulative significance in the course of the development of civilization. Meaning in history is defined by the *telos*, the conscious end, or else by its *entelechy*, by the immanent, largely unconscious goal provided by the society and its culture. Thus Husserl speaks of the entelechy of European culture and of the telos of *theōria*, or philosophical speculation, inaugurated by the Greek philosophers.

Thus phenomenological method may be applied by the historian of culture to the comparative study of past cultures or to the living cultures of the present with a view to recording and interpreting their symbolic, regulative ideas and the significance of these for their cultural life-worlds. Without consciously realizing it, E. B. Tylor, for example, presented an implicit phenomenological analysis of the evolution of religion from primitive animism to monotheism and found the belief in spiritual beings to be the common core of all religious belief. Culture history, to be meaningful, must be more than a chronicle of social and cultural events; it must interpret and explain the direction of cultural events by reference to the ideals which they intend to realize. This is precisely what the cultural evolutionists attempted

24. *Ibid.*, p. 139.

to do when they indicated a pattern of progress in the evolution of human culture, a pattern which was marked by the growth of rationality and scientific thought. Their fundamental error lay, not in attempting to demonstrate meaning in history, but rather in assuming that culture history is subject to natural laws of evolution and that it is unilinear and uniform for all societies. It was only after this normative, rational ideal of progress was converted into natural law by the sociologists Comte and Spencer and by the evolutionary anthropologists who followed them that twentieth-century social scientists began to question the idea of progress itself. As a humanistic ideal of which historians may be conscious, it may well be revived.

As a transcendental phenomenologist, Husserl accepted the ideal of civilization in the darkest hours preceding the Second World War. In his *The Crisis of European Sciences and Transcendental Phenomenology* he wrote:

> To be human at all is essentially to be a human being in a socially and generatively united civilization; and if man is a rational being (*animal rationale*), it is only insofar as his whole civilization is a rational civilization, that is, one with a latent orientation toward reason or one openly oriented toward the entelechy which has come to itself, become manifest to itself, and which now of necessity consciously directs human becoming. Philosophy and science would accordingly be the historical movement through which universal reason, "inborn" in humanity as such, is revealed.[25]

Here Husserl is speaking the language of Hegel's *Phenomenology,* viewing the phenomena of culture in historical perspective.

Husserl, the philosopher of culture history, is very much concerned with the transformation of the life-world and with the realization of the meaning of man as a civilized human being existing in society. The uniqueness of culture or civilization lies in its being a product of human intelligence, and it can be understood only phenomenologically, i.e., in relation to the meaning it has in the lives of its human subjects and creators. Phenomenological philosophy, when applied to culture history and to the history of ideas, enables the historian and cultural anthropologist to appreciate the significance of normative, regulative ideals in providing a direction and immanent goal (entelechy) for man and his civilization.

25. *Ibid.,* pp. 15–16.

EXISTENTIAL CULTURE AND THE CULTURAL *Lebenswelt*

THE CONCEPT OF THE *Lebenswelt* is the connecting link between modern anthropology and phenomenology. Contemporary anthropologists frequently describe cultures as "the designs for living" historically constructed by man for life in society. A culture represents one possibility of existence which has been realized in a particular ecological environment. The task of the ethnologist is to describe and re-present conceptually the life-world of the society he is studying. Every ethnological study of a given culture is an abstraction from that culture in the sense that it is a construct or conceptualization based on observation of the social life of a given community. The primary reality is the existential or actual life-world of the members of a society in its ecological environment; the secondary reality is the abstraction of the anthropologist who attempts to reconstruct or "reconstitute" the life of the society in the symbolic form of language.

Each cultural life-world is a subjective world; it is the historic world created by human effort and thought which has meaning and value for the members of that society at a given time and place. *A culture is an intersubjective system of meaningful experiences, institutions, activities, symbolic expressions of ritual and art, together with their products, which are shared by the members of a given society.* The culture as recorded by the anthropologist in his descriptive analysis is an abstraction from the lived experiences and life-styles of the subjects of a particular culture. Those social and cultural anthropologists who derogate culture as an abstraction distinct from the actual behavior of man in society, as did the late Kroeber, Kluckhohn, and Radcliffe-Brown, have failed to distinguish the abstractions of the anthropologist, who provides knowledge *about* a culture, from the existential cultural experiences and processes of the subjects *of* the culture. Anthropologists have tended to confuse the abstract, objective essence of a culture and the concrete, subjective essence manifest in the actual social interactions of individuals in society. If there is to be a science of cultural anthropology, then the anthropologists must refer to the existential or actual experience of the people who live by, and for, their cultural norms as the ground of reference by which to judge the truth or falsity of the cultural constructs. The cultural life-world is the ground or basis for the cultural abstractions or conceptualizations of the anthropologist. The life-world of a given society must be taken as empirically given; it is not in itself a construct of the anthropologist.

A phenomenological and existential approach to culture is ultimately a humanistic one which affirms the proposition that all culture is relative to man and that man is the measure of his culture. *All human forms or modes of culture are processes and products of human work and of the intentional consciousness of man in adapting to the necessary conditions of nature and the ecological environment.* Hence a phenomenological, existential, humanistic approach to culture need not lead to a "spiritual anthropology," after the manner of Cassirer, Husserl, and other Neo-Kantian philosophers, all of whom tend to assume the idealistic thesis that symbolic forms of consciousness are "constitutive" of cultural reality. It is possible to adopt a realistic epistemology and ontology and to retain the duality of nature and of culture, as the present writer has done in his *Theoretical Anthropology*, and yet recognize that culture is an attribute of man and that its very existence is unintelligible apart from the intentional consciousness and work of man in his ecological environment. Similarly, a phenomenological-existential view of culture precludes the culturological view of both idealists and materialists, such as Leslie White, who regard culture as if it were an autonomous natural process independent of man, a reality *sui generis,* subject to its own laws of development. The only alternatives are *not* a spiritual anthropology, concerned with the symbolic expressions of the human *Geist,* or else a naturalistic, materialistic culturology, which views culture as a natural process controlling and determining human essence and existence. A humanistic, existential, and phenomenological approach recognizes the role of intentional human consciousness and creative activity in interacting with the ecological environment to produce a cultural life-world relative to human needs and aspirations.

A phenomenological view of culture precludes the reduction of cultural phenomena to any other mode of experience and yet also recognizes that all cultural phenomena are correlative with natural law and natural processes to which they must conform.

The anthropologist studies man as a part of nature subject to natural law in interaction with his ecological environment. But man is also a being with an intentional, autonomous consciousness, which is the source of his experience of nature and of his cultural creativity, which is not given by nature. Cultural reality introduces a new dimension of experience not given by the order of nature; it is a mode of reality which has to be willed into existence through human work and invention. For the anthropologist, man is both the subject and object of his cultural experience; he is both free to create his cultural life-world and yet is determined by it once it has been created and brought into existence. This is the ultimate "paradox of human subjectivity: being a subject for the world and at the same time being an object in the world," as Husserl puts it.[26] Unlike Husserl's, however, the position taken here does not require a transcendental epochē, which would transform everything objective into something subjective.[27] It is sufficient to recognize the role of the intentional mind, the role of the subject, in transforming nature into culture; we need not reduce nature to culture. Nature and culture remain as essential polarities of existence. The paradox of human subjectivity is resolved, not by reducing nature to culture, but by recognizing the fact of man's intentional consciousness, the fact of man's freedom to construct his cultural life-world while remaining subject to natural law and the cultural determinism of his own natural and cultural life-worlds. Husserl would preclude the reduction of cultural phenomena to any other mode of intentional consciousness, but he does not hesitate to advocate the transcendental epochē, or reduction of objectivity to subjectivity, thereby reducing nature to culture, as Cassirer and the Neo-Kantians before him attempted to do. By retaining the duality and polarity of nature and culture, as advocated here, the reality of culture is maintained without reductionism to other phenomena, and the ontological reality of both nature and culture is retained without ontological or transcendental reductionism.

26. *Ibid.*, p. 178.
27. *Ibid.*

MODERN ETHNOLOGY AND THE METHOD
OF CULTURAL RELATIVISM

THE CONCEPT OF THE LIFE-WORLD, introduced by Husserl, links together the natural and historical sciences by providing a universal object for all subjects. The life-world is the world as given in experience prior to critical reflection, the world as experienced by man in society and in a given ecological environment, and it includes his experience of the world of nature as well as the world of his culture. The cultural anthropologist or ethnologist studies and records the cultural life-worlds of human society and in the name of "ethnoscience" attempts to reconstruct the cognitive maps of their symbolic modes of experience, such as their art, rituals, and systems of belief and logic. A phenomenological approach to the study of human culture is at the same time an existential approach, since the anthropologist records the lived experiences of given subjects at a given moment of their history. The task of the anthropologist is not merely to give an objective account and to record the traits and artifacts abstracted from a given culture, as one writes a catalogue of merchandise, but to describe and interpret the intentional meaning and the intersubjective symbolic meanings of the behavior and the interactions of the members of a given society.

Since the life-world of each society is subjective, in the sense that it is relative to the cultural and historical experience of each society, the task of the cultural anthropologist requires him to employ "the method of cultural relativism," that is, he must describe and intuit each life-world from the perspective of the subjects of that culture rather than from the perspective of some alien culture, such as his own. Each life-world is ethnocentric in the sense that it is relative to the people of a given society. The ethnographer must first describe in detail, and "objectively," the life-world of his subjects as he has observed it himself or as his native informants have described it to him. That is why the cultural anthropologist endeavors as far as possible to become a "participant observer" in order to get the immediate feeling and subjective perspective of a participant in the culture, a perspective which no outsider or alien can appreciate fully.

The method of cultural relativism may be said to be the *method of objective ethnocentrism*. If the anthropologist interprets the data he perceives from the perspective of his own culture, then his judgments and evaluations are said to be ethnocentric in the sense that they reflect the subjective prejudices of his own life-world rather than the facts of the life-world he is observing. It is in this latter sense that anthropologists are taught to avoid "ethnocentrism" in the interests of objective ethnology and social anthropology. As a scientist, the cultural anthropologist and sociologist is objective and impartial in recording the ethnocentric, subjective life-world of a particular society, usually other than his own, and he must at the same time *avoid* being "ethnocentric" in his interpretation of that alien culture (by introducing his own subjective cultural perspective into his evaluations and interpretations). This taboo against "ethnocentrism" may be called *the ethnocentric epoché or reduction* to distinguish it from Husserl's epoché of objective science and his transcendental, subjective epoché, which is the phenomenological epoché involved in suspending the natural attitude toward the world.

It should be noted here that the cultural anthropologist does not practice total ethnocentric epoché, since to do so would put him out of business. The anthropologist performs only a partial epoché or reduction in suspending his own ethnocentric culture the better to intuit the ethnocentric life-world of another culture. The cultural anthropologist may be regarded as a Leibnizian "monad," but a monad with windows out upon the life-worlds of others, which he can intuitively perceive as a phenomenon of his consciousness. To be an anthropologist requires the possibility of intuiting and participating in the cultural life-worlds of societies other than one's own or of treating one's own life-world as a phenomenon to be investigated *as if* one did not really belong to it. To be objective about the cultural subjectivity of others and one's own society, that is the paradox of consciousness which renders a scientific study of culture possible.

The natural scientist attempts in principle to transcend the ethnocentric life-worlds of his own and other societies in order to achieve an objective, transcultural truth concerning the world of nature. The natural scientist attempts as far as possible to transcend his ethnocentric life-world, and he may be said to strive for a total ethnocentric epoché, although that is a regulative ideal rather than an objective to be fully realized. The history of scientific thought bears ample evidence of the progress of science in its attempt to transcend ethnocentric, purely subjective theories. The natural scientist is always experimenting to test pragmatically the relevance and conformity of his scientific theories and hypotheses to the existential, ontological reality of nature, and he is prepared to modify his theories to conform to the facts of his experience of nature. He attempts in principle to eliminate and transcend his ethnocentric, subjective life-world in order to achieve a common single world of science valid for all men; and he measures his success by the expanding horizons of his life-world and by the ability of rational men to participate in this one world. In a normative, ideal civilization, rational men also strive to emulate the natural scientist and to conceive and imagine a unity of civilization, a unity of the cultural life-world with universal validity. The philosophical anthropologist and phenomenologist believes it possible to transcend the multiplicity of cultural life-worlds and to intuit the possibility of a rational civilization based on a scientific knowledge of man in nature. The cultural anthropologist, in the meantime, is concerned with the historic facts of culture as they exist and are perceived in the variety of life-worlds. Perhaps the conflict of these life-worlds and their incompatibility with one another existentially may yet serve as a stimulus for expanding the horizons of cultural life-worlds also.

Conclusion: The Synthesis of Phenomenological Method and Scientific Anthropology

The practical, heuristic significance of phenomenological method lies in the thesis of the nonreducibility and relative autonomy of each basic form or category of cultural experience. As applied to social and cultural anthropology, this means that culture is to be regarded as having an objective essence or being of its own as a natural phenomenon and that it is not to be reduced, or explained away, as if it were reducible to some other kind of phenomena, e.g., those of geography, biology, psychology, or sociology. This led cultural anthropologists to maintain, as a principle of their methodology, that all culture is to be explained through culture (*Omnis cultura ex cultura*) and not through the phenomena of any other science. Culture was said to be autonomous in the sense that it is a closed system and that cultural phenomena can be explained only through other cultural phenomena. In practice, this meant that cultural anthropology was essentially a historical science, which utilized the cultural data of the past to explain those of the present or used the cultural phenomena of one area to account for the diffusion of cultural traits to another area. In American cultural anthropology in particular, under the leadership of Franz Boas, the concept of culture became the central unifying concept of anthropology, and historical method became the established method. Taken simply as an affirmation of the reality and non-reducibility of cultural phenomena, the claim is a valid one. It is only when culture becomes reified into an ontological entity *sui generis,* capable of acting and existing independently of man—as it tended to become in the theory of the "superorganic," as advocated by Kroeber prior to 1948, and in the culturology of Leslie White—that one commits what I have termed "the culturalistic fallacy." The anthropologist has then passed beyond phenomenological method into ontology and metaphysics. In an existential, phenomenological anthropology, the subject and object of culture must not be separated in principle, and culture must not be regarded as an entity or process independent of human consciousness.

The essential attitude of phenomenological method is its subjectivity, its reference to a transcendental ego and consciousness as the source of meaning. As opposed to the naïve method of a naturalistic epistemology and behaviorism in psychology, which tend to assume that objects, things, and modes of behavior have an intrinsic meaning in themselves, phenomenological method is radically subjective in that it refers all meaning back to a transcendental subject who is the source of meaning and for whom alone meaning is valid. Phenomenology as a philosophy and ontology does tend toward idealism and spiritualism insofar as it maintains the primacy of *Geist* or spirit as the constitutive source or foundation of all phenomena. Husserl in particular is opposed to the metaphysical dualism of Descartes and, in agreement with the Neo-Kantians, tends to substitute a form of spiritual monism for the duality of nature and culture. It is possible, however, to utilize phenomenological method in the cultural sciences without accepting the spiritual anthropology implied in Husserl's phenomenological idealism.

This is why it is essential to distinguish, as Marvin Farber and other commentators have done, between phenomenology as a method of scientific research, on the one hand, and phenomenology as an ontology and spiritual anthropology. Phenomenological method is compatible with Hegelian, Marxist, Neo-Kantian, and Existentialist philosophies and with any other philosophies of science which make their appeal to the phenomena of experience and the intentionality of human consciousness. Phenomenological method is especially significant for the development of a humanistic existential science of social and cultural anthropology. Hitherto, anthropologists have tended to employ phenomenological description and intuition rather implicitly in their studies of ethnological method, ethnoscience, religion, and anthropological linguistics. By making us conscious of the role of human consciousness and intentionality in the cultural process, phenomenology may combine with anthropology to produce an authentic humanistic science of anthropology. In particular, the concept of the *Lebenswelt,* or life-world, introduced by Husserl may provide the basis or ground for a synthesis of the natural and cultural sciences in harmony with a humanistic philosophical anthropology.

PART II

Phenomenology
and Sociology

Philosophy, Science, and Everyday Life

Thomas Luckmann

AT THE END of an illuminating analysis of the extra-scientific presuppositions that went into the making of modern physical science, Edwin A. Burtt wrote almost half a century ago: "An adequate cosmology will only begin to be written when an adequate philosophy of the mind has appeared. . . ."[1] This was the conclusion to which Burtt was led after a survey of historical evidence on the formation of scientific thought during the period from Copernicus to Newton. What is required for a foundation of scientific knowledge is more than a science that analyzes "nature" and its structure. We have such a science and its achievements are well known. What is required is also more than a science that analyzes man as part of nature. We have such a science as this, too, and its results, considerable even today, promise to become more impressive in the future. But what is required in addition is a science that analyzes man as that peculiar part of nature that is not only capable of understanding "nature" but also of understanding itself as part of it. We do have sciences that are beginning to grapple with this peculiarity of man's position in nature, but it must be conceded that our knowledge here is uncertain and there is much confusion about the methods appropriate to such sciences.[2] And,

1. Edwin Arthur Burtt, *The Metaphysical Foundations of Modern Physical Science* (1924; rev. ed., Garden City, N.Y.: Doubleday, n.d. [1932]), p. 324.
2. Modern philosophical anthropology represents the most significant response to the joint challenge to philosophical reflection offered by evolutionist biology, historicism and structuralism in the social sciences, and the beginnings of ethology (Julian Huxley, Jakob von Uexküll, and

[143]

finally, what is required is a philosophy that provides clear and reliable methods of reflection on the nature of the evidence on which these various sciences are founded, *and* on the nature of the evidence on which such a process of reflection itself can be firmly based. The philosophy of the mind called for by Burtt must therefore be more than a narrowly conceived philosophy of science. In fact, Burtt postulates the need for a general and critical theory of knowledge, "critical" to be understood as an extension of the Kantian sense of that word. Obviously, this need has not been fully met to this day, but it is my conviction that under certain conditions phenomenology, and especially the program and the achievements of Husserl's last work, can satisfy it.[3]

Husserl saw that modern science, having separated itself from philosophy, no longer provided answers to certain elementary questions that men have asked at all times. He also saw that the empiricist tradition in modern philosophy (going back to Locke and Hume) and modern science was beginning to formulate as a problem something that to him too was a problematic

---

others). Adolf Portmann is a biologist and ethologist as much as a philosopher. Max Scheler's philosophical anthropology, on the other hand, is still strongly marked by metaphysical speculation. Better known to philosophers in the English language is Ernst Cassirer's study of symbolic forms. Arnold Gehlen's work is directly linked to the theoretical concerns of cultural anthropology and sociology, but for a number of reasons has generally exerted influence only in German social science. The most important nonreductivist and nonidealist philosophical connection between the problems of biological and sociological theory is established in the work of Helmuth Plessner. The relevance of his thesis on the "eccentric position" of man in nature and the implications of this thesis for an account of the "natural artificiality" of man as a body and as a social and historical being are slowly being discovered outside the German cultural milieu despite a lack of translations. An English appreciation of Plessner, as well as of Portmann, Buytendijk, and Kurt Goldstein, can be found in Marjorie Grene's *Approaches to a Philosophical Biology* (New York: Basic Books, 1968). A brief but interesting Marxist critique of modern philosophical anthropology, and of the way in which sociologists use its resources in their theorizing, is presented by Paul Walton, Andrew Gemble, and Jeff Coulter, "Philosophical Anthropology in Marxism," *Social Research*, XXXVII (Summer, 1970), 259–74. For a kind of response *avant la lettre*, see Plessner's "De Homine Abscondito," *Social Research*, XXXVI (Winter, 1969), 497–509.

3. Edmund Husserl, *Die Krisis der europäischen Wissenschaften und die transzendentale Phänomenologie* (The Hague: Nijhoff, 1962); English translation by David Carr, *The Crisis of European Sciences and Transcendental Phenomenology* (Evanston, Ill.: Northwestern University Press, 1970; hereafter cited as *Crisis*).

consequence of the separation of science and philosophy, i.e., the naïve self-sufficiency of science and its inability to examine its own presuppositions. But Husserl was convinced that this tradition was not radical enough in its attempt to clarify the foundations of science, and that it would not be able to resolve the "crisis" of modern science, its divorce from basic and meaningful questions of human life.[4]

There is an urgent need, then, for philosophical clarification of the human activities in which cosmologies originate—including that apparently privileged and indubitable cosmology that is associated in the popular mind with modern physical science. Like its mythological and theological predecessors, this scientific variant of cosmology is self-sufficient, i.e., it claims to provide a satisfactory account of its own foundations. It thus evidently believes that it has already answered the need stated by Burtt, if indeed it is at all inclined to admit the legitimacy of that need. But it is precisely this naïve, metaphysically motivated self-sufficiency that cannot stand up to critical philosophical examination, any more than could its mythological and theological predecessors. No critical theory of science can accept the assumption that the scientific cosmology has found the Archimedean point from which both an understanding of the universe *and* an understanding of this understanding can be reached in one single move. And, in contrast to the nonreflexiveness of the mythological and theological cosmologies, the modern, self-sufficient scientific cosmology has not even succeeded in providing plausible answers to the human quest for a subjectively meaningful location of the self in the universe.[5]

4. "In this perspective empiricism seems to contain a tendency to the scientific discovery of the life-world which is familiar to everyday experience and yet unknown to science. . . . Here it must suffice to note that the achievements of the mathematical sciences, and more generally, of all sciences committed to a physicalist approach necessarily became problematic to empiricism as it directed its attention to the concretely experienced, historically relevant world which is the topic (human society, culture) of scientific investigation in certain scholarly traditions in the humanities. The demand for a clarification of the theoretical activities which produce the constructs of science, a clarification in the context of and in relation to the life-world, was evidently present in this situation. Such a clarification was to establish the meaning and the 'scope' of science" (*Crisis* [German ed.], p. 449; my translation).

5. In an appraisal of Husserl's view of science, Herman Lübbe puts it succinctly: "In its modern form European science for the first time no longer fulfills its old function to provide man with a reasonable grasp

We are, of course, certain of the productivity of scientific methods, and we cannot doubt that useful knowledge has accumulated in various particular sciences. And yet we remain uncertain of the basis of such knowledge, and doubts linger on as to the extent to which scientific methods are capable of reaching the realities of human life. To put it simply, each science taken singly is impressive; all sciences put together make for a sorry cosmology. It is no solution at all to the problem to declare cosmological questions meaningless and to reduce science to the status of a cognitive technology. This merely leaves the field to the irrational ideologies of scientism and antiscientism. It is dangerous to try to suppress the need for a critical clarification of the foundations of science and the activities in which sciences and cosmologies originate. The philosophy of science has wider obligations than those to which, in recent times, it thought it could limit itself as a result of the technical specialization of the sciences and the academic compartmentalization of philosophy.

This is not to denigrate the usefulness of the contributions that have issued from recent philosophy of science within its self-imposed "professional" limits. The reconstructed logic of science, as Abraham Kaplan aptly calls it,[6] tends to an idealization of the complex structure of scientific knowledge. But reconstructions may effectively influence constructions: it is the quality of the reconstruction, not the fact that it is reconstructed, that is important. If the reconstructed logic stands in a sensible relation to what Kaplan calls the logic-in-use, and to what Norwood R. Hanson describes as the logic of theory-finding as opposed to the logic of theory-using,[7] it can help to reveal the syntax by which statements in the sciences are constructed and aid in the clarification of the canons by which the validity of conclusions is evaluated. Having overcome its early inclination to ignore the processes of concrete scientific inquiry, the philosophy of science may contribute to the formulation of rigorous method-

and reasoned consciousness of his existence in the whole of being. To the contrary, it successively dissolved this consciousness. It thereby released man to metaphysical disorientation. In a manner of speaking it threw the individual subject back upon himself and his isolated certainty of himself" ("Husserl und die europäische Krise," *Kant-Studien,* XLIX [1957–58], 228; my translation).

6. Abraham Kaplan, *The Conduct of Inquiry* (San Francisco, Calif.: Chandler, 1964).

7. Norwood Russell Hanson, *Patterns of Discovery* (Cambridge: At the University Press, 1958).

ologies for science. It may help in the description of the theoretical activities that constitute science as currently carried on. But these contributions form only one part of its legitimate task.

The philosophy of science must not stop short of an investigation of those activities that are the basis for theory of any kind, including scientific theory. These are the activities that it is nowadays fashionable to call *praxis,* referring to the full range of human conscious activities in the intersubjective and historical world of everyday life. Only a clarification of this universal basis of theory can hope to show the significance of scientific knowledge for human life and establish its legitimate place among other forms of knowledge, theoretical or pretheoretical. Karl Popper describes clearly and simply the common theoretical interest of science and philosophy:

> There is at least one problem in which all thinking men are interested. It is the problem of cosmology: *the problem of understanding the world—including ourselves, and our knowledge, as part of the world.* All science is cosmology, I believe, and for me the interest of philosophy as well as of science lies solely in the contribution which they have made to it.[8]

The task of the philosophy of science goes far beyond the immediate concerns of the methodologies of the physical sciences. It consists in giving a convincing account of the relation of science to theoretical activities in general, and of the relation of these activities to common sense and everyday life. It simply will not do to refer this task to an empirical discipline—such as the psychology of cognition, or even the sociology of knowledge—for *final* adjudication. Such a procedure leads to an obviously vicious circle.

An attempt to avoid that circle involves the search for a controlled, independent perspective on both science and common sense. The question about the foundations of science, its place among other forms of knowledge, and their common origin in everyday life is, first of all, a question about an appropriate method of answering questions of that kind. Clearly, the method must be at least as reasonable and subject to control as the methods of scientific reasoning—but it must also be reflexive and give an account of its own presuppositions. Much depends

8. Karl R. Popper, *The Logic of Scientific Discovery* (New York: Basic Books, 1959), p. 15 (italics mine).

on the initial view of the problem. One can easily relapse into the circularity of scientific rationalism instead of retaining the controlled reflexivity of a critical theory of knowledge. This danger, I think, is what Burtt had in mind in juxtaposing a philosophy of the mind to a cosmology. And it is at this point that Popper decides to remain within the universe of scientific discourse. This strategic decision is foreshadowed in a highly personal view of a great philosophical tradition:

> Its most important representatives during the last two hundred years were Kant, Whewell, Mill, Peirce, Duhem, Poincaré, Meyerson, Russell, and—at least in some of his phases—Whitehead. Most of those who belong to this group would agree that scientific knowledge is the result of the growth of common-sense knowledge. *But all of them discovered that scientific knowledge can be more easily studied than common-sense knowledge* [italics mine]. For it is *common-sense knowledge writ large* [italics Popper's], as it were.[9]

This view seems rather one-sided in the case of Peirce and Whitehead, and perhaps also of the Russell of *Human Knowledge*.[10] It definitely does not do full justice to Kant. One may agree that scientific knowledge can be more easily studied than common-sense knowledge. But that, at best, justifies a beginning, not an end, and it does not resolve the question of method. By no means does it justify what is presented as a conclusion: that scientific knowledge is a (magnified) replica of common-sense knowledge. Popper, I am sure, was induced to make this formulation by his understandable polemic against a conception of science that would sever it from any sensible connection with everyday knowledge. His account of "corroboration" alone is sufficient proof that he does not assume a relation of simple isomorphy between science and common sense. Unfortunately, a perfectly legitimate decision to concentrate on an analysis of the structure of scientific knowledge is dressed up, by virtue of this unjustified claim, as a general theory of knowledge.

Husserl also made what appears in retrospect as a strategic

9. *Ibid.*, p. 22.
10. Bertrand Russell, *Human Knowledge* (New York: Simon and Schuster, 1948), a work in which Russell devotes considerable space to a discussion and to some descriptive analysis of common-sense knowledge. He does show certain connections and similarities between science and common sense, but his main aim is to point out the differences.

decision: not to accept the claim of modern science to be the ultimate form of human knowledge. In three of his major works, one early and two belonging to a later phase of his thought, Husserl investigated the foundations of formal logic.[11] By the method, first, of phenomenological psychology and later of transcendental phenomenology, he traced the origins of logical and mathematical thinking to the activities of consciousness in what he came to call the *Lebenswelt*, that is, the pretheoretical and theoretical levels of the world of everyday life. But it is his last work, the *Crisis*, which initiated a new phase of philosophical reflection on science. In it he effectively demolished the "ultimacy" pretensions of the modern scientific cosmology. For superficial if not silly reasons, and often from sheer ignorance, this has been taken as an "attack" on science, whatever that may mean.[12] It should not be necessary to stress that Husserl does not question the validity of science—as far as it goes. The question remains, of course, how far *does* it go? [13]

It is significant that in answering this question Husserl im-

11. *Logische Untersuchungen* (1900; Tübingen: Niemeyer, 1968); English translation by J. N. Findlay, *Logical Investigations* (New York: Humanities, 1970); *Formale und transzendentale Logik* (Halle: Niemeyer, 1929); English translation by Dorion Cairns, *Formal and Transcendental Logic* (The Hague: Nijhoff, 1970); *Erfahrung und Urteil* (1938; 2d ed., Hamburg: Claassen and Goverts, 1948); English translation by Spencer Churchill and Karl Ameriks, *Experience and Judgment* (Evanston, Ill.: Northwestern University Press, 1973).

12. Some years ago Maurice Natanson warned against the misappropriations and misrepresentations of phenomenology: "In particular, the legend of the *Lebenswelt* lends itself or has been made to lend itself to a critique of rationalism and natural science which is, I think, not only mistaken but inimical to phenomenology" ("The *Lebenswelt*," *Review of Existential Psychology and Psychiatry*, IV [Spring, 1964], 134). Things have taken a turn for the worse in the meantime. Having first provided general absolution for mild "humanistic" confusions, misconceptions of phenomenology later gave rise to some academic subcultures whose resemblance to phenomenological analysis is purely incidental.

13. Aron Gurwitsch puts it concisely: "*It is the historical significance of Husserl's Galileo analysis to challenge and even to abandon the acceptance of science as an ultimate fact and rather to see in it a problem.* Husserl is far from questioning the technical, or, more precisely, the intrinsic validity of science, and nothing could have been further from his mind than dismissing it in any sense. What is in question is not science itself, nor any particular scientific theory, but the interpretation of science" ("Comments" on Herbert Marcuse, "On Science and Phenomenology," *Boston Studies in the Philosophy of Science*, Vol. II: *In Honor of Philipp Frank*, ed. Robert S. Cohen and Marx M. Wartofsky [New York: Humanities Press, 1965], p. 294; italics original).

mediately confronts the problem of method. In this respect, at least, his importance equals that of Descartes and Kant. If Husserl initiated a new phase in philosophy and in the philosophy of science, it is as much by having developed a method for determining the validity of science as by having destroyed the "ultimacy" pretensions of the scientific cosmology. The elementary phenomenological epochē, the various reductions, eidetic variation, and so on, combine in accounting or being able in principle to account for the presuppositions of phenomenological psychology and transcendental phenomenology—which, in turn, have clarified or are capable of clarifying the constitutive structures of conscious activities upon which everyday life as well as science is founded.[14] In short, Husserl developed a method of philosophical analysis that is rationally controlled (and in this sense "scientific") *and* reflexive. The method permits an approach to the question "How far *does* science go?" that does not end in a vicious circle.

It is perhaps more obvious to this generation than it was to its predecessors that this question goes far beyond the boundaries of a single academic discipline. It is a fundamental philosophical question for modern man. In an age when science—which, after all, *is* a human activity—is either deified or satanized, it is also an eminently political question. Far from being destructive of science, Husserl's demolition of the "ultimacy" claim of the scientific cosmology and his attempt to establish firm foundations for science provide a sound basis for determining its human significance. One may hope, on a smaller scale, that his efforts will also help to overcome the curious arrangement whereby in a prototypical philosophy department a faithful Carnapian "covers" science while an existentialist "takes care" of "subjective meaning" and a neo-quasi-neo-Marxist

14. I know of no resumé of the methods of phenomenological analysis that could adequately substitute for the study of Husserl's work. Dorion Cairns's systematic presentation of Husserl, which served as a source of instruction to a generation of students, has not yet found its way into print. Discussions of Husserl in the work of Alfred Schutz, Aron Gurwitsch, and other first-generation phenomenologists were rarely expository. Among the numerous brief introductions, one that is particularly clear and useful is Maurice Natanson's "Phenomenology: A Viewing," in his *Literature, Philosophy, and the Social Sciences* (The Hague: Nijhoff, 1962); see also Herbert Spiegelberg, "The Essentials of Phenomenological Method," in *The Phenomenological Movement: A Historical Introduction*, 2d ed. (The Hague: Nijhoff, 1965), II, 655–701.

proclaims the political and social irrelevance of what his colleagues are doing.

THE COSMOLOGICAL PARADIGM IN SOCIAL SCIENCE

BOTH THE GENERAL PROBLEM, i.e., the cosmological validity of science, and the question about the proper way to approach this problem are particularly urgent when "cosmology" is taken to refer not only to a systematic explication of the physical universe, but also to a theoretical account of the social world. The reasons why the problems of validity and method should be especially crucial when the reality of human activities is involved are obvious, at least in a general way. They have been taken up under different headings in what is by now a voluminous literature.[15] Nevertheless they will bear some discussion from the point of view I am taking here.

To begin with, one should register profound wonder that anyone should ever have wanted to exclude the social world from the theoretical concern of cosmology. The world of man *was* included in mythological and theological cosmologies, as a matter of course *and* as a matter of overwhelming interest, during most of the history of human thought. This changed in Western thinking after Galileo. Since his time, some philosophers and scientists have excluded the reality of human activities from cosmology. It is my contention that they do so for reasons (perhaps I should say motives) that are not subjected to rigorous and critical reflection. Other philosophers and scientists are once more including the social world in the scientific cosmology. I contend that they do so for reasons that are just as naïve as those of the other group. I may be putting things too sweepingly and dramatically, and I shall have to be more cautious presently. One thing that can be maintained with confidence, for the moment, is that the distinction between a "physical universe" and other domains of reality, e.g., a "social world," is derived from the metaphysical presuppositions that went into the making of

15. Two examples of the literature I have in mind here are the hundreds of books and, probably, thousands of articles on historicism and on the so-called value freedom of social science. For a good overview of the latter, see Hans Albert and Ernst Topitsch, eds., *Werturteilsfreiheit* (Darmstadt: Wissenschaftliche Buchgesellschaft, 1971).

the modern scientific cosmology. This distinction must therefore not be exempt from critical examination. The division of reality into a physical world and a world of human affairs occurred as part of a global process of "rationalization." It was a milestone in the depersonalization of mythological views of the world, a process described by Max Weber as *Entzauberung*.

This division of reality stands at the end of concatenated theological, philosophical, and scientific traditions, and at the beginning of a historical movement of thought that led to the situation characterized by Husserl as the "crisis" of modern science. The motives for this division had their source in the theological cosmology of the Middle Ages. To say that man attains a divine level of knowledge by virtue of mathematics was not merely a *façon de parler* for Galileo. Nor did his opponents underestimate the possibilities inherent in his view. In a universe whose reality is guaranteed by its mathematical structure, man as well as God becomes problematic in a way that was entirely alien to the older cosmologies, however much they may have differed among themselves in other respects. In the new vision of reality man requires ad hoc explanations just as much as God.

The ontological and epistemological sources (to the extent that it is possible to isolate these more technically philosophical components from the general cultural background) that fed into the stream of the new cosmology can be traced to shifting patterns of influence of opposing philosophical traditions; in Galileo, Platonism won over Aristotelianism.[16] However, reference to the complex origins of these perspectives tells only part of the story; the other part consists of the unique blending of these perspectives into a new vision of the universe. This new vision became clear with Copernicus, who postulated the mathematical structure of the universe. Against the opposition of traditional empiricist philosophy, this postulate was transformed into an article of belief which is taken for granted in the modern cosmology. It did not become entirely immune from critical examination, but philosophical questioning generally proceeded along the innocuous line that the postulate should, perhaps, not be given an ontological but "merely" an epistemological interpretation.

The cosmological plausibility of this view was decisively

16. Alexandre Koyré, "Galileo and Plato," in *Roots of Scientific Thought,* ed. Philip Wiener and Aaron Noland (New York: Basic Books, 1957), pp. 147–75.

strengthened when it was combined with Galileo's doctrine of primary and secondary qualities, and still later, with Newtonian mechanics. Galileo's idea of primary and secondary qualities is expressed in his famous statement that "Whoever wants to read a book, must know the language in which that book is written. Nature is a book and the characters in which it is written are triangles, circles and squares." [17] It can be paraphrased less elegantly as follows: Only the primary qualities can be expressed exactly, i.e., mathematically; the real, objective, absolute reality consists of primary qualities; only what can be expressed mathematically is truly, objectively, absolutely real. This is not much of a syllogism and it probably was never formulated in quite that manner. It is an example of what C. S. Peirce analyzed as abductive reasoning. [18] According to Peirce, abduction is a form of reasoning which guides many common-sense procedures and is also an important strategy of theory-finding in science. In this particular instance abductive reasoning on a grand scale seems to have been involved in the historical construction of a cosmology.

The Copernican postulate of the mathematical structure of reality, the Galilean doctrine of primary and secondary qualities, and the notions of causality generally associated with Newtonian mechanics (Newton's own strong strain of prudent empiricism notwithstanding) combined to produce a new view of reality whose persuasiveness was probably based as much on its extraordinary aesthetic appeal as on its continuous popular verification in the successes of applied science and technology. As is the nature of systematically articulated views of the world, the cosmology was expansionistic within science and imperialistic outside of it. New areas that were to be investigated scientifically were subordinated to the new cosmology. [19] At the same time, the

17. Quoted in Gurwitsch, "Comments," p. 300 (see Galileo Galilei, *Il Saggiatore* [Florence: Edizione Nazionale, 1965], VI, 232).
18. C. S. Peirce used the terms "hypothesis," "abduction," and "retroduction" to describe the process of abductive reasoning. See his *Collected Papers*, 8 Vols., Vols. I–VI, ed. Charles Hartshorne and Paul Weiss (Cambridge, Mass.: Harvard University Press, 1931–35), especially II, 372–88; V, 112–31; and VI, 311–32. For abduction as an interactional phenomenon, see Richard Grathoff, *The Structure of Social Inconsistencies* (The Hague: Nijhoff, 1970), especially pp. 40–75.
19. "The conviction that sooner or later all science is mechanics dies hard: for three centuries science has been dominated by notions of inertia,

cosmology was not restricted to formulations of "laws" and "hypotheses" about restricted dimensions of the universe. The notions of domains of reality [20] and levels of explanation [21] belong to a later period in which philosophers and scientists had already begun to confront the "crisis" of the scientific cosmology. But as long as the arrogant doctrine of primary and secondary qualities prevailed, the ontologically and epistemologically modest conception of domains or levels had no chance to emerge.

In contradistinction to older cosmologies, the expansionism of the new scientific cosmology was checked, at first, by the problem of fitting man into its scheme. The conception of man was more resistant to change than was the conception of the universe. As long as man was cut from the pattern of the old cosmology, he could not be fitted into the tight clothes of the new. Descartes did not hesitate to deliver the human body (and the poor beasties) to the icy winds blowing in the new universe. But not, alas, the human soul.[22]

For some time the cosmological situation was thus characterized by uncertainty, inconsistency, and incipient implausibility. What was traditionally, and plausibly, connected as part of one comprehensive reality was split asunder. Radically different styles of thought which were completely incompatible with one another were prescribed for the knowledge of man (and God) and for the knowledge of the rest of the universe. This split

---

impact and resultant velocities. This has affected our understanding of causation" (Hanson, *Patterns of Discovery*, p. 65).

20. Making use of suggestions from various sources, especially from William James, George Herbert Mead, and Husserl, Alfred Schutz developed a theory of "domains" as "finite provinces of meaning," i.e., based on a characteristic experiential and cognitive style. See his "On Multiple Realities," in *Collected Papers*, Vol. I: *The Problem of Social Reality*, ed. Maurice Natanson (The Hague: Nijhoff, 1962), pp. 207–59.

21. The notion of levels of explanation was, of course, one of the central issues in the long debate on "reductionism" in science, especially after its revival in Neurath's program of "unified science." I may refer here to two sensible discussions in the *Symposium on Sociological Theory*, ed. Llewellyn Gross (Evanston, Ill., and White Plains, N.Y.: Row, Peterson, 1959): Abraham Edel, "The Concept of Levels in Social Theory," pp. 167–95, and Herbert Hochberg, "Axiomatic Systems, Formalization and Scientific Theory," pp. 407–36.

22. A very special act is required to account for the human soul: "I had described after this the rational soul and shown that it could not be in any way derived from the power of matter, like the other things of which I had spoken, but that it must be expressly created" (René Descartes, *Discourse on Method*, trans. Elizabeth S. Haldane and G. R. T. Ross [Cambridge: At the University Press, 1931], I, 117–18).

had been prepared for a long time. Judaism, a major step in the *Entzauberung* of the mythological universe, had already singled out man, the member of the elect tribe, as standing in a special compact with God.[23] But the Thomistic reconciliation of Christianity with Greek philosophy successfully refitted man into the over-all scheme of creation. Meanwhile, beneath the official doctrines the world view of the folk tradition had always retained the essential structure of the old mythologies. The separation of man from the universe in the newly emerging cosmology, on the other hand, gave rise to a metaphysical disorientation that within a century or two had repercussions in the culture of all social classes.

In order to cope with this cosmological inconsistency, attempts were begun to justify the expulsion of Adam from the new cosmology or to recast the conception of man so that he would fit into it smoothly. The attempts carry the trade-mark of abductive reasoning; they are neither inferences nor deductions but leaps from familiar premises to an unknown order of things that is made comprehensible by assimilation to the premises. Such movements are not entirely unlike leaps of faith. It is therefore not surprising that two contradictory ways of resolving this cosmological inconsistency emerged in the course of time.

One solution runs as follows (if I may be allowed to retrace the abductive steps in a less than complimentary fashion): Man is part of nature; nature consists of primary qualities; man is reducible to primary qualities; there is no world of human affairs for which scientific understanding is not possible, in principle, through a reduction to the mathematical manifold of space and time (here the Newtonian conception of causality is occasionally thrown in for good measure). The leap to the other solution takes off from the other foot: Man is not reducible to primary qualities; the special origin of his soul—or the uniqueness of his experience—cannot be mathematized; man is not part of reality in the sense in which nature is real (this is one of the sources of the Cartesian difficulty); therefore there can be no science of man (except of course under the wholly subordinate aspect of man as a "machine").

These "conclusions," still generally unexamined, are at the

23. See Max Weber, *Ancient Judaism*, trans. and ed. H. Gerth and D. Martindale (Glencoe, Ill.: Free Press, 1952).

heart of the methodological controversies of social science. It hardly needs to be added that these controversies are the social science variant of the general crisis of modern science. I shall not pursue directly the wider topic of to what extent phenomenology, by clarifying the origins of theoretical activities in the world of everyday life, provides a philosophical foundation for all science. I shall turn instead to look closely at one important part of the wider question, the elementary problem of social science methodology. I hope I have already shown the historical relativity—which does not necessarily mean falseness—of the ideas that prevented the emergence of a social science which did not try to follow the precepts of the new cosmology. I am not afraid of overstating my case by saying that Copernicus, Galileo, and Newton are *malgré eux* the main figures, not of social science, but of the methodology of modern social science. Their new cosmology severed social science from its ancestry.

The rapid growth of social science in the past quarter-century, the specialization of disciplines and the increasing technical sophistication of their methods, the attempts at extending paradigms across disciplinary boundaries and at constructing a unified theory, as well as the urgency of the social problems that can only be resolved—or so it is commonly thought—if social science reaches the "maturity" of, and collaborates with, physical science and technology: all this may explain, and, perhaps, partly justify, the loss of memory that is widespread among contemporary social scientists. The long tradition of systematic reflection on human conduct in society is no longer alive. The historian will no doubt trace some contemporary theoretical paradigm by way of Marx and Hegel to a Gnostic source. In a playful mood, he may point to a similarity between some idea of Veblen's and a half-forgotten observation of Saint-Simon. A political scientist may appeal to hallowed ancestors in Aristotle, Pomponazzi, or Machiavelli. A linguist may make his reverence before Panini, a sociologist may bow to Montesquieu. Occasionally, someone may even want to shake his fist at what he takes to be a dangerous survival of, for example, Platonism. But these ritual invocations are usually mere frills and ornaments in scholarship, whose live, subjectively grasped intellectual sources are much more recent. The works of earlier centuries have less influence on contemporary social science than the discovery of pre-Socratic beginnings of non-Euclidian geometry has on a land surveyor in Alaska. To the average social scientist the idea of a specialized history of social science appears stranger than did the need for a professional history of physical science to the ordinary physicist of pre-Sartonian days; he sees himself as the practitioner of a science that is in its infancy. Social science as we know it today (and as it knows itself) is a child of Modernity writ large. It traces its descent into the nineteenth, perhaps as far back as the late eighteenth century. Beyond that begins the prehistory of social lore and isolated philosophical speculation. And still further back are the Dark Ages of utter ignorance concerning human conduct.

I do not intend to examine here all the reasons for this peculiar partial amnesia. Nor do I want to plead for the inclusion of Thucydides in the training programs of social scientists. Appeals do not revive dead traditions. The contemporary historian of ideas and the future historian of social science need not be told their business, and the thoughtful social scientist knows more or less clearly that he is carried on "the shoulders of a giant." My reminder here has a different purpose. I want to stress an important consequence of the modernity-image that prevails in social science today. In sharp contrast to physical scientists, social scientists find that they cannot look backward to an autonomous tradition of philosophical reflection on their enterprise. The most promising candidates to membership in such a tradition, Vico, for example, are sweepingly disqualified as mere speculative "metaphysicians." The philosophy of science until very recently was a philosophy of physical science. The methodology of *social* science is a child of Galilean *physical* science.[24] In this perspective it makes little difference whether the child is abjectly docile or wildly rebellious, or, to change the metaphor, whether man is thrown out of the modern scientific cosmology or locked into it.

24. I am using the term "Galilean science" in the sense employed by Husserl in *Crisis*. It corresponds approximately to what I have referred to as the new cosmology or the Copernican-Galilean-Newtonian view of the world. Gurwitsch puts it as follows: "Husserl, when he speaks of Galileo, does not mean the historical figure of that name who lived at a certain time, any more than by Galilean science he means the scientific work actually done by that historical figure. Rather Galilean science denotes the science inaugurated by Galileo. The name is used as a symbol for the historical development of modern science from, roughly speaking, 1600 to 1700, that is, the constitution of classical physics and even beyond" ("Comments," p. 292).

THE "CRISIS" OF SOCIAL SCIENCE

MOST SOCIAL SCIENTISTS and almost all those philosophers who like to instruct social scientists on their business persist to this day in allowing the Copernican-Galilean-Newtonian view of the world to impose upon them the basic perspective in which they look on themselves and on the goals of their theoretical activities. They continue to take for granted the assumptions that the universe is deceptive yet fully knowable; that the appearances given to prescientific man, an inferior "subjective" species easily befuddled by secondary qualities, hide a structure of "objective" primary qualities; and that discovery of this ultimate reality depends on the supreme and autonomous form of knowledge, (numerical) mathematics. Despite Hume and others, they cling to an apparently ineradicable push-and-pull notion of causality to explain how it all hangs together.[25] Revolutionary elements of seventeenth-century philosophy and science, abductively transformed into an eighteenth-century cosmology, almost routinely transmitted to the nineteenth century as a paradigm of physical science, thus form the unexamined background of methodological reflection in social science well into the second half of the twentieth century.

The same paradigm, however, gave rise to elementary methodological positions in social science which seem to their adherents to be irreconcilably opposed. It should be recalled that the early phases of the new cosmology were characterized by an elementary inconsistency which stimulated abductive reasoning along two main lines (as summarized above), depending on whether the inconsistency was to be eliminated or legitimated. The fundamental methodological controversy in social science is at best a continuation and at worst a petrification of these efforts.

One side of the controversy makes the "big leap forward." Man is subordinated to the newly found principles. He *cannot* be merely a bundle of secondary qualities, he *has* to be part of nature. And because "nature" is the mathematical manifold

25. For a discussion of this important aspect of the problem, see Mario Lins, *Foundations of Social Determinism*, trans. George Reed (Rio de Janeiro: Livraria Freitas Bastos, 1959).

representing the primary qualities of true reality, the hunt for the primary qualities of human existence is on. The Cartesian reservation on the human soul is given up and an intrinsically consistent man-machine solution replaces it. Through analogy with astronomy and mechanics, a plausible interpretation of anatomical and even physiological findings appears possible. But while the solution appears logical, the application of the logic to the study of human affairs leads to results whose absurdity is not diminished by the fact that they form part of the routine background of our thinking as social scientists. The hope that, by discovery of primary qualities to which measurable values can be attached, social science will finally become "exact" (a word with powerful emotional appeal for Neo-Pythagorean romantics) waxes eternal. No matter how sophisticated the technical discussion of the logic and the logistics of science, the guiding vision of social science on this side of the methodological controversy is of a closed mechanical universe whose objective qualities are numerical.[26]

Failure of the vision has resulted in two varieties of frustration. The inability to determine the primary qualities of man as a social, political, and historical being by transforming him into a walking inventory of instincts or drives, into a *homo œconomicus, homo sociologicus,* game-strategist, personality subsystem of an action system, and the like, inspires recurrent movements of cosmological reductionism. If the "soul" will not play by these particular rules, out with it! The man-machine will play by them, and therefore it is invited into the part vacated by the "soul." The man-machine becomes a symbol of hope to those proponents of reductionism who must try to secure unlimited extensions of credit for their program. The other variety of frustration is that of the sensitive souls who, after an early training in some self-consciously "scientific" discipline, develop ideological guilt feelings or aesthetic phobias about the language of cybernetics,

26. "The physical sciences have dominated applied mathematics for so long that many scientists and mathematicians have mistakenly assumed that non-divergence is necessary before prediction is possible. Consequently the physical sciences have been called the 'exact sciences,' while the biological and social sciences have been mistakenly labelled the 'inexact sciences'" (E. C. Zeeman, "The Geometry of Catastrophe" ["Thinking by Numbers," no. 13], *Times Literary Supplement* [December 10, 1971], pp. 1556–57).

systems analysis, simulation, or even old-fashioned structural-functionalism. They are easily converted to the soft belly faction of the other side of the methodological controversy.

The other side of the controversy not only refuses to leap but, one is tempted to say maliciously, hesitates to walk. Most of its adherents, seeing the absurdity of the consequences, deny the applicability of the premises of the new cosmology to man, while at the same time uncritically accepting those premises for the rest of creation. Man therefore has to be removed as far as possible from nature, "nature" being nothing but a measurable space-time manifold. Furthermore, the pushes and pulls of vulgar matter cannot apply to the "historicity" and the "uniqueness" of the human mind (these are the words of emotional appeal on *this* side of the fence). Therefore there can be no social *science*, there can be only artistic and intuitive reconstructions of the unfolding of the mind. These idiographic narratives have to have a logic, a structure, a style different from the man-machine analysis of human affairs. The palpable inapplicability of the new cosmology to human affairs provokes not merely a legitimate rejection of a numerical-mechanistic conception of social science, but an enduring inability to reexamine the problem of formalization and mathematization independently. The adherents of this side of the methodological controversy do not dream of challenging what they take to be the laws of the land. They are fully satisfied with a cosmological Human Exclusion Act. Let us have our hermeneutics, they insist, and you can have your cybernetics!

Neither side of the watershed, of course, possesses a common program. Neurath's claim that "empiricists" and "rationalists" have joined in a movement of "unified science" whose platform could be called "logical empiricism" or "empirical rationalism" was exaggerated when it was originally made in 1938, and the movement has not become any more unified since then.[27] Since the seventeenth century philosophers have presented a wide variety of positions on logic, scientific method, causality, inference, and so on, which followed most of the imaginable combinations of Baconian empiricism and Cartesian rationalism.

27. Otto Neurath, "Unified Science as Encyclopedic Integration," in *International Encyclopedia of Unified Science,* ed. Otto Neurath, Rudolf Carnap, and Charles Morris, Vol. I, no. 1 (1938; 2d ed., Chicago: University of Chicago Press, 1955).

Nevertheless, logical empiricism serves to designate the modern philosophical center of the one side of the watershed. In science, it combines with various philosophically more or less purified versions of "positivism." It is not *necessarily* reductionist, but it often is; it is not *necessarily* behaviorist, but again it often is.

Meanwhile, the sources on the other side of the watershed can be characterized, in a general way, as Neo-Platonistic and idealistic. Among its more extreme adherents the Hegelian heritage is obvious. Roughly speaking, one may consider the historicists, Dilthey, most Neo-Kantian philosophers, e.g. Rickert, idealistic phenomenologists, and the "picture-book" variety of phenomenologists as belonging here. Winch's interpretation of Wittgenstein,[28] as well as so-called "critical sociology" in Germany and some Neo-Marxists (claiming to go back to the "early" Marx of the *Frühschiften*) in other countries have their *methodological* origins on this side of the divide. Seen through Neo-Kantian and idealistic interpretations Max Weber can also be placed here. But these interpretations miss his heroic effort to tunnel through the range to the other side. Despite the inconsistencies in his methodological rhetoric, Weber seems to me to have passed more successfully than any other major social scientist the Scylla and Charybdis of the cosmological paradigm in social science.[29]

In sum: the search for a *mathēsis universalis* of human affairs was—and is—abandoned by both sides. One side stopped looking because it thought it had found it already, and was content to let the concrete problems and the recalcitrant "facts" of the social sciences look out for themselves. The other side never started looking because it was convinced there was nothing to find. Both sides thus contributed to the social science variant of the crisis of modern science.

The crisis is not to be confused with the "reactionary" and "revolutionary" attacks on the limited but, within this limitation, necessary and legitimate autonomy of science. Nor is it simply a matter of romantic impatience with the also limited but legitimate rationality of science. Attacks and cavils of this kind are

28. *The Idea of a Social Science* (New York: Humanities Press, 1965).

29. For an interesting recent critical appreciation of Weber that does not try to make him over into a positivist or phenomenologist, see W. G. Runciman, *A Critique of Max Weber's Philosophy of Social Science* (Cambridge: At the University Press, 1972).

not new, and despite their present vociferousness they are probably less dangerous today than earlier in the century when they were associated with powerful totalitarian political forces. The crisis of social science is not caused by its technological implications, despite the recurrent fear, recently reacting to Skinnerian chimeras, that social science is about to find the key to the total manipulation of the human mind. Nor is it a crisis of substantive theory or of research procedures, if these terms are understood narrowly. The logical and logistic problems of the organization of ideas arising in social science, as in any similarly complex social institution concerned with the acquisition and transmission of knowledge, are so normal that they hardly deserve to be called "crises," though it is true that the ideological, technological, theoretical, and procedural problems connected with social science appear more serious at the present time than ever before.[30] In part this impression may be attributed to the well-known generation effect: every generation views the state of the world with more profound concern than did the previous one. In part, however, these contemporary alarms are genuine symptoms of the "crisis" of social science in the sense in which I am using it, i.e., in strict analogy to Husserl's application of the term to Galilean physical science.

The fundamental function of theory is to suggest meaningful solutions to basic problems of everyday life, to help men in their orientation to the universe. One would hope that science would do this more successfully than its cosmological predecessors. In order to perform this function, however, theory must first give a meaningful account of the concerns of everyday life. Description and explanation are inextricably interwoven. Furthermore, scientific theory is distinguished from the mythological and theological accounts from which historically it emerged (and which vestigially survive in it)[31] by its degree of *explicit* systematization and formalization of knowledge and by its commitment to a teachable and public method for the acquisition of knowledge. The method is to be rational and empirical (both words subject to varying interpretations but each

30. A thoughtful discussion, by a physical scientist, of some of the recent Doomsday prognostications about science can be found in Harvey Brooks, "Can Science Survive in the Modern Age?," *Science*, CLXXIV (October 1, 1971), 21–30.

31. See Ernst Topitsch, "Mythische Modelle in der Erkenntnislehre," *Studium Generale*, XVIII, no. 6 (1965), 400–418.

roughly having a common core-meaning). The empirical acquisition of knowledge, its rational interpretations, and its public transmission are to be controlled by a community of investigators, to borrow an apt Peircean reformulation of the old concept of the republic of scholars. Communication within this community, however, and just as importantly, with the larger community of noninvestigators, is founded in some presumably determinable but inevitably circular manner on the intersubjectivity of ordinary experience. In short: scientific theory is description as well as explanation; communication in science rests on communication in everyday life.

This circularity (science–ordinary experience–science) has an important consequence for social science. The subject matter of social science, the sociohistorical reality of everyday life, is not only a problem in the sense in which "physical nature" as a universe of "objects" is a problem to science, but a problem of epistemological reflexivity as well. According to Husserl, the crisis of science resulted from the alienation of the idealized and formalized products of theoretical activity, of "logic" and "mathematics" reified as structural principles of nature, from their sources in the *Lebenswelt*. I submit that because of the peculiar reflexivity of social science, its estrangement from its sources is a bigger threat to its elementary theoretical function than the illegitimate reifications in physical science are to *its* cosmological purpose. In social science it is not only the products of theoretical activities that are uncritically reified; under the prevailing cosmological paradigm the producers themselves are in constant danger of reification.

It is of course not enough merely to speak of "alienation" and "crisis" in a general way. I hope I have succeeded in a more specific diagnosis by tracing the present symptoms in the methodology of social science to an underlying cause. The cosmological paradigm of Galilean science was imposed, for a number of reasons, on social science and on the philosophy of social science, and kept them in a state of double naïveté. [32] In the first place, the sources of science in the theoretical activities of idealization and mathematization, and the foundation of these

32. In *Crisis* Husserl distinguishes the naïveté of Galilean science and logic from the naïveté of the natural attitude of everyday life. See also *Cartesian Meditations*, trans. Dorion Cairns (The Hague: Nijhoff, 1960), especially pp. 152–53.

activities in the praxis of everyday life, were suppressed. This is a form of blindness which social science shares with physical science. Social science not only very properly took over the logical form of reasoning (the historic achievement of the combination of empiricism with rationalism) from physical science; it also very improperly pretends to the same (illegitimate) *epistemological* autonomy of scientific knowledge (which is its historical *hubris*). The second aspect of naïveté is the exclusive property of social science. It is a blindness concerning the nature of the subject matter of social science. It consists in a metaphysical elimination of reflexivity.

I am reasonably confident that the diagnosis is correct. It would be tempting to stop here, because I must confess that I am much less confident of the cure than of the diagnosis. Nevertheless, having come this far in the identification of the problem, I should like to try to suggest the direction in which I think the solution is to be found. In pointing to it I shall use as signposts certain important suggestions in Husserl's *Crisis* [33]

33. The reader beware! I am not giving a faithful rendering of Husserl's work *in toto*. I think that the extrapolation of the suggestions which I am taking mainly from *Crisis* can be justified. But Husserl probably would not accept these extrapolations as being within the frame of transcendental phenomenology. In *Crisis* there are passages which suggest a train of thought with which my proposal is incompatible, at least on the surface. See, e.g.: "For the realm of souls there is in principle no such ontology, no science corresponding to the physicalistic-mathematical ideal, although psychic being is investigatable in transcendental universality, in a fully systematic way, and in principle in essential generality in the form of an *a priori* science" (*Crisis*, p. 265 [italics mine]); "for an objectivity after the fashion of natural science is downright absurd when applied to the soul, to subjectivity, whether as individual subjectivity, individual person, and individual life or as communally historical subjectivity, as social subjectivity in the broadest sense" (p. 337). Much depends on what one means by "after the fashion of natural science." If it refers to Galilean science, *d'accord*. But a "science" a priori, a transcendental eidetic phenomenology is not the only alternative. Cf. Husserl's own statement: "[Corrected] experience—either as communal experience and reciprocal correction or as one's own personal experience and self-correction—does not change the relativity of experience; even as communal experience it is relative, and thus all descriptive assertions are necessarily relative, and all conceivable inferences, deductive or inductive, are relative" (p. 336). An "open," empirical, science whose "objects" are "relative" and "descriptive" statements should be just as legitimate as a science whose "objects" are (numerically) mathematized qualities. For an interesting discussion of ambiguities in Husserl's notion of *Lebenswelt* and correlative

and in the opus of Schutz.[34] Again I shall leave aside the general problem of the crisis of science, to whose solution Husserl devoted his last work, and concentrate instead on the methodological consequences of the second aspect of the naïveté of social science mentioned above.

I have suggested that the crisis of social science, to the extent that it is separable from the general crisis of science, is its inability to come to terms with its peculiar epistemological reflexivity. The underground waters of the Galilean cosmology continue to feed the rivers on both sides of the methodological watershed, the only important difference being that some flow east and the others west. The epistemological reflexivity of the enterprise is either wished away because it is bothersome, or else it frightens the practitioners back into a mythological or theological mode of thought. The result is that neither side has produced a *mathēsis universalis* appropriate to human affairs.

I suggest that a solution to the crisis of social science might be found if the search were taken up again. I maintain that a *mathēsis universalis* of the *social* world has not even been programmatically established in what, roughly speaking, is the positivist tradition. I also maintain, however, that the cosmological goal of a *mathēsis universalis* must include human conduct on all its levels; the Human Exclusion Act is just as unconstitutional in science as it is in philosophy. The unity of science does *not* presuppose a reductionist metaphysics. I am convinced, and I hope I have shown the reasons for my conviction, that the goal of a *mathēsis universalis* for human affairs cannot be reached by simple analogy to the ideal of mathematization in Galilean cosmology. This ideal is too closely tied to a numerical conception of what is "objective" and "empirical." A *mathēsis universalis* appropriate to the social world will have to be truly independent of Galilean cosmology. It will have to be based on the premise of the epistemological reflexivity of a science of human conduct. A science that describes and explains the con-

---

ambiguities in his view of an (a priori) science of the *Lebenswelt*, see Natanson, "The *Lebenswelt*," especially pp. 130–32.

34. See especially "Common-Sense and Scientific Interpretation of Human Action," *Collected Papers*, I, 3–47; "Concept and Theory Formation in the Social Sciences," *ibid.*, pp. 48–66; and "Phenomenology and the Social Sciences," *ibid.*, pp. 118–39. His work constitutes an essential contribution to the philosophical foundation of social science.

structions of social reality must be able to develop a program of formalization (and a theory of measurement) that is appropriate to the constitutive structures of everyday life.[35]

The diagnosis of an illness is not its cure, nor is the naming of a medicine that is not yet on the market. I am aware of that. Yet I think that these two steps are important, at least for redirecting attention from symptoms to causes.

The existence of a crisis in social science is not generally perceived, unless one considers as instances of such perception the utilitarian dissatisfactions with its lack of predictive efficiency on the part of "practical men of research and business" or the amusing conceit of bourgeois sociologists that bourgeois sociology is doomed. Among social scientists the "crisis" in the sense in which I am using the term is only half seen on one side of the methodological Big Divide, and then denied with almost as much conviction as on the other side. This failure of observation of course does not strengthen my case, but it does not necessarily weaken it. If the diagnosis is correct, both sides have good reason to ignore the existence of a crisis common to both sides. It is more flattering to assume that it is not social science but the opposing side that is in critical condition. The epistemological, theoretical, procedural, and ideological difficulties that undeniably exist in social science can then be attributed to the senility of an established church or to the wrongheadedness of a newly emerging sect.

The controversies among various schools of thought *do* concern genuine issues of substantive theory, investigative technique, and occasionally also of methodology. But because every indication of the critical condition of the patient is attributed to a serious but localized infection (structural-functionalism, *structuralisme*, neopositivism, "critical theory," transformational grammar, componential analysis, symbolic interactionism, statistical historiography, games and simulation theory, econometrics, ethnomethodology, etc.), the scattered symptoms are not recognized as forming part of a syndrome which has a single cause.

35. This, I take it, is the wider aim of Aaron Cicourel's *Method and Measurement in Sociology* (New York: Free Press, 1964). At this stage of methodological discussion his book admittedly and understandably has a programmatic flavor. Cicourel's detailed critique of the unreflected use of (numerical) mathematics in various research procedures is particularly valuable.

I have already indicated that in my view the solution to the crisis of social science lies in the formulation of a *mathēsis universalis* appropriate to human affairs. Because of the illustrious history of the concept of *mathēsis universalis* the statement of the program in the abstract makes it appear even bolder than it is. I shall come back to what I see as its main promise and its most serious difficulties; I hope that taking the program at least one step beyond its present degree of abstractness will help prevent unnecessary misunderstandings. But first it should be recognized that the need for such a program is not widely felt, which is not surprising. Empirical theory and research are only possible on a foundation of things taken for granted. It is impossible to make everything problematic at the same time. In addition, the reluctance of the practitioners to make their methodological naïveté a topic for reflection is not only understandable, it is a secondary indication of the crisis we have been discussing. But the intrascientific difficulties of methodological communication have a parallel in the intraphilosophical difficulties of communication *about* social science (and social reality)—not to speak of the traditional difficulty of communication between philosophers and social scientists. There are several reasons why the crisis of social science is not perceived in various philosophical traditions; and I expect that these traditions will find the program of a *mathēsis universalis* for social reality either absurd or superfluous for highly divergent reasons.

I would not be surprised if logical empiricists and positivists of various persuasions should forget their differences and agree on the absurdity of the goal I have advanced. Is not the mathematization of nature including, of course, social reality already achieved in principle? Why should there be an intrinsic relation between the algorithms of theoretical operations, i.e., the generalized syntax of science, and the interpretations of the algorithms with respect to particular domains, i.e., the semantics of specialized sciences? The Galilean paradigm suggests obvious answers to these questions. The need for taking into account the epistemological reflexivity of social science will be denied. As for the implied question about the "conditions of the possibility" (to apply the Kantian expression) of social science, that is an impermissibly idealist and transcendentalist query. The history, psychology, and sociology of science including, of course, social science, and of philosophy including, of course, the philosophy of science, will provide an empirical account of the conditions under which science and philosophy originate and operate.[36] That must suffice. And as for the sense and import of social science, that is a matter of value judgments, political decisions about social uses of knowledge, and so on, which science can treat as empirical facts and analyze for their consequences. That, again, must suffice. Need I say that the chief weakness of this line of reasoning lies in its faith in the Münchhausen trick of pulling oneself out of a swamp by one's own pigtail. Respect for rationalism and empiricism as essential elements in the historical "rationalization" of cosmologies is one thing. It is another thing to accept as an article of faith the "ultimacy" claim of science and resign oneself to the viciously circular theory of knowledge that claim entails.

Transcendental phenomenologists, on the other hand, will find the program superfluous. They will maintain that Husserl's conception of the universal structures of the *Lebenswelt* is only meaningful in connection with his idea of transcendental phenomenology as a rigorous a priori science. What can social science add to this? Physical science can be presumably left to its naïve theoretical *technē*. But any program for social science other than one that makes it part of a transcendental eidetic enterprise is a relapse into a naïve naturalism.

I have already stated some of the reasons for my reluctance to adopt a position which postulates a supreme "discipline of all disciplines" and anticipates an ultimate "fulfillment" of science and philosophy. It is one thing to consider the crucial question of the transcendental conditions of knowledge and to adopt a rigorous method of philosophical reflection grounded in immediate experience. It is another thing entirely to abandon the unity of science in its cosmological sense and basic logical structure for the sake of an illusory quest for absolute and total certainty of knowledge. To do this, it seems to me, is to abandon the idea of a descriptive-phenomenological foundation of cumulative empirical sciences, confusing it with that of a perennial "first philosophy." [37]

There is another group of academic philosophers who see neither the crisis of social science nor, of course, the need for

36. See Richard Bevan Braithwaite, *Scientific Explanation* (1953; 3d ed., Cambridge: At the University Press, 1956), pp. 20 f.
37. See Natanson, "The *Lebenswelt*," pp. 133 f.

programs to overcome it. The reason here is simple: they do not see social science. A formulation of MacIntyre's is so apt and amusing that I may borrow it despite the difference in context: "The second major head on which the symposiasts seem to agree is their refusal to allow that the natural sciences have as yet happened. . . ."[38]

UNIVERSAL AND HISTORICAL STRUCTURES OF EVERYDAY LIFE

THE PROGRAM OF a *mathēsis universalis* for social reality is stated provocatively—on purpose. It should be made clear at the beginning, however, that the aims of the program are weaker as well as stronger than the two terms *mathēsis universalis* may suggest separately and jointly. The aims of the proposal, stated one way, are to institute a search for possibilities of formalization that are genuinely independent of the Galilean cosmological paradigm. Stated in another way, the aims are to generate some principles for the construction of a metalanguage into which the observational languages of the various social sciences could be translated with a controlled decrease of historical specificity and without loss of the intrinsic significance of observational statements. "Formalization" and "metalanguage" describe the goals of the program but they do not specify them exactly; I am using the terms in a sense that is not identical with their common employment in technical discourse. Before clarifying my use of these terms, however, I want to anticipate an even likelier misunderstanding by stating explicitly that the proposal does not imply a revival of notions concerning a separate "logic" of social science.

Kant's critique of the "transcendent" use of concepts provided a transcendental foundation of knowledge in the activities of human consciousness. In its historical context, however, Kant's critical theory of knowledge can be seen as an attempt to purify the epistemology of physical science of the powerful traces of Galilean cosmology. After Kant—and Hume, who woke Kant from his "dogmatic slumber"—the merger of rationalism and empiricism from which was fashioned the hard core of

---

38. Wolfe Mays and S. C. Brown, eds., *Linguistic Analysis and Phenomenology* (London and Basingstoke: Macmillan, 1972), p. 43.

modern science was obliged to meet higher standards of epistemological sophistication. The influence of Kant on Peirce may
serve as an illustration of this point.

The attempts to provide a philosophically adequate foundation for social science, however, generally still took a Galilean
view of physical science, and that well into the first half of the
twentieth century. It was this view that was either adopted uncritically or rejected completely. Up to the generation of Rickert,
Dilthey, and Weber—and in some quarters for a generation beyond them—the conviction prevailed on both slopes of the
methodological Big Divide that in social science one had to opt
for the Galilean model or against it. *Tertium non datur!* Those
who rightly decided that the model offered neither theoretical
nor technical and procedural solutions to the problems they were
facing therefore searched for a special form of logic which would
permit generalized interpretations of unique, value-oriented
human actions and the equally unique products of human action
as, for example, art. This search led into one of the major dead-
end streets in the philosophy of social science. As far as I can
judge, no plausible argument was advanced that justified a
radical distinction between a *general* logic of explanation in
social science on the one hand and in physical science on the
other.[39] That such arguments were tenaciously believed may be

39. The question of a special logical form of social science was recently revived by Karl-Otto Apel (see especially "Szientistik, Hermeneutik,
Ideologiekritik," *Man and World*, I [1968], 37–63; and "Wittgenstein und
das Problem des hermeneutischen Verstehens," in *Zeitschrift für Theologie
und Kirche*, LXIII, no. 1 [1966], 49–87) and Jürgen Habermas (see his
two major studies on this problem, "Zur Logik der Sozialwissenschaften,"
in *Philosophische Rundschau*, special publication 6 [Tübingen: 1967], and
Knowledge and Human Interests, trans. Jeremy J. Shapiro [Boston:
Beacon Press, 1972]; and, among his articles, especially "Der Universalitätsanspruch der Hermeneutik," *Hermeneutik und Dialektik*, ed. Rüdiger
Bubner, Konrad Cramer, and Reiner Wiehl [Tübingen: Mohr (Siebeck),
1970], pp. 73–103, in which he defines his agreements and disagreements
with the central figure of hermeneutic philosophy, H. G. Gadamer). Apel
and Habermas offer a polemical interpretation of physical science and of
what they consider its official philosophy, positivism. They subject the
foundations of the Galilean cosmology to legitimate criticism but present
their discussion, at least by implication, as a general analysis of physical
science and its philosophical foundations. No doubt they are right in pointing out the serious shortcomings of "positivist" methodology in social
science. To a global view of a reductionist physical science, based on a
manipulative and operationalist theory of measurement, they oppose, in
the end, a discipline of hermeneutic interpretation of cultural configura-
tions of meaning. Their perspective is not entirely dissimilar to that of

partly attributable to the fact that the refutations of such proposals were generally of a rather simple-minded Galilean variety
and sometimes absurdly reductionistic.

But with Dilthey and even more so with Weber the first
signs announcing a shift in orientation appear. The question
of a special logical form of the social and historical sciences re-
ceded into the background. Weber himself clearly recognized it
as a pseudo-problem and in his rebuttal of Stammler's "refuta-
tion of materialistic history" insisted on the generality of the
"logic" of explanation in science.[40] Slowly there emerged another
question, in various formulations, in which words as hetero-
geneous as "meaning," "intention," "purpose," "motivational
nexus," "rationality of goals and ends," "semiotic context," "sign-
oriented behavior," "norms," and "roles" appeared as key terms.
With Dilthey's program of a general descriptive historical psy-

Wittgenstein as described by Winch. Habermas sometimes comes close to
the notion of a protosociology (analogous to the protophysics of Lorenzen)
but shies away from it, mainly, I think, because he finds it difficult to conceive of a theory of measurement appropriate to sociohistorical reality.
Both Apel and Habermas take the methodological leap into language as the
transcendental "condition of possibility" of intersubjectivity, of knowledge, and of science, and, at the same time, as the ultimate *explicans* and
explicandum of social and historical reality. This leap is motivated in part
by their serious concern with what I have called the epistemological reflexivity of social science: communication itself shows a "first-order"
reflexivity. I agree that the "professional" philosophy of science cannot
serve as a substitute for a critical theory of knowledge. But I do not find
their solutions plausible. Habermas, for example, suggests at one point a
linguistic-psychoanalytic "metapsychology" (*Knowledge and Human Interests*), and at another point a "theory of communicative competence" as
the frame of hermeneutic interpretation ("Der Universalitätsanspruch der
Hermeneutik"). These suggestions have recently been taken up elsewhere
(see, for example, Johannes Fabian, "Language, History and Anthropology," *Journal for the Philosophy of the Social Sciences*, I [1971], 19–47). I
cannot agree that the epistemological reflexivity of social science entails a
radical dichotomy between social and physical science—let alone a
dichotomy based on differences in "logical form." The insistence of Apel
and Habermas on the radical difference between the two kinds of science
has other than purely methodological motives. It derives from a number
of premises on the nature of "nature" as against "history." It is also connected with the curious assumption that physical science is founded on a
technological, essentially capitalist praxis, whereas "critical" social science
is to become a historical praxis of emancipation.

40. Max Weber, *Gesammelte Aufsätze zur Wissenschaftslehre* (Tübingen: Mohr [Siebeck], 1922), pp. 291–359. Incidentally, this essay should
be reread by all those social scientists who have been hypnotized by the
recent upsurge of discussion in English and American philosophy on the
meaning of "following a rule."

chology and Weber's systematic combination of the "interpretation" of human action with "causal" explanation, the new
question began to replace the search for special logical forms as
a central issue in philosophical reflection on social science. The
question is how the "field" of social science is to be identified
and how the constituent elements in the "field" are to be recognized and defined. Kaplan puts it quite simply: "Behavioral
science is occupied with what people do, but the 'what' is subject
to two very different kinds of specification." [41] It is a mistake to
bypass answering the question by pointing to some higher
rationality presumably at work in forming the tradition- and
context-bound but apparently decisionist definitions of problems
by scientists in a given discipline, or even worse to refer it, by
default of a critical philosophy of science, to the academic
division of labor. It is also a mistake to trivialize the question
about the identification of constituent elements or "units" by
referring it exclusively to the level of specific investigative
techniques, such as participant observation, coding, and the
like.[42]

The answer to this question should bring out whatever it
is that distinguishes social science from physical science and
whatever is common to the various social sciences. It is definitely
not a matter of logical form. The logic of social science is the
logic of science—if various rather general modes of explanation
can indeed be given this designation because of their common
origin in human logic as an idealized form of theoretical activity
and because of their common cosmological purpose. There are,
however, more specific styles of explanation which are deter-

---

41. Kaplan, *Conduct of Inquiry*, p. 358. Kaplan introduces here the
useful terminological distinction between act and action. To say that social
science is interested in the explanation of *actions* does not imply that in
their explanatory frames data from ecology, ethology, neurophysiology,
and so on, are not to be used in a full causal analysis of a given problem.
It does, however, state a level of interest, and withdraws credit from
metaphysical reductionism. For an interesting attempt to work back to
that level of explanation from positions influenced by some forms of reductionism, see George A. Miller, Eugene Galanter, and Karl H. Pribram,
Plans and the Structure of Behavior (New York: Holt, Rinehart, and
Winston, 1960).

42. This seems to be the tendency of Hans Albert in his highly interesting and highly polemical "Hermeneutik und Realwissenschaft," *Mann-
heimer sozialwissenschaftliche Studien*, III (1971), 42–47.

mined by specific explanatory aims. These are associated with various disciplines. The specific styles of explanation, while themselves instances of more general modes, are tied to the substantive theoretical problems which the various disciplines confront, and the problems derive in their turn from the subject matter with which a discipline is concerned. I suggest that the family likeness in the explanatory problems faced by the disciplines of social science, from history to linguistics and very definitely including sociology, is due to the peculiarities of the areas over which they claim academic jurisdiction, and that these peculiarities originate in the structure of the domain over which social science implicitly, at least, also claims cosmological jurisdiction. The domain is the domain of human action and of its objectivated results. It is the constitution of the domain and the explanatory aims that are bound to it, rather than the logical form by means of which the domain is explained, that account for the difference between social and physical science.

It should not be, but it probably is, necessary to add that this does not mean that the domain (and its science) is to be considered autonomous within the over-all paradigm of cosmological "causal explanation." [43] It certainly does not imply that human action is the only thing of interest with respect to man or, for that matter, that an account of human action need not take in data from other explanatory frames which, however, are then subordinated to the explanation of action. What it does mean is that there is an autonomous theoretical interest in a level of explanation that is irreducibly that of human action. The identification of the domain of social science is determined by the human interest in the understanding of human action. The interest is theoretical but prescientific; the theoretical interest, in turn, originates in the praxis of everyday life. This interest is cosmological, entirely legitimate, and ineradicable. The theoretical interests of social science must represent this interest in the logical form of science.

The identification of the domain and of its constituent elements is not merely a matter of several levels of analysis in a "unitary" science, in the sense that different aspects of phe-

43. See Weber, *Zur Wissenschaftslehre*, especially pp. 322–34 and 509 f.; cf. also Geoffrey Madell, "Action and Causal Explanation," *Mind*, LXXVI (1967), 34–48.

nomena may be deducted and placed in a "deductive system." [44] It is that, but in a way which is trivial in the present context: the domain *does* happen to be the domain which is the foundation for the production of cosmologies of science and of operational-instrumentalist decisions on levels of analysis. No doubt the domain, and the production of cosmologies, and the decisions on levels of analysis, can be and should be made objects of empirical analysis. But even the most sophisticated sociology of knowledge is an insufficient answer to the problem of epistemological reflexivity in social science (we are back with Münchhausen, an utterly self-reliant but not entirely plausible gentleman).

An alternative and less problematically circular, because methodologically controlled, reflexive account of the constitution of the domain and its elementary structures is provided by the phenomenology of the *Lebenswelt*. The radical return to the immediate evidence of conscious experience provides an evidential starting point unavailable in common sense and scientific theory. The method of reduction permits controlled reflexiveness on the presuppositions of the method, of the evidence, and of their communication to others. The circle, as Husserl fully recognized, remains. But it is not viciously naïve.

The program for a *mathēsis universalis* of social reality is a proposal for a phenomenology of the universal structures of everyday life; it is to serve a methodological purpose in social science by supplying a matrix for the empirical analyses provided by the disciplines that deal with and "explain" the concrete historical structures of everyday life. The matrix is not "theory," i.e., it has no direct connection to the logic of explanation. Nor is it merely a regional taxonomy based on classificatory decisions. It is founded on a rigorous method that uncovers and clarifies invariant structures of the conscious activities in which human action is constituted.

---

44. Cf. this quotation from Morris R. Cohen and Ernest Nagel: "It follows that there is a *plurality* of systems, each of which may be explored in isolation from the others. Such a plurality of systems may, indeed, constitute a set of subsystems of a single, comprehensive system, but we have no evidence for such a state of affairs. In any case, it is not necessary to know this comprehensive system in order to explore adequately any one of the many less inclusive systems" (*An Introduction to Logic and Scientific Method* [New York: Harcourt, Brace, 1934], pp. 140–41). See also Hanson, *Patterns of Discovery*, pp. 134 f.

It is now easy to see why it is somewhat inexact to describe the program of a *mathēsis universalis* for social reality as a proposal for formalization appropriate to human affairs. Formalization generally refers to the establishment of systems of symbols and of rules governing the combination of symbols. When I speak of formalization in the present context I am not thinking of the general logic of the rules that govern the combinations of symbols. I am not thinking of a general logistics of operations on statements about social reality as distinct from a logistics of operations on statements about some other kind of reality. Just as I see no reason to accept the claims in favor of a special logical form in social science, I cannot easily conceive of a need for (or indeed the possibility of) a special algorithm for the universe of human action. It may very well be that there are serious difficulties in the "recasting of verbal theories as causal models," [45] and that the specific mathematical operations performed on statements about social reality within some explanatory paradigm leave a large residue of dissatisfaction. This is surely due in some measure to the inappropriateness of the specific operations. But I suspect that in large measure such dissatisfaction can be traced eventually to unsatisfactory solutions to the problems of identifying the "field" and defining the "units" in the field. I suspect, in other words, that the dissatisfaction stems from a frustration of the theoretical interest in the level of human action and its objectivations, not from a failure of the mathematics involved. [46]

45. Hubert M. Blalock, Jr., *Theory Construction* (Englewood Cliffs, N.J.: Prentice-Hall, 1969), p. 27.

46. "Mathematical techniques can often be applied to good effect even when the known facts have to be somewhat distorted to feed them into the mathematical machinery. But in the case of current algebraic grammar the amount of distortion, while not great, conceals just the most important fact about natural human languages: the fact that they are (technically speaking) 'ill-defined' systems, like table-manners or football or governments, rather than 'well-defined' systems like logic or mathematics." Thus Charles F. Hockett, disowning, as gracefully as only a scholar of his stature could, substantial parts of his own essay "Language, Mathematics and Linguistics" (*Current Trends in Linguistics,* Vol. III: *Theoretical Foundations,* ed. Thomas A. Sebeok [The Hague: Mouton, 1966]) in an author's précis of the essay published in *Current Anthropology,* IX (April–June, 1968), 128. Presumably all "natural systems" are ill defined, more or less. It is of course the "more or less" which offers room for further debate on what it is that is being defined. It will hardly do, however, to object to Hockett that "to the extent that natural language is an 'ill-defined' system, it is not language" (Eugene Verstraelen in a comment, *ibid.,* p. 149).

And that leaves us again with the problem of the constitution of social reality in human action. The formalization of "the rules of the game" presents no intrinsic difficulty—for any particular game in "nature" or "social reality." The difficulty arises from the fact that in society everybody is playing many games at the same time, and that the rules define the players, and the players define the rules.[47]

Furthermore, the proposal for a *mathēsis universalis* appropriate to social reality has no *direct* bearing on the question of quantification in social science. In principle, counting noses and performing operations on numerical items are methodologically rather harmless; taken in isolation, the practice is no more dangerous in social science than anywhere else. But it does become methodologically explosive because it is tied to the identification of the units in the field. It has to be decided *what* is to be counted. Indirectly, then, the problem of quantification, like the problem of formalization, is connected with the problem of the constitution of the domain and the level of explanation that is pertinent to a given explanatory interest.

I am led to suggest that what appears as a triad of the simplest theoretical activities: identification (observation)-counting-classification, is anything but that. A burning methodological issue centers around the implicit theory of measurement in social science. This issue is most acute in disciplines with a general explanatory aim, such as sociology and social anthropology, which try to account for *all* the games, less acute in disciplines with a relatively restricted region of investigation, such as linguistics, and least acute in disciplines with a sharply defined explanatory interest, such as economics. But in all social

47. The point is made by Ernest Gellner: *"The constraints, the 'rules' within which social life is played out, are themselves a consequence of the game. . . .* A 'structural' account of a society is an account of how this comes to be: how the game itself generates and sustains the limits within which it is played. This is the really crucial fact about sociological method. This manner of formulating it shows why the task is so much harder than that of a chess analyst, who has no need to explain just why the players will not knock over the board, why the rook will not move diagonally, and so forth" ("Our Current Sense of History," *European Journal of Sociology,* XII, no. 2 [1971], 170; italics original). Gellner maintains, incidentally, that language is less complex than "society," an assertion which makes sense in one way but seems debatable in another. The complexity is not simply a function of the "natural system" out there but also of the ("ill"-) *definition* of the system and its elements. It is instructive to compare Gellner on language with Hockett on football (see n. 46).

science disciplines the theory of measurement carries the imprint of the Galilean cosmology.[48] A methodologically legitimated decision on what is to be counted is generally avoided. In other words, the researcher unwittingly adopts individual or official, bureaucratic, common-sense taxonomies. Such decisions do not produce data whose comparability is warranted. All too readily the problem is glossed over by post hoc technical "validation" and submerged in displays of numerical mathematics whose items originated in "coding decisions." [49] The fact that we all do it cannot defend us against the accusation of methodological naïveté.

No Galilean primary qualities having been discovered in human conduct, assortments of secondary qualities are measured as if they directly represented primary ones. The consequence of social science naïveté concerning its epistemological reflexivity is, on the most prudishly hidden level of "operationalized" research procedure, measurement by fiat.[50] Cicourel describes the problem as follows:

> If the "rules" governing the use of language to describe objects and events in everyday life and in sociological discourse are unclear, then the assignment of numerals or numbers to the properties of objects and events according to some relatively congruent set of rules will also reflect a lack of clarity.[51]

I should merely add that the rules governing the use of language in everyday life are typically unclear in some necessary degree to ordinary speakers. Cicourel's statement should not be misconstrued as implying that the clarity of the rules governing the

48. It is hardly surprising to come across statements such as these: "The terms of classical Newtonian theory are, like those of social science, all concepts referring to what can be observed. The relatively simple structure of such a powerful theory has, to put it moderately, not yet been deployed to its fullest advantage by social scientists" (May Brodbeck, "Models, Meaning, and Theories," in Gross, *Symposium*, p. 401); and: "Talking about the meaning of people's movements does not suggest that the way of ascertaining its presence is not the same as the way of ascertaining the meaning of anything else" (Quentin Gibson, *The Logic of Social Enquiry* [New York: Humanities Press, 1960], p. 52).

49. For an excellent discussion of this and of related problems, see Cicourel, *Method and Measurement*, especially chap. 1.

50. The term was used by Warren Torgerson (*Theory and Method of Scaling*, [New York: Wiley, 1958], p. 21) and taken up critically by Cicourel (*Method and Measurement*, pp. 12 f.).

51. *Method and Measurement*, p. 15.

use of language to describe objects and events in *sociology* presupposes the clarity of the rules governing the *ordinary* use of language. Rules and "rules" in his statement are not strictly equivalent.[52]

Hochberg defines formalization as the replacement of descriptive signs in an axiomatic system by mere marks.[53] The proposal of a *mathēsis universalis* for social reality is thus not a proposal for full formalization but merely for partial formalization. The "descriptive signs" are statements on human conduct in ordinary language or, if one wishes to become technical about it, in an observational language in which the statements of actors are reformulated in one translation step and linked to statements of (actor-) observers.[54] These are to be "represented,"—not by mere marks, e.g., geometrical figures, but by statements on elementary structures of human conduct. It must be added immediately that the specific form of attentiveness to the ordinary language of the actors that characterizes some traditions in social science such as, for example, some symbolic interactionists and ethnomethodologists in sociology, ethnoscientists, "cognitive" anthropologists, etc., in social anthropology, and ethnographers of communication and componential analysts in anthropological linguistics, does not presuppose an established matrix of universal, invariant structures of everyday life which rigorous phenomenological analysis should yield. Nor does such attentiveness suffice in and by itself to generate such a matrix—but such traditions find direct methodological justification in this matrix. This does not mean that other traditions are to be excommunicated by some new methodology, but their research procedures can be shown to be more naïve than absolutely necessary in the

---

52. Cf. Weber, *Zur Wissenschaftslehre*, especially pp. 322–45, in which he introduced a regional German card-game (*Skat*) to social science literature. Cf. also Gellner's class-game and his discussion of Chomsky's notion of "rules" in language (Gellner, "Sense of History").

53. "Axiomatic Systems," p. 427.

54. Even Felix Kaufmann's well-known phrase, "every interpretation of social facts presupposes a fundamental interpretation, namely, that of the underlying physical fact as a social fact" does not specify adequately the complex constitution of "social facts" and of the recognition of social facts (*Methodology of the Social Sciences* [1944; 2d ed., New York: Humanities Press, 1958], p. 166). For an interesting account of typification of social reality based on an original synthesis of Peirce, William James, Schutz, and Gurwitsch, see Grathoff, *Structure of Social Inconsistencies*, chaps. 4 and 5. See also Kaplan, *Conduct of Inquiry*, pp. 32 f.

matter of operational definitions of the field and its units. More-over, to the extent that unit-identification procedures, partial formalization of units, theoretical explanation, and methodological reflection on the entire theoretical enterprise are empirically connected, this naïveté does have repercussions.

The proposal of a *mathēsis universalis* for social reality is thus a proposal for formalization only in a loose sense of that term. In fact, it is a proposal for a *mathēsis universalis* in a restricted metaphorical sense. Its basic aim can be stated as the formalization of a matrix of elementary and universal structures of human conduct. In a way that is open to debate, the proposal takes up Husserl's notion of a science of the *Lebenswelt* and reformulates it as a proposal for a phenomenological foundation for the methodology of social science, inasmuch as that methodology cannot avoid being concerned with the peculiar problem of the structure of the domain that is undeniably constituted in human action.

The motive for and the foundation of the program are one:

as soon as we consider that the life-world does have, in all its relative features, a *general structure*. This general structure, to which everything that exists relatively is bound, is not itself relative. We can attend to it in its generality and, with sufficient care, fix it once and for all in a way equally accessible to all. As life-world the world has, even prior to science, the "same" structures that the objective sciences presuppose in their substruction of a world which exists "in itself" and is determined through "truths in themselves" (this substruction being taken for granted due to the tradition of centuries); these are the same structures that they presuppose as a priori structures. . . .[55]

The phenomenology of the *Lebenswelt* is not to be taken as a substitute empirical method, as a kind of teutonically glorified subjectivistic social psychology or a cousin of analytic philosophy in Continental masquerade clarifying the concepts of ordinary and scientific language.[56] The descriptive phenomenology of the *Lebenswelt* is ultimately based on the phenomenological method of radical reduction and attention to the experience of intentional acts in originary evidence. It is thus philosophically

55. Husserl, *Crisis*, p. 139 (italics original).
56. For a critique of such misconceptions see Maurice Natanson, "Phenomenology as a Rigorous Science," *International Philosophical Quarterly*, VII (March, 1967), 5–20.

legitimated by a critically reflexive account of the knowledge of experience. In other words, the descriptive phenomenology of the natural attitude in everyday life has its methodological foundation in phenomenology as a transcendental critique of knowledge. For this reason it satisfies the need for a "philosophy of the mind" described by Burtt. It can offer the guarantee of continuous epistemological reflexivity, which is an essential condition of the philosophical foundation of social science.

Yet I believe that it is legitimate to suggest a more specific function for the descriptive phenomenology of the invariant structures of the world of everyday life: that is, to provide the general matrix, appropriate to the level of human action, for statements on human conduct articulated in historical vernaculars. Such a matrix offers a satisfactory solution to a fundamental problem of social science, the problem of the comparability of historical data. And, obviously, all the data of social science are historical.

To put it more precisely:

1. The data of social science are preinterpreted.[57] Interpretation of experience (and action) is a constitutive element of the data; we do not have "raw" data to which are added common-sense interpretations which are to be discarded by means of some "purifying instrument," if only we could find one (this is the old cosmology!).[58]

2. Interpretations are made in, and bound to, ordinary historical languages. The data of social science are therefore from the outset irrevocably part of historical worlds of everyday life: they are constituted in human action and experience as historically specific contexts of significance and motivation.

The universal structures of everyday life could serve as a matrix for such data, as a kind of metalanguage for the historical languages in which data on human action must necessarily be presented.

Such a matrix must meet two requirements. It would have to

57. In several methodological writings Schutz clarified the complex interdependence of the interpretations and preinterpretations that constitute the data of social science.

58. In view of misunderstandings (which shall charitably remain anonymous) I hasten to add that Schutz never suggested that *explanations* in social science must reproduce common-sense explanations.

meet the criterion of subjective adequacy in the sense in which Weber introduced the term. The "translations" of the statements (but not necessarily of their theoretical explanations) from the historical languages into the metalanguage or, more appropriately, the protolanguage, would have to be plausible in principle if not in immediate fact to the speakers-actors who produced the statements. The matrix would also have to be based on genuinely universal structures of the world of everyday life. It is not sufficient to generalize some apparently elementary features of a given common-sense view of man and society. This procedure cannot substitute for the phenomenological *epochē*, as witness the ethnocentric "picture-book phenomenology" of the twenties and, I might add, of the sixties as well.

The protolanguage consisting of the strict phenomenological account of the universal structures of the world of everyday life would thus represent a formalization (in the sense that it would not be another ordinary historical language) of statements on human conduct articulated in ordinary languages. The proposal is neutral with respect to the problem of logical form of explanation and of theory construction, except that it is motivated by and subordinated to the cosmological interest in the explanation of human action. At the same time, the proposal is intimately tied to a demand for a theory of measurement in social science. Measurement of human actions and their objectivations must be based on a two-level account: of the invariant structures underlying typifications of social reality (and thus co-constituting social reality), and of the invariant structures underlying linguistic articulation of historically variant concrete typifications of human action in human experience.

This program for the solution of a central problem of the methodology of social science is still just that: a program. Nevertheless, some important prerequisites for accomplishing the aims of the program have been met. Husserl himself, Gurwitsch, Schutz, and some other phenomenologists have been filling in the over-all contours of the *Lebenswelt* originally sketched out by Husserl. Still, much work remains to be done there. As for the specific use of descriptive phenomenology in methodological reflection, this essay is a tentative step in that direction. And finally, as for the replacement of the implicitly Galilean theory of measurement in social science by an epistemologically reflexive one, work on this task has begun in various movements in social science that are close to or even claim descent from phenomenology (symbolic interactionism, ethnomethodology, ethnoscience, and others), as well as in other quarters that have no particular inclination to look for philosophical foundations in phenomenology, as in the increasingly rewarding work on universals in language by linguists of various theoretical persuasions, anthropological linguists working on ethnographies of speaking, and others who would perhaps dislike to be labelled but whom I would call "structuralists" sensitive to epistemological reflexivity.

A synthesis of these varied efforts in phenomenology and in the various approaches in the several disciplines will require more than an addition of individual results. It will require continual reflection on the sources and consequences of epistemological reflexivity in social reality and social science.[59] Without such reflection the relevance of science in general and social science in particular can be assumed but not explicated. And inability to explicate its relevance is a symptom of crisis.

POSTSCRIPT ON THE CIRCLE

ALAS, THERE ARE NO ABSOLUTE CERTAINTIES and there are no definitive resolutions of fundamental "crises." It is good to

---

59. I refer here only to the contribution to the theory of measurement. It is not my purpose to evaluate in detail the merits of the various approaches in producing accurate and relevant descriptions, although I may say that in my opinion some of the best work in this regard is being done in the approaches that pay attention to the "indexical" (to borrow Garfinkel's expression) features of communication. Nor am I proposing to assess the respective contributions of these approaches to theory, and thereby to the cosmological purpose of science. I would merely like to offer my opinion that some of these approaches are lapsing into a new empiricism. This empiricism differs significantly from the old "positivistic" empiricism in its descriptive sophistication, but its romantic self-sufficiency makes its more extreme versions almost as much of a threat to the cosmological purpose of science as its "positivistic" opposite number. The most cogent presentation of a point of view on sociology that is based on concerns similar to mine but whose conclusions are diametrically opposed to the one I have presented here can be found in Harvey Sacks, "Sociological Description," *Berkeley Journal of Sociology*, VIII (1963), 1–16. The *Lebenswelt*-romanticism that can be observed on the fringes of ethnomethodology and symbolic interactionism is generally absent from the converging developments in social anthropology and ethnolinguistics.

have friends who point out the facts of life![60] My argument which contained as an important step in its chain of reasoning a critique of a historical process of cosmological abduction relies in its proposal for a solution to the crisis in social science on abductive premises. I maintain that the circle in which I have become entangled is inevitable but not vicious. I suggest that it offers clarification for a scientific-cosmological enterprise. It does not resign itself to the inner circle of viciousness that characterizes the thinking of the modern descendants of the scientistic theory of knowledge. It is only fair, however, to let the reader judge whether the outer circle is not as tightly closed as the inner.

The physical and social sciences are engaged in a common cosmological enterprise. The enterprise follows certain general rules whose structure is analyzed in the logic of science and whose origin can be reconstructed historically. On that level it can be decided whether the sciences have the structure of hypothetico-deductive systems, whether notions of verification should be replaced by the concept of corroboration, whether or not over-all paradigms change in a revolutionary fashion, and so on.

These theoretical activities presuppose still more general activities of the mind. The idealized rules for these activities can be "operationalized" in a logistic system and traced back to their origins in everyday activities. In radical philosophical reflection following a precise rule of evidence (transcendental reduction, i.e., attending to phenomena as they "present" themselves), the structures of theoretical and pretheoretical activities are clarified and traced back to their foundation in active and passive syntheses of consciousness. This is a process of explication that starts with and returns to the most direct evidence available: inspection of immediate experience. The analysis points at all levels of the foundational structure of experience to its embeddedness in the *Lebenswelt*, the world of everyday life.

The descriptive phenomenology of everyday life which is ultimately founded on this radical method describes the universal structures of subjective orientation and action: lived space, lived time, the elementary structure of face-to-face situations,

---

60. This particular fact was pointed out by Hansfried Kellner.

the levels of anonymity, the biographical-historical subscript to all experience, the lived intersubjectivity of communication in everyday life, and so on. To the most general discoveries of the "geology" of the *Lebenswelt* these "geographic" analyses of a descriptive phenomenology thus add some basic surface contours.

But now one discovers "correlates" of these descriptions in the descriptive results of "naïve" empirical sciences and, indeed, of aesthetically filtered common-sense observation. That discovery is an invitation to embrace the pretheoretical immediacy of the *Lebenswelt* or to join the traditional cosmological enterprise of "naïve" science. There is no reason to decline the invitation, individually, as long as the differences in cognitive style, method, universe of discourse, and purpose are not extinguished.

And here another round starts. Theory in all sciences involved in the cosmological enterprise takes a number of things for granted which become problematic upon reflection:

1. The unity of experience among men in different societies throughout the course of history. Philosophically speaking, this refers to the problem of whether "mankind," a "transcendental ego," an "empirical species," or whatever, is the transcendental subject of knowledge.
2. The givenness and the possibility of communication. Philosophically speaking, this refers to the problem of *the mathēsis universalis.*

Social science rests upon an additional presupposition: that the ordinary, culturally and historically highly variable common-sense definitions of reality are "objective" data (sales, suicides, fathers, presidents, and so on). Philosophically speaking, this is the problem of the epistemological reflexivity of social science and of the human constitution of the domain under investigation.

With this problem we are back with the *Lebenswelt* as the foundation of science, and as the foundation of the field of social science. And we start with reflection on the presuppositions of a particular historical enterprise, science, in which our elementary cosmological interest is historically invested. The method of reflection must be "rational" and must be based on immediate evidence. And that is where we came in.

The solution to the epistemological reflexivity of social reality and social science which I proposed is not a definitive solution at all. It starts a process of reflection, however, in which the quest for certainty about "starting points"—to be found in a radical philosophical method—is abductively joined to the cosmological interest in understanding the universe of which we are part—to be satisfied, more or less plausibly, more or less effectively, and perhaps *less* naïvely, by science.

Sociology and Existential Phenomenology

Edward A. Tiryakian

THE CENTRAL CONCERN of this paper is to indicate the general relevance of phenomenology for sociological research, both theoretical and empirical. To do this, it will be necessary to explicate major features of the phenomenological approach as a pertinent general frame of reference. Consequently, in the first part of this essay I shall focus on the sociological importance of such cardinal features of phenomenology as intersubjective consciousness, the constitution of social objects in acts of perception, and the uncovering of a priori structures of perception by the phenomenological method.

While this discussion is essentially for the benefit of sociologists having little prior exposure to phenomenology, I hope that it will also instill in other readers a greater awareness of the intrinsic importance of sociology for the continuing self-reflection of existential phenomenology. As general inquiries of knowledge grounded in the experience of the *Lebenswelt,* sociology and phenomenology are by the nature of their subject matter profoundly intertwined, since both are ultimately concerned with the rigorous description of the patterning of intersubjective consciousness. The reciprocal contributions of each to the other may be broadly stated thus: existential phenomenology can provide sociology with a more adequate methodological foundation than the latter has at present, and sociology can provide phenomenology with empirical data on the social nature, forms, and transformations of consciousness in social space and social time, thereby grounding philosophical reflection, or at least preventing it from overlooking the sociohistorical matrix of human consciousness.

The second section of this paper will present certain aspects of my research on modern colonialism in Africa as it relates to the general context of the first part. The aim is to indicate the feasibility of a phenomenological orientation in dealing sociologically with a complex sociohistorical phenomenon such as African colonialism. Heretofore, most current applications of phenomenology in American sociology have been at the microsociological level; but if phenomenology is to provide a general method of inquiry for the social sciences, the method should also apply to investigations transcending face-to-face interaction, such as macrosociological, historical situations. After all, the early applications of the phenomenological method in European sociology (by such figures as Max Scheler, Karl Mannheim, and Georges Gurvitch) were in this direction. This essay seems an appropriate opportunity to redirect phenomenological interest to problems of macrosociology as a complement to phenomenological investigations at the micro level.

What I shall not provide in these pages is an overview of past relationships between phenomenology and sociology, nor shall I seek to assess current thinking and research in sociology having a phenomenological inspiration.[1] However, it might be mentioned in passing that albeit still a minuscule part of the totality of ongoing sociological endeavors, the phenomenological orientation in American sociology is probably receiving greater recognition now than at any previous time. This is due to several interrelated developments: (*a*) the dissemination in English within the past decade of the works of Edmund Husserl and Alfred Schutz (who "translated" much of Husserl into sociological reflection); (*b*) the explication of these works by such figures as Maurice Natanson, Thomas Luckmann, and Peter Berger; (*c*) further explication and research by a new generation of sociologists, including Jack Douglas, George Psathas, and Peter Manning; (*d*) the imaginative school of ethnomethodology

1. I have covered some of the earlier developments in my article, "Existential Phenomenology and the Sociological Tradition," *American Sociological Review*, XXX (October, 1965), 674–88. An excellent recent volume relating phenomenology to current sociological concerns is that of Paul Filmer, Michael Philipson, David Silverman, and David Walsh, *New Directions in Sociological Theory* (London: Collier-Macmillan, 1972).

(strongly influenced by Husserl and Schutz among others) that has developed around Harold Garfinkel, who has attracted in recent years a host of talented sociologists (including Lindsey Churchill, Peter McHugh, Aaron Cicourel, Harvey Sacks, and Egon Bittner).

In addition, it might be suggested that there are other factors in the increased receptivity to phenomenology, particularly among younger sociologists. Outside the academic setting, there is a new questioning of the meaning and worth of the industrial-technological order; if a previous generation saw it as a source of blessing for mankind, a more recent view sees it not as a panacea but as a source of debasement and depersonalization—in effect, a "pollution" of subjectivity. The object-oriented positivistic methodology which has dominated sociological research is tacitly linked to the industrial-technological order, and the increasing tendency to question the adequacy of the latter carries with it a questioning of the adequacy of the former. The new availability in English of a substantial body of phenomenological and phe-nomenologically derived writings makes possible an alternative paradigm for sociological inquiry in a period when there is a growing awareness that sociology itself is undergoing a state of crisis.[2]

It is not very helpful to speak of a "crisis of sociology" without specifying what aspects of the discipline are in this state. A full elaboration of this topic would take the paper too far afield; I will merely suggest that an essential element of the crisis of sociology today is a crisis in explanation: that is, the inability of the discipline to provide a rigorous scientific accounting for the sociohistorical *Lebenswelt* which frames social action. There is an increasing realization that the paradigmatic frame of sociolog-ical inquiry needs to be overhauled to enable sociology to explain the real (i.e., lived or experienced) social world and its far-reaching transformations in modern society. I would further suggest that the crisis of sociology is a reflection of the crisis of Western social science in its attempt to provide truly scientific

2. This theme underlies recent writings in the area of the sociology of sociology, notably Alvin W. Gouldner, *The Coming Crisis in Western Sociology* (New York: Basic Books, 1970); Robert W. Friedrichs, *A Sociology of Sociology* (New York: Free Press, 1970); Edward A. Tirya-kian, ed., *The Phenomenon of Sociology* (New York: Appleton-Century-Crofts, 1971).

and valid knowledge, a theme of the utmost concern to Husserl, particularly in his last writings.[3] Phenomenology, for Husserl, offered the possibility to reconstruct the foundations of scientific and philosophical knowledge by going "to the things themselves"; as an extension, the phenomenological method may help sociology redirect itself to the disclosure of social phenomena themselves as the ground of sociological knowledge.

It is one of the subtle ironies of history that phenomenology historically arose as an attempted response to a general crisis of scientific knowledge (not in its amount but in its validity) as formulated by the methodology of positivism. For positivistic methodology, which traces its origin to Auguste Comte (the founder of sociology), was itself a historical response to the crisis of knowledge in European society at the beginnings of the industrial-technological social order which has stamped modern society up to our time.

THE CENTRALITY OF INTERSUBJECTIVE CONSCIOUSNESS

Two CENTRAL THEMES in phenomenology are those of "consciousness" and of "world." Despite the different meanings that Edmund Husserl's writings have taken on for his various interpreters, and irrespective of the controversies that have thus arisen, it is commonly agreed that phenomenology has as a central task the radical description and analysis of human consciousness, including the general problem of how consciousness is constituted in its modes of intentionality. In other words, a fundamental question of phenomenology is: how do we go about experiencing in our subjectivity that which we do experience, and how can we as phenomenologists put into relief how reality is structured and perceived in acts of consciousness?

As to the centrality of the world, Husserl's method of analysis for investigating how consciousness is constituted, namely, the famous process of phenomenological reduction, leads directly to the "grasping of the world . . . as phenomenon. It is not a question of making it appear in its factual reality . . . but in its

3. Edmund Husserl, *The Crisis of European Sciences and Transcendental Phenomenology: An Introduction to Phenomenological Philosophy,* trans. with an Introduction by David Carr (Evanston, Ill.: Northwestern University Press, 1970).

immanent reality of consciousness." [4] Phenomenological analysis thereby "reveals not the cogito alone but . . . consciousness-of-the-world, consciousness constituting the meaning of the world." [5]

It is important here to dwell on the themes of consciousness and world, for the "special relationship" between phenomenology and sociology is grounded in the sociality of both consciousness and the world, and, dialectically, in the phenomenological status of the world as social reality.

Students of Husserl's writings hardly need to be reminded of the master's growing interest in the relevance of the social as his thinking about phenomenology evolved. It might be said that from the *Cartesian Meditations* to *The Crisis of European Sciences* the founder of modern phenomenology traced the steps from micro- to macrosociology, i.e., from the problem of the existence of the Other for the ego to consideration of the structure of the historical community. The great contribution of phenomenology to the corpus of philosophy—its Copernican revolution—lies in its attachment of cardinal significance to intersubjectivity and in its realization of an experienced world (the *Lebenswelt*) which is constituted in manifold intentional acts of intersubjective consciousness. In this respect, phenomenology may be seen as the first real social philosophy. Further— and the consequences of this realization may lead to a major rethinking of sociological methodology—*phenomenology may also be seen as the first adequate philosophical grounding for sociology* (and other social sciences).

The significance of the social in Husserl has been explicated by René Toulement,[6] and brilliant elaborations of Husserl's pioneering efforts in this direction have been made by Alfred Schutz.[7] What is crucial here is to place in relief what implications

4. Pierre Thévenaz, *What Is Phenomenology?*, trans. James Edie, et al. (Chicago: Quadrangle, 1962), p. 46.
5. *Ibid.*, p. 47.
6. See *L'Essence de la société selon Husserl* (Paris: Presses Universitaires de France, 1962).
7. *Collected Papers*, 3 vols., (The Hague: Nijhoff, 1962–66), Vol. I, *The Problem of Social Reality*, ed. Maurice Natanson; Vol. II, *Studies in Social Theory*, ed. A. Brodersen; Vol. III, *Studies in Phenomenological Philosophy*, ed. I. Schutz; *The Phenomenology of the Social World*, trans. George Walsh and Frederick Lehnert (Evanston; Ill.: Northwestern University Press, 1967); *On Phenomenology and Social Relations*, ed. Helmut Wagner (Chicago: University of Chicago Press, 1970).

the irreducibility of intersubjective consciousness has for both phenomenology and sociology.

To begin with, in describing how consciousness is constituted so as to arrive at the transcendental ego, or pure subjectivity, phenomenology (first through Husserl and later through Heidegger) discovered the presence of the Other. That is to say, my efforts at self-awareness take me immediately to an awareness of the Other as self and as self-for-me; reciprocally, my embodied self is also a self-for-Other.[8] In other words, selfhood is not a fixed thing; it emerges and manifests itself in the presence of the Other—the social Other who is ambiguously both object and subject for the acting self or ego. (Sociology adds to this phenomenological insight the multiplicity of the Other, including the "significant Other.")

Equally fundamental to subjectivity is another form of intersubjective consciousness present in selfhood, one reflected in language as autonomous but much less appreciated by traditional philosophy, namely, that of the "we." To paraphrase Paul Ricoeur, it is this form of intersubjective consciousness which constitutes any and every social community; [9] it is presupposed by sociologists and anthropologists as a primary given, whereas it is the end point for phenomenological philosophy.[10] Peter Koestenbaum in his otherwise admirable introduction to Husserl's *Paris Lectures* unwittingly indicates this in his exposition of Husserl's conception of the phenomenological reduction. What is it that is revealed experientially as the pure subject of acts of consciousness? It is, he states, an "I-pole":

> a core from which all intentional streams of experience radiate. . . . This I-pole, the *terminus a quo* of all experience, is everpresent, yet cannot be apprehended in the normal way in which objects are apprehended because the disclosure of this I-pole con-

8. See my essay, "The Existential Self and the Person," in *The Self in Social Interaction*, ed. Kenneth J. Gergen and Chad Gordon (New York: Wiley, 1968); also R. D. Laing, *The Divided Self* (London: Penguin, 1965).

9. Paul Ricoeur, *Husserl: An Analysis of His Phenomenology*, trans. Edward G. Ballard and Lester E. Embree (Evanston, Ill.: Northwestern University Press, 1967), pp. 135 f.

10. To be sure, quite a bit of American sociology has shown little appreciation of the "we" in social life; the collectivistic movements of recent years may force a reappraisal of Durkheim's notion of the "conscience collective."

travenes the characteristic intentional structure of consciousness. This I-pole is the transcendental Ego or the transcendental subject.[11]

What this view neglects is that the "I-pole" of subjectivity is not the sole *terminus a quo* of all experience, that there is a "we-pole" which is not antithetical to it but which can also claim phenomenological status as "a core from which . . . intentional streams of consciousness radiate." This transcendental subject is not just "I"; it is also "we," revealed in experience as a primary form of consciousness. It comes to the fore particularly in collective gatherings and in periods of effervescence, revolution, war, and calamities in which the social time and social space of daily life become greatly contracted.

It might be pointed out in passing that the interdependence of the "I" and the "we" as coexistent in selfhood is indicated in the etymology of consciousness, that is, "con-sciousness." The forms, structures, and acts of consciousness partake, latently or manifestly, of this intersubjective component, which is an integral aspect of the self as subject. Realization of the "we-pole," which is embodied in various intersubjective relationships stemming from it (the "we" of the family, the neighborhood, the region, the nation, the professional or occupational group), not only points to the transcendence of the self (in the sense that the self transcends the body though incarnate in the body) but also leads to the discovery of the world as having a phenomenological status beyond its immanence in *my* reality. That is, my reality is a shared or a conjoint reality.

True, the world exists there *for me:* in this vein it is the ensemble of meanings that I experience in my encounters and relationships within the totality of my spatiotemporal horizon; every subject, every self has a world constituted by and for him. But there is side by side a world constituted by and for *us,* by and for every "we." The realization of this multiple reality of the world presented in the experience of the "we," that is, the phenomenological discovery of the togetherness of being as consciousness (the *Mitsein*), enlarges the horizon of the self and of the social.[12] Intersubjective consciousness, as I have been sug-

11. Peter Koestenbaum, Translator's Introduction to *The Paris Lectures,* by Edmund Husserl (The Hague: Nijhoff, 1964), p. xlix.
12. For a more extensive discussion of intersubjective consciousness, see Schutz, *Phenomenology of the Social World,* esp. pp. 163–81.

gesting, is not grounded solely in the "I-pole" ("I-you," "I-he," "mine-yours," etc.); it is also constituted by multiple "we-poles" ("we-they," "ours-theirs," etc.), which are both immanent and transcendent for the self. And this linkage of ego to the world as a social reality—a dynamic linkage, because of the continuous modification of the structure and contents of consciousness in the socialization process from birth to death, to say nothing of abrupt changes in the subject's attachment to the world—implies that for the self the intentionality of consciousness is directed not only to the Other understood as a single subject-object but also to the Other as a collectivity (both "we" and "they").

Thus, when phenomenology embarks on its journey to explore the stream of consciousness, it soon meets the ocean of inter-subjective consciousness, which is also navigated by sociology—an ocean which contains various forms of social consciousness: class consciousness, racial consciousness, religious conscious-ness, ethnic consciousness, generational consciousness, and na-tional consciousness, among others. It is these, ultimately, which when activated constitute the world as a primary dynamic social reality, a reality constituted by the multiplicity of intersubjective consciousnesses intending acts with and against one another in the ecological adaptations and maladaptations of human sub-jects.

These prefatory remarks have sought to suggest the inter-dependence of phenomenology and sociology. Let us now turn to view in greater detail salient features of existential phenome-nology and examine how these may have value for the sociologi-cal enterprise.

Characteristics of the Phenomenological Orientation

In seeking to characterize phenomenology as a gen-eral frame of reference, or as a complex mode of analysis, it is useful to emphasize that a primary concern of phenomenology is the radical description of how we as human subjects experience the world in acts of consciousness. Stated differently, phenom-enology puts the accent on how human subjects confront and are confronted by phenomena which manifest themselves to consciousness. Phenomenology is a dynamic conception of re-ality because of its focus on consciousness, and it is thereby congruent with a sociological approach that emphasizes change or mutability as endogenous to social phenomena. This relationship will be elaborated later.

The phenomenological focus on subjectivity derives from the basic phenomenological inquiry into the structure of consciousness by which we perceive what is nonself and in terms of which we orient ourselves in our comportment toward the external reality of the nonself. For phenomenology, consciousness is not simply a given, nor is it an irrelevant factor in the true scientific description of empirical reality; it is a cardinal aspect of that reality, so that we cannot adequately describe what we perceive there in front of us without describing our perception and consciousness of what is external. Consciousness, for phenomenology, is not something passive, a receptor of stimuli, like the fixed prism of a camera; it is the self in its subjectivity intending toward the external, that is, projecting itself to the outside in activities. In acts of perception, we organize things "out there"; we perceive not discrete entities but rather, as Gestalt psychology has shown, wholes or sets which we find meaningful and which we take to be related to other wholes.

In this respect, the reality of objects is given in and by perception. Perception involves a transaction between the subject and the nonself (or the subject's field), whereby in consciousness *things* outside the self are transformed into *objects* to and for the self, an object being a meaningful entity in a perceptual field. That is, the self in its active subjectivity constitutes [13] reality by means of an intentional reaching for things outside itself, to which (and to whom) it bestows meanings and expectations and in terms of which the self orients itself in its activities. These meanings and expectations, which give us the significance of objects in experience, cannot be deduced from the physical properties of objects; they are fundamental structures of perception, the ground of experience which is not itself a physical referent but without which objects would not be constituted. Stated somewhat differently, *meaning is inherent in perception.*

13. The term "constructs" might be used here, provided it is not thought of in a purely intellectual sense, since the experience of reality for the self also entails emotions and feelings about that which is perceived and to which the self relates. For a complementary discussion, see Thomas Luckmann and Peter Berger, *The Social Construction of Reality* (New York: Doubleday, 1966).

This is not because meaning inheres in that which we perceive, whatever it may be, but rather because meaning is inherent in the structure of perception, that is, in the activity of consciousness directed externally from the self.

Thus, if an act of consciousness is always the consciousness *of* something (what may be called the "phenomenological postulate of intentionality"), it is also the case that whatever is an object is always an object *for* or *to* a subject (what may be called the "postulate of subjectification"). This implies that a given entity or phenomenon—a chair, a political event, a person—will take on different meanings and be perceived differently by different subjects, depending on their perspectives, on how they situate themselves or are situated in relation to the entity or phenomenon in question. An object, then, is not (as common sense would hold) something definite or specific "out there"; it is at least an entity *and* the set of meanings attached to that entity by a subject.

If an entity becomes an object to a subject in terms of the set of meanings that entity has for the subject, this does not mean that an entity will be the same object (i.e., have the same meaning or the same set of expectations) for different subjects. An entity will appear as a different object for subjects having different meanings for what they perceive, though each may think that other subjects are perceiving the same entity (that is, each may think that the entity is manifesting itself as a phenomenon the same way for every other subject). Only an observer who is not involved as a subject in the situation can be aware of this, which I will call "the Pirandello effect." Several factors go into producing this effect, which is particularly pronounced when social objects or social phenomena are involved. One factor is the social relationship between the subject and the entity in question, including status and power differentials, not only between subject and object, but also between different subjects perceiving the same social object. Another factor is the term used by different subjects to characterize or label a given entity: to call a social object a "pig" or a "police officer" is to attach different meanings to the entity, and suggests a different perception of that object. It also structures a different set of responses from the entity.

Yet another factor in producing the effect is the social time-space location of the subject: the meaning of a phenomenon will vary with the distance of the subject from the entity in question.

This latter proposition cannot be stated in a simple linear relationship, however; for example, the romantic period, including the events of 1830 and 1848, may be said to have had one set of meanings for a succeeding generation that reacted against it, say that of the Victorian age; to mean something else to a still later generation which largely ignored it, say the interwar generation; and finally, it may seem very proximate to our own generation of the 1960s and 1970s. As a social phenomenon, then, the romantic period is not a fixed entity which can be objectively grasped once and for all; as a sociohistorical object it is what it means to all those who situate themselves as subjects, or take a position, in relation to it.

If the meaning which constitutes an object is, in fact, multiple, not only will a given entity manifest itself differently to different subjects, but it will also evoke different reactions. Again, this is particularly the case with social objects. Every entity has or is a multiplicity of meanings. An entity is not fixed as to what it is; it is a set of possibilities, some of which become actualized by some subjects, others by other subjects. To the extent that a given social entity (a person, a group of persons, a social movement) is perceived and acted on in terms of one and only one set of meanings, as if this were all there is to the entity, we can speak of that entity being "overdetermined," or, perhaps better, "reified." Ultimately, for a subject to reify a social entity, to reduce it to one and only one set of meanings, is to deny the subjectivity of the Other. It is also, unwittingly, to deny one's subjectivity for the Other; if I treat the Other as having one and only one meaning, this reciprocally leads the Other to see in me one and only one set of meanings, so that reification of the object dialectically leads to reification of the self (at least in relation to the social object in question).

It might be well to interpose here that while I have stressed that an object, particularly a social object, is multimeaningful and manifests itself as an object by virtue of how it is perceived by subjects, I am not saying that an object has an infinity of meanings. The person as a perceiving subject is not an isolated monad. In the typical socialization process (or rather in the socialization process as it is typically seen through the Cooley-Mead prism of sociological writings), the person comes to internalize in his perceptual structure the meanings of objects (including social objects), activities, events, and situations which are communally held by the social group(s) of which he becomes a member. The "we-pole" of subjectivity provides an essential aspect of the self's perceptual awareness in the form of a ground of common meanings of objects and indications of how to approach them or situate oneself in relation to them ("common sense" is, in this respect, the pragmatic, typical, or public definition of the meaning of things, as validated by the evidence of tradition). The "we-pole," an end point of any given socialization process, reduces the heterogeneity, though it does not eliminate the multiplicity of meanings. Naturally, if the socialization process facilitates the communication of meanings within a group, it also enhances perceptual differences of strategic objects between groups.

Borrowing a term from Husserl's analysis of intentionality, I wish to designate by the term *noema* the set of meanings attached to an entity as that entity is experienced by a subject. An entity and its meanings together constitute an object for a subject. The noema is, essentially, the subject's understanding of an entity (or a set of entities) as an object for him manifesting itself in perception. Part of the understanding of an object is the extent to which it fulfills the subject's expectations of the object's manifestations. By the term *noemata* I will designate the totality of meanings and understandings of the object for all subjects experiencing that object. Objects, both physical and social, necessarily have multiple meanings. Take, for example, an object in our sphere of perception which common English language terms a "house." The perceptual experience of this object (comprising several entities but presented in perception as a whole) for its owners (for whom it is their property, and if they are resident-owners, also their home) will differ qualitatively from that of a burglar, an overnight visitor, a tax assessor, or an urban redeveloper. The same applies for any social object, including, to take another example, the one commonly designated as a "woman": for one subject she is "wife," for another "mother," for another "coworker," and so forth. The perceptual appearances of this person interacting with others will vary depending on the relationship of roles and the interaction process (in which every social object is also a social subject). If we wish to define the object socially, then, we have to take into account all meanings of that person qua social object, and it is this totality that is conveyed by the term "noemata."

In part, then, our perception of social objects is not an *immediate* experience of them, but rather a *mediated* experience. We perceive what is external to us, including others, in a multi-layered medium of meanings constituting an "assumptive frame of reference," which I shall refer to in abbreviated form as AFR.[14] The AFR is a general orientation to the world within which human subjects act and react toward others, make projects, and evaluate events. It is a general perceptual structure which we bring to situations and in terms of which we formulate explicit "definitions of the situation," to make use of William I. Thomas' important concept. The AFR is not, however, an object for us, hence not something which qua subjects we are aware of; it lies in the tacit domain of consciousness.

The AFR is multifaceted and multidimensional. It is composed in part, but only in part, of ideas and representations we make of the world on the basis of empirical knowledge, which could, on reflection, be stated by the subject in the form of verbal propositions. It also consists of generalized feelings and sentiments about the world or parts of the world, including groups of others; these feelings cannot be rendered verbally, yet they are an integral part of the perceptual act. Another component of the AFR is imagery; we perceive objects not only as they are but also in terms of the images we have of them, which we may have had before we encountered the objects. Images are in part constituted by the activity of consciousness reflecting upon what it has perceived and giving it form and contour, or they may be the product of imagination, that is, generated by consciousness without reference to any concrete entity in its sphere of perception. It lies beyond the scope or the intention of this paper to undertake an examination of the complicated inter-relationships between perceived objects, images, imagination, and the imaginary. But it is germane to note in passing that, *particularly with social objects*, the reality before us, in terms of which we act and react, is one which our AFR grafts to images we have of objects and relations between them. That is, when we perceive and evaluate social situations, or react to persons and social events, we do so at least in part in terms of the mean-

14. The notion of the AFR is derived from that of the "assumptive world" in the writings of Adelbert Ames. See Hadley Cantril, ed., *The Morning Notes of Adelbert Ames, Jr.* (New Brunswick, N.J.: Rutgers University Press, 1960).

ings of the imagery these persons or events represent. Since subjects are seldom aware of their own imagery, much less that of others, it is entirely possible that the same entity (event, person, etc.) may be perceived in terms of very different images, which give that entity qua object a very different meaning for the respective subjects.

Perception, as a transaction between the AFR and external reality, has the important quality of being *morally evaluative* of what it perceives; the ordering and evaluating particularly of social objects is at the same time a *consciousness of* and a *conscience of* them. The expectations we have of the Other or others involve not just cognitive expectations but also moral expectations—for example, that the person who lives next door does not belong to a "subversive organization," that our closest friend can be trusted to keep the secrets we tell him, that the president of the United States does not have money from a foreign power accumulating in a Swiss bank account, that our spouse will not leave our household if we fail to get a promotion or a raise in salary. It is on the basis of such moral expectations that we talk about some things to some persons and not to others, that we act in some ways to some persons and not to others, and so forth.

It should be understood that if I have suggested that we perceive objects in part in moral terms, I am not proposing that we hold the same moral expectations for all other persons. A given society will recognize, juridically or otherwise, that some of its members are not expected to fulfill moral expectations held of others—typically, young children are given "exemptions" in most societies, as are those declared "insane," and so on. Only in utopias is it the case that the entire population is expected to, or does, fulfill the same moral expectations. How a subject perceives another person in moral terms is, needless to say, of significance in structuring not only his interpretations of the other person's acts, but also in structuring his own comportment vis-à-vis that person. If the other person is seen as belonging to a different moral community (that is, belonging to a significantly different "we" than that of the self), the subject may allow himself to suspend the typical norms of conduct which structure his interaction with others belonging to the same moral community.[15]

15. Harold Garfinkel brings out the conditions under which a social object can be presented as belonging to a morally different (and inferior) community in his article "Conditions of Successful Degradation Cere-

The point is that in perceiving social objects and their ordering (the ordering may be a set of relationships between others or a set of related or sequential activities of the same person), the moral aspect of the object is always a component of its meaning to the subject.

I have sought to draw attention to the fact that the a priori structures of our acts, in the light of which we perceive and evaluate what we encounter in our situations, are in part moral "screens"; the AFR is, among other things, a general set of moral meanings and moral expectations. It follows that a given object or phenomenon—a person, the conduct of two persons, the activities of a person in relation to the subject or to others—does not have one and only one moral meaning; for this would imply, contrary to what we have been saying, that perception is merely the simple transmission of sensations or "untouched" photographic impressions, leading to automatic responses, and not involving any transaction between perceiver and perceived.[16] While an object, particularly a social object, usually manifests one moral meaning to a perceiving subject, it is always capable of manifesting different moral meanings. When a social object fails to fulfill certain moral expectations held by the subject, perception of it is severely jarred; that is, there is an "explosion" (or, perhaps better, an "implosion") of the noema—a loss of meaning of the object to the subject. The noema can also "explode" if the perceiver comes to experience the object as pertaining to a different category of events and objects than the one previously assumed or perceived. Either situation will lead to the social object being reassigned in the moral universe of the subject and to a reinterpretation of the object's previous manifestations (in the case of a social object, its previous activities).

As a hypothetical illustration, take the case of a student who

---

monies," *American Journal of Sociology*, LXI (March, 1956), 420–24. This is a more general aspect of what Gresham Sykes and David Matza have termed, in reference to juvenile delinquency, the technique of "the denial of the victim." See "Techniques of Neutralization: A Theory of Delinquency," *American Sociological Review*, XXII (December, 1957), 664–70.

16. I shall assume the reader's familiarity with the arguments developed by Maurice Merleau-Ponty in his extensive studies: *Phenomenology of Perception*, trans. Colin Smith (New York: Humanities Press, 1962); *The Structure of Behavior*, trans. Alden L. Fisher (Boston: Beacon Press, 1963); and *The Primacy of Perception*, ed. and trans. James M. Edie (Evanston, Ill.: Northwestern University Press, 1964).

courts a girl, dates only her, buys her small gifts, and tells her that she means everything to him. We can assume, at least for the purpose of the discussion, that she will interpret his activities pretty much in accord with his public manifestations (i.e., "He is seriously interested in me and wants to marry me"). But now, suppose a close "friend" of the girl's feels obliged to inform her that the boy comes from a much humbler economic background than she does, and had been heard telling a friend that one of the reasons he had come to college was to "marry wealth." With this development, we would probably witness the girl's rein-terpretation of the boy's actions toward her, involving a profound change in his moral significance.[17] In turn, it is more than likely that the girl would change her own comportment toward the fellow in question.

When the cognitive meaning of an object changes for a sub-ject, the perceptual adjustment will be much smaller than when the moral meaning changes, for changes in moral meaning are accompanied by changes in affect toward the object, while changes in cognitive meaning seldom are. To limit the discussion, an object can be said to "shift" its moral position from a "positive" to a "negative" or "indifferent" zone (the latter two are not the same, though they do overlap), or from a zone of moral indiffer-ence to a positive or negative zone, or, finally, from a negative zone to one of the other two. The more an object is perceived as occupying a central position in either the positive or the negative zone (poles which are expressed in everyday speech as "love-hate," "good-evil," "friend-foe," and the like), the more sharply in focus, so to speak, is the object in the subject's perceptual field. And as the moral meaning of an object waxes or wanes in in-tensity, the "size" of the object in relation to other entities in-creases or decreases proportionately, although an observer could not detect and measure "objectively" such changes.

The above propositions should be familiar to readers through historical, biographical, and everyday experience—the experi-ence, for example, of seeing a social object "sacralized" and lifted out of the realm of morally indifferent, "profane" objects, as in the case of the veneration of John F. Kennedy and Charles de Gaulle in their respective countries, or the more typical experi-

17. The friend's effectiveness in leading the subject to perceive a "significant Other" in a very different (moral) light could be described as "the Iago effect."

ence of enamorment when one suddenly "only has eyes" for a certain person. In these instances, the moral meaning—of "holiness" or "sacredness"—tends to envelop the object's manifestations so that the object "can do no wrong"; in fact, a social object which is perceived as sacred will not be seen as belonging to the common universe of objects at all, but rather as an entity so extraordinary as to be a nonobject. It might be said that instead of reflecting the light of perception, such entities are themselves luminous, radiating a light for the subject. But it might be noted in passing that social objects can also be perceived in terms of extreme moral negativism, as creatures of evil. These, too, are very salient in the perceptual sphere of the subject, and are seen "in a dark light." A characteristic aspect of this perception is that such entities are seen as belonging to a different moral universe, and not as social beings belonging to humanity.

The everyday, face-to-face situations we experience with our fellow men (friends and foes) are those of microsociology; as individuals we experience changes in the moral meaning of others, and we alter our comportment as a function of our changing experience. But the remarks just made about the moral meaning of objects also apply in the broader sphere of collectivities, including national collectivities. Thus, when one country goes to war against another, most of the population of the one country typically comes to perceive most of the population of the other country—especially that part of it in uniform—in a different moral light. "They" come to be seen as a homogeneous, immoral community, and at the same time "they" become much more important than neutral countries, who occupy, in the perception of the first country, a place of relative moral indifference.

Change in the perception of the moral meaning of other entities or collectivities is of course not an automatic procedure, but requires the acceptance by a public of a new moral interpretation of the collectivity or entity in question. As Jacques Ellul has argued so well, the effectiveness of modern propaganda in mass society lies in its not being perceived and in its agents not being identified; or if they are, they must provide an interpretation of their activities such that these are perceived as being for the welfare of others, as a public service, and the like.[18] This implies

18. Jacques Ellul, *Propaganda: The Formation of Men's Attitudes*, trans. Konrad Kellen and Jean Lerner (New York: Knopf, 1965).

that an effective technique of neutralizing propaganda is to identify (if possible) publicly those seeking a change in the moral meaning of the entity in question and to assert that such a change would materially (economically, politically) benefit those seeking to bring it about. This will be more effective than countering the propaganda with cognitive arguments.

I have tried to suggest that when an actor finds a different moral meaning in an entity, he will alter his behavior toward it, even though the physical properties of the entity may have changed very little or not at all. As a corollary of the famous theorem of W. I. Thomas, we can propose the following: If actors come to perceive an entity (social or nonsocial) as having a different moral meaning than they had previously believed, there will be real changes in their behavior toward that entity. That is, the social consequences of changes in consciousness are real, even if there have been no real changes in the physical properties of the object. But changes in moral meaning may reveal new facets of the entity to the public. As an example, in very recent years we have discovered pollution, which is now a complex entity manifested in a variety of things, from the exhaust of automobiles, to the mercury level in fishing waters, to beer cans in ponds; these physical conditions were present years before, yet were for the most part treated with moral indifference by the public. They were not perceived as part of a social problem, which, as all social problems, involves a moral dimension. But once the moral meaning of the situation was accepted by enough people, which involved a growing sentiment of outrage and indignation (components of negative moral experiences), a vast number of things came to be perceived as part of the same pollution phenomenon, and this realization has led to a variety of societal and corporate actions (legislation, new processes for disposing of wastes, new companies or subsidiaries set up to market new antipollutants, etc.).

These considerations do not lead to a denial of the reality of pollution. What is of interest in this phenomenological discussion are the noemata structuring the collective perception and experience of pollution (or whatever the referent may be). As I shall argue shortly, the focus of a sociological investigation conducted with a phenomenological orientation is on the meanings relating an object of social consciousness to its subject (whether the subject is an "I" or a "we" and whatever the object may be).

This leads us to some methodological considerations which will be familiar for the most part to students of Husserl and of phenomenology, but which are still something of a novelty for much of sociology.

THE BRACKETING OF THE NATURAL ATTITUDE

EARLIER, I HAVE STRESSED the theme that phenomenology is a consciousness of the structure of consciousness, and that this structure is one of meanings and representations, not a physical entity. Phenomenology seeks to describe rigorously how phenomena manifest themselves to conscious subjects—that is, to describe the primary world of experience, wherein subject and object are not passive, inert, or merely in exposure to one another, but are related to one another in experience. The phenomenological approach seeks to return to the primary manifestations of phenomena in experience, "to the things themselves"; it seeks to observe phenomena clearly, to uncover their sense or senses.

In order to see things as they manifest themselves, the phenomenologist abstains from viewing things through what Husserl called "the general thesis of the natural standpoint," namely, from the presupposition that there is a factual world that has a being out there, a world which is knowable and measurable by us, and hence objectively grounded in nature (or in the nature of things).[19] Phenomenology "places in brackets" this "natural attitude." This methodological heuristic device (the *epochē* or abstention from the natural attitude) is not meant to deny the reality of the world, or of what the natural attitude asserts is "out there." Its purpose is rather to reveal the a priori structures or presuppositions of consciousness in terms of which what we perceive makes sense or has meaning for us.

What are these a priori structures of consciousness, and what is their sociological relevance? As an extension of Durkheim's epistemological position developed in his later writings (notably in *The Elementary Forms of the Religious Life*), I understand a priori structures not in the Kantian sense as being innate in the mind, but instead as arising in the processes of interaction and socialization. They constitute the person's AFR, which the subject

19. Edmund Husserl, *Ideas*, trans. W. R. Boyce Gibson (New York: Macmillan, Collier Books, 1962), p. 96.

"brings" to or "projects" in social situations in which he participates (face-to-face involvement in a situation is not necessary as one can participate from a distance). The a priori structures are a complex set, and include sociolinguistic categories for grouping social objects and events; cognitive categories (e.g., scientific and ethnoscientific) for relating and grouping physical objects in nature; routine procedures and conventionalized reactions for dealing with typical social events in the subject's situations (occupational, domestic, and others); ideas, images, presuppositions, and social theories (for example, causal models of why certain persons or groups act the way they do); and cosmological theories (on, for example, what ultimately accounts for things happening the way they do).

Using these a priori structures without, for the most part, being aware of doing so, subjects orient themselves to others as objects "out there" who are part of an objective world, which can be objectively known and accurately described. Persons operating in the natural attitude will not consider that the procedures and schemas, the models and interpretations which they tacitly hold and use in approaching, situating, relating to, and interpreting the Other will structure how the Other manifests himself to them. This is the case not only for the layman but also for positivistic sociologists who implicitly believe that there is an objective social reality that can be grasped and depicted accurately, preferably by quantitative formulations free from subjective distortions. These sociologists for the most part fail to recognize that their a priori structures and the operations which stem from them are not different from those of laymen. The empirical results obtained are not, therefore, faithful and direct depictions of an external reality "as it really is"; they are products of acts of consciousness, collectively organized and accepted by practicing sociologists, acting on external referents.

To "bracket" the a priori structures of consciousness means to consider these structures as data, very important phenomenological data, and not to treat them as sources of error. This is in contrast to *both* the positivistic perspective, which identifies such structures (e.g., observer "bias") as sources of errors in measurement which must be reduced to a minimum or accurately accounted for, *and* the Marxist perspective, which sees such structures as ideologies to be unmasked. Both these perspectives have their own a priori structures of consciousness about social reality (theories, models, etc.) which are not brought to the fore. For a sociologist operating in a phenomenological perspective, there is a suspension of belief in the truth or falsehood of assertions about the world, or parts thereof, which he finds subjects making. A major interest guiding the phenomenological investigation is how subjects experience a phenomenon in terms of their a priori structures, and how these structures can be brought to light. For in bringing the modalities of experience to light—in relating, for example, moral judgments of subjects about the future of their country to a priori structures such as presuppositions and images about the world—the phenomenologist does not start with some thesis that he will seek to demonstrate, nor does he organize his research so as to test some hypotheses or tease out of the data some statistically significant relationships. The merit of the phenomenological approach lies in the fact that it allows the social phenomena under examination to manifest themselves in experience—in the experience of their participating subjects, and in the experience of the researcher as well. The phenomena are not forced into the mold of an a priori research design; at least there is no premature or predetermined delimitation of essential parameters or variables.

The phenomenologist will, to be sure, begin with a problem or a social phenomenon he wishes to understand: the appeal of urban communes to middle-class youth, the meaning of becoming unemployed among highly trained and well-educated persons, the rise of antiwar protest movements among veterans. Whatever it is that starts him off—a puzzling problem in the sociological literature or a chance observation in a subway—the researcher will seek to observe in a spirit of naïveté, abstaining from making judgments as to what is true or false, significant or trivial about a given social condition, or what is the source of that condition. He abstains from the "common-sense" interpretation made by his fellow men (laymen and scientists), but he will treat their interpretations and procedures themselves as data to be examined in the attempt to understand the social condition or phenomenon under consideration. The spirit of naïveté, of wonderment at how things are, is of paramount importance; it should enable the researcher to see social phenomena in a fresh perspective, akin to the insights of the child or the fool in singling out essential aspects of interpersonal relationships.

What the bracketing procedure enables us to do is twofold.

First, it allows the sociological observer to relate social phenomena to the way in which they are experienced by subjects in a situation; since subjects are always in a situation, the phenomenological investigation will concretize and personalize social phenomena even while it seeks the essences of these phenomena, their fundamental meaning in and for social action. By directing his attention to the primacy of experience, the researcher is returning "to the things themselves." By perceiving how the phenomenon is experienced by the subjects of the situation, he gives the emphasis to approaching and seeking to understand the phenomenon from the interior, rather than initially treating it as an inert thing to be manipulated at will.

Second, the bracketing procedure enables us to see the phenomenon more globally, for to be liberated from the natural attitude (or to sublimate it in a Hegelian sense) means to be freed from the restrictions of conventional ways of seeing things and events, including the limitations of our sociopolitical perspectives. Obviously, this means that the sociologist who takes Husserl's methodology seriously and applies it to the social world must be willing to undergo a certain estrangement from his colleagues' perception of social phenomena; in many ways this may lead to a position of profound solitude and alienation very much like that experienced by the anthropologist, as described by Beidelman.[20] In any case, the phenomenological approach leads us to perceive alternative meanings to a given arrangement of social objects or social conditions. Suspending judgment on the validity of the assertions of the natural attitude enables us to see hidden sides of social phenomena and covert meanings to social relationships, so that we may even find that what makes good sense to the natural attitude may sometimes appear to be non-sense in a more global phenomenological perspective. There is some similarity here with psychoanalysis, which unveils a layer of meanings in psychic phenomena different from their common-sense interpretation.

These methodological considerations can now be developed into a broader characterization of existential phenomenology as it relates to sociology. In particular, the question of how ex-

20. Thomas O. Beidelman, "Some Sociological Implications of Culture," in *Theoretical Sociology: Perspectives and Developments,* ed. John C. McKinney and Edward A. Tiryakian (New York: Appleton-Century-Crofts, 1970), pp. 499–527.

istential phenomenology may be applied in sociological research will constitute the concluding section of this discussion.

PHENOMENOLOGY AND SOCIAL CHANGE

EXISTENTIAL PHENOMENOLOGY MAY BE SEEN as a general methodological orientation, rather than as a substantive theory. It is an orientation which may be used in practically any sociological investigation (including, to be sure, the sociological investigation of sociology). Above all, it is an orientation that seeks to find the structure of social phenomena in their meanings, meanings which are grounded in the experience of social subjects. Meaning is not seen as a given but as problematic, as something to be discovered. Existential phenomenology is a relational approach to social reality, asserting a fundamental nexus between social subject and social object, the nexus being the meaning-structure in terms of which the object is perceived by the subject and in terms of which the subject is disposed to act. But this nexus is not a solid, physical structure, any more than a social object is a solid. The meaning-structure which gives a configuration to the social object, can grow or diminish in intensity relative to other objects (as when we say that some thing or some person "has come to mean everything to me" or, on the contrary, "no longer means anything to me"). Related to this is the problem of commitment and the transmission of collective commitment from one generation to another, a problem partly dealt with by Max Weber in the question of the "routinization of charisma." [21] Phenomenology does not lead to the solution of the question of how the meaning-structure of phenomena is retained by successive generations, but the nature of the conditions under which there is a transformation in the meaning-structure of an object would be a relevant question for research.

Existential phenomenology lends itself to a view of social reality which sees the social world as ambiguous but orderly, as multidimensional but not determinate. This view stems from the consideration that social actors for the most part find meaning in what they do in concert with one another, that organized and

21. Max Weber, *The Theory of Social and Economic Organization*, trans. A. M. Henderson and Talcott Parsons, ed. with an Introduction by Talcott Parsons (New York: Free Press, 1964), pp. 363–73.

institutionalized society makes sense to most people. A broad set of shared meanings is held at various levels of consciousness and constitutes a certain social rationality. This set of meanings, which has specific manifestations in specific social groups, under-lies procedures and practices which put these meanings into action and whose results are normally interpreted so as to validate, even if only tacitly, the meanings in question.

Yet, if shared meanings form one side of the social currency, ambiguity forms the other side, for several reasons. First, in everyday life we tend to assume that others share our perspective, that they experience and interpret social phenomena in the same way we do; in fact, the sense of the same phenomenon, object, event, or series of events may be understood very differently by different groups of subjects. Second, and related to the above, we seldom put our expectations and the conditions under which these may be violated by ourselves and by others on the line; moreover, while we tend to act as if there is a congruence of ex-pectations, we have little knowledge of the limits within which the Other (or others) will allow fluctuations in the manifestations of the self and still define the self as retaining its essential mean-ing, that is, as living up to expectations. Third, the moral mean-ing of a social phenomenon, which is a cardinal element in how the phenomenon manifests itself to the subject, is frequently based on a partial perception and is not grounded in personal experience. From a more global perspective, or one based on more total experience, the moral meaning of a social referent may appear a good deal less clear. Thus, the moral meaning of the "proletariat" (industrial workers, blacks, peasants, and so on) may be rudely jolted for many "progressives" from upper-middle-class backgrounds after direct contact with and experience in trying to lead the former; likewise, the moral meaning of civil authority may be equally jolted for other middle-class persons upon first seeing and experiencing police activity in the streets or the operations in some courts.

As a method of inquiry, existential phenomenology em-phasizes the social subject as an embodied consciousness, who is in a here-and-now situation which includes other embodied consciousnesses; some elements of the situation are perceived as meaningful, others are not, and those elements that are meaning-ful are not of the same order of meaning. The subject's conscious-ness of the situation, including his reactions to elements that he defines as part of the situation (whether such elements are physically present or not), is, to reiterate earlier remarks, structured by moods and feelings as well as by the intellect. It is partly because our experience of what is outside us (or of what is nonself) is grounded in feelings relating us toward that which we perceive and experience, that "existential" seems an appropriate qualifier for a social science orientation focusing on phenomenology.

A major theme of phenomenological investigation is the attempt to describe social experiences and the way in which subjects experience and structure their social world, with particular emphasis on the categorizations and typifications used to delineate the contours of that world. It is in the study of the structures and interaction processes of everyday social life that most of what can be called existential phenomenology has been carried out, which particularly reflects the influence of Erving Goffman on the one hand, and the more phenomenologically explicit and methodologically rigorous research of Harold Garfinkel on the other.[22]

There is a "macro" dimension to existential phenomenology in relation to sociology, a dimension more developed in European than in American sociology. The embodied consciousness of subjectivity, or selfhood, exists in a sociohistorical milieu, which is a structure of our experience, a constituent part of the horizon of our perception. The self's experience of the social world, or more broadly of the ambient world (*Umwelt*), is not the experience of an isolated monad. The moods, feelings, and cognitive experience of subjectivity are also reflections of the *collective* representations, moods, and aspirations of a given historical moment or epoch shared by a group of contemporaries. This collective set of feelings and representations, of commonly lived experiences, helps to constitute one form of intersubjectivity: the historical peer group or generation. I use the term "generation" not in a narrow demographic sense but in the more global sense of a cohort of subjects who have experienced and perceived a

22. See Erving Goffman, *The Presentation of Self in Everyday Life* (New York: Doubleday, 1959); *Asylums* (New York: Doubleday, 1961); and *Interaction Ritual* (Chicago: Aldine, 1967). Major writings of Garfinkel are "Perception of the Other: A Study in Social Order" (Ph.D. diss., Harvard University, 1952); and *Studies in Ethnomethodology* (Englewood Cliffs, N.J.: Prentice-Hall, 1967).

series of events and situations in a similar way—a cohort that is both marked by historical events and itself marks history with its actions.

These remarks lead me to propose that the relevance of an existential phenomenological approach to sociology extends beyond the description of the structure of the everyday life-world to the description of sociocultural change, that is, of transformations in the matrix of the everyday life. Viewed phenomenologically, the question of sociocultural change focuses on perceptual transformations in the collective consciousness and the collective experience of reality, including changes in the moral meaning and imagery of the social world, and, following commitment to a new imagery, changes in the patterns of ordering social relationships. Basically, then, I am suggesting that the core of social change involves changes in the dominant meaning-structure of a collectivity's experience of the world; or, to state it differently, the problem of social change directly involves the question of under what conditions the constellation of perceptual images, meanings, presuppositions, and the like which make up a civilization's natural attitude comes to be displaced by another, or in any case no longer remains operative. That is, under what conditions or in what ways do the noemata explode, leading to sustained alterations in the actions of subjects?

Several research problems are related to these questions, such as the location in the societal structure of sources of an alternative consciousness of reality, the conditions under which a group whose consciousness of reality has heretofore been considered "marginal" may succeed in having its experiences of the world accepted by a wider public, and the conditions under which a collectivity withdraws affective meaning from a set of objects, or, alternatively, finds a new meaning in them. Such phenomena as the loss of meaning of the monarchy or the emergence of regional nationalism in politically autonomous countries (such as France and Yugoslavia) come to mind as illustrations of the last point.

In passing I would like to suggest that Max Weber's seminal study of the role played by the Protestant ethic in the development of modern, rational, bourgeois society is in fact a model of a phenomenological study of social change.[23] Weber emphasizes

23. Max Weber, *The Protestant Ethic and the Spirit of Capitalism*, trans. Talcott Parsons (New York: Scribner's, 1958).

the critical transformation of the moral meaning of work for Western man. The imagery of mundane work was transfigured by the Reformation, and particularly by Calvinism and the Puritans with their notion of the "calling" attached to each occupation, so that it came to be perceived as the major vehicle of salvation; this involved transferring the source of salvation from the sacraments, an other-worldly vehicle, to this-worldly practical activity. And in the process, the hierarchy of the clergy lost the meaning of sanctity it had held for the faithful. The correctness of Weber's thesis or the adequacy of his documentation is not at issue; the point is that Weber's analysis of the vast social changes attending the modernization of Western civilization may be cited as an instance of a phenomenological approach to sociology. He identified the dominant mentality of modern, secular, rational society, and sought to locate in the data of history the origins of this mentality in a concrete social group which was "marginal" in its early setting. Weber was concerned with getting to the essence of the modern capitalistic spirit and sought to do so by understanding the assumptive frame of reference of ascetic Protestantism, concretized in Calvin's perception of reality and that of his later followers.

Weber's study involves long-term transformations of comportment and social structures. More dramatic, perhaps, are short-term transformations in social consciousness and experience of the world. There is a vast descriptive sociological (or sociologically relevant) literature dealing with collective behavior, including panic behavior, mob behavior, disaster behavior, and the like, too diverse and voluminous to be cited here but deserving greater attention than has been given to it.[24] This literature is an

24. In terms of this paper, special mention deserves to be made of a remarkable empirical study done on the French student revolutionary movement of May, 1968, by Alfred Willener, *L'Image-action de la société ou la politisation culturelle* (Paris: Seuil, 1970); English translation by A. M. Sheridan Smith, *The Action-Image of Society* (London: Tavistock, 1970). The study was undertaken while the dramatic events were unfolding; that is, the phenomenon imposed itself on the researchers who were located within it, rather than watching from the exterior. The attempt to account for a sociocultural phenomenon "characterized by its very interiority" was a "methodological crisis in the pursuit of understanding," leading the investigator to develop, for his sociological analysis, a method of hermeneutics (p. 282). Besides the richness of the descriptive materials, the methodological reflections are extremely rewarding for a phenomenological consideration of how to decipher the meaning of social events (pp. 281–85).

important source of comparative and phenomenologically significant data on how actors in rapidly changing sociophysical conditions, actual and/or imagined, come to perceive and act upon the social world from a quite different perspective than their everyday one. Such a change in perspective is manifested in the spontaneous collapse of traditional status differentiation as a basis for interaction, changes in the experience of time as a structure of social interaction, and so forth. Broadly speaking, studies of disasters and social crises complement studies of everyday life by indicating the limits of the meaning-structure of social interaction and by placing in relief what intersubjective orientations and meanings remain under extreme conditions.

AFRICAN COLONIALISM

IN THE FOLLOWING PAGES I will discuss briefly something intermediate between Weber's analysis of long-term transformations of Western consciousness and the short-term transformations examined in disaster studies. It will be based on materials derived from my research, which aimed at providing a sociological analysis of the modernization of sub-Saharan Africa. The discussion will indicate how a phenomenological approach may be of use in the sociological interpretation of a complex sociohistorical situation, in this case colonial Africa. In the process I hope to illustrate several points made earlier in the explication of existential phenomenology. It would not be appropriate here to present detailed information about the research, which will be reported more fully at a later time; for the present, I shall explore the issues raised by a phenomenological approach addressed to a macrosociological investigation.

The materials used in this study were gathered over a period of approximately ten years, beginning in the late 1950s. Firsthand data were gathered in the field by the researcher during visits to a number of African countries, and include observations recorded in diaries and field notes, as well as interviews and informal discussions with various people living in Africa (Africans, Europeans, Levantines, Asiatics). These data were supplemented by information obtained from the great variety of documents and publications available: archival materials (reports of administrators, etc.), contemporary analyses by social scientists, statistical reports, and earlier books on Africa by journalists, freelance writers, explorers, administrators, and missionaries, only some of whom had been in Africa.

The goal of the research was to provide sociological theory with an adequate analysis of a type of society hitherto neglected, namely, colonial society. Sub-Saharan Africa is an apt terrain for this type of study, since practically all of it was colonized by European powers; moreover, the time period is relatively short, roughly including the period between 1885 (the date of the Berlin Conference) and 1960, the "Year of Africa."

In treating colonial Africa as a social phenomenon, localized in time and space, I am starting with a tacitly phenomenological endeavor, namely, the quest for a constellation of experiences and meanings—in other words, intersubjective essences—underlying the various empirical settings. An alternative approach, commonly reflected in ethnographic and political science studies, stresses the peculiarities of the locale, its language, culture, or political system. Given the great variety of African environments, ethnic and linguistic groups, and colonial policies and influences, one could despair of finding essences or even uniformities. Yet, my approach has led me to view colonial sub-Saharan Africa as a total social situation. In part this stems from the decision to treat the theme of African unity, expressed by so many black writers, not simply as ideology or utopia, but also as a formulation of a commonly shared sociohistorical situation which needs to be brought to light by careful investigation. Second, amid the variety of settings I visited—from highly urbanized areas to predominantly nonurban ones, from areas with a substantial number of Europeans to those with just a token European population, in countries or colonies having had apparently quite different European regimes—my experiences and observations pointed to strong similarities in the structure of social interaction between whites and blacks and in the attitudes of whites toward black Africans and toward whites overseas or "back home."

In "bracketing" judgments about the nature of the colonial experience, it was immediately obvious that the manifestation of this experience changed considerably in the public image over a relatively short period of time. Until World War II, the great part of the literature on Africa either extolled the moral meaning of colonization (e.g., that colonization was uplifting Africa from its state of moral, economic, and political backwardness) or simply accepted it as a fact; criticisms of colonialism by both Europeans and Africans were for the most part directed not at its premises (i.e., the existence of colonies politically attached to a metropolitan state as the source of the economic, political, and cultural evolution of the colony) but at failures to realize these premises (e.g., the failure of assimilation in French colonies through the policy of giving Africans a civil status different from that of French citizens). After World War II, and particularly in the 1950s, there was a vast change in the moral meaning of colonialism; from being viewed as a positive moral phenomenon uplifting backward masses, colonialism came to be seen in negative moral terms, as the incarnation of evil. This transformation of consciousness, both in Europe and in Africa, took place, paradoxically, without a deterioration of economic conditions in sub-Saharan Africa, and with, if anything, an improvement in the political conditions of Africans in most colonies.

The central problem of the study was therefore how to account for changes in the meaning of colonialism, among both blacks and whites, over a relatively short period of time. To pursue this question, it became obvious early in the research that attention would have to be given to the meaning of colonialism in the pre–World War II period, which led to an examination of the images of Africa held by Europeans at various periods, starting with the latter half of the nineteenth century as the effective beginning of the modern colonization of sub-Saharan Africa. Subsequent readings and reflection suggested that I could make use of the notion of "generation" by typifying the African colonial situation over three periods: the first colonial generation corresponded to the period from, approximately, the Berlin Conference in 1885 to World War I; the second, to the interwar period; and the third, from the end of World War II until roughly 1960. An extensive part of the research has been to construct an "ideal type" representing the characteristics of the interaction between whites and blacks in the colonial situation of each period.[25]

It also became clear after reading the accounts of European explorers, administrators, missionaries, and others, that many

25. Although this is not the place to discuss extensively this conceptualization, it might be noted that in the European population we consider there to be significant differences in the "world" of the first-generation "colonizer," that of the second-generation "colonial," and that of the third-generation "settler."

interpretations of experiences in Africa and with Africans were, in fact, part of an assumptive frame of reference based on the existential and cultural conditions of Europe. That is, perception of the African situation was screened by how the subjects perceived and experienced the European world. To understand a phenomenon such as the colonization of Africa, therefore, one is also forced to delve into certain themes and images which have nothing to do specifically with Africa, but which become implicit components of the structure of the perception and experience of that phenomenon. This makes the sociological analysis of the colonization of Africa much more complex, but at the same time adds depth to the sociological understanding. So, for example, it became clear that the colonial situation could not be reduced in essence to the "racial factor," although the image of racial superiority/inferiority was one component. Another element of the situation is suggested by the fact that several accounts depicted blacks in somewhat the same perspective as that in which the Victorian bourgeoisie perceived and evaluated other elements of the population at home, notably women and the working classes. A related aspect of the Victorian ethos, the repression of affect in interpersonal relations, also seems to have been extended to Africa: Africans were judged "barbarians" or "wild" because of their direct expression of feelings in a variety of situations, and some Europeans were said to be "going native" or engaging in what would have been judged deviant behavior (sexual transgressions, verbal and physical violence against Africans, etc.) "back home." Black Africans became the object of sexual stereotypes just as did blacks in the American South; the colonial situation permitted whites to engage in sexual conduct considered taboo in the European setting, and this was justified by images of the promiscuity of Africans (the exotic "Black Eve" figuring prominently in stamps, posters, and other representations of Africans). Even missionary activity, particularly by Protestants, was an extension of the nineteenth-century European cultural setting: the formation of industrial missions reflected the notion that salvation is a this-worldly activity to be organized in a rational work ethic.

This discussion has just scratched the surface of the sort of analysis that it was necessary to undertake in trying to come to grips with the sociohistorical matrix of African colonialism. Yet I hope it indicates that in trying to uncover the meanings, experiences, and structure of perception of subjects involved in a common situation, one must investigate a much wider network of phenomena which have a bearing on their experiences of the situation.

The phenomenological orientation of the research has also led to other considerations. Corresponding to the problem of uncovering the components of colonial consciousness—the sources, values, ideologies, and characteristics of those who were active agents of the colonization of Africa—is the related problem of delineating the components of decolonization, that is, the sources of the consciousness which rejected the premises of colonialism, and the location of these sources in the social structure. The movements of nationalism and independence, both forms of political consciousness, represent the climax of the process of decolonization. However, two other currents played essential roles. The first was the movement of religious independence in many parts of Africa before World War II (Kimbangism in equatorial Africa, the Harris movement in West Africa, and others), frequently organized around black prophets who had a vision of a new order that questioned the very premises of the colonial social order—at a time when that order was accepted by assimilated intellectuals and black civil servants. The second was the movement of cultural independence, which was particularly marked among black intellectuals coming together in France to form the movement of negritude, a truly revolutionary cultural movement negating the primary cultural premise of colonization, that is, the superiority of Western civilization with its rationality, technology, and all the rest. As in the case of colonization, to understand the process of decolonization in Africa one has to extend the field of inquiry outside Africa. Garvey's "Back to Africa" movement in Harlem, for example, was an important influence in the development of Kimbangu's movement in the Congo, just as surrealism and the figure of André Breton in France did much to stimulate the development of negritude (which in turn is of significance in understanding the Black Power movement).

If the existential phenomenological approach has made this sociological research more *extensive*, it has also led to a more *intensive* study of the nature of the colonial phenomenon. That is, I have attempted to grasp from within the essence of the colonial situation, in the fashion of eidetic reductions from specific and contingent manifestations. Although this warrants greater elaboration than can be presented adequately in these pages, I would like to propose that perhaps the essence of colonialism, as manifested in the African situation, is that of *alienation*. The notion of alienation is not a new one in social philosophy, having been discussed by Hegel, Marx, and Kierkegaard over a century ago; more recently, its significance for sociological analysis has been noted by an increasing number of writers.[26] However, there are limitations to this literature: either it abstracts individuals from their social situation, treating alienation as a psychological variable, or else it focuses on the alienation of industrial work and/or Western society. I therefore propose to add a comparative dimension to the notion of alienation by suggesting that it is an essence of the colonial situation as it manifests itself in intersubjective consciousness.

In its objective aspects, economic alienation—i.e., the alienation of land—was one important aspect of colonization. Land which was used and integrated in the traditional sociocultural setting (including land set aside for sacred purposes, allocated to deities, and so on) was estranged and placed at the disposal of Europeans for rational economic purposes. Since land is not only a physical resource, but has symbolic significance as well (e.g., home-land), the alienation of the land for economic purposes within an essentially foreign economy was instrumental in changing the experience of Africans from one of feeling-at-home to one of being no-longer-at-home. Second, alienation involved the *estrangement* (which is indicated in the etymology of "alienation") of the colonized population from its own cultural matrix; this aspect of alienation involved the denigration of traditional African dress, religion, education, and language, so that these came to be felt as "alien" to Africans seeking to become accepted by colonial society. The colonial premise was, so to speak, that the traditional culture was inferior, and that if Africans accepted Western culture they would progress and come to share the European way of life. In fact, this did not happen, or only for a privi-

26. Among these the following may be cited as representative: Melvin Seeman, "On the Meaning of Alienation," *American Sociological Review*, XXIV (December, 1959), 783–91; John Horton, "The Dehumanization of Anomie and Alienation: A Problem in the Ideology of Sociology," *British Journal of Sociology*, XV (December, 1964), 283–300; and Joachim Israel, *Alienation from Marx to Modern Sociology* (Boston: Allyn and Bacon, 1971).

leged few, and even these came to feel that they were still "less equal" in certain regards. The awareness of alienation, of estrangement from home, and ultimately from self, was strikingly felt by Africans (and other blacks) when they went overseas, particularly to the metropole for higher studies: their situation made them aware of being aliens in a white world and at the same time of having been alienated by the white world from their own roots. This led several of them to a *prise de conscience*, to a new consciousness of the meaning of the colonial situation in its fundamentally alienating character—alienating and uprooting those accepting assimilation into a culture foreign to their own authentic being. From this we can describe decolonization as a complex process of liberation, of reexperiencing the world, involving first the realization that one has been alienated in terms of how one perceives and evaluates the world, and second, the quest to return to the cultural roots, to "feel at home again" in the culture that one had rejected. It is in this respect that one can examine various themes in the negritude movement to place into relief the experience of the colonial situation.

But alienation as an essence of the colonial situation involved other subjects besides those who were colonized—it also involved the colonizers. The latter were, after all, aliens. Africa was not their home; home was overseas, in the metropole. Yet they came to feel that the colony was theirs, and although it was not their home, it was not to be entrusted to the "natives" either. The "natives" were seen either as instruments for the maintenance of the colony or else as an unwanted alien presence. But alienation also operated on the alien population in another way. The materials I have surveyed indicate that, particularly in the case of third-generation whites, the colonial situation produced an increasing alienation from the metropole. Persons returning "home" for visits after prolonged stays in Africa began to feel out of place; the ways of life, the climate, the syles of comportment all seemed unfamiliar. Moreover, especially by the 1950s, and notably in Belgium, the returning colonials were treated in the metropole as aliens and as morally reprehensible for being "colonials." They reacted with moral indignation to what they saw as the pronative policy of the home government and the metropolitan public; but underneath this, I would suggest, was the experience of having been betrayed and dispossessed—the same experience as that felt by Africans.

Cursory as this discussion has been, I hope it has indicated how a phenomenological approach can be fruitful in the sociological analysis of a large-scale social situation. Of course, such a situation cannot be analyzed solely in this vein. The researcher must take into account the historical dimension of the situation, its demographic aspects (for example, changes in the structure of the white population), economic factors, and the like. But the phenomenological aspect of the investigation has been invaluable in baring alienation as a key structural factor of the African colonial situation, which helps make sense of much that might otherwise remain obscure.

CONCLUSION

THERE IS A VAST AND FRUITFUL FIELD of exchange between existential phenomenology and sociology, a field whose potential fruits have been only partially cultivated heretofore. It is ultimately up to philosophers to examine the relevance of sociology for producing further refinements in the philosophical reflections of existential phenomenology. Conversely, existential phenomenology has multiple applications for sociology: as (1) a general theoretical frame of reference, sensitizing us to the nature and fundamental role of intersubjectivity in the structure of social interaction; (2) a source of reflection on the researcher's awareness of himself in his actions, that is, on the engagement of his subjectivity with the objects of his consciousness; and (3) a catalyst to the broadening of our horizon of sociological problems and explanations.

Much of the corpus of sociology, including its techniques of research and its conceptualizations of social reality, has been linked to the development of a technological, industrial society and the ecological changes of that society. The physicalistic and mechanistic models of this society produced by sociology (models taken from the natural sciences and economics) gave scant recognition to consciousness and subjectivity. Familiar with these models "from the inside," natural scientists have become more aware of their limitations, especially in relation to social phenomena, than many social scientists who have dominated the growth of their disciplines.

In the post–World War II period, existentialism and phenomenology have been the intellectual sources of a reaction in the academic setting against the overobjectified view of man—in philosophy, in psychology, and more recently in sociology. Unfortunately, much of the debate has been more polemical than dispassionate, with the existential phenomenological camp treated as something of a pariah in many sociology departments, or as a subversive notion to be kept from the minds of youth so as not to corrupt them. Although I consider myself a "militant" for the phenomenological cause in sociology, I hope that the need to be one will be short-lived, and that the constructive role of existential phenomenology in the sociological division of labor will soon be perceived and accepted by the patricians and the plebes alike. Side by side with vast technological changes having major social consequences, we are witnessing vast upheavals in forms of intersubjective consciousness: the formation of a counterculture, the explosion at the cultural level of the noemata of the Protestant ethic, and the sexual revolution, among other phenomena. For sociology to be able to deal adequately with the technological and the intersubjective mutations that characterize our contemporary society it will have to use both complementary methodologies of positivism and phenomenology. This, it seems to me, is a prerequisite for the future viability and growth of the sociological enterprise.

PART III

Phenomenology and Psychology

Theoretical Problems in Phenomenological Psychology

Joseph J. Kockelmans

MANY PHILOSOPHERS interested in the philosophy of science believe there is something wrong with the epistemological status of the psychological sciences. Some even go so far as to say that these sciences have been in error from the very beginning: that since psychology was originally interwoven with philosophy, it was for many centuries unable to "mature" and find its own way as an empirical science. Even when psychology began to withdraw in the nineteenth century from the influence of philosophy, it fell in turn under the sway of the natural sciences (Herbart, Wundt). Those who hold this view contend that to this day psychology has never been able to find its own "innermost self." "Naturalism," "psychologism," "objectivism," and "physicalization" are the principal labels that have been used to refer to the "disease" from which psychology has suffered since its first attempts to break away from philosophy. However, a growing number of people in Europe as well as in the United States now share the opinion that it is phenomenology which can offer everything necessary for the solution (at least in principle) of the basic problems connected with the epistemological status of psychology.

In my opinion, although there is undoubtedly a core of truth in these considerations, the case is nonetheless overstated, and the real problems are much more complicated than many authors have initially realized.[1] For this reason I wish to deal here with

1. Although all phenomenologists subscribe to this view of psychology, most of them (at least in some sense or other) share my reservation in regard to the oversimplification of the facts. Cf. Edmund Husserl, "Phi-

[225]

some of the basic *theoretical* problems which I think phenomenological psychology must face if it is ever to fulfill Husserl's original intention: namely, that it be an eidetic, aprioric, and purely descriptive science of man's psychic life, which could occupy a mediating position between empirical psychology and phenomenological philosophy.[2]

In considering these problems I wish to take as my point of departure a brief summary of Husserl's final ideas on the subject and an outline of the reflections which led to his view [I]. Then I shall present a description of the two predominating reinterpretations of Husserl's original view and explain why I feel that one of these views is to be preferred above the other [II]. Following these historical considerations I shall attempt to answer the question of what, precisely, is to be understood by the expression "empirical science," as I feel that misunderstanding in this area has been the source of much confusion [III]. Finally, I shall endeavor to justify my own view in regard to the meaning and function of phenomenological psychology, and will then proceed to develop this view in greater detail [IV].

In reading the second, third, and fourth sections of this essay it is very important to keep in mind that empirical psychology is no longer the hesitating, "groping" science it was when

---

losophie als strenge Wissenschaft," *Logos,* I (1910–11) 289–341; *Phänomenologische Psychologie* (1925) (The Hague: Nijhoff, 1962) (hereafter cited as *Ph P*); *Die Krisis der europäischen Wissenschaften und die transzendentale Phänomenologie* (The Hague: Nijhoff, 1954), English translation by David Carr, *The Crisis of European Sciences and Transcendental Phenomenology: An Introduction to Phenomenological Philosophy* (Evanston, Ill.: Northwestern University Press, 1970). J.-P. Sartre, *L'Imagination* (Paris: Alcan, 1936); *Esquisse d'une théorie des émotions* (Paris: Hermann, 1939); Stephan S. Strasser, *Phenomenology and the Human Sciences* (Pittsburgh, Pa.: Duquesne University Press, 1963); B. Delfgaauw, "Verantwoording der phaenomenologische psychologie," *Nederlands Tijdschrift voor de Psychologie en haar Grensgebieden,* IX (1954) 78–83; F. J. J. Buytendijk, "Die Bedeutung der Phänomenologie Husserls für die Psychologie der Gegenwart," *Husserl et la pensée moderne,* ed. H. L. Van Breda and J. Taminiaux (The Hague: Nijhoff, 1959), 78–98; Jan Linschoten, "Fenomenologie en psychologie," *Algemeen Nederlands Tijdschrift voor Wijsbegeerte en Psychologie,* LV (1963), 113–22; *Auf dem Wege zu einer phänomenologischen Psychologie* (Berlin: de Gruyter, 1961); *Idolen van de psycholoog* (Utrecht: Bijleveld, 1964); Aron Gurwitsch, *Studies in Phenomenology* (Evanston, Ill.: Northwestern University Press, 1966). For a more complete bibliography, see: Joseph J. Kockelmans, *Edmund Husserl's Phenomenological Psychology* (Pittsburgh, Pa.: Duquesne University Press, 1967), pp. 352–59.

2. Husserl, *Ph P,* pp. 46–51.

Herbart and Wundt first tried to lay its foundations. However, it was the work of the early psychologists with which Husserl was familiar: Wundt, Herbart, Paulsen, Brentano, Stumpf, Ebbinghaus, and Dilthey. Empirical psychology as we know it today is for the most part behavioristically oriented. But when I speak of "empirical psychology" in this essay, I do not intend that this term be applied to any one particular school or trend within empirical psychology. Rather, what I do have in mind is a certain ideal which in my opinion has only partially materialized today. By "empirical psychology" I mean the scientific study of man's behavior (or orientation toward the world) which makes use of empirical methods only and holds all philosophical and quasi-philosophical issues outside its own realm of investigation.

Since the time of Husserl's original investigations in this regard, the philosophy of science has been able to point to many important logical, methodological, and epistemological issues with which Husserl himself was only partly familiar. In what follows I wish to make explicit use of some of these insights.

Since this essay is not meant to make a positive contribution to either empirical psychology or phenomenological psychology, but rather to contribute something to the "foundations" of these sciences, it is obviously philosophical in character. This means among other things that it is written from a determinate philosophical point of view. Although space limitations preclude my clarifying and justifying this view here, I feel nevertheless that I at least owe my readers a "label" for my own philosophical conception. Formulated as concisely as possible, the reflections which follow have been inspired by "existential phenomenology." I have explained this view elsewhere and so shall limit myself here to listing those publications that are relevant.[3] In order to make my perspective as broad as possible, however, I shall try to keep the immediate influence of this conception to a minimum. I am convinced that what I shall say from this particular point of view could also easily be reformulated from some other related philosophical perspective.

3. Joseph J. Kockelmans, *World in Science and Philosophy* (Milwaukee, Wis.: Bruce, 1969); *Phenomenology and Physical Science* (Pittsburgh, Pa.: Duquesne University Press, 1966), pp. 13–91.

[1] Husserl's View on Phenomenological Psychology

A FEW INTRODUCTORY REMARKS are necessary for a proper understanding of Husserl's view on phenomenological psychology.[4] I wish first of all to call attention to the fact that Husserl originally studied mathematics and physics. However, while studying mathematics at Leipzig, he also attended some lectures in philosophy given by Wilhelm Wundt; and later, in Berlin, when he was studying with Weierstrass, Kummer, and Kronecker, Husserl attended lectures in philosophy given by Friedrich Paulsen. But it was in Vienna, where he received his degree under Königsberger, that Husserl met Brentano, who had a great influence on him—not only on his decision to become a philosopher and to devote his entire life to the cause of philosophy, but also on his whole way of thinking. Through Brentano, Husserl came in contact with the works of Hume, Mill, and Bolzano. In 1886 Husserl became Stumpf's assistant at Halle; Brentano had advised Husserl to go there in order to become more familiar with Stumpf's ideas on the relationship between philosophy and psychology.

Given these facts, it is understandable that Husserl was originally interested in the philosophy of mathematics, that he approached the subject from the viewpoint of psychology, and that he originally became entangled with psychologism, that is to say, the tendency which reduces all basic philosophical problems and notably all epistemological issues to mere psychological questions. To be sure, Husserl never defended an extreme form of psychologism (Stumpf had warned him of all the dangers such a position would entail), but with his background and original interest it was almost impossible for Husserl not to have made certain fundamental mistakes which necessarily follow from adopting a psychological approach to philosophical problems.

The same historical data explain, also, why Husserl uses the expression "empirical psychology" to mean, exclusively, the scien-

---

4. See, with regard to this section in general: Max Drüe, *Edmund Husserls System der phänomenologischen Psychologie* (Berlin: de Gruyter, 1963); Kockelmans, *Edmund Husserl's Phenomenological Psychology*, 87–301; *Phenomenology: The Philosophy of Edmund Husserl and Its Interpretation* (New York: Doubleday, 1967), pp. 418–49.

tific study of consciousness. Following the tradition which was quite generally accepted in Germany around 1880, Husserl adopted the point of view that psychology should limit itself to being an empirical investigation of conscious phenomena and that the study of all "bodily accompaniments" should be left to biology and physiology. There can be no doubt about the fact that, at least prior to 1894, Husserl believed that a psychology of consciousness could make a substantial contribution to solving the foundational problems of mathematics. Several ideas which point in this direction are found in his first writings, *Über den Begriff der Zahl* (1887)[5] and *Philosophie der Arithmetik* (1891).[6]

Influenced by Frege's criticism of his original view and by some publications of Natorp, Husserl gradually became aware of the fact that he, indeed, had made several important mistakes in his attempts to determine the relationship between psychology and mathematics. A careful examination of the pertinent literature as well as of his own original position led him to recognize two seemingly conflicting views: (1) psychologism is unacceptable; and (2) it is nonetheless true that a certain type of psychology can make a substantial contribution to the foundations of mathematics and logic. Husserl's criticism of psychologism constitutes the main theme of the first volume of *Logische Untersuchungen* (1900), whereas the second volume of the work (1901) defends and develops the second "thesis."[7]

In the first volume of *Logische Untersuchungen* Husserl came to the conclusion that mathematical and logical axioms are true regardless of whether or not man thinks of them. Their truth is independent of man's thinking of them; they have a being which is not subject to the factual functioning of man's consciousness. If logical and mathematical propositions are true, it is not because man's thinking functions properly in formulating them, but because these propositions have validity in themselves. Thus, Husserl concludes, we must accept the fact that there is a universe of ideal entities, such as the world of numbers, geometrical entities, logical generalities, and so on, the validity of

5. Edmund Husserl, *Über den Begriff der Zahl* (Halle: Heynemann-Beyer, 1887).

6. Edmund Husserl, *Philosophie der Arithmetik* (Halle: Pfeffer, 1891).

7. Edmund Husserl, *Logische Untersuchungen*, 2 vols. (Halle: Niemeyer, 1900–1901).

which is independent of the psychical activities by which these ideal entities are apprehended by man.

In the second volume Husserl tried to answer the question of exactly how these ideal objects are given to consciousness. That is why the most important theme of this volume consists in the descriptive investigations concerning the psychological experiences which are inseparably connected with the ideal objects of logic and mathematics. For a closer consideration of the ideal objects themselves reveals that they have their own characteristic being-in-itself and being-for-itself to which their pure truths refer in an a priori way, and which make them what they are regardless of their being counted or thought of. On the other hand, we must realize that these objects arise only out of our subjective psychic activities and experiences. How then can we explain this strange correlation between these ideal objects of pure logic and the subjective experiences which constitute them?

In trying to provide a general theory concerning logical and mathematical acts of knowing as they relate to logical and mathematical ideal entities, Husserl originally believed that he could use some of the basic ideas of Brentano, Stumpf, and Dilthey, who, in their own ways, had already pointed to the necessity of adding a "decriptive" psychology to the traditional empirical psychology.

In 1901 Husserl thought that the intent of this discipline was to apply reflexive intuition to those thought processes of the mathematician and logician which had remained hidden up to then, and to work out a complete, *eidetic* description of these experiences by radically and consistently working back from the relevant categories of the ideal objects to the corresponding modes of consciousness in which these objects become conscious to man. At the beginning it was not yet very clear how to accomplish this questioning back from the ideal objects to the subjective experiences in which they emerge as conscious. One thing was clear, however: the methods used by empirical psychology would be of no help; only those methods which make use solely of careful *analyses* and *descriptions* of psychic experiences on the basis of an *immediate intuition* could be meaningful here. But where must analysis and description take their point of departure? Obviously in the only things we consciously know, namely, the ideal objects. By elaborating upon Brentano's conception of intentionality, Husserl found another link in the chain, which was to lead him finally to the solution of this basic problem.

Brentano had already understood that the basic characteristic of all psychic experiences is to be found in their intentionality; however, he had limited himself to an "external" and merely classifying, descriptive consideration of intentional experiences. He had not yet realized the enormous task of going from the various classes of objects back to the manifold modes of consciousness in and through which we become conscious of these objects. Such regressive analyses show that consciousness is not something that becomes conscious of its objects in a merely passive way; rather it does so by achievements which come about in many different forms of syntheses and are always intentionally and "teleologically" oriented toward the truth concerning the ideal entities.

But the essential element was still missing in these considerations. For when one turns from the ideal objects of logic and mathematics to the acts of consciousness which give rise to them, it soon becomes clear that the activities in which these objects come to the fore cannot be of a merely empirical and accidental nature. The experiences out of which these objects arise as conscious entities must possess their own essential and always identical structures. Thus, there must be an a priori in psychology which corresponds to the a priori of the formal *mathēsis universalis*.

Out of all these reflections, a completely new conception of the nature of psychology arose. This new, descriptive psychology, or phenomenology, is devoted to the study of an entirely new theme, namely, intentionality. More importantly, however, this descriptive psychology strives to become a nonempirical, thus an a priori, science. Instead of speaking about factual human subjects living in a concrete world, descriptive psychology deals with the ideal essence of the knowing subjectivity as such. Starting with a concrete case as an example, phenomenology tries to bring to light descriptively its essential structure and characteristics and then, in unconditioned universality, its ideal possibilities.

As early as 1903 it became clear to Husserl that in addition to this new kind of psychology there was a place and a need for a "transcendental phenomenology." For the aprioric psychology which arose within the limited sphere of *mathēsis universalis* was not able to furnish a radical explanation for all foundational problems. It became evident that even an aprioric psychology cannot, itself, posit and answer all epistemological problems in a fundamental way. Only in the first volume of *Ideen* [8] (1913) do we find for the first time a complete, methodically developed foundation for a universal science of transcendental subjectivity. Such a foundation, however, cannot be developed without a transcendental reduction, that is, a radical change of attitude by means of which everything which is not, or cannot be made, apodictically evident is excluded from the philosophical reflection. Transcendental phenomenology can employ only those pure descriptions which remain within the realm opened up by the reduction, and which emanate there from a pure intuition of essences on the basis of intentional analyses.

Thus, in 1913 Husserl was convinced that, as far as man's *consciousness* is concerned, three scientific approaches are possible. First, there is the empirical-psychological approach which was realized in very imperfect form in the psychological studies written around 1900. Secondly, there is phenomenological psychology, which is a further development of Brentano's descriptive psychology and Dilthey's *verstehende* psychology. Finally, there is the genuinely philosophical approach of transcendental phenomenology, an initial outline of which Husserl had given in the first volume of his main work, *Ideen*.

From this brief historical survey one can see why Husserl later defined phenomenological psychology in the following way: It is an aprioric, eidetic, intuitive, purely descriptive, and intentional discipline which is concerned with man's consciousness and which, furthermore, remains within the realm of the natural attitude (that is, which does not employ the transcendental reduction).[9] Husserl tried to clarify and justify this conception of phenomenological psychology in the many manuscripts and lecture courses he prepared between 1913 and 1938. His main concern in these later investigations was to determine the nature and function of this discipline more carefully, and in particular

8. Edmund Husserl, *Ideen zu einer reinen Phänomenologie und phänomenologischen Philosophie. Erstes Buch: Allgemeine Einführung in die reine Phänomenologie*, 1st ed., 1913 (The Hague: Nijhoff, 1950); English translation by W. R. Boyce Gibson, *Ideas: General Introduction to Pure Phenomenology* (New York: Humanities Press, 1931).

9. Husserl, *Ph P*, p. 46.

to explain its relationships to other sciences as well as to philosophy, taken as transcendental phenomenology. Since space limitations do not permit me to go into detail on this subject, I shall briefly mention only those concepts in these later investigations that are of immediate relevance to the main topic of this paper.

Between 1913 and 1923 Husserl was mainly concerned with constitutional problems. As a result of investigations in this area he came to the conclusion that his view of phenomenological psychology as presented in the first volume of *Ideen* was still somehow inadequate, in that the distinction between phenomenological psychology and transcendental philosophy had not yet been fully established there. It became clear, also, that phenomenological psychology was not only very important for the development of empirical psychology, but also could have a vital function in regard to transcendental phenomenology. These were the reasons why Husserl believed that more *radical* investigations concerning phenomenological psychology were indispensable. He dealt with the topic explicitly in various lecture courses prepared between 1923 and 1927 and devoted a substantial part of his last book, *Krisis*,[10] to the function of phenomenological psychology for transcendental philosophy.

In the lectures published posthumously in 1962 as *Phänomenologische Psychologie*,[11] Husserl describes phenomenological psychology as one of many "regional ontologies," a term that harked back to the theory of science with which he had fully dealt for the first time in the first volume of *Ideen*. After establishing an essential distinction between facts and essences, Husserl argued there [12] that this distinction necessarily leads to a correlative distinction between sciences of facts and sciences of essences. He furthermore contended that concrete empirical objects, together with their material essences, have their places in highest material genera, "regions" of empirical objects. Since every empirical object has its own essence, each regional essence must have a corresponding "regional ontology," just as there is a "regional" empirical science or set of sciences that corresponds

10. Husserl, *Crisis*, pp. 191–265.
11. Husserl, *Ph P*, pp. 221–22.
12. Husserl, *Ideas I*, pp. 55–59; see also: C. Lannoy, "Phaenomenologie, ontologie en psychologie in het werk van Edmund Husserl," *Tijdschrift voor Philosophie*, XI (1949) 391–416.

to the "region" of empirical objects. Accordingly, Husserl concluded, every empirical science which deals with the empirical entities belonging to a given region will be essentially related to a corresponding regional ontology. In other words, every factual empirical science has its essential counterpart and theoretical basis in an eidetic ontology. For instance, an "eidetic" science of physical nature in general (= ontology of nature) corresponds to the natural sciences, insofar as there is an *eidos* corresponding to actual nature that can be apprehended in its purity. Similarly, we can say that corresponding to all empirical sciences of man's *psyche* there must be a regional ontology of the *psyche* and this is phenomenological psychology.

In the first volume of *Ideen* Husserl had already suggested that each empirical science, in addition to having its own corresponding regional ontology, also necessarily presupposes a *formal* ontology which is common to all empirical sciences. He usually refers to this formal ontology with the Leibnizian term *mathēsis universalis.*[13] In *Phänomenologische Psychologie* Husserl adds to this that all empirical sciences also presuppose a general *material* ontology which he calls the general ontology of the world of immediate experience as such.[14] The function of this latter science is to explain all the eidetic structures which are found in all entities and events which constitute the subject matter of all empirical sciences and their corresponding regional ontologies. Since all regional ontologies and even the general ontology of the world of immediate experience as such must be founded ultimately in transcendental phenomenology,[15] the relationship between phenomenological psychology and empirical psychology on the one hand, and phenomenological psychology and transcendental phenomenology on the other, is immediately evident. Phenomenological psychology must give a firm basis to the empirical investigations of man's conscious life, whereas it, in turn, must be radically founded in transcendental phenomenology. Whereas empirical psychology deals with psychic facts, phenomenological psychology deals with the essential structures

13. Husserl, *Ideas I*, pp. 55–56, 59–62, 158–60, 309–11.
14. Husserl, *Ph P*, pp. 64–97.
15. Edmund Husserl, *Ideen III: Die Phänomenologie und die Fundamente der Wissenschaften* (The Hague: Nijhoff, 1952), pp. 23–24; *Erste Philosophie* (1923–24), 2 vols. (The Hague: Nijhoff, 1956–59), I, 212–18; *Ph P,* 52–72.

(*eidē*) underlying and governing these facts. On the other hand, whereas phenomenological psychology and transcendental phenomenology have the same subject matter, namely, the eidetic structures of man's intentional consciousness, phenomenological psychology, which does not make use of the transcendental reduction, investigates intentional consciousness from the natural point of view, while transcendental phenomenology examines it from a transcendental and thus absolute point of view.[16]

In this survey of the genesis of Husserl's conception of "phenomenological psychology," I have purposely omitted an element which somehow conflicts with Husserl's entire approach to the problem, and which, if it had been studied systematically by him, might perhaps have led to different conclusions.[17] Obviously, Husserl has always known that what he calls the "psychical" is found only as it is interwoven with the spatiotemporal reality of the human body. He has known, also, that the psychical, precisely as it is found in the living subject which perceives, strives, wills, thinks, acts, and behaves in many other ways, can indeed be chosen as the subject matter of scientific investigation. Although Husserl originally paid little attention to this possibility, after 1900 he continuously returned to it, stating that the science which seeks to study psychic life just as it manifests itself in the plenitude of our experiences, and therefore as it appears in the concrete interwovenness with the living body, should be called "psychophysical psychology." In his view this discipline frequently degenerates into naturalism in its attempt to explain the psychical exclusively on the basis of material bodily events, as is done for example in classical behaviorism. "Psychophysical psychology" obviously must accept the fact that the psychical never occurs in the world without a foundation of the physical, but it must at the same time maintain the insight that the psychical as such has its own typically essential characteristics and therefore has its own realm of lawfulness.

If one wishes to study the psychical purely as such, the first problem to be dealt with is the question of whether the *purely* psychical can be sufficiently separated from the physical so as to form the subject matter of a pure psychology which must operate in addition to psychophysical psychology. Husserl was of the

16. Husserl, *Ph P*, pp. 324–28; 344–49.
17. Drüe, *Husserls System der phänomenologischen Psychologie*, pp. 55–57.

opinion that before answering the question we must first clarify the characteristics of psychical experience itself and of the psychical data it brings to the fore. To that end we must concentrate our attention on our immediate experiences. These experiences allow us to discover the psychical as such merely by means of *reflection,* thus by means of a change in our normal, natural attitude. In the natural attitude we normally concentrate on things, their characteristics, and values, but bypass the psychical acts of experience through which we get to know these things. But the act itself cannot be revealed except by reflection, and such a reflection can be applied to every experience. In this reflection we turn away from the things, their characteristics, and values and try instead to contemplate the experiences themselves, in and through which things and their different aspects become revealed. Husserl calls these intentional experiences "phenomena." The essential characteristic of a phenomenon thus consists in the fact that it is a "consciousness-of-its-object." *Pure psychology* is concerned with these phenomena exclusively.

It is possible, Husserl argues, to assume two different theoretical positions in regard to these pure psychical phenomena: We can accept them as psychical facts and stop there, or we can shift our attention and concentrate on the very *essence* which, at the same time, manifests itself in these facts. In the first case we become involved in a pure, factical, scientific psychology, that is, a psychology which investigates psychical facts only after removing those physical components which in reality are always connected with the psychical. The object of such a psychology is the study of human experiences apart from all bodily and physical components. Actually, however, such a pure psychology is often closely related to psychophysical psychology. Taken together, Husserl concludes, these two sciences form what is usually called *empirical psychology.*[18]

The investigations of this pure, factical, scientific psychology need to have as their foundations a pure *eidetic* and *aprioric* psychology. This latter, namely, phenomenological psychology, restricts its activities, too, to the realm of the purely psychical, and concentrates then on the very *essence* of the psychic phe-

18. Husserl, *Ideen I,* p. 395; *Ph P,* pp. 217–22, 285, 324–28; *Crisis,* pp. 211–15, 224–26.

nomena rather than on their factual aspects. In so doing it must first reduce facts to "unities of meaning" (phenomenological-psychological reduction) and then reduce these concrete unities of meaning to their invariable structures (eidetic reduction).

Anyone who reflects critically upon this position will find a basic inconsistency in this view in that phenomenological psychology as such is unable to account for the essential structures of psychic phenomena as we actually experience them. Husserl has felt this inconsistency, but to the best of my knowledge has never taken it very seriously. Obviously, this is due not to any lack of flexibility on his part, but rather to the position in which empirical psychology (insofar as Husserl was familiar with it) found itself at that time. Referring to the fact that phenomenological psychology must provide us with the fundamental concepts which, in describing the a priori structures of the psychical as such, must govern every possible psychological description, he notes explicitly that a typical problem manifests itself here. For, he says, the a priori of *empirical* psychology is much more extensive than that which is explained by phenomenological psychology. *Empirical* psychology as a science of the psychical which manifests itself in the given world as a real moment, and thus belongs to nature as psychophysical datum, is also to be co-founded, therefore, by the a priori of physical nature. The necessary consequence of this is, Husserl continues, that *empirical* psychology is based on the empirical and aprioric sciences of nature, also. *Ultimately it is even founded in its own a priori, which belongs to the psychophysical as such.* In other words, the a priori of empirical psychology is not exclusively phenomenologically psychological, for it depends not only on the essence of the psychical, but also on the essence of the physical, and more particularly upon the essence of psychophysical organic nature as such.[19]

These short remarks do not do justice to Husserl's conception of the meaning and function of his phenomenological psychology. But I hope nevertheless that they contain all the elements necessary for an understanding of the further developments of Husserl's ideas by other phenomenologists, a subject to which we may now turn our attention.

19. Husserl, *Ph P*, pp. 324–28.

[II] FURTHER DEVELOPMENT OF HUSSERL'S ORIGINAL CONCEPTION

MANY PHILOSOPHERS AND PSYCHOLOGISTS have been most favorably impressed with Husserl's conception of the meaning and function of "phenomenological psychology." And yet only a very few actually employ his insights without major modifications. The reasons for this seem to be twofold. First there is the fact that our contemporary conception of the subject matter, meaning, and function of *empirical* psychology is considerably different from the one Husserl had in mind. On the other hand, the major difficulties experienced by those who have studied Husserl's ideas are not to be found in that fact alone, but must be traced back to the transcendental phenomenology on which Husserl's explanations concerning phenomenological psychology are founded. Since both of these reasons are very important for a genuine understanding of the development which has taken place since Husserl's death in 1938, I shall comment on them briefly before going into detail regarding that development itself. First, I should like to make some very brief historical remarks on the origin of empirical psychology and on the position in which Husserl found this science in 1880.[20]

Before Descartes's time the term "psychology" was used exclusively for the philosophical study of the phenomena characteristic of the lives of men and animals. Although Descartes remained substantially within this tradition, nonetheless he laid (without his knowing it) the theoretical foundation for an *empirical* investigation of these phenomena.

At a certain moment in his development Descartes (influenced by others) came to the insight that it should be possible to conceive of the human body as a beautifully organized and extremely complicated machine. He thought he could develop this idea without in any sense endangering human values because, before explicitly materializing this idea, he had already "saved"

20. Cf. G. Gusdorf, *Introduction aux sciences humaines: Essai critique sur leurs origines et leur développements* (Paris: Presses Universitaires de France, 1960) pp. 88–93; E. Boring, *A History of Experimental Psychology* (New York: Appleton, 1957), *passim*; Kockelmans, *Edmund Husserl's Phenomenological Psychology*, pp. 36–38 *passim*.

the genuinely human values by stating that man is substantially soul. Once it is accepted that all genuinely human phenomena can and must be explained by analyzing the "thinking substance," there can be no danger for human values if one attempts to explain all other phenomena which seem to accompany the "genuinely human phenomena" by appealing to mechanical forces and laws governing the automaton in which the human soul dwells.

Thus, in his attempt to account *philosophically* for the mode of being characteristic of man, Descartes claims that man consists of two separate and distinct substances, each of which is to be studied by a different discipline. Man's spiritual substance forms the proper subject matter of metaphysics, whereas man's body must be studied by "physics," which is related to metaphysics as the trunk of a tree is related to its roots.

When we look at Descartes's investigations concerning man from our *contemporary* point of view, it is clear that he succeeded in founding an *empirical* science of the human body, and that he achieved this only at the expense of an ontological separation between man and his body. Metaphysics leaves the study of the human body to physics, but in so doing must pay the price of excluding the human body from the human reality. To make it a fitting subject for scientific investigation, the human body is to be estranged from man himself. After splitting the human reality into two different and independent parts, Descartes was at a loss to restore the unity which all of us experience in our everyday life. His attempts in this direction in *Les Passions de l'âme* and *Correspondance* failed completely.

Closer analysis reveals, furthermore, that Descartes's vision of man becomes understandable only in the light of an implicit Neo-Platonic point of view. While remaining within the temper of his time, Descartes tried to account for man as spirit, man as person, in terms of a spiritualistic metaphysics which finally reaches back to the philosophies of Augustine and Plato. On the other hand he wanted to account for the fact that (as far as his body is concerned) man can be brought within the realm of science. Proceeding along these lines, he indeed prepared for a strict science of the human body, but this science was no longer a science of man. Descartes's mechanistic anthropology is perhaps a genuine mechanics, but it is surely not a genuine anthropology.

At any rate, Descartes's importance to empirical psychology lies especially in the fact that his research concerning the human body laid the foundation for the later physiology and physiological psychology, whereas his studies of consciousness, on the other hand, formed the basis for a future psychology of consciousness. It was to take many years before an explicit physiology as well as a psychology of consciousness would be developed, and there is no doubt, either, that many other factors influenced the development of these sciences. It would be fruitful to follow this development closely during the period between 1650 and 1880, when, from the first biological and physiological investigations, phrenology and psychophysiology gradually developed under Bell, Magendie, Müller, and others, and when, on the other hand, scientists under the influence of Locke's and Hume's empiricism later developed empirical psychology by subjecting the "ghost in the machine" to principles and laws analogous to those governing Cartesian physics, thus creating what Stuart Mill aptly calls a "mental chemistry." Only then would it become clear how under Fechner, von Helmholtz, Herbart, and Wundt these two empirical sciences, prepared in the Cartesian doctrine of the "ghost in the machine," could come to full development, and how later, at the beginning of the twentieth century, they could merge into what we now call "empirical psychology."

We have already pointed to the fact that Husserl originally understood "empirical psychology" as Wundt's psychology of consciousness. Husserl undoubtedly followed the development which took place in psychology after 1900, but there is little evidence that he was in any sense sympathetic to the new ideas then appearing. In 1927 he still believed that the shortcomings of nineteenth-century psychology could and should be corrected not by pursuing the basic ideas of classical behaviorism, which he conceived of as a form of "naturalism," but by admitting a "phenomenological psychology" in addition to the psychophysical psychology and the psychology of consciousness with which he was familiar since the days he had been in contact with Wundt.

Today the situation is obviously quite different. When one speaks of "empirical psychology," one very seldom has in mind what Wundt and Ebbinghaus understood by the term; most people conceive of empirical psychology as that scientific study of man's behavior which makes use only of empirical methods. And the question we have to answer today is whether or not such an empirical psychology is meaningful and whether or not such a conception of psychology presupposes a "phenomenological psychology" somehow analogous to the one Husserl had in mind. Since it is my intention to return to this question in the final section of this essay, let us consider now the second, more important reason why many contemporary phenomenologists have developed Husserl's views far beyond the perspective of his *transcendental* phenomenology.[21]

In this context it is perhaps meaningful to indicate first of all some of the major "problem areas" involved. To begin with, there is Husserl's idea that philosophy is a presuppositionless, rigorous science, and connected with this view the idea that philosophy's main task consists in providing a solid foundation for all other sciences. This explains why Husserl demands that no philosophical insight can be accepted as such if it is not founded upon apodictic evidence. Such evidence cannot be reached except by performing the transcendental reduction whose main task is to eliminate everything that is not, or at least cannot be made, apodictically evident. Then there is Husserl's conception, the origin of which is equally found in Descartes and Kant, that consciousness is the privileged *locus* where all philosophical problems are to be decided. Husserl seldom, if ever, talks about man as such; when he speaks of man, he always does so in terms of "consciousness." From this it becomes understandable that he conceived of intentionality merely as the essential characteristic of consciousness, and notably of cognitive activities. Husserl did not sufficiently realize that man himself is intentional in each mode of his behavior as man, and that for this reason it makes good sense to speak of man in terms of ek-sistence.[22] Finally, Husserl did not sufficiently

21. Kockelmans, *Edmund Husserl's Phenomenological Psychology*, pp. 314–51, and the literature quoted there, particularly: Strasser, *Phenomenology and the Human Sciences*, pp. 245–320; Ludwig Landgrebe, *Philosophie der Gegenwart* (Bonn: Athenaeum, 1952), chap. 1; *Der Weg der Phänomenologie* (Gütersloh: Mohn, 1963); W. Biemel, "Husserls Encyclopaedia-Britannica Artikel und Heideggers Anmerkungen dazu," *Tijdschrift voor Philosophie*, XII (1950) 246–89; Paul Ricoeur, *Husserl: An Analysis of His Phenomenology*, trans. Edward G. Ballard and Lester E. Embree (Evanston, Ill.: Northwestern University Press, 1967); Hans-Georg Gadamer, *Wahrheit und Methode: Grundzüge einer philosophischen Hermeneutik* (Tübingen: Mohr, 1960).

22. The term "ek-sistence" was introduced by Heidegger. In *Being and Time* he used the German term "Existenz"; since *Letter on Humanism* he

realize that all human phenomena are intrinsically historical and that thus they cannot merely be analyzed and described but must necessarily be interpreted (hermeneutics). These and other similar reflections have been the reasons why many philosophers and psychologists interested in Husserl's conceptions finally associated themselves with the existentialist interpretation of Husserl's philosophy as given by Heidegger, Sartre, Merleau-Ponty, and others.

In trying to characterize the move from transcendental to existential phenomenology more adequately, one encounters very great difficulties. Anyone who has, if only superficially, gone through the "existentialist" literature knows how arduous and delicate a task it is to arrive at a characterization which would be equally applicable to the philosophical conceptions of Heidegger, Jaspers, Marcel, Sartre, Merleau-Ponty, and others. Thus, in trying to describe the events which occurred between 1927 and 1948 we can by no means satisfy ourselves with the remark that during this period the merging of "phenomenology" and "existentialism" was brought about.[23] For without further specification neither the term "phenomenology" nor the term "existentialism" has a clear meaning. It seems more useful, therefore, to characterize the new style of philosophy by briefly comparing it with Husserl's original conception of phenomenology. Here again we shall limit ourselves to just those aspects which are immediately relevant for our theme.

After World War I profound dissatisfaction developed over the way in which realism dealt with ontological problems; yet the feeling of uneasiness about Husserl's idealism was equally as strong. Husserl's identification of being and being-object called for sharp criticism, and the new generation of philosophers cer-

---

has usually employed the word "Ek-sistenz" in order to avoid misunderstanding. The term "ek-sistence" does not have the meaning which the word "existence" normally has in English, nor the meaning of the technical term "existentia" as opposed to "essentia." The term expresses the idea that man's essence is to be understood in terms of "standing out" (ek-sistere). Man is certainly a "subject," but he is an ek-sisting subject that always places itself outside itself in the world. Man essentially stands out toward the world in which his fellow men and the things appear to him in the way they are. In Heidegger's view no genuine mode of man's being can be conceived which is not a mode of being in and toward the world.

23. Heidegger's *Being and Time* appeared in 1927, Merleau-Ponty's *Sense and Non-Sense* in 1948.

tainly could not be persuaded to accept the idea that the existence of an anonymous consciousness, an "impersonal" consciousness, as Husserl called it,[24] that is to say, a consciousness of nobody, contains the solution for all ontological and epistemological problems.

For Husserl, being is being-object-for-consciousness, and as such being is constituted by transcendental consciousness. This implies that all modes of being and all regions of beings correspond to different modes of constitution. The final reason for Husserl's adopting the view that being is a priori the correlate of consciousness is to be found in the fact that Husserl wanted to arrive at something genuinely unquestionable which as such can be the ground of all that is. Husserl believed that this absolute root consists in transcendental subjectivity. Now if transcendental subjectivity must indeed be the ultimate ground of all that is, then this means that all that is must ultimately be constituted in and by this subjectivity. Thus all being must be dissolved in the subjectivity's consciousness of it; transcendental subjectivity becomes the only absolute and real being.

Later phenomenologists have offered several major objections to this view. First of all, they say, if phenomenology as the process by means of which we let things manifest themselves characterizes the standard method of philosophy, then this conception of philosophy presupposes that originally there is something which is not yet manifest and in that sense still hides itself. That which is not yet manifest does not consist in the constitutive activities of a transcendental ego, but in the being of beings (the things themselves) and the totality of all meaning or the world within which these things can appear as meaningful.[25]

Another objection is connected with Husserl's conception of the ego. For Husserl, transcendental subjectivity as the ultimate source of all meaning is as such worldless. Later phenomenologists claim that the relationship between the human subjectivity and the world belongs to the very *essence* of that subjectivity *as finite*. In other words, where Husserl tries to free the ego

24. Edmund Husserl, Ms. 37 IV 26, quoted by Drüe, *Husserls System der phänomenologischen Psychologie*, p. 242.
25. Martin Heidegger, *Being and Time*, trans. John Macquarrie and Edward Robinson (London: SCM, 1962) pp. 49–63; William J. Richardson, *Heidegger: Through Phenomenology to Thought* (The Hague: Nijhoff, 1963), pp. viii–xxii.

from the world and everything which is mundane by means of his reductions, later phenomenologists claim that the human subjectivity is essentially being-in-the-world and only as such discloses the world. For them Husserl's pure ego is merely an artificial abstraction which is to guarantee the apodicticity of philosophy's understanding of the world. In fact, however, such a conception hampers our understanding of man's own mode of being (his ek-sistence, his standing-out toward things and the world), and, in the final analysis, the world itself.[26]

Anyone who adopts the point of view suggested by existential phenomenology obviously must give up the idea of a presuppositionless philosophy and the possibility of ever being able to reach apodictic evidence in regard to the world. Among other things this means that philosophy must pay full attention to the fact that being shows itself and hides itself at the same time and, thus, that a certain negativity, a certain experience of "nothingness," always accompanies our experience of being.[27]

Another consequence of this conception of phenomenology is that the starting point of philosophy is found not in an epistemology of certain theoretically cognitive activities, but rather in an analytic of man's being as being-in-the-world. For, from the preceding reflection, it would appear that the new generation of phenomenologists is trying to find access to genuine ontology by way of an analytic of the "tragedy" of man's ek-sistence, which obviously is intrinsically finite, temporal, and historical. To these writers, an existential analytic of man's being is the means of elucidating the general framework in which basic ontological problems can be formulated and philosophically dealt with. But this means that the existential analytic of man's being, in a certain sense at least, has to play the role of classical epistemology.[28] It is even possible in such an analytic to show that certain fundamental epistemological problems are quasi-problems and to explain why and how they could ever have arisen in Descartes's day. This means, furthermore, that it is meaningless to try to talk about man in terms of "pure consciousness," "pure ego," and "transcendental subjectivity."

26. Joseph J. Kockelmans, "Husserl on World-Constitution," in *Analecta Husserliana*, ed. A.-T. Tymieniecka (Dordrecht: Reidel, 1971), pp. 11–35.
27. Richardson, *Heidegger*, pp. 16–24.
28. Heidegger, *Being and Time*, pp. 244–56.

Finally, existential phenomenology claims that Husserl's postulate of radical presuppositionlessness must be replaced by the basic principle of hermeneutics. Philosophy then becomes identified with a universal ontology based on a hermeneutical interpretation of man's being as being-in-the-world. The Cartesian view to which Husserl subscribes, namely, that every philosopher must begin his philosophy by taking his point of departure in something which is apodictically evident, strikes the new generation of thinkers as unreasonable. At the very moment the philosopher begins to reflect, he has already engaged himself in the world, society, history, language. It is impossible to eradicate all of this by means of the transcendental reduction. The phenomena, the things themselves, must be accepted by the philosopher the way they really are, but this can be done only by interpreting them on the basis of a conception of the world which is already there before the philosopher can begin to reflect. But although the philosopher cannot deny that in doing so he takes his point of departure in presuppositions, he obviously cannot content himself by accepting them without further investigation. He must try to understand his own presuppositions and must bring that of which they are the presuppositions into a unity with these presuppositions themselves by means of a hermeneutic unfolding. In other words, the ontological presuppositions are justified by what is ontologically unfolded, clarified, and justified, thanks to the hermeneutical interpretation of the meaning as this manifests itself historically.[29]

These few remarks certainly do not adequately characterize the difference between Husserl's transcendental phenomenology and existential philosophy. As we have indicated, if we were to go into greater detail it would become clear, also, that very deep differences of opinion are to be found among authors such as Marcel, Heidegger, Jaspers, Sartre, and Merleau-Ponty. But as we return now to our main theme, phenomenological psychology, we may perhaps say that, notwithstanding the innumerable differences in the phenomenological movement as a whole, there are only two major currents to be distinguished as far as phenomenological psychology is concerned.[30] For those who adhere to the first conception there is no longer a determinate discipline

29. *Ibid.*, pp. 61–63; Gadamer, *Wahrheit und Methode*, pp. 250–89.
30. Kockelmans, *Edmund Husserl's Phenomenological Psychology*, pp. 332–43.

called "phenomenological psychology" which is to be carefully distinguished on the one hand from empirical psychology, as the term is traditionally used, and on the other hand from phenomenological philosophy. Human reality, they believe, cannot be studied with the help of empirical methods, and for this reason a descriptive and interpretative phenomenological psychology is to be substituted for what is commonly called "empirical psychology." In this case, the term "phenomenological psychology," like the expressions "Gestalt psychology" and "behaviorist psychology," refers to a current in contemporary psychology which defends a conception of psychology quite different from that defended by most other trends and schools in psychology.

The second group of authors holds that the term "phenomenological psychology" still refers to a determinate discipline which is to be distinguished from empirical psychology as well as from philosophy. Following Husserl more closely, these authors claim that phenomenological psychology is to furnish empirical psychology with the necessary foundation for its empirical investigations by means of a descriptive and interpretative explanation of the human meaning of the phenomena with which empirical psychology deals in its observations, experiments, tests, and so on. Instead of claiming that empirical psychology in the traditional sense of the term is impossible, these authors contend that the results of an empirical approach of the human reality is bound by typical limitations and that it is precisely these limitations which make a phenomenological psychology necessary.

In this part of the essay we have seen that two different conceptions of phenomenological psychology are found in contemporary phenomenology. One conceives of phenomenological psychology as a trend in contemporary psychology, the other uses the term to refer to a distinct discipline to be distinguished from empirical psychology. Although I find the second view preferable, it is nonetheless important to dwell for a moment on the arguments which can be set forth in favor of the first conception.

The members of the first group of phenomenologists claim that their particular approach to psychology applies in an analogous way to all the other sciences of man, and that it is advantageous to study the problems of psychology within the much broader context of the sciences of man in general. Furthermore, they are of the opinion that the sciences of man, and psychology and sociology in particular, have from the very outset attempted to imitate the empirical sciences of nature, although it has gradually become evident, according to this view, that such a "physicalization" of the sciences of man leads to serious problems. Because of the seriousness of these problems, the authors in question claim that one must draw the conclusion that there is an essential difference between the sciences of nature and the sciences of man. Explaining this position in greater detail, most of these authors defend the view that we must contrive a new set of methods which both guarantee intersubjectively valid conclusions and yet respect the specifically human character of man, that is to say, that man as man is the originator and organizer of his own world.[31]

In this connection the crucial problem for any empirical science of man is the following: How can man *as man* be made the "object" of empirical investigation? Upon closer consideration it becomes evident that this question has several aspects. First of all, the scientist who deals with individuals and groups as originators and organizers of their respective "worlds" must certainly include his own science in these worlds, because it is evident that individuals and especially societies are deeply influenced by modern psychology and sociology. However, such an inclusion means that the one who studies the human sciences changes his own subject matter as and because he studies it, so that the question must be asked: Where, then, is the firm foundation that is needed in the pursuit of a supposedly "objective" empirical study.[32]

This first group of phenomenologists asks a further question: Is not the creation and also the organization of a world an expression of human freedom? Although the life of an individual and the "culture" of a group reveal a definite style, still the question must be asked as to whether or not it is possible, empirically, to investigate free activities. If "being free," for instance, should mean "to be able to do whatever one wants," including "being able to be unreasonable, immoral, unsocial, unjust, and inhuman," how would it be possible to describe these changeable

31. Strasser, *Phenomenology and the Human Sciences*, pp. 5–7.
32. *Ibid.*, pp. 7–8.

beings, to compare their behavior, to characterize their realizations, and to discover general laws applying to them?[33]

Finally, individual human beings as well as social groups are sensitive to values, they are attracted to purposes, and they make projects. But how is it possible to "measure" values? And even if we agree that there is an "objective hierarchy of values," and that the appreciation of values gives rise to the motives which determine man's actions, how do we know what an individual man or a group is going to decide and to choose? Here, are we not fully in the realm of the purely subjective, in which no real science is possible?[34]

We may say at this point that all of these questions indicate reasons why the problem of the empirical study of man as man places us in a dilemma: Either we accept the idea that the only empirical method possible is that used in the empirical sciences of nature, which in fact renders an empirical science of *man as man* impossible, or we accept the possibility of an empirical science of *man as man,* a view requiring first a proof that a second form of "objectivity" in the realm of the empirical sciences is possible, and then a delineation of its fundamental characteristics. If we adopt the first point of view and see physics as the model science and the example to be followed in every kind of empirical research, we must demand that the conceptual framework, method, and scientific apparatus to be used in the different sciences do not deviate *essentially* from those of physics. We may admit, of course, that *accidental* modifications will be possible in the application of empirical methods to the various realms pertaining to the study of man, but must demand that in these accidental modifications attention be paid to the continuum running from physics to chemistry, biochemistry, biology, physiology, and the behavioristic currents in psychology and sociology. The consequence of this point of view will necessarily be that the empirical sciences of man will cease to deal with what is typically human, because it is clear that the methods used by the empirical sciences of nature cannot be applied to human behavior *as such,* since those methods abstract, and must abstract, from certain aspects which are essential for human behavior *as such.* For the method of the empirical

33. *Ibid.,* p. 8.
34. *Ibid.,* pp. 8–9.

sciences of nature is based on a complete abstraction from the human subject. The goal of "objective" science is to achieve a systematic explanation which is universally valid and subject to controlled verification by anyone at any time; such an explanation must be "causal" and, therefore, must deal with a world of "facts" which in themselves are precisely independent of the subjectivity of the observer. Finally, the rich and variegated realm of life-world experiences must be reinterpreted in terms of experiments involving a limited and controllable number of variables which can be codified in abstract mathematical formulae or by some similar symbolic construction.[35]

If, however, we adopt the second point of view, which accepts the possibility of an empirical science of *man as man,* we may admit that man as part of nature can be studied legitimately as a body among bodies. But on the other hand, we must maintain simultaneously that as regards a total and integral explanation of human behavior *as such,* we are in need of more subtle and less abstract methods of investigation, because we are concerned here first and foremost with the experiencing subject himself, the world of meaning and value which depends on the free and personal intervention of the subject, and also on the not-yet-free and not-yet-conscious decisions of man taken on the level of the unconscious (Freud), or the "owned" human body (Marcel, Sartre, Merleau-Ponty).

Faced with this dilemma, these phenomenologists feel that a choice between the two possibilities is not very difficult. If it is really true, they say, that empirical science must leave outside the competence of a strictly scientific method considerations such as the proper activity of the behaving subject as such, thus making impossible any explanation of why it is that my life has meaning and value for me, and if empirical science, furthermore, has to abstract from the intentionality, the purposiveness, and the finality of my behavior as it is experienced by me, as well as of the gestural and linguistic expressions of those purposes and meanings, then we need a different type of method, because these aspects are precisely constitutive to human behavior as such.[36]

Speaking for myself, I am convinced that modern science

35. *Ibid.,* pp. 21–25.
36. *Ibid.,* pp. 25–26.

has found an acceptable solution for some aspects of the problems mentioned and, furthermore, that contemporary philosophy of science has made a great contribution toward clarifying the issues and suggesting answers for a great number of them. All of this notwithstanding, there still remains the disturbing question of whether *man as man* is a valid subject for empirical investigation. As far as this question in particular is concerned, the phenomenologists just referred to certainly make a point, but it seems to me that they have not succeeded in bringing the genuine issue clearly into focus. In my opinion this is mainly because they never stipulate what precisely is to be understood by the expression "empirical science" and just what element in the empirical methods it is that exactly precludes an empirical study of man as man. Furthermore, while some people claim that the existing empirical methods are to be adapted to the requirements of each particular subject, and others speak of the necessity of developing completely new methods, to the best of my knowledge, no one has ever specified precisely what these statements mean from a practical standpoint. For this reason I want to try now to make more explicit just what the expression "empirical science" stands for.

[III] WHAT IS MEANT BY THE EXPRESSION "EMPIRICAL SCIENCE"?

BEFORE ATTEMPTING TO SPECIFY exactly what is meant by "empirical science," we should take note of certain distinctions which will help us to avoid confusion and misunderstanding. First of all, it is an obvious fact that the empirical sciences themselves can be studied from different perspectives. They can be studied from a historical point of view in the history of science, from a social point of view in the social sciences, from a logical point of view in the logic of science, and from a philosophical point of view in either epistemology (Neo-Kantianism) or fundamental ontology (existential philosophy). The most universal practice in the neopositivist literature notwithstanding, I feel that in this particular context it is necessary to make an explicit distinction between logic of science and philosophy of science, and in the case of the latter to speak of ontological rather than epistemological reflections. From the viewpoint of existential phenomenology this standpoint can be defended in the following way. Logic of science does and must presuppose certain conditions which of necessity must be fulfilled on the part of the scientific praxis of the scientists as well as on the part of the subject matter of investigation, although logic itself and taken as such does not and cannot make these conditions a theme of *logical* investigation. In Kantian philosophy the study of these conditions was assigned to epistemology, taken as critique of reason, whereas in existential philosophy the study of these conditions is given to fundamental ontology, for reasons to which I have already alluded in Part II. In justifying their point of view, phenomenologists argue along the following lines. The problem of specifying the conditions of possibility under which a science dealing with a determinate region of things from a determinate point of view can be developed and then expressed in statements which can be logically analyzed, as is done de facto in logic of science, refers in the final analysis to a basic conception of man in general, and to the ontological status of his different orientations toward the world, notably to his theoretical orientation, in particular. Studying the essence of man and the ontological status of his orientations toward the world is a matter not of logic or epistemology but of fundamental ontology.[37]

In this connection, furthermore, it is important to make a distinction between science taken as process (*in actu*) and science taken as result (*in habitu*). When one speaks about "logic of science," one seldom speaks directly about science as process, but mainly considers science as result and as already expressed in linguistic statements of a natural or artificial language. Logic, then, is interested in the logical relationships between the statements in which the results of science as process are expressed.[38] This relationship can be described, for example, in terms of a deductive-nomic scheme. Ontology of science, on the other hand, as we have said, is principally interested in science *in actu*.

Thus the question as to what precisely is to be understood by an "empirical science" can be answered from either a logical

37. For a more detailed justification of this view, cf. Joseph J. Kockelmans, *World in Science and Philosophy*, pp. 77–168.
38. Richard S. Rudner, *Philosophy of Social Science* (Englewood Cliffs, N.J.: Prentice-Hall, 1966), pp. 4–18.

or an ontological point of view. From a logical point of view, one could say, perhaps, that a science is considered empirical if it fulfills the following conditions:

1. It approaches its subject matter by formulating hypotheses which must fulfill conditions that are to be further specified.
2. It tests its hypotheses by means of procedures which are guided by criteria whose precise meaning and function are to be further determined.
3. It explains its hypotheses by relating them to laws or lawlike statements in a way which must be articulated in greater detail.
4. It verifies its explanations by using a principle of verificacation which must fulfill certain conditions that are to be further specified.
5. It follows certain rules in formulating the definitions of its basic concepts.

In formulating these conditions it is not my intention to claim that they are necessary and sufficient conditions; nor do I feel it to be my task here to specify them in greater detail.[39] My only purpose in setting up this provisional list of conditions is to call attention to the fact that in approaching the problem from this point of view it is very difficult to see why it should be said that empirical sciences of man are impossible, or even why they should be seen as confronted with problems which are intrinsically different from those met in the sciences of nature.

However, if we approach the same problem from an ontological perspective, the situation will be quite different. By adopting an ontological standpoint and taking science as process, one could then say, for instance, that the expression "empirical science" refers to a certain kind of *theoretical* knowledge which proceeds systematically by using typically *empirical* methods. This circumscription could be further explained along the following lines. The term "theoretical" is used to exclude all forms

---

39. For a possible specification of these conditions, see, for instance: Carl G. Hempel, *Aspects of Scientific Explanation and Other Essays in the Philosophy of Science* (New York: The Free Press, 1965); Wolfgang Stegmüller, *Wissenschaftliche Erklärung und Begründung* (Berlin: Springer Verlag, 1969); Stegmüller, *Theorie und Erfahrung* (Berlin: Springer Verlag, 1970).

of knowledge which are already found on a more primordial level, namely, on the level of our concernful dealing with things and careful dealing with our fellow men. It is typical for the *theoretical* attitude that in it man confines himself to "observing" the world in such a way that he is no longer completely engaged and involved in it. Man comes to a theoretical kind of knowledge only when he "holds himself back" from any manipulation or utilization, from his work, his fabrications, his activities, and, in a word, from his life in and with intramundane things. The result of this change of attitude is that the things which man initially "manipulated" within the framework of his original, environmental world now receive a new character; they are no longer ready-to-hand, but become now present-at-hand; man no longer wants to do something with things, but confines himself now to being interested merely in the way things look (*eidos*). This is possible only by detaching them from their original, environmental world, by letting them appear exclusively in a frame that is no longer immediately related to man and his "practical" concern, and, finally, by stripping things as well as man's approach to them of all limits and limitations typical for the environment in which man originally encountered these things.[40]

The expressions "systematically" and "empirical methods" are added to the definition in order to distinguish this particular type of theory from all nonsystematic, theoretical looking-at-things, as well as from philosophy and all other eidetic ways of knowing things theoretically (regional ontologies). What is meant by "typically empirical methods" is still to be specified.

Toward this end we may take as our point of departure the general reflections which follow. Each empirical science which de facto has developed deals with a determinate realm of things, as well as with the things which belong to this realm, from a determinate point of view or perspective. From this we may conclude that there is no empirical science which claims, or rightly can claim, to deal with all things from all possible points of view. Positively formulated, this means that each empirical science must begin by somehow delineating its realm of investigation and by projecting the ontological structure necessary if a given thing is to be a valid subject matter for investigation by that particular science. In the physical sciences, for instance,

40. Heidegger, *Being and Time*, pp. 86–90, 244–50.

nature is projected mathematically. That is to say, it is decided in advance that considering the totality of all things which could be studied scientifically (the totality of all things which man encounters in his theoretical attitude as merely present-at-hand), only those which in a certain sense can be quantitatively determined will be taken into consideration. Once this decision is made, the basic concepts to be used in this science are determined, and a fundamental option is made in regard to the concrete methods to be used and the conception of truth that will guide this theoretical endeavor.[41] For my purpose here it is of utmost importance to stipulate that this determination of the formal aspect under which the things that belong to a certain region are to be investigated necessarily comprises formalization, functionalization, and some kind of quantification.[42]

Formalization means here the description of things or events with respect to their formal properties; formalization, therefore, necessarily implies abstraction of some material or contentlike elements in preference to a group of formal characteristics. *Functionalization* refers to the consideration of phenomena which are already formalized in terms of other formalized phenomena, according to the general scheme "if *p* then *q*" or any further development of this scheme. Formalization and functionalization give the scientist the possibility of describing phenomena with the help of general *rules* and *laws*. *Quantification* refers to the process by which the relationship between condition and conditioned is described by employing numbers or other mathematical entities. It is evident that when these procedures are applied the original phenomena become reduced to more or less ideal entities which are abstract in comparison to the originally given phenomena.

Thematization, which comprises all of these steps, and adopts in each science a different form determined by the subject matter of the relevant science, opens up for scientists the possibility of questioning a certain region of intramundane things under a determinate, comparable aspect within the general perspective prescribed by the abstract scheme "if-then." In materializing this possibility systematically, scientists thematize these things in such a way that they can no longer be in-

41. *Ibid.*, pp. 408–14.
42. Linschoten, *Idolen van de psycholoog*, pp. 24–27.

terrogated within the science in any manner except that which has been, in principle, already determined by that thematizing project. In view of the fact that in all natural sciences formalizing functionalization is connected with quantification (without which it would be impossible to reach a high degree of accuracy), the expression "comparable" of necessity takes on the meaning "countable or measurable," both terms to be taken in a broader sense.[43]

Turning once again to the sciences of man and to psychology in particular, we see clearly that the question of whether or not *empirical* sciences of man are possible, and if so within what limits, is not *primarily* one of whether or not the statements of the human sciences can be systematically related to one another in a determinate way, but is connected, rather, with whether or not man's behavior allows for a thematization which essentially includes idealization and formalization. It is clear here, also, that the question of whether or not one is to allow for mathematization in this context is a derivative and secondary one, and that it can perhaps be answered most easily by conceiving of mathematics in a sufficiently broad way.[44]

It seems to me that, where the first question is concerned, it is apparent that, if applied to human phenomena, idealization and formalization necessarily imply that an important part of the meaning of the human phenomena must be left out of consideration. This is not to say, however, that consequently an empirical science of man is impossible, but merely that such a science has meaning within relatively narrow limits, and that, therefore, there is a place and need for another approach to human phenomena which is neither philosophical nor empirical.[45] I hope to develop these views more systematically in Part IV.

If my reflections are indeed valid, then it is not so difficult to understand why most phenomenologists have trouble in understanding the position of the logician, for whom an empirical science of man is obviously possible, and why conversely it is difficult for logicians to see the point of the phenomenologists, for whom it is apparent that a formalizing thematization within the realm of the human sciences means leaving out of considera-

43. Kockelmans, *World in Science and Philosophy*, pp. 155–66.
44. Linschoten, *Idolen van de psycholoog*, pp. 27–37.
45. Buytendijk, "Die Bedeutung," pp. 89–94.

tion what is most interesting, namely, the genuinely human meaning of these phenomena, a meaning which is *essentially* determined by man's facticity.

[IV] PHENOMENOLOGICAL PSYCHOLOGY AS A DESCRIPTIVE AND INTERPRETATIVE SCIENCE OF MAN

IN THE PREVIOUS SECTION I have tried to explain what I believe should be understood by the expression "empirical science," and in what sense this expression can be meaningfully applied to a scientific study of man. I have defended the thesis that empirical sciences of man are possible, and that each of these sciences tries to explain, at least in principle, a particular, clearly delineated aspect of man's life taken individually or socially. I have indicated, also, that such an explanation of man necessarily implies an "idealization" of the phenomena to be investigated in that this type of explanation necessarily involves formalization, functionalization, and perhaps some sort of quantification. Finally, I have argued that the "reductive models" to which such a way of thematizing man's life necessarily leads objectively describe and relate certain aspects of man's orientation toward the world, and that these "reductive models" are relatively poor in content in comparison with the immediately lived experiences which they are supposed to explain.

It is often said that the application of empirical methods to man's life must make an abstraction of precisely those aspects which, from a human point of view, are *exclusively* relevant, and that for this reason an empirical science of man is, if not impossible altogether, at least practically meaningless. Although I think there is a core of truth in this consideration, it seems to me nonetheless that the case is overstated. In evaluating the situation one has to realize, first of all, that no kind of theoretical knowledge can describe and explain the concrete as concrete. Furthermore, in representing man's orientation toward the world with the help of reductive "models," we must, indeed, set aside certain aspects of man's life which, taken concretely, are of the greatest importance; but we must realize, too, that in so doing we gain the possibility of defining certain aspects of man's behavior unambiguously, and of describing them in connection with other similar phenomena. Finally, it certainly is not true that an empirical investigation has to set aside *completely* all the aspects of man's behavior which, from a typically human point of view, are essential, such as meaning, purpose, value, finality, and so on. Contemporary literature shows that under certain conditions these aspects of man's orientation toward the world can be examined in an indirect way.[46]

All this, however, does not mean that an existential phenomenologist defending this point of view is insensitive to the problems to which his opponents really wish to point. If the view defended here necessarily implied a return to what Husserl called "the physicalization of the sciences of man" and to "naturalism," I could not subscribe to it. To recognize the limitations of the application of empirical methods to man's life is one thing; to claim that such an application is meaningless altogether is another. While I admit the possibility and importance of the empirical sciences of man, my major concern is with the question of whether in addition to the empirical sciences there could not be developed a science of man that would somehow "compensate" for the losses which the limitations essentially connected with an empirical approach necessarily entail. The desirability and necessity of such a new discipline have already been defended by Mach, Brentano, Stumpf, Dilthey, and others. It is not too difficult, on the basis of ideas taken from Husserl, Heidegger, and Sartre, to adapt their motivations to the point of view defended in this essay, and I propose to do that next.

The meaning and function of a descriptive science of man

A first question which we must try to answer is: What exactly does the expression "descriptive science of man" mean? In attempting to answer this question again, let us look first at Husserl's view on the meaning and function of his "phenomenological psychology," taken as the regional ontology of the psychical.[47]

We have seen that Husserl understands a "regional ontology" to be an aprioric, eidetic, intuitive, and purely descriptive

---

46. Linschoten, *Idolen van de psycholoog*, pp. 31–38.
47. See in general: Ludwig Landgrebe "Seinsregionen und regionale Ontologien in Husserls Phänomenologie," in *Der Weg der Phänomenologie*, pp. 143–62; Lannoy, "Phaenomenologie in Husserl"; E. Levinas, *Théorie de l'intuition dans la phénoménologie de Husserl* (Paris: Vrin, 1963), pp. 20–22.

science of the basic structures of the entities belonging to a certain region of beings. Since each regional ontology is a science to be carried out within the realm of the natural attitude, regional ontologies are *not philosophical disciplines.*

Husserl defends the necessity for "regional ontologies" by pointing to the fact that there is a gap to be filled between the empirical sciences and transcendental phenomenolgy. "Regional ontologies" presuppose the existence of the empirical sciences in the order of time, but they are not founded on these sciences or their results. The fundamental principles of "regional ontologies" are—on the contrary—to be brought to light by an accurate reflection, analysis, and description of the very essence of the entities belonging to a certain region. Because the extension of the different regions cannot be determined a priori and, on the other hand, because the precise delineation of the different regions cannot be the task of the empirical sciences which precisely presuppose this delineation, the different "regional ontologies" have to take their starting point in a "general ontology of the world of our immediate experience." It is clear that in Husserl's view the "regional ontologies" must find their ultimate and radical foundation in transcendental phenomenology, because without transcendental phenomenology the "regional ontology of the world of our immediate experience" is left in suspension as far as its foundations are concerned.[48]

Taking the foregoing into consideration, one sees that an existential-phenomenological view of science does not exclude regional ontologies. On the contrary, it even seems to require such "additional" sciences, although it is true that existential phenomenology describes the meaning and function of these ontologies in a different way.

For, if we realize that, notwithstanding the results obtained in them, time and again in the empirical sciences of man (to which we wish to limit ourselves here) important problems arise which cannot be solved with the help of the empirical methods *as such,* we can see that there is not only room, but even a certain need for these "additional" sciences, focusing all their attention on those aspects of man's orientation toward the world which the empirical sciences have had to leave out of consideration because of limitations essentially connected with the meth-

48. Husserl, *Ideas,* pp. 56–62, 158–63, 185–88.

ods employed. The difference between such a descriptive science and the correlative empirical sciences is that, whereas the empirical sciences focus attention on "facts," the descriptive scientist must first and foremost be faithful to the general and necessary structure of the phenomena to which these facts refer.

Provisionally we may say, then, that in this context the expression "descriptive science of man" means that regional ontology which tries to bring to light the essential and necessary structures of all the various modes of orientation toward the world which are characteristic of the entities belonging to the region of human beings. Such a science is of importance not only for empirical psychology, but also for all other empirical sciences of man.

It is not too difficult to determine the relationship between this regional ontology and the empirical sciences of man. The only problem is whether such a descriptive science is to be called a philosophical or nonphilosophical discipline. There can be no doubt that the answer to this question will depend largely on what one understands by the term "philosophy." Husserl answered this question by stating that "phenomenological psychology" is not a philosophical discipline because it does not make use of the transcendental reduction. Existential phenomenology rejects Husserl's reductions and must try, therefore, to motivate its answer in a different way. It seems to me that one could justify such an answer along the following lines. Given the fact that in existential phenomenology it is quite generally accepted that philosophy as such deals with the "Whole" (= *the* world in its historical development) and with man's place and function within this "Whole," [49] whereas the descriptive sciences focus attention only on the basic structures of the entities which together constitute a determinate region, that is, a *limited* realm of beings, it seems proper to defend the thesis that a descriptive science of man is not a philosophical discipline.

49. Heidegger, *Being and Time*, pp. 21–27, 227–28; Maurice Merleau-Ponty, *Le Visible et l'invisible* (Paris: Gallimard, 1964), 142–71; English translation by Alphonso Lingis (Evanston, Ill.: Northwestern University Press, 1968), pp. 105–29; Jean-Paul Sartre, *L'Etre et le néant: Essai d'ontologie phénoménologique* (Paris: Gallimard, 1943), 11–34; English translation by Hazel E. Barnes, *Being and Nothingness* (New York: Philosophical Library, 1956), pp. xlv–lxvii; Alphonse de Waelhens, *La Philosophie et les expériences naturelles* (The Hague: Nijhoff, 1961), 189–211; Kockelmans, *World in Science and Philosophy*, pp. 3–13.

Many phenomenologists, however, are of the opinion that although this standpoint could perhaps be defended in the case of other descriptive sciences, nevertheless it is unacceptable the moment the descriptive science of man comes into the picture. These authors substantiate their point of view by positing that the determination of man's place and function within the "Whole" necessarily implies a description of the essential structures of the various orientations of man toward the world, and vice versa. That is why, according to them, it is not meaningful to make a distinction between a descriptive science of man and philosophical anthropology.

Although many phenomenologists thus believe that the function ascribed to the descriptive science of man by Husserl and Sartre could be fulfilled by a philosophical anthropology in the style proposed by Heidegger in *Being and Time* or by Merleau-Ponty in his *Phenomenology of Perception*, it is my opinion, nevertheless, that it is preferable *not* to reduce this descriptive science of man to a philosophical anthropology. In maintaining this standpoint I am guided especially by the following considerations.

First of all, I agree that the determination of man's place and role within the "Whole" necessarily implies a description of the essential structure of man as man. However, I do not see that this statement requires that there be no point in making a distinction between a descriptive science of man and philosophical anthropology. I do not think that the function of a descriptive study of man presupposes an explicit orientation toward the question concerning the meaning of the "Whole," a question which (provided it is properly understood) in my opinion is the only fundamental philosophical question. Although the descriptive science of man, as well as philosophical anthropology, tries to delineate the essential structure of man as man, each of these sciences tries to materialize this task with a completely different intention.[50]

Furthermore, it should be evident that in this essay the desirability and necessity of a descriptive science of man has been defended solely on *methodological* grounds. Taken from this point of view I see no reason why, merely on the basis of those considerations, we should draw conclusions which would imply

50. Sartre, *Esquisse d'une théorie des émotions*, pp. 53–54.

that every scientist should adopt an existential-phenomenological viewpoint in philosophy. For, if it were really true that the empirical sciences of man necessarily require a phenomenology of man and society, understood as a philosophical discipline, on *merely methodological grounds* which have their origin in the "foundational crisis" of those sciences, then empirical investigations *as such* would be possible and legitimate only within the horizon of an existential-phenomenological philosophy. Obviously this is nonsense.

I shall try to formulate this statement in another way in order to avoid misunderstanding. If one defends the thesis that the empirical sciences of man are to be thought of as sciences which *necessarily* develop on the basis of, and also in the horizon of, a phenomenological philosophy, this standpoint *necessarily* requires that one be of the opinion that (1) all empirical sciences must be founded in a philosophical view of man and science, and (2) that this philosophical view is to be taken in the sense of a phenomenological philosophy. That would mean that any scientist who does not adopt *this philosophical* point of view is unable to account for the *human* meaning of the phenomena considered, and to really deal with man *as* man. It is precisely in the hope of avoiding such dangerous consequences that I am inclined to admit the existence of a nonphilosophical descriptive study of man between philosophy and the empirical sciences of man, because such a science *does not and cannot affect the scientific status of those sciences.*

To put it differently, when a psychologist, for instance, speaks of fear and undertakes in a test situation to determine something concrete about someone's being-afraid, what he then describes as fear must evidently be intersubjectively recognizable by every fellow scientist as what all of us experience as fear. An eidetic, intuitive, descriptive study of man seems to suffice to materialize this ideal. I see no reason why scientists should have to adopt the same point of view in regard to the question of the "Whole" in order to be able to agree on the very essence of a human phenomenon which everyone can experience immediately, at least in principle.

Whatever philosophical standpoint a scientist implicitly or explicitly adopts, he needs, in addition to his empirical investigations as such, a descriptive science, especially in the realm of the sciences of man. For, first of all, the scientist dealing with the sciences of man must be able to demarcate exactly the requirements which must be fulfilled by his empirical methods in order to be really able to investigate man's orientation toward the world; and this is impossible if he does not understand this orientation toward the world with respect to its essential structure and typically *human* modifications. Furthermore, summarizing the conclusions to which his investigation leads him, the scientist must try to reinterpret the results of his empirical investigation in terms of the immediately "lived world" in order to restore the human meaning to these results.

In adopting this point of view I am, however, influenced by still another motivation, which was implicit in my rejection of a "phenomenological psychology" as a school or trend. It is my conviction that in the realm of the empirical sciences there is no room for schools and trends in the sense in which we find them in philosophy. As long as we continue to find schools and trends in an empirical science, we know without going any further that the science in question is still not yet "mature," that it has not yet reached the level of a "strict and rigorous" science. Returning to the question under consideration, if we now conceive of "phenomenological psychology" as a philosophical discipline and if we demand, furthermore, that such a discipline be essential for an accurate understanding of the results of the empirical sciences, then once again we are introducing schools and trends into the realm of the empirical sciences of man. However, this cannot be understood in such a way as to imply that there ought to be a univocity of conviction in the sciences of man such as that found in physics and chemistry. The meaning of my remarks is only that I do not believe that the differences in conviction, and the disparity in terminology which is the necessary consequence of it, have to be so deep-seated that one is forced to speak of schools and trends whose *basic principles* exclude each other. It is my conviction that all of these differences, which ultimately have their origin in an explicitly or implicitly adopted philosophy, can be "neutralized" to a great extent, as soon as the influence of the adopted philosophical view of man and society on the empirical sciences is mediated by a descriptive study of man on which, otherwise, the influence of some kind of philosophy will have been naturally unavoidable. But even here the differences do not have to be so profound that a descriptive study written by a scientist adopting this philosophy cannot be understood or accepted by a scientist affiliated with another kind of philosophy.

Finally, it is self-evident that many of the differences just mentioned do not have to exist at all, in that they are exclusively the consequence of a lack of methodology and logic. It seems to me that logic of science could have an extremely fertile domain of investigation in this area.

Methodological considerations

Although I have repeatedly used the expression "descriptive science of man" in the ideas just presented, the meaning of this expression has been indicated in only a rather indirect way. Referring to Husserl's phenomenological psychology, understood as the "regional ontology of the psychical," I pointed out that what Husserl *intended* by this expression seems to be very important and that, indeed, there is a need for a descriptive science of man which can fill the gap between philosophy and the empirical sciences of man. In order to make our conception of this descriptive science of man more concrete, we must now focus our attention on the problem of the methods such a science must employ in order to reach its goal. In so doing I shall again take my starting point in Husserl's view and try to indicate briefly in what sense I think this view is to be reinterpreted.

We have seen that Husserl defines "phenomenological psychology," understood as the regional ontology of the psychical, as an aprioric, eidetic, intuitive, descriptive study of the psychical which—although it is to be carried out within the realm of the natural attitude—nonetheless presupposes a certain phenomenological-psychological reduction. The most important methods to be used in this science are, according to Husserl, "the method of free variation" and "intentional analysis." [51]

From what has been said, it is clear that I agree with Husserl regarding the function and subject matter of the science in question. The difference between Husserl's view and the one I am defending here is mainly a matter of the philosophical view from which the conception is defended. However, as I said before, the difference in philosophical orientation, and the difference in terminology which is the necessary consequence of it,

51. Husserl, *Ph P*, pp. 46–51, 72–87.

by no means immediately affect the essential structure and function of the science in question. Although there is a great difference in motivation and terminology, what is intended in both points of view is the same, as far as its essential structure and function are concerned.

In my opinion an analogous point of view is to be adopted in regard to the methods to be used in such a descriptive science. As we have seen, Husserl held that the method of free variation is essential to every regional ontology. This method is to be used in connection with intentional analyses, and both these methods are to be carried out in regard to phenomena which must be taken as "unities of meaning." This realm of phenomena itself is to be brought to light by means of a special phenomenological-psychological reduction.

From our criticism of Husserl's phenomenology it will be clear that in the view defended here there is no room for a reduction in Husserl's sense. What is to be brought to light are the essential structures of the fundamental modes of man's orientation toward the world as they are immediately "lived" in our being-in-the-world. With respect to the procedures which are to be used in doing so, a phenomenological-psychological reduction is superfluous.

But what about Husserl's intentional analysis and his "method of free variation"? In trying to answer this question I wish first to describe in a few words what Husserl himself understood by these methods. In the critical evaluation of Husserl's thoughts on these subjects, I hope to make it clear that this conception is to be not only reinterpreted but also extended. For it appears that in a descriptive science of man methods other than the ones used in a descriptive science of nature are necessary. The reason is that typically human phenomena cannot just be described as one would describe stones: They are to be interpreted, because they are intrinsically historical and as such function within a historical context. In other words the "real" meaning of human phenomena can never be brought to light without hermeneutical and dialectical methods which, as it were, follow on the heels of the "logic" which is intrinsic to and characteristic of these phenomena themselves. But this reinterpretation and expansion notwithstanding, I hope to be able to show, also, that for a limited domain of phenomena the two methods remain important.

The method of free variation.[52] Although the "method of free variation" and "intentional analysis," as Husserl conceives of them, belong together in principle, and from a practical point of view should go hand in hand, I wish, nevertheless, to deal with them separately, as Husserl himself always does.

Husserl adopts a priori the point of view that phenomenology is either a science of essences or it is no science at all. That is why it is so important for his conception of phenomenology that he be able to account for our knowledge of essences. In regard to essences Husserl adopts a point of view which at first sight seems to imply a contradiction. On the one hand he says that our knowledge of essences must take its point of departure in our knowledge of facts as these are ultimately given to us in perception; on the other hand he claims that our knowledge of essences is in no way dependent upon our knowledge of their concrete and factual realizations in the world—in other words, that essences are known to us by means of an original intuition. Husserl solves the apparent contradiction by claiming that it is possible to achieve an essential insight into the very nature of things by disengaging the essences from everything which is accidental to them, although they themselves are originally never given to us without these accidental features. The process which mediates between our knowledge of facts and our intuition of essences is what Husserl calls "ideation." [53]

In order to explain what is meant by "ideation," we must first call attention to the fact that Husserl uses the term "essence" to indicate *what* a thing is. Every essence can be expressed by an idea. Every empirical and individual intuition of our immediate perception can be transformed into an essential insight by means of "ideation." The object of such an insight is the corresponding *pure* essence or *eidos*. This *eidos* is a new kind of object: Just as the datum of individual and empirical intuition is an individual object, so is the datum of essential intuition a pure essence. Consequently, essential insight is a new kind of intuition; and, if it is insight in the strict sense of the term, it is a primordial object-giving act which grasps the essence in question in its authentic reality. Essential intuition, according to its very nature, is based on an individual intuition, although it does not presuppose any

52. *Ibid.*, 72–87.
53. Quentin Lauer, *The Triumph of Subjectivity* (New York: Harper & Row, 1958), pp. 69–73.

apprehension of an individual's reality. Hence it is certain that no essential intuition is possible when consciousness cannot freely direct its regard to an individual counterpart. Conversely, no individual intuition is possible unless there is a free possibility of carrying out an act of ideation. However, according to Husserl, all this does not alter the fact that the two kinds of intuition are fundamentally different.

The pure essence can be exemplified intuitively in data of our immediate experience, but also in data of pure fantasy. For instance, if in the play of fantasy we produce melodies, through ideation we can secure from this source a primordial insight into the pure essence of a melody. The question is, how, precisely, is this to be accomplished?

Husserl says that every experienced or fancied object can be interpreted as an *example* of a certain *eidos* and, therefore, as a prototype of possible modifications by a series of free variations in fantasy. Let us suppose that all these variations remain similar to the same prototype; then the complex of new instances produced in fantasy are permeated with an invariant, identical content, in terms of which all these arbitrary variations remain congruent, while their differences remain irrelevant. It is this invariant element which imposes limits on possible variations of the same prototype; it is that element without which an object of this kind can neither be thought of nor intuitively imagined. The intuition of the *eidos* is founded on the manifold of the variants produced in the process of arbitrary and free variation. This intuition of the *eidos*, however, consists in an active apprehension of that which was passively preconstituted in fantasy.[54]

It is my opinion that an important methodical device is contained in these considerations, particularly if the method of free variation is combined with intentional analysis. On the other hand, we have to realize that its practical applicability within the realm of a descriptive study of man is rather limited and that Husserl's conception of essences is to be reinterpreted from an existential point of view. In this regard Merleau-Ponty remarks that the essences about which Husserl speaks cannot be an end in themselves; they have only the meaning of a means. For it is

54. *Ibid.*, pp. 73–78. See also: Husserl, *Ideas I*, pp. 46–51, 180–93; *Ph P*, 72–87; *Erfahrung und Urteil: Untersuchungen zur Genealogie der Logik*, ed. Ludwig Landgrebe (1st ed., 1939; Hamburg: Claassen, 1954), pp. 410–28.

precisely our effective involvement in the world which is to be understood and made amenable to conceptualization, because it is this effective involvement in the world which polarizes all our conceptual particularizations. The need to proceed by way of essences means not that the study of man has to take them as its final objects but, on the contrary, that our ek-sistence is too tightly bound to the world to be able to know itself *as such* at the moment of its own involvement. In other words, our ek-sistence requires insight into the field of ideality in order to become acquainted with and to prevail over its facticity.[55]

Intentional analysis. Phenomena which not only "bear" meaning but which first and foremost "constitute" meaning, phenomena to which most of the fundamental modes of our orientation toward the world belong, cannot be adequately described solely by employing the method of free variation. It is for this realm of phenomena that Husserl proposes descriptive analyses, which—because of the fact that the phenomena to be analyzed and described are essentially intentional—are called intentional analyses. Let us now discuss what Husserl means by an "intentional analysis" and determine its exact function within his phenomenological philosophy as a whole.

According to Husserl, phenomenology tries to found every knowledge in evidence rooted immediately in intuition which, in turn, grasps the immediately given in itself as adequately as possible. Evidence, therefore, is ultimately identical with adequate self-givenness.[56] Husserl believes that by means of the transcendental reduction a field of transcendental experiences given in such evidence is brought to light. These transcendental experiences appear to be intentional experiences. But when the experiences are essentially intentional, it is not only the experiences themselves as such that are apodictically evident, but also their *cogitata,* provided, at least, we consider them exclusively inasmuch as they are immediately given in these experiences. The transcendental phenomenological reflection, thus, enables

55. Maurice Merleau-Ponty, *Phénoménologie de la perception* (Paris: Gallimard, 1945), pp. ix–x; English translation by Colin Smith, *Phenomenology of Perception* (New York: Humanities Press, 1962), pp. xiv–xvi.

56. Edmund Husserl, *Die Idee der Phänomenologie* (1907), ed. Walter Biemel (The Hague: Nijhoff, 1950), p. 59.

us to analyze and to describe the *cogitata* just as they were meant (*noemata*) and to describe the cogitations (*noeses*) correlated to these *noemata*.[57]

However, we have to realize here that consciousness is not just a whole made up of data that are like matches in a box; instead it is constituted of different types of syntheses, because that which is meant is, practically speaking, never identical with that which immediately appears.[58] Intentional analysis is guided by the fundamental insight that every consciousness is a meaning of its object meant, but that at any moment this something meant is more than what is explicitly given at that moment. The intending beyond itself which is necessarily implied in any conscious act must be considered an essential moment of every act.[59] In addition, the phenomenologist not only has to question the intentional object purely as such, but must also describe the noetic multiplicities of consciousness and their synthetic unity, which alone make up our intentional object in its essentially necessary unity.[60]

The most universal type of these analyses is indicated by the following scheme: *ego cogito cogitata*. In the particularization of this universal type, the intentional object plays the role of a transcendental guiding clue to the typical infinite multiplicities of possible cogitations. The point of departure is necessarily the given object taken "straightforwardly" at this particular time. From it, reflection goes back to the mode of consciousness taken at that time, and then to the potential modes of consciousness included horizonally in that mode; then to those in which the object might be otherwise intended as the same, such as perception, retention, recollection, expectation, etc. And all those types become more complicated in their noetico-noematical structure, inasmuch as the intentional object is more particularized.

Each type brought to the fore in this way is to be asked about its noetico-noematic structure and is, thus, to be systematically explained with respect to those modes of the intentional flux that

57. *Ibid.*, pp. 59–60.
58. *Ibid.*, pp. 70–72.
59. Edmund Husserl, *Cartesianische Meditationen und Pariser Vorträge*, ed. Stephan Strasser (The Hague: Nijhoff, 1950), pp. 83–84; English translation by Dorion Cairns, *Cartesian Meditations: An Introduction to Phenomenology* (The Hague: Nijhoff, 1960), pp. 46–47.
60. *Cartesian Meditations*, p. 47.

pertain to it, and with respect to the modes of their horizons and the intentional processes implicit in their horizons.[61] We may say, therefore, that intentional, or noetico-noematical, analyses are those phenomenological procedures in and by which every concrete experience is analyzed and descriptively explained with respect to its noetical and noematical sides on the basis of immediate intuition, and in which all the potentialities implicitly contained in its inner and outer horizons are descriptively unfolded and uncovered.[62]

The phenomenologists who objected to Husserl's view of philosophy as a radical and rigorous science, the phenomenological reduction, and his theory of evidence seldom explicitly mentioned intentional analysis in their description of phenomenology as a method. Heidegger claims that the originally given phenomena are not so much to be analyzed and described as interpreted according to the laws and rules of a phenomenological hermeneutics.[63] Marcel and Sartre have pointed to the fact that phenomenology's method primarily consists not in analysis and description but in a reinterpreted Hegelian dialectics.[64] Merleau-Ponty feels that intentional analyses are to be replaced by ek-sistential analyses.[65] Although it is not my intention to suggest here that these remarks are unimportant, I believe nevertheless that most of the later phenomenologists have underestimated the practical value of Husserl's view. I do agree with the authors mentioned above that in an existential-phenomenological context, Husserl's view is to be reinterpreted, and also that it is to be completed. As I see it, Merleau-Ponty in particular is correct in claiming that existential analyses must take the place of Husserl's intentional analyses of consciousness, for the simple reason that in existential philosophy Husserl's basic concept of intentionality is replaced by the modern view of man's ek-sistence.

61. *Ibid.*, pp. 47–53.
62. *Ibid.*, p. 40.
63. Heidegger, *Being and Time*, pp. 61–63, 200–202, 486–87.
64. Gabriel Marcel, *Journal métaphysique* (Paris: Hermann, 1935), pp. 10–15, 135–45, 261–62; Martin Heidegger, *Holzwege* (Frankfurt a.M.: Klostermann, 1950), pp. 105–92; Maurice Merleau-Ponty, *Sens et non-sens* (Paris: Nagel, 1948), pp. 125–39; English translation by Hubert L. Dreyfus and Patricia Allen Dreyfus, *Sense and Non-Sense* (Evanston, Ill.: Northwestern University Press, 1964), pp. 71–82; Walter Biemel, "Das Wesen der Dialektik bei Hegel und Sartre," *Tijdschrift voor Philosophie*, XX (1958), 269–300.
65. Merleau-Ponty, *Phenomenology of Perception*, pp. 137–38, 326–27.

However, I also agree with Ricoeur [66] that, if for every problem one goes immediately to the "existential project" and the "movement of ek-sistence" which entails all authentically human conduct in the way Sartre conceives of it, one takes the risk of missing the specificity of the problems, and of pushing the contours of the different modes of orientation toward the world in a kind of indistinct existentialist monism which tells the same story repeatedly when speaking about emotions, sexuality, speech, imagination, perception, etc. I believe that when we take Husserl's intentional analysis in the sense of Merleau-Ponty's reinterpretation, it will prove to be a methodical instrument of inestimable value for a descriptive science of man, although it is and remains true that this procedure is to be completed by hermeneutical and dialectical procedures.

Hermeneutics and dialectic

Thus far I have been arguing that man's behavior can be legitimately studied empirically, provided one is aware of the limitations of such an approach to man's orientation toward the world. Moreover, I have defended the view that man's behavior can be studied on a second level by means of descriptive methods analogous to those proposed by Husserl in his phenomenological psychology, though I am aware that such an approach has its typical limitations also. Neither one of these two approaches, taken singly or together, can explain the complete meaning of man's behavior. The reason for this is that all forms of man's orientation toward the world are *essentially* historical phenomena whose genuine meaning remains hidden to empirical as well as descriptive methods. This is why I feel that these methodical possibilities must be completed by hermeneutic and dialectic procedures.[67]

Protagonists of the hermeneutic conception believe that the most important revolution which has taken place since the beginning of our modern era has been the fact that man is becom-

66. Paul Ricoeur, "Méthodes et tâches d'une phénoménologie de la volonté," *Problèmes actuels de la phénoménologie,* ed. H. L. Van Breda (Paris: de Brouwer, 1952), pp. 115–23.
67. Hans-Georg Gadamer, *Wahrheit und Methode,* pp. 162–360; *Le Problème de la conscience historique* (Louvain: Publications Universitaires, 1963); Gerard Radnitzky, *Continental Schools of Metascience* (Göteborg: Akademiförlaget, 1968), pp. 4–77.

ing aware of the genuine meaning of history. If it is true that all meaning is intrinsically historical, then it seems to follow that we must be prepared to accept the historicity of *all* that is present and thus, also, the relativity of all present opinion. In our contemporary world it is quite a common phenomenon that in philosophy as well as in politics we encounter a multiplicity of views. Those who defend these views do not always see the relativity of their own conceptions, but many philosophers today are prepared to admit the possibility of a multiplicity of relative points of view which in principle cannot be overcome in an all-encompassing synthesis. The idea that there should be an all-encompassing view which is true and valid for all men at all times is being given up by an increasing number of people, philosophers and politicians alike, and the renunciation of this idea has had a strong influence on the modern sciences of man, which try to employ this basic awareness in a methodical way.

The conception was developed first into a method for the historical sciences in the strict sense of the term; later it was employed in an analogous way in other sciences of man. Using this method and following the rationale upon which it was ultimately based, modern science began to refuse naïvely to follow a tradition, or for that matter a certain body of truths admitted by a tradition. Modern science takes a reflective position in regard to everything handed down by tradition, and this attitude, when concretized into a method for the sciences of man, is known as "interpretation." [68]

People usually speak of interpretation when the meaning of a written text is not evident at first sight; in such a case the text is to be interpreted according to rules. Today, interpretation is applied not merely to difficult texts and complicated verbal traditions, but to everything which has been handed down to us by a tradition. For example, we commonly speak of the interpretation of a historic event, the interpretation of a mode of behavior. What one means to say in all these cases is that the meaning which presents itself to our understanding does not unveil itself without mediation; thus it is necessary to look through the immediate meaning in order to find the genuine meaning which was originally hidden. [69]

68. Gadamer, *Le Problème*, pp. 7–9.
69. *Ibid.*, pp. 9–10.

Today many scientists share the opinion that interpretative methods can and should be used in the human sciences. For our purpose here it is important to realize that the genesis and interpretation of this conviction are connected with a dramatic development that has taken place in modern philosophy since the time of Hegel. It is well known that in the development of their philosophical views Descartes and Kant were oriented toward the mathematical and physical sciences, whereas Hegel and many post-Hegelian philosophers such as Marx, Nietzsche, and Dilthey were inspired in their philosophical conceptions by the historical and social sciences. Thus, when we talk today about *hermeneutics,* there is more involved than the question of providing a new foundation and opening up new methical perspectives for the sciences of man; what is at stake, also, is the attempt to assure a new and genuine foundation for philosophy. At any rate, after this brief reflection it should be more easily understood why so many contemporary phenomenologists have attempted to reformulate Husserl's conception of phenomenology and, also, why these same authors defend the necessity of applying hermeneutic methods in the sciences of man.[70]

For we have seen that Husserl maintained Descartes's ideal of a presuppositionless philosophy. Later phenomenologists no longer adhered to this ideal and consequently had to abandon certain favorite themes of Husserl's thought as well. The question has been raised repeatedly as to whether Descartes really did proceed without presuppositions and whether such a demand does not necessarily lead to an infinite regress. Heidegger, Sartre, and Merleau-Ponty have shown convincingly that the Cartesian ideal does not agree with man's phenomenological situation, because the philosopher's thinking is always already situated. The most convincing reason, however, why they find the Cartesian ideal of a philosophy without any presuppositions impossible consists in the essential historicity of my own ek-sistence and, therefore, in the essential historicity of my authentic philosophy.

Philosophy today is expected to be, not a "system built in a vacuum," but an authentic interpretation of man's ek-sistence. Such an interpretation of something which is not transparent in itself is to be provided by hermeneutics. Negatively, the herme-

70. *Ibid.,* pp. 10–12.

neutic attitude is one in which the philosopher does not claim the ability to begin his work in an acosmic and unhistorical consciousness. Positively, it is characterized by the fact that the philosopher considers his own ek-sistence, in its transcendence toward the world, to be pregiven.

The consequence of this view is that every philosophy possesses only a hermeneutic value. No matter how systematically and rigorously the philosopher may proceed in his own thinking about the meaning of the "Whole" and man's place and function within it, the result to which he comes can never be more than an interpretation. For the philosopher cannot rise above the course of history, the social praxis, and the culture of his time, and, therefore, he must recognize that it is possible to attempt a different philosophical interpretation from the vantage point of a different historical or cultural situation. He has to abandon the dream in which all philosophers work together in building up one and the same "immutable" and eternal system. Such a dream is based on the illusion that there is one infallible method for the discovery of truth, which is to be conceived either after the model of the empirical sciences (empiricism), or after the model of the logico-mathematical sciences (rationalism), thus making it inevitable for science to become the norm of philosophy and for philosophy to drown again in scientism.[71]

The *contemporary* hermeneutic attitude, which is the most radical rejection of all forms of scientism, has its origin in Heidegger's *Being and Time*.[72] There Heidegger has posited that the meaning of all phenomenological description, taken merely from a methodical point of view, lies in interpretation. The *logos* of a phenomenology of man's mode of being has the character of a hermeneutic in the primordial sense of the term: It is a question of interpretation.[73]

Heidegger has obviously asked the question here as to precisely what it means to "interpret" such a nonsymbolic "fact" as man's mode of being. In trying to answer this question he claims that all interpretation *aims* at the "genuine" meaning of the thing

71. Strasser, *Phenomenology and the Human Sciences*, pp. 231–40, 249–51.
72. Heidegger, *Being and Time*, pp. 61–62, 200–202, 275–78, 358–64, 476–87.
73. *Ibid.*, pp. 61–62.

to be interpreted, thus presupposing that what is to be interpreted has meaning and that this meaning is originally hidden, at least in part. Now as far as man's mode of being is concerned, it is not difficult to show that it admits of such an interpretation, in that its "genuine" meaning is originally always hidden in part. This is due to the fact that man's being is essentially temporal and historical, so that each concrete form of behavior, that is, each concrete orientation toward the world, is embedded in the history of the individual as well as in the history of the community to which this individual belongs. As Heidegger formulates it, the very essence of man's being consists in his having-to-be on the basis of an equally primordial being-able-to-be. As having-to-be, man's being is always oriented toward possibilities which lie beyond itself; on the other hand, as being-able-to-be, it is always co-determined by the past, that is, its past as well as the past of the community. But, Heidegger continues, not only is man's being capable of interpretation; it also requires interpretation in that man has an unavoidable tendency to forget his own privileges. For, first of all, man is inclined to lose himself in his concernful dealing with things. But in addition, in his everyday life he is continually threatened by the danger of losing his authentic self by submerging in the "they." It is obviously true that man's being implies selfhood; but one must realize also that in his everyday life man usually cultivates the averageness of the impersonal "they." Hermeneutics, then, must take its starting point in the "fallenness" which is characteristic of the everyday mode of man's being; thus, swimming against the current and sometimes even using "violence," it must try to bring to light the genuine meaning of man's being.[74]

Seen from this perspective, hermeneutics can thus be defined as an attempt at bringing to light the usually hidden meanings which motivate the concrete modes of man's orientation toward the world. And since hermeneutics tries to unveil hidden meanings of phenomena which are inherently historical, it must employ methods which go far beyond *mere* descriptive analyses of what is immediately present. But if this is so, then it is clear also that hermeneutics is important for all disciplines which deal with human phenomena. Gadamer has shown this convincingly, and

74. Herbert Spiegelberg, *The Phenomenological Movement*, 2 vols. (The Hague: Nijhoff, 1965), I, 323–24.

it will be helpful at this point to paraphrase some of the basic insights he has come to on this subject.[75]

In order to explain the relevance of hermeneutics for the sciences of man, it is important to note first that historic knowledge, that is, genuine knowledge of intrinsically historical phenomena, cannot be described after the model of an objectivist conception of knowledge, because this knowledge itself is a process which as such has all the characteristics of a historical event. Even as historians, sociologists, and psychologists, that is, as representatives of contemporary methodical sciences of man, we are members of an uninterrupted chain by means of which the past addresses itself to us. Whereas in the natural sciences this undeniable fact does not immediately affect the subject matter of investigation (because the latter is taken out of the historical context by means of a process of idealization or demundanization), here this fact has an immediate influence on our understanding of man's behavior (since this cannot be taken out of its historical context without depriving it of its *genuine* meaning).

In making this claim we are immediately reminded of one of the basic rules of hermeneutics: the hermeneutic circle. Since there is a circular relationship between a whole and its parts, the anticipated understanding of the whole is to be comprehended by means of the parts, despite the fact that it is only within the light of the whole that the parts can play their clarifying roles. This can easily be explained by giving an example. When one begins to translate a text written in a foreign language, one starts to structure the text with the help of a provisional understanding of its subject matter as suggested by the title, context, similar or analogous texts, etc. This is true for the text taken as a whole as well as for its major parts, and ultimately even for the individual sentences of which it consists. During the process of translation this provisional idea guides the work, but it will be corrected or even rejected on the basis of a more careful study of the parts of which it consists. What every translator aims toward is the complete coherence of this anticipated meaning with the "final" meaning; for this is the only criterion for an understanding of the text.

Although the hermeneutic circle has been examined by many

75. Gadamer, *Le Problème*, pp. 65–87; *Wahrheit und Methode*, pp. 250–90.

people, notably Schleiermacher and Dilthey, most authors have approached the problems with which the circle confronts us either from a subjective or from an objective point of view. Consequently, they all have believed that hermeneutics can show us how *to transcend* the circle and come to a genuinely objective point of view.

It was Heidegger's existential analytic that first made it possible for us to understand the real meaning of the circular structure of our understanding. Concerning this circle Heidegger writes:

> But if we see this circle as a vicious one and look out for ways of avoiding it, even if we just "sense" it as an inevitable imperfection, then the act of understanding has been misunderstood from the ground up. . . . What is decisive is not to get out of the circle, but to come into it in the right way. This circle of understanding is not an orbit in which any random kind of knowledge may move; it is the expression of the existential *fore-structure* of Dasein itself. It is not to be reduced to the level of a vicious circle, or even of a circle which is merely tolerated. In the circle is hidden a positive possibility of the most primordial kind of knowing. To be sure, we genuinely take hold of this possibility only when, in our interpretation, we have understood that our first, last, and constant task is never to allow our fore-having, fore-sight, and fore-conception to be presented to us by fancies and popular conceptions, but rather to make the scientific theme secure by working out these fore-structures in terms of the things themselves. [76]

It is clear that in *Being and Time* the positive, *ontological* meaning of the circle is emphasized for the first time; this dimension was lacking in Schleiermacher as well as in Dilthey. Anyone who wants to understand something should adhere to "the things themselves" and try to rid himself of prejudices, regardless of whether they have their origin in his personal life or in the tradition he happens to find himself in. What is to be found out is what has been the case, not what should have been the case, or what I and other people wish had been the case.

Take a historical document. As soon as the interpreter has found some elements which he understands, he projects a provisional conception of the meaning of the whole text. But this first understanding of certain parts has been motivated not only

76. Heidegger, *Being and Time*, pp. 194–95.

by the sentences found in the text, but also by the general context in which, in his view, such sentences should fit. To understand "the thing" which emerges before him in this way means to project a provisional conception which is *to be corrected* as the reading of the text proceeds. Eventually he will have to adopt another point of view in regard to the text and its over-all meaning, but this new perspective, too, is perhaps to be broadened, changed, specified. In all of this, "the thing itself," as it emerges for him in the process of deciphering, keeps guiding him. And it is this perpetual oscillation of interpretative conceptions which Heidegger tries to describe in the text just quoted: namely, our comprehension of something in terms of a process in which we form ever new projects (as long as the situation requires this). Anyone who does so continuously runs the risk of getting entangled in his own prejudices and of finding that the conception he has projected does not conform with "the thing itself" as it emerges before him. That is why the continuous task of our comprehension of something consists in the elaboration of projects which are authentic and proportionate in regard to the thing to be brought to light. The only form of "objectivity" found in such a process consists in the fact that one's anticipation becomes confirmed while, in reading the rest of the text, one tries to test this anticipation on "the thing" that emerges before him. Thus each interpretation of a text must begin with a reflection by the interpreter on his own preconceived ideas, which result from the "hermeneutic situation" in which he finds himself. He must try to legitimize them, that is, to clarify their origin and value.

From this it follows that the hermeneutical task as Heidegger conceives of it does not consist merely in recommending a method. On the contrary, he attempts to radicalize that understanding which everyone endeavors to bring about when he tries to comprehend something. What we encounter in our attempt to understand a text or a historical phenomenon is already found in all forms of our understanding, provided the subject matter of our understanding in the latter case is something intrinsically human and for that reason essentially historical. In all these cases in which man tries to understand something human, he has to follow the "same" procedure. He begins by assuming that such and such is the meaning of the phenomenon under consideration. Many factors play a part in this preconception of the meaning of a phenomenon: my personal outlook on the world, my moral standards, my religious views, the tradition I belong to and live within, my knowledge of the field connected with this phenomenon, my interest, and so on. Obviously my main guide in forming my preconception is that which already shows itself here and now, however partially this may be. Hermeneutics does not demand that one give up these "subjective" codeterminants of one's preconceptions; it does not require that one try to come to an "objective neutrality" in regard to the phenomena; such neutrality is impossible, and it is not desirable, either. The hermeneutic attitude asks merely that one be willing to qualify prejudices as prejudices, and to take opinions for opinions, and to give them up the moment the phenomenon, the pattern of behavior, the thing, the text, appears to be incompatible with them. It is only when one adopts this attitude that one gives a text, a form of behavior, a phenomenon, a thing the possibility of manifesting itself in its being-different, of showing its truth against the preconceived ideas which we originally tried to substitute for it.

Another aspect of the hermeneutic circle that has become manifest through Heidegger's investigations is its lack of mere formality. Schleiermacher and Dilthey speak only of a formal relationship between a whole and its parts; they speak of a dialectic between our "guessing" about the meaning of the whole and our later explanation of it by means of the parts. In this romantic conception of the circle, the circular movement is not the result but a deficient, although necessary, form of investigation. Schleiermacher suggests that once we have gone through the circle we finally reach certainty; at that moment our circular form of understanding is no longer necessary; our original preconception has then been verified (or falsified) and is no longer needed as such. Heidegger, on the contrary, defends the thesis that our comprehension of the text never ceases to be determined by the anticipatory impetus of our preconception.

There is even more. We have just said that all comprehension must be characterized as a totality of circular relationships between the whole and its parts. Now we have to add to this that these circular relationships themselves must be characterized by our anticipation of a "perfect coherence." This means that in the final analysis only an interpretation which is intrinsically coherent in itself, as well as with all its parts, can be admitted. This requirement could still be understood in a purely formal way. However, if one reflects on the meaning of this requirement, it becomes clear that the coherence we assume to be present in a series of phenomena *transcends* this series in that it is also assumed as referring to what happens to be the truth, thus the things themselves represented by them. Let us again take the example of a historic document. When I claim that a text must be coherent in order to be understandable, I make this claim because I am convinced that this coherence is a necessary condition if the text is to describe the truth, and if I am thus to find the truth via a historico-critical analysis of the text. What I am ultimately interested in are the things themselves, not the way in which they have been handed down to me. In other words, the anticipation of perfect coherence presupposes not only that the text is an adequate expression of an idea, but also that this idea corresponds with what is actually the case. All hermeneutics tends toward the things themselves in such a way that these things are accessible and, in principle, capable of being comprehended by everyone. Where man's behavior is concerned, we have to realize that here, too, a certain coherence must be assumed; for without coherence man's behavior could not be genuinely meaningful.

We have already seen that hermeneutics does not deny the existence of prejudices in its interpretations, provided the term "prejudice" be taken in its neutral sense and stand for preconception, anticipatory judgment (prejudgment). By means of its critical methods, hermeneutics endeavors to separate false from true prejudices, that is, prejudices which blind from prejudices which clarify. Prejudices are dangerous as long as one does not recognize them as such. But one would not be able to recognize them if they had not already been at work. It is very possible that unobserved prejudices have determined people's opinions concerning many things. In looking back critically upon a set of phenomena, it is often possible to unmask false prejudices. But this is possible only after one has been provoked by these prejudices.

Let us suppose that we come across a prejudice which seems unacceptable. Let us assume further that we substitute another anticipatory judgment in its place. In this case the second "prejudice" cannot be conceived of as the "definitive truth"; that would again mean a return to a naïve thesis of objectivist historicism. Such a conception forgets that the prejudice which was denounced and the "prejudice" which was substituted for it both belong to an uninterrupted chain of events of which both are members. The original prejudice continues to play an important part, albeit a different one than before. Everyone knows that it is difficult to give up a prejudice and substitute a new conviction in its place. The reason for this is that the new conviction can never be presented as the eternal truth. And what is more, the new conviction can never be adequately specified if it does not have a connection with the prejudice which was given up. It is by opposition that convictions become evaluated.

Here a new element presents itself: the *dialectic* between old and new. The original, implicit prejudice, which was not yet understood as prejudice, functioned within an over-all conception concerning a set of phenomena. My new conviction is not in harmony with that over-all conception. Adopting a new conviction means giving up my original over-all understanding of that set of phenomena. Thus a dialectical process begins to take place between what is mine, though it is still inauthentic, and what is authentic but not yet mine. The universal mediator of this dialectic is called "interrogation," and this interrogation never reaches a point where it becomes impossible to replace an implicit prejudice by something "alien" which I will have to make mine if I am really willing to comprehend a set of phenomena.

It seems to me that the importance of these reflections for a descriptive science of man is obvious. We can appreciate this at once when we realize that each mode of man's behavior constitutes an integral part of a whole which, in the final analysis, comprises not only this man's life in its entirety but also the life of the society to which he belongs. Yet in my opinion this does not alter the fact that the other methods discussed are important, also, in that they enable us to shed light on aspects and details which can serve to deepen our hermeneutic understanding of man.

Experiential Phenomenology

Eugene T. Gendlin

IN THIS CHAPTER I will first outline a little of the basic approach of the philosophy of experiencing, and then show how its application has led to some research advances in psychology.

I will begin by formulating what I consider the basic unsolved problem of current philosophy. I will first discuss phenomenology and linguistic analysis from the vantage point of the philosophy of experiencing, but I hope to be both fair and clarifying. If I attribute to them certain explicit understandings which perhaps they often lack, it is because clarification is like that: what one clarifies is in a sense already there—in another sense, not.

I will then outline some systematic relationships between experience and verbalization, some characteristics of experience in the process of being explicated, and some few points of method. With these I will hope to have made a new phenomenological approach, one which solves the basic problem by approaching it quite differently.

I will then show the application of this new approach in psychology.

THE PROBLEM

IN THE WESTERN TRADITION of philosophy, experience (and nature) has usually been interpreted as basically a formal or logic-like system. This was done through a philosophical analysis of the basic assumptions of knowledge or science. These assumptions were then attributed to experience. Experience "must be" such-and-so, the philosophers said; otherwise science or knowledge would be impossible.

Philosophers have not agreed on their analysis of science or knowledge, and therefore also not on what they attributed to experience. For instance, those who held that knowledge is basically mathematical and consists of unit steps, each repeatable, considered nature and experience to be a system of that same sort. Thus the forms required by knowledge were read into nature and experience.

Some philosophers made this reading-in quite explicit, in which case experience was held to depend frankly on the nature of thought (Idealism, so-called); others preferred to present this reading-in backwards, so that experience was said to be the origin from which knowledge received its forms. Either way, experience (or nature) was inferred to have the kind of forms, relations, and connections which knowledge requires. Either way, therefore, the needs of knowledge (as analyzed) governed what was said of experience or nature.

Since Schleiermacher, Dilthey, Husserl, Heidegger, Sartre, Merleau-Ponty, Wittgenstein, Ryle, and Austin, this approach has gone out of style. Instead, it is now widely held that experience need not, and in fact does not, have the same character as logic, science, or knowledge. Experience is not organized like a verbal scheme. What we say in philosophy should be based on experience, not read into it.

The crucial problem has two parts: (1) If experience is not like a verbal scheme and we do not wish to say that it is, then how can we say anything at all about it without imposing a verbal scheme? and (2) If we wish, in some way, to appeal beyond logical schemes to a sense of "experience" not yet organized verbally, in what way do we have such "experience" present and available for an appeal, and in what way does experience give "yes" or "no" answers, so that some statements will be "based" on it and some statements not?

Although my major concern is with phenomenology, let me say a little about linguistic analysis in these regards, because both these philosophies stand or fall with this problem.

Linguistic analysis, following Wittgenstein and Austin, examines how words are used in the context of ordinary situations: these philosophers find the use of a word quite unlike the logic scheme the word embodies, and quite unlike its logical relations to other words. For example, although "voluntarily" and "involuntarily" are logical opposites, they are used in entirely different kinds of situations. One does not use them to mark the same thing in either its presence or absence, as opposites would do. Ryle says, rather, that "voluntarily" is a word of affirmation or denial ("not voluntarily") that we use when something "morally fishy" has been done and we want to assign or withhold blame.[1] "He did not do it voluntarily" means the morally fishy act was not his responsibility. "Involuntarily," on the other hand, belongs to muscle jerks, reflexes, or automatic behavior. A man might shoot someone not voluntarily but in self-defense; yet we would not use the word "involuntarily" unless the trigger was released by accident.

This kind of approach moves beyond logical and philosophical schemes and instead analyzes situations of ordinary living. Our living in situations is said to be a great deal more complex than any scheme. Situations, and how we differentiate and act in them, involve a great many distinctions which we "know," and which are marked in language use. But this "knowing" is not like knowledge or science; it is rather like "knowing how" to do something—perhaps how one does it cannot be explained, at least not easily. Yet one "knows" when to use a given word, and when it would be inappropriate. The complexity and distinctions of our situations have developed with language; hence linguistic analysts use language as the lead from which to discover these differentiations and to make explicit what situational characteristics are being differentiated.

Linguistic analysts, therefore, appeal to something beyond the logical relations of words, beyond the "models" implicit in them, and beyond any philosophical scheme of the kind formerly considered to be basic to experience. For example, the discussion just alluded to is in some way a philosophic discussion of will, choice, and responsibility, yet no scheme of "free will" or "determinism" is used. Neither are the purely logical relations of the words to be trusted. Linguistic analysts appeal beyond schemes and logic, they appeal to our knowing how to act, speak, and live

1. S. Cavell, "Must We Mean What We Say?," in *Ordinary Language*, ed. Vere C. Chappell (Englewood Cliffs, N.J.: Prentice-Hall, 1964).

in situations. But what sort of appeal, what sort of basis for an appeal, is involved here? [2]

Austin says our actions and uses of words in situations are organized very differently from the way a flat system of words is organized. He denies that a word has a "handy denotation" to which it refers.[3] For one word there is not necessarily one thing. Philosophy appeals beyond words to something that is not organized in a one-to-one relation to words, and does not have units and relations that are the same as words and their logical relations. Linguistic analysis only looks like an analysis of language. What is actually analyzed is something very different: namely, our "knowing how to use" words in situations.

This knowing how to use a word involves knowing all the complexities of the situations governing its use. It is possible to try to explicate what these are, and linguistic analysts attempt this. But in so doing, they inevitably give this "knowing how" a verbal scheme which the "knowing how" is not. They verbally organize the maze of situational detail in just certain ways, even while asserting that action-in-situations cannot be so organized. We can see this clearly in the way in which linguistic analysts differ among themselves as to when such an explication has been achieved. Austin did not agree with Ryle that our knowing how to use "voluntarily" was rightly explicated by saying that we use it in "morally fishy" situations to assign or withhold blame. Austin says that we do not use the word to determine whether the act is blameworthy or not: a child may give a gift "voluntarily," or because his mother made him give it; in neither case would his action be morally fishy. With this example to argue from, Austin changes much of Ryle's explication of how we use "voluntarily."

How is it that the same knowing how which grounded Ryle's earlier explication now grounds Austin's differing one? Clearly, the verbal organization of neither the one of these explications nor the other can claim to set out "the" complex organization of situational aspects implicit in our "knowing how."

This brings us to the second part of our problem. Even if we accept the fact that, although these philosophers set themselves the task of getting at experience rather than imposing a scheme

2. E. T. Gendlin, "What Are the Grounds of Explication?," in *The Monist*, XLIX, no. 1 (January, 1965).

3. J. L. Austin, "The Meaning of a Word," in *Philosophical Papers* (Oxford, 1961), pp. 29–30.

on it, they end by imposing a scheme after all, we can still ask: Did they involve the not-yet-verbalized experience in some way? Did they merely impose a scheme, or did they use their sense of "knowing how"? How did they use it? In what way do they have this "knowing how"? Surely, not only in the form of the scheme and not only after they state it. Surely, they will tell us how they have this "knowing how" and use it to make their explication.

Even here we will get no satisfactory answer. The philosophers exhibit their "knowing how" to use a word by using it in action. When analysts try to explicate this "how," they talk about various situations. They propose examples, which force us to admit that some are possible and some are not. It is not possible to say, "He did the shooting under orders; therefore he did it involuntarily." The word seems to mean the right thing, yet in that example it doesn't. It sounds wrong. This means it feels wrong; it gives one a sour, discordant feeling. If someone now says, " 'Involuntarily' belongs with muscle jerks or accidents, not with being compelled," this feels right. (Still, quite possibly it isn't right.)

Now, what is this "feels right" or "feels wrong," which seems to be the ultimate court of appeal? One intends to appeal to the situations directly, for the decision as to what words can and cannot be used in them, but actually one appeals to "what feels right" in them, or "feels wrong." Linguistic analysts do not actually go out and observe situations directly. They would not accept an empirical statistical study of the use of the word, because more people use words in a sloppy way than use them rightly. Can "rightly" mean only that it feels right?

Can "feeling" be used in this way? Isn't it a "private datum"? Isn't feeling a poor criterion for philosophy? Why and how does it work? Why and how does feeling seem to allow some organizations or schemes to be imposed upon it, and not others? (And some of these may be found "wrong" later.) What the philosopher organizes and defines (some of the situational details) was somehow, puzzlingly, "implicit" in the feeling. Does it really all come down to feeling?

Phenomenologists similarly hold that language and living developed together (and continue to do so), that experience and situations are together (just as our sense of "knowing how" to use a word and the situations in which we use it are together). "Being-in-the-world" is Heidegger's way of defining humans as beings-in, as experiencing-in situations.[4] According to Heidegger, situations are differentiated with language, and linguistic distinctions are thus in the very texture of the situations with which we live.

Husserl and Merleau-Ponty discuss the experiential sense which guides our use of language, an "emotional sense" [5] which "fills" [6] verbal sound patterns (which are empty in a language foreign to us). Experience, language, and situations are thus inherently connected.

Phenomenologists also hold that while language is part of the situations in which we live, experience and the life-world are not like a system of words or concepts. Phenomena cannot be equated with schemes, and it is an error to impose schemes on them. Thus, Heidegger argues that every statement, or truth, "stands in some kind of approach," and depends on it. That is to say, the world cannot be rendered as such, but only through some (historically developed) scheme.

To get beyond this, Heidegger seeks "an approach that would not be again merely an approach." Rightly, he envisions that, having gained perspective on the variety of possible schemes and approaches, and their historical development, we would not now simply settle for another scheme. But what else is possible? There Heidegger stops. This next step will be the work of a whole culture, he says, not of one man. It is a conundrum which affects every philosophy which refuses to equate experience or world with a scheme. On the one hand, it appeals to that experience in a way that should be corrective of schemes; on the other, the result has to be again a scheme, and attributes to experience the nature of a scheme.

Husserl may be said to be the first to base philosophy, quite explicitly and deliberately, on an examination of experiencing as we actually live, have, and are, rather than regarding "expe-

4. M. Heidegger, *Sein und Zeit* (Tübingen: Niemeyer, 1927); English translation by John Macquarrie and Edward Robinson, *Being and Time* (London: SCM, 1962).

5. M. Merleau-Ponty, *Phénoménologie de la perception* (Paris: Gallimard, 1945); English translation by Colin Smith, *Phenomenology of Perception* (New York: Humanities Press, 1962).

6. E. Husserl, *Logische Untersuchungen*, 3 vols., 3d ed. (Halle: Niemeyer, 1921–22), Vol. II, pt. II, Investigation VI; English translation by J. N. Findlay, *Logical Investigations* (New York: Humanities Press, 1970).

rience" as already imposed upon by the requirements of one view of science, as had been done traditionally. Husserl found, for example, that the notion that experience comes in colors, sounds, smells, etc., is a notion already derivative from a philosophical scheme which analyzes experience into certain handy units. Ordinary experience is of trees, doors slamming, kids crying— not of colors and sounds. (Austin makes the same point many decades later.) Thus Husserl finds the whole "life-world" implicit in experience, even when he first brackets all questions as to what exists and seeks to examine only experience as such.

Although Husserl resisted schemes that have been read into experience, how could he himself organize his own analysis of experience? What about such schemes as cognition versus emotion versus conation (which he used)? What about noesis versus noema, or, simply put, process and object, as organizing notions in his work? What about the individual as the starting point (as compared, for example, to Heidegger's different starting point) and the ensuing difficulties about other egos? These are only examples of a larger fact: the phenomenologist has set himself a seemingly impossible task, that of examining and describing lived experience without imposing schemes upon it. But to "examine" and to "describe" are activities which inherently involve schemes.

Husserl was aware of this problem. Each period of his work is followed by a period in which he again undercut his own assumptions and schemes; as he said, whereas others built edifices, he only dug further into the ground, and he meant by this something both good and bad. Good because it was his self-set task to undercut schemes and assumption systems; bad because he knew that in some sense he was failing at this task.

He had to fail in this regard, since, on the one hand, he wanted to study the structure of experience without importing a scheme, and yet, on the other hand, any studying, describing, laying out in words and distinctions must, after all, employ some scheme and some organizing parameters. Could he claim that his distinctions and organizing parameters were themselves "the" structure of experience?

That we cannot grant Husserl such a claim is shown by the fact that other phenomenological philosophers set out "the" structure of experience quite differently. And again, is not each phenomenologist involved in a contradiction, claiming both that experience is preschematic and that the scheme arrived at is true of it?

The second part of our problem is also a problem for phenomenology. The second part is: Even if we grant that a scheme is being imposed, what, if anything, is a "phenomenological basis"? How do we have it and how do we use it? Are phenomenologists simply claiming unwarrantedly, in the most puerile fashion, that they have some kind of mysterious direct line into not-yet-verbalized experience, without being able to show us even a trace of it? Or is there something clearly explainable that can be called a "phenomenological basis"? Granted that experiencing is never to be equated with a verbal scheme, and granted that it does not contain some verbal "the" scheme, and granted that each phenomenologist does use, and thereby in some sense imposes, a scheme in his verbal descriptions, is there any difference left between phenomenologically grounded assertions and those which are not so grounded?

For example, if you say to me, "You are tired," then if you intend your statement phenomenologically, you will consider it false if I do not feel tired. On the other hand, if you are not proceeding on a phenomenological basis, you might still retort, "I can tell from looking at you that you are tired," or, "I know you have been working for eighteen hours now, and I know that anyone who has worked that long is tired." Roughly, these two assertions are based respectively on empirical observation and on logical deduction.

These three types of bases for statements—phenomenological, empirical, and logical—are not unrelated. For example, it is possible to say, "Because of what I saw you do, and because of what I can figure out, I think you will feel tired if you stop working and lie down for a while." Here a phenomenological basis is used (if I don't feel tired then, you will admit that you were wrong), but it is asserted in the future and predicted because of the inherent connectedness of situations, logic, and experience.

Our example is much too simple. Also, it raises some well-known problems about just whose experience shall be a phenomenological basis, whether such direct experiences are "private," how these can be grounds for assertions, and other questions. But the example illustrates how a statement may be phenomenological if one seeks to make some direct experience the court of appeal for its correctness or falseness.

In order to assert truth and falsity these philosophers *seek* to appeal to direct experience, beyond schemes and assumptions. Can we say more than that? Can we say that in some way this appeal works?

We know the appeal does not work univocally, since these philosophers frequently disagree with each other. How then, does it work? Husserl discusses,

> Expression and what is expressed [are] two layers that are congruent, one covers the other. . . . One must not expect too much from this image of layers, expression is not something laid on . . . rather it affects the intentional underlayer . . .[7]

Clearly, here Husserl gets at something beyond the image of layers that he uses in saying it. How can you tell that this is so? How can you tell if it is right? How can you tell that the image of layers is wrong?

Husserl says expression "is congruent" or "covers" what is expressed (and for this the layers image does nicely); but it also affects what is expressed (and for this the layers image fails, he says). Thus Husserl himself says right here that the verbal schematizing he uses is wrong. Something more than the verbal schematizing is operating, or else we would have nothing more than a statement which is at the same time being called wrong.

Notice that we have more than just the sentence, so that we do not lose everything when we discard the sentence. How do we have this experience of what Husserl is getting at by "an expression covers"? How do we have this experience of what Husserl means by "expression . . . affects the intentional underlayer," in a not-yet verbally schematized way, so that we can first agree to the scheme of layers and then also agree that the scheme of layers is wrong? How are both of these agreements possible, despite the fact that "covers" really contradicts "affects": if the expression changes what it purports to be congruent with, how then is it congruent with it? Clearly the verbal scheme or metaphor fails, and yet we have something more.

Without a further, much better, treatment of these questions

7. Husserl, *Ideen zu einer reinen Phänomenologie und phänomenologischen Philosophie: Erstes Buch* (The Hague: Nijhoff, 1950), par. 124; English translation by W. R. Boyce Gibson, *Ideas: General Introduction to Pure Phenomenology* (New York: Humanities Press, 1931; paperback ed., New York: Collier Books, 1962) (present translation slightly modified).

we can only say that we *feel* how an expression fits when it succeeds in expressing; we can say only that we also often *feel* a change in what we are expressing in the process of expressing it. But would one want to make "feeling" the final judge of philosophic discourse? After so much careful thought, will we say that whatever we feel to be right, is right? Since so much of what the other fellow feels is obviously wrong, we can only view this kind of basis with doubt.

This passage just quoted from Husserl is not only an example of appealing beyond the verbal metaphor one uses; the passage is itself about the fact that verbalizing "affects" an experience.

The basic unanswered question of current philosophy, then, seems to be: How can lived experiencing be a basis for assertions? Both major current philosophies claim such a basis, claim that this basis lies beyond the verbal and logical schemes of assertions, claim to correct schemes by means of it, and yet have shown neither how we have and use this lived experience as a basis for assertions, nor how the result is more than simply another imposed scheme.

It is scandalous that current philosophy appeals to something beyond verbal schemes, and yet claims that its assertions are "merely" read off, or that they "merely" state this something. It is as if, having said that direct experience or knowing how is not a scheme, contemporary philosophers pretend that it shows its schematic organization on the very face of it.

But as we have seen, when looked at more closely, these philosophers do go by something other than schemes made or found, just as they claim to do. But because these philosophers fail to examine just what their basis is and how they use it, therefore they have left it in this unexamined state of mere feeling.

But can there be a solution to this problem? If saying involves schematizing and organizing, how can it not impose scheme and organization? If experience is used as a basis and is not a set stable structure, must it not be merely vague and felt?

A new beginning

To arrive at a solution and a successful phenomenological method, we must make a fundamental turn, and a new beginning. We must look at the situation sideways, make a ninety-degree turn, so to speak. Instead of standing only on statements, deploring that we can speak about experience only through them, let us stand to one side and look at both statements and experience as they affect each other.

Let us free ourselves from that perspective in which experience is to be rendered without the statement having an effect upon it. Obviously, we cannot state experience, as it is unstated. Let us take the bull by the horns and study the ways stating can affect experience. In this way we make a field of study out of what was an embarrassment.

We cannot study experience as it is when it is not studied; we cannot state it as it is when it is not stated. What we can do is to study it in the process of being stated. From this new approach we take our standpoint neither in statement, nor in an experience that we can say nothing about. Rather, we study both experience and statement as they occur in the process of affecting each other. What many different effects may they have on each other?

I will try to show in the following section that this turn, this new approach, has borne fruit.

Situations, language, and feelings

We have seen that external situations, language, and feelings are intimately related, yet each may independently establish truth criteria. Thus a sentence might be called true or false either because it stated or failed to state a definite empirical observation, or because it followed or failed to follow logically from other statements, or because it explicated or failed to explicate a directly felt experience. It is often useful to make quite clear the basis on which a sentence is intended to rest. However, these three types of truth criteria are not independent of each other, really, since situations, words, and feelings are inevitably interrelated.

Thus, while phenomenologists intend their sentences to rest on their success or failure to explicate direct experience, they should make it clear (and I have tried to show that they often *do* make it clear) that feelings, situations, and language are inherently involved in each other. Thus, although Husserl began not with these interrelations but rather with direct experience, he soon found these interrelations in that experience.

Wittgenstein's argument against "private data" was that the use of words is governed by situations and our actions in them, not by what it feels right to say. The way in which the word is objectively used is the criterion for its use. "Look on the language game as the *primary* thing, and look on the feelings, etc., as you look on a way of regarding the language game . . ." [8] This means not that I do not have feelings, or that they are not complex and organized, but rather that Wittgenstein asks us to make the behavior in situations the criterion for feelings, rather than the reverse. Linguistic analysts first honor, then disobey this dictum, since they first assume that what feels right to say is governed by objective situations, and then proceed to state the marks of these situations, by using what feels right to say in them as the criterion.

Experience is always already organized by, or in, situations. Language is used to distinguish situations and to differentiate aspects of them. When we want to study experience and statement in relation to each other, it must be clear that they are always already related, and that both are related in turn to situations. Thus we will not be studying "pure" experience as if it were some kind of putty; rather, experience is always organized by the evolutionary history of the body, and also by culture and situations organized partly by language. Although language is always involved in the complex organization of experience, it is never all that is involved in it. The role of language does not get at all of an experience. But neither are you relating statement to experience for the first time when you explicate. Language is already involved in experience.

For example, the different rooms in a house and the activities that go on in them are developed and differentiated along with the words and phrases used in these activities. Even the house cat experiences each room and its activities differently. Although the cat does not use the words that go with these differences, nevertheless these words are, in a way, implied in the different experiences the cat has with the different rooms. Observable situations are related both to the cat's experiences and to the words that for us structure some of the aspects of these experiences.

Thus when direct experience serves as a basis for statements, it does not do so apart from situations: situational structure is implicit in it. But we can also *further* structure situations with feelings and words, and in explication we do so.

8. L. Wittgenstein, *Philosophic Investigations* (New York: Macmillan, 1953), p. 656.

The argument against private data has been mistaken by some to imply that one's statements about one's own feelings are incorrigible, that they cannot be found to be in error (or true, therefore). But this is a misunderstanding. We will show that one can both be mistaken and can later correct what one said and believed about one's feelings. But when one states (or corrects) a feeling, one states aspects of the situations in which one has the feelings.

But just as feelings do not have some simple verbal-schematic structure, neither do situations. The complex and arguable nature of the marks for when we use a simple word have already shown that. It may be quite an objective matter, but it is not one that can simply be observed. To delineate situations involves simplifying and further organizing, imposing further patterning upon what is already very complexly patterned. The situations we live in do not come in "handy denotation" packages, nor in any single set of already cut-out units.

We must therefore assert both that experience is already organized in part linguistically and situationally, and that in using experience (or situations) to ground statements upon, we further organize it. We must assert *both* that this further organizing is not the pattern of the experience, *and* that it does have something to do with the way the experience is already organized. To state this in the reverse order, the organization of experience is not the kind which we set out in a verbal pattern, although what we do set out in such a pattern has something to do with the experience's own kind of organization. (And, since these are related, with the situation's own kind of organization.)

We must examine and explicate situations, feelings, and language in their relations to each other, realizing that explicating gives them a still further relation.

Functional relations and characteristics of experiencing

In *Experiencing and the Creation of Meaning* [9] I have set out seven "functional relationships" between experiencing and words. I will cite four of these briefly, to show that we can study these relations in action, and to clarify our later discussion.

1. *Direct reference* is a use of words to set off, separate out,

9. E. T. Gendlin, *Experiencing and the Creation of Meaning* (New York: Free Press, 1962), pp. 91–137.

set up some "aspect" of experience which can thereby be called "this" or "that" experience, or "an" experience. The words used may very well be demonstrative pronouns—or they may be somewhat descriptive. Yet what they say is so obviously vague and untenable literally that it is clear that they only "point," if they do anything.

For example, when I spoke of "that feeling" which an inappropriate explication gives one, I was directly referring to your having such a feeling. If you did not have it and had never had it, I might arrange to give it to you, but the phrase "that sour feeling" would not in itself give it to you.

Thus direct reference is a use of words such that *an* experience is thereby set out. But the words alone do not convey or call out the experience: one must know already with what approach and in what situation to look, and the directly referring phrase must have a result which is definitely not simply that phrase. The result must be a distinguishable aspect of experience which now stands out, so that one can say, "Yes, I know what *that* is." (You might now say, "But I wouldn't call it 'sour' . . . ," and you might propose another word that I might agree is a better word. Still, my phrase would have succeeded in directly referring.)

It is perfectly possible for the direct reference to either fail or be misunderstood. Though words do structure experience further (into "this" or "an" aspect), nevertheless the experience is not totally the result of schematizing, entirely up to how schematizing proceeds. It is not the mere result of schematizing, since the direct experience may appear, or it may not. If not, then you have *only* the words. If it does appear it talks back— which may lead you to discard the very words that let it emerge.

We see now, that, far from there being a "pure" preorganized experience which might first be verbalized, even the existence of "an" experience such as "this" one is already a further organizing we have made. To be sure, it need not be words, exactly, which do this, although it can be words. It could be a certain pointing and differentiating attention; we feel "this" and "this" and "that." Hadamard [10] says he often uses dots rather than words, putting a dot down for each separable aspect as he separates them.

2. *Recognition* is my term for the way in which words seem

---

10. J. Hadamard, *The Psychology of Invention in the Mathematical Field* (New York: Dover, 1945), pp. 76–77.

to have "their own" experience, which they call out in anyone. (Or, we might say that if one is in the kind of situation that gives one that feeling, one then finds that the word comes.) The word seems to call out the feeling, and if we fail to get it we fail to "recognize" the word. The feeling seems to call for that word. If one has the feeling, then the word comes. (One has the feeling in a situation, so the word seems to explicate the situation as well.)

The relationship between words and experience appears here to be a one-to-one relation—the word says the experience, the experience calls for that word. Actually, the experience is much more complex and much different, and if you directly refer to a "recognition feeling" which seems paired with a word, you will find that you could use a great many other words to say what it is. Similarly, there are quite complex situational aspects which give us this feeling and make this word come. But to try to state the recognition feeling differently is quite another relationship between experience and words. For the moment we want to set out this very ordinary, seemingly one-to-one relationship, of words and "their" recognition-feelings, so that each gives you the other.

To make this quite vivid, suppose you are in some situation and feel a certain way for which you know there is a word. You might find yourself unable to think of the word. You then have only "that feeling," to which you can directly refer, but for which you are unable to think of the word. (You can describe this aspect of experience in a roundabout way, seeking to give another person the same sense of the situation so that he might come up with the word. This is again another relation of words and experience, one in which you seek to create the experience in others, not by calling it out with the word, but by putting them, actually or vicariously, through many events until they have it.)

3. *Metaphor* involves novelty. Here words are used in such a way as to create a new experience. The metaphor or simile is literally about some other situation or experience but is now used about this situation or experience. A metaphor requires direct reference; you must be able to point directly to the experience the metaphor is now about, and permit the metaphor to apply to it. Understanding the metaphor requires a recognition of the usual use of the words. Then, if the metaphor succeeds, some new aspect of the present experience should emerge.

Some people would like to say that such a new experience (and new aspect of a situation, for as usual these are together) is not really new, that the similarity already existed between the present situation and the one that the metaphor derives from. But this is to assume that the world consists of already cut-up, handy "similarities" that only await noticing. Rather, the metaphor involves a further creative organizing, as in direct reference. An aspect of experience emerges, and in the case of metaphor, a new one. Many such new aspects could metaphorically be made to emerge, if one brought many other areas of experience to bear on the present one.

4. *Comprehension* occurs when an experience or feeling has no regular words, when these must first be made. Usually such words cannot be made up anew, but must consist of new arrangements of extant words, used in a fitting way. As we have seen, if a metaphor is presented to you, it creates a new experiential aspect. But now, let us say you already have the experience and you seek to make words for it. To fashion a new verbalization of an experience or a feeling, you must perform the metaphoric task (so that the old words make a new experiential aspect), but this new aspect must be very close to the one that you already have. Comprehension thus involves direct reference (to *this* experience you want to verbalize), as well as recognition (the experience or feeling the words usually arouse), and also metaphor (the use of these words to create a new experiential aspect). All three functional relationships are used in such a way that the thereby-made aspect shall be the one you already have, which was to be verbalized.

This is the relation in which words are said to "feel right" or "sound right"; but note how much more complex it is, once the various relations of words and experience are set out. By no means do we need to let it remain at a "feeling right."

There are a number of aspects involved in "feels right," which have just been explicated here. Unless the other relationships are clearly set out, this one cannot be understood. Even without understanding, that is to say, even if you reject my description of each relationship, it is helpful at least to separate the direct reference power of a statement, if it has any, from the (usual or novel) recognition power the words may have. Thus a statement purporting to state some aspect of experience may have direct reference power. It may only half succeed, but by its context, and by what you already have, you may get the experiential aspect it sets out. And yet you may want to reject—not that there is such an aspect—but the way in which the sentence formulates it. This distinction enables us to keep the experiential aspect a statement refers to, at the same time rejecting what the statement says ("I know what you're getting at, but you can't put it that way").

Our earlier examples—"that sour feeling" of an inappropriately used word, and Husserl's "an expression covers"—were attempts at comprehension. In both instances we kept the experiential aspect referred to, but rejected these statements as comprehension.

This short presentation of four relationships in which verbalizing affects experiencing shows that there is a fruitful field of study here, and may invite you to look at the fuller treatment of these relationships.

Experience is never entirely caught in any one relationship to words. It is always possible to refer directly to the experience, to apply patterns from other areas of experience to it, and to permit new aspects of the experience to emerge. Thus there are usually a series of steps or successive versions in an explication.

Neither the first verbal patterning nor the second, and neither the first set of "aspects" of the experience nor the second set, *is* exactly the experience. Experience can never be equated with our assertions. Rather, we can say something about experience in relation to the fact that one can always schematize further and get, or fail to get, certain experiential results. What character does experience have which is revealed in this fact that we may always schematize further in these different relationships?

To be able to be further schematized is a very striking characteristic of experience. In *Experiencing and the Creation of Meaning* I examined this possibility of further schematization under nine headings. Here I will use only three: We will find that, in the process of being *further* schematized, experiencing has no definite units, is responsive to any scheme, and is capable of being schematized by any other experience.

Experiencing is "nonnumerical." We can see this from the fact that direct reference can be made in many ways, each of which sets out some further "this" or "an" aspect. Experiencing does not come as a unit, or set of units, already cut in it. If it does, still quite other units can be set out from it. Although the recognition a word calls forth (or the situation which calls for a certain word) seems superficially to be packaged as a unit by that word, a situation is always potentially multiple. It can always be further differentiated, cut up, unitized.

Experiencing is "multischematic." Something unique (and not just anything you like) will emerge when you apply any scheme. Even if you keep a directly referred aspect "constant," it will respond differently to different schemes. Even when a scheme already seems to do well to organize an experience, other schemes can be applied and will have different results.

Experiences are "interschematizable": I mean by this that any experience (you need direct reference before you have "an" experience) can schematize any other, or be schematized by any other. This is hard to believe and needs examples. You can use any experience as a way of patterning another. Thereby commonalities will, as it were, fall out. With these, you can talk about either experience.

For example, consider what you were doing just before reading this, and use that activity to schematize our discussion. Perhaps you were on a bicycle ride with a friend. Yes, some parts of our discussion were uphill struggles, just as were parts of the bicycle ride, and some were easy and smooth and downhill. (Note: once you apply this bicycling experience to our discussion, you get just certain parts of it which were uphill and just so many. You can't have it just any way; unfortunately you can't have it all downhill. Any scheme applied gives you just certain results.)

Isn't it near madness to claim that any experience can be a scheme for another? Does this mean everything is everything? And it seems mysterious that any experience already contains something that will fall out as common with any other experience. Isn't this a metaphysical assertion? But, no. All we are saying is that a common aspect *can be created* in the process of schematizing one experience by the other; we don't say such an aspect *was* there, before.

We are discussing experience in terms of what *can be created*. What, then, *is* experience? The word "is" applies to experience only as held static, symbolized in some way, and hence it applies only to both experiencing and its symbolization as a compound.

Here then, is "the" structure of experiencing, not indeed as it "is," but as it is in regard to the next, or any further symbolization!

Nonnumerical, multischematic, and *interschematizable* together make up a type of order obviously different from the logical kind. But now, do not these three terms themselves constitute a scheme? Yes, of course. But their value lies in what they say we can *do:* we can directly refer and unitize; we can apply a scheme and see what we get; we can apply another experience and then schematize and see what we get.

It is quite true that "this" aspect of experience which I am setting forth here, and naming "the character of experiencing," could be formulated very differently than I did above. Not necessarily three but more or fewer characteristics could be set out. One could merge the "nonnumerical" and "multischematic," since they imply each other; one could merge the distinction between extant schemes and schematizing by another experience, thus merging the second and third characteristics. One could then apply some other scheme or experience to lay it out again, and differently. This is one fact we are finding as a characteristic of experience.

The problem now is whether we must think of this fact as a limitation on thinking, or whether there is not, here, the beginning of a more powerful method, closer to the nature of experience and living, which we may develop.

In *Experiencing and the Creation of Meaning* I presented eight points of method. Here I can only briefly touch on method.

For example, if I directly refer to, and then formulate, some aspect of experience, my formulation will have many logical implications. Must I be trapped by them all? Must I, on the contrary, lose all logical precision? Neither.

I can use any formulation and see what effect it has. If it makes me lose hold of what I wanted to formulate, I will retreat from it immediately. If, on the other hand, it makes new "aspects" of the experience stand out, and especially if these aspects seem important or troublesome, I will hold on to them. It may take a lot of fruitful work for me to find another way to formulate these new aspects, and to examine how my second formulation alters them and whether the difference is important to me, just now.

Two different formulations may be equivalent in regard to some directly referred-to aspect of experience—but only equivalent for the moment and in regard to the present point I want to make. One more step of thought, work, or action, and I might have to retract the asserted equivalence, for now the difference may be important.

I can even insist, in the case of two equivalent formulations, that since their words differ they must be capable of schematizing something different for me, and this can be pushed until it happens, and pushed further until it happens usefully.

Although most thinkers do not intend their schemes to be used in this way, any scheme can be employed as an open scheme—that is to say, it can enable us to refer directly to aspects of experience which may be formulated in a different, and possibly a better way, with many further aspects emerging.

One can be systematic and precise about which of these sort of steps one takes at any given juncture in one's thinking.

Signposts of the explication process

Let us return to our previous example, which, as we have said, was much too simple. You say that I am tired. If you consider your statement to be phenomenological, you will consider your statement wrong if I do not feel tired.

Your statement invites me to see if I am tired. How would I do that? Not by reviewing how long I have worked, and not by looking in the mirror. I can attend to my body directly and see if I find there what is called "tired." That is direct reference. Until you asked me, I paid no attention. Now, in reaction to your words, I seek to set up such "an" experience as we call "tired." If I cannot do so (and, note, this is not a matter of choice), your statement was wrong. Let us suppose that I agree I am "sort of tired."

Let me show how much further we can go than when we first considered this example.

Now suppose I say, "I am not exactly tired, but I *am* getting a little weary." It is clear that here you were definitely right in some way. Your words succeeded in "directly referring." They were also close in what they conveyed; they were pointing in the right direction. (I might have said, "No, I have a slight toothache.") We do not know as yet why I prefer "weary" to "tired" —they seem to be indistinguishable. "Weary" might perhaps include along with "tired" some sense of some long, drawn-out cause for being tired, and indeed we have been working all day and all evening. (It is this sort of experiential sense of how a word is used, which the linguistic analysts explicate.)

We must note that I probably did not feel tired until you said so. Your saying it made it true by leading me to create, specify, set out, distinguish (these words are equivalent here) "an" experience. Before I tried to refer to it, it wasn't there; now that I do, it is.

Yet, the feeling must be there; I do not just make it. Trying to refer to it, trying to see if I am tired, doesn't always make that feeling. Since now it did, for me, I would want to say that it *was* there before, only I didn't notice it. Of course, as a "this feeling" it certainly was not there before. (Yet the case is different than if you had suddenly made me tired, perhaps by telling me some heavy news. There is a continuity between how I remember being before, and my direct reference now to this tired feeling: thus the tired feeling is a newly set-out aspect *of* the over-all experience I was attending to.)

Suppose I now continue to explicate why "weary" seems to be true for me, and "tired" doesn't. I may say next, "Well, it's sort of not tired, but tired-of. That's why I said 'weary.' I don't feel like going on to this next job we have to tackle now. It's too tough."

Having said this, which is a more exact version of how I feel (as well as an explication of the use of the word I preferred), I might say, a moment or two later, "I feel like going out and having a good time. I am *not at all tired*—just so we don't have to get into this next job, it's too hard to do."

Now I am actually denying flatly what seemed above to be "in the right direction," though I really feel no different. I am still talking about "the same thing," and, despite the flat denial of what I said, I hold that what I say now is what my feeling really "was."

As I continue now to say just what it is about the next job that seems so tough, I may say, "Well, it isn't exactly hard to do, but what *is* hard is that I know they won't like how I'll do it." And then, *"The job is really easy."* And, again, further, "It isn't so much that I care what they think of it; it's just this one way I care, and that's a way that they're right, really. Gee, *I don't care at all what they think!* But this one criticism they'll make, I know they're right about that. It's really what *I* think that I care about." And, further, "I could help it, but I would have to take a day off to study up on how to do it right, and I don't want to do that."

And, again, "Really, *I do want to.* Every time I hit this sort of thing I wish *so much* that I could take the time off to learn how to do it, but I just can't give myself the time off. It would seem like a whole day with nothing done. I don't feel any trust in myself if I go and do something that isn't a part of the routine we call work, just doing something because I'd like to do it." And, later, "Hell, I'll do it tomorrow."

This aspect of experience—its vast capacity to be further schematized and unitized in relation to verbalization, and thereby revealing aspects which, we now say, it most truly "was," has not been recognized at all in philosophy until now. Therefore no systematic method has been devised for the various kinds of steps involved in explication.

It is clear from the example that one's own feelings *can* be stated falsely by oneself, and later corrected. There can be several steps in such correcting.

How may we get at the truth criteria involved in calling such steps a "correcting"? Both feeling and situation are internally complex and capable of having this complexity explicated verbally in various ways.

It is an error to think of situations as already cut up neatly and tritely, so that they need only to be observed and stated, just as it is an error to think of feelings as featureless masses unrelated to situations or words. We have feelings in and of situations. Conversely, situations are not physical facts but predicaments for people's living, desiring, and avoiding. Situation and experience cannot be separated, and both have the characteristic I attributed to experience: they can (and often must) be explicated further.

Thus, again considering our example, I can neither make anything I wish of my feeling and situation, nor can I regard them as given in a defined way. I must structure the situation further. This further structuring must go beyond the way in which the situation is cut and defined—at least in situations that are a problem for me. On the other hand, I must remain in accord with something about the situation—or else no realistic, feasible course of action will emerge. The sense in which I must remain in accord with the situation can be stated as its "non-

numerical, multischematic, and interschematizable character."
Although in this brief chapter I deal chiefly with the relation
of words and experience, I must say here that speaking and
thinking are special cases of action. Experience and situation
are always already organized, but are capable of being further
schematized and organized not only by verbalization but also
by actions. Again, such further structuring can occur in a variety
of ways, but it is never arbitrary. For any given action you will
get only just what you get, not merely anything at all. In phenomenological explication, as in ordinary action, you must not
only interpret a situation, but you must also apply your organization if you are to live in the situation further. That is very different from merely imposing some logical or attractive way of
organizing it, and then being able to leave and let it go at that.
Thus explication differs from mere deduction. One deals with
not only the words and statements but also the experience and
situation, and what is or is not revealed in them.

The relationships between experience and verbalization show
this character of explication: each relationship involves not only
words but a certain effect in experience which they elicit or fail
to elicit. One cannot simply wish for the words to have this effect.
For example, although I might wish my phrasing to have the
power to create an experiential aspect in you, it might fail to
have that power. I may wish a word to produce a certain recognition feeling and "be the word for" that, yet it may not be. And,
of course, I may from the start wish that my statement not be
accepted but used only for its direct reference power; yet it may
fail to have such power for you, even in the context and with all
you know. Thus each of the relationships I have cited is, in a
way, its own truth criterion—if it happens at all.

Therefore, if we can be sure that a given chain of thought or
speech is a true phenomenological explication, then we can at
least be sure that it will move a step forward in some way. Thus
there are truth criteria not for a single statement alone but for
a kind of process, a kind of step, each step in relation to an
earlier one.

To restate what we have already said, the following *signposts*
help us to recognize when phenomenological explication is going
on and when it is not. When phenomenological explication occurs:

(*a*) Precise defined meanings of words and the defined aspects of situations are used, but they can be further structured and redefined in ways that would not follow from the extant definitions.

(*b*) Something more than what is defined is employed. A not yet cognitively clear sense, feeling, or experience is used. This experience enables one to be dissatisfied with the words and definitions one has. Without it one would have only the statements and would have to either accept or reject them. In explication, on the other hand, a statement often serves to enable a step to be taken, and yet the statement cannot be accepted. Something directly referred to is involved in addition to statements.

(*c*) Aspects, and aspects within aspects, of this experience can be found.

(*d*) Demonstrative words such as "this" or "it" are used importantly, and yet such words alone convey little or nothing.

(*e*) Several different descriptive words may be used for the "same thing," despite the fact that literally they mean different things. Such different words can have quite different effects even in regard to the present experience, and one may ignore this, or pursue it.

(*f*) Previous assertions which enabled important steps forward may later be flatly denied.

(*g*) Whatever one now says is held to be what the experience "was" all along.

(*h*) Earlier false steps are believed to have been in the right direction, despite the fact that they are flatly contradicted now.

(*i*) What is at first simply physically "felt" becomes explicated in words that are about situations and world (not in feeling-tone words such as "dull" or "sharp" or "intense").

(*j*) Despite revealing new aspects and despite its changing, what is talked about is held to remain "the same" (not *literally* "the same"; it is obviously capable of various organizations and aspects).

If we accept the explication process of steps instead of a good or bad, single-step statement, we are in the position of caring less about "what" the statement says and more about "how" it relates and affects the experience: we are interested in the effects of the statement.

We have already cited some characteristics of an explicative step. Although its ultimate truth value is not firm, but depends on what subsequent steps will reveal, its characteristics as explication (or not) are quite firm.

In regard to our initial problem, we have denied that explication statements simply describe, state, or read off experience without changing it. Instead, we propose a method in which a statement can be used as exactly relative to the change it makes in the experience, or—more fairly said—to the kind of relationship it has with experience in the process of being further schematized. There are several such relationships that need to be distinguished. Each enables us to determine a statement's use as relative to that relation. Thereby certain specific methodic moves also become specifiable.

We rejected "feels right" or "sounds right" as a criterion, and instead found the several specific relationships involved. Explication always involves direct reference—and may succeed relative to that relationship—yet it may fail to achieve verbalizations we can accept. Far from being right if it feels right, such a statement is likely to succeed in directly referring and yet fail quite obviously in what it formulates. Even if the failure is not obvious, there is always the possibility of further differentiation of new aspects, as well as further formulation.

This phenomenological method makes the process, relationships, and steps of explication (rather than any given statements) basic. As I will now try to show, this shift from what is said to how it is related to experience has basic applicability to many fields.

The method may seem as if it launches us on an endless progression, but even here there are methodic ways of knowing when a desirable stopping point is reached; again the stopping point is not a final statement *of* an experience, but rather a way of structuring words or situations adequately so that some living, some action, or some intellectual task may be carried out. With respect to the final nature of experience there is no stopping point to statement, because the nature of experiencing vis-à-vis further structuring is precisely that it can be further structured, and in several different ways. There are steps rather than statement.

I have tried to show that this avenue can lead to a systematic analysis of relationships between verbalizations and experience, a systematic characterization of experience in these relations, and systematic rules of method.

The strategy of looking at the "how" of a process, rather than at the "what" of single step statements, has many applications. Let me cite one.

In ethics, for example, it is said that a person has "reasons" for his actions, even if these are not always apparent to him. But what an oversimplification it is, then, to adduce these reasons—without taking into account the nature of experiencing as characterized here!

In ethics, one must first recognize this character of experiencing. One must then see that any "reasons" stated may bear the several kinds of relationships to experience that we have outlined or alluded to. Further steps of explication are always possible. It will be better, for a philosophical ethics, to turn ninety degrees, and instead of calling some reasons good and others bad, to characterize the kind of decision-making process that arrives at "good" results. There is much adulation of spontaneity and feeling-expression today, but only some actions and speakings are related to feeling-experience in this good way. A different kind of relation obtains in impulsive behavior which is worse and less grounded than thinking alone. Still a third type of relation obtains for people who have explicit "reasons" that are not even explications of the experiencing leading to the action. Even a fourth relation is possible: one may truly have explicit "reasons" for an action (truly, that is to say, not as a rationalization or disconnected cover for experienced reasons) that are experiential and yet have nothing to do with what the reason is or says—as when a person tries to act in accord with some principle not for its own sake, but because he wishes to be loyal to a certain group holding that principle. Here we would need to explicate his experience—not of that reason and not the experience leading to the action, but of what led him to such loyalty to that group.

I cannot discuss ethics here. The single paragraph above illustrates, however, that the strategy of a ninety-degree turn may be fruitful in a variety of fields. The strategy is one of characterizing the "how," and of allowing the "what" to change step-by-step—being very precise, however, about these steps.

I will now discuss the application of experiential philosophy to psychotherapy research and psychology generally.

PSYCHOTHERAPY THEORY AND PRACTICE

IN PSYCHOLOGY, TOO, the shift has been a basic and fruitful one: from the consideration of only structures and patterns to the consideration of the structure-experiencing relationship. This cross-cutting type of variable, the phenomenological consideration of the relationship of statements or thoughts to experiencing, has been found fruitful in psychological research.[11] I want to report in detail one chain of such research which has become important in that field.

In psychotherapy it is common for a patient to work on a direct referent, "an" experiencing he feels quite strongly and yet does not cognitively understand. The kind of sequence illustrated by our example of "tired" is quite common. Not one, but a whole sequence of explicative statements occurs, each step bringing a shift in this so-called "same" experiencing. The change wanted in psychotherapy is not some final true statement but the continuation-and-change in the bodily felt experiencing which occurs in such steps.

All psychotherapists and psychotherapy patients know the difference between statements that are merely true and—much rarer—statements which make an experiential difference. Every psychotherapist has found that interpretations are often ineffective even when they are quite correct. One can say something about oneself which one understands quite well, and which one feels ought to be different; yet there is no change. One's feelings and behavior remain as they were, even though one can now explain the problem, trace its origin, and show why and how the change is desired. Freud [12] discusses the fact that the intellectual acceptance of an interpretation does not necessarily make a difference in the way a patient feels and acts. The task of psychotherapy is not to devise correct interpretations, but as Freud said, to "work [them] through," to concretely live and experience the trouble and its change. Freud said that this was the most crucial

11. E. T. Gendlin, "Galvanic Skin Response Correlates of Different Modes of Experiencing," *Journal of Clinical Psychology,* XVII, no. 1 (1961), pp. 73–77.
12. S. Freud, *Beyond the Pleasure Principle* (New York: Bantam Books, 1959).

part of any analysis, but he said very little about how to make it happen. We are told that it happens in transference, that is to say, in the relationship between patient and analyst, but the process is left as a rather obscure struggle. Most of Freud's writings concern *what* human beings typically find in these explorations, what interpretations may be about, but he says very little about *how* interpretations may be effective in this process of working-through, and why so often they are not.

Fenichel, who systematized most of Freud's work, is more specific: An interpretation, to be effective, he says, must be given

> only at one immediate point, namely where the patient's immediate interest is momentarily centered, . . . interpretation means helping something unconscious become conscious by naming it at the moment it is striving to break through. In giving an interpretation, the analyst seeks to intervene in the dynamic interplay of forces, to change the balance in favor of the repressed in its striving for discharge. The degree to which this change actually occurs is the criterion for the validity of an interpretation.[13]

The phenomenological approach is, of course, much more familiar with the problems of dealing with direct experience. Phenomenologists reject the Freudian explanatory concepts (such as theoretical "forces"), and therefore would reject the above explanation of why some interpretations are effective. But in rejecting the Freudian concepts (of "forces" and of the "unconscious"), phenomenologists are not quite able to account for all the observations Freud was concerned about. Some interpretations are effective and elicit material seemingly not there before, which, however, in some way, is experienced also as always having been there. However, with the philosophic method I have outlined, a more powerful phenomenology can both reject Freud's explanatory scheme and still hold to the direct experience and observation he described. In every effective psychotherapy, the patient feels an experiential shift as a result of (some few) effective interpretations, whether made by analyst or patient. Many other statements have no such effect.

If we look phenomenologically, but with our new method, at what Freudians mean by the "unconscious," we note that—at least in the above instance—they mean the common occurrence

13. O. Fenichel, *The Psychoanalytic Theory of Neurosis* (New York: W. W. Norton, 1945), pp. 25–32.

in which a person will for a time have confused but quite conscious feelings, which then later "shift" and "open up into" statements which seem to state what the earlier confused feeling really was.

To so restate the "unconscious" is to restate it in terms of a relationship between experience and explicatory statements.

Let us further delineate psychotherapy by using terms that concern the relation between experiencing and statement. It is one task of philosophy to criticize the concepts used in science and to fashion new and better kinds of concepts. Let us see if we have done so.

As we have seen, it is very common in psychotherapy for a patient to have a difficult and confused feeling for which he cannot find the proper words—at least not for some time. Not only can he not find words, but the feeling itself is also confused and partly closed to him. He would not say, "I know what I feel but I can't find words." He would say, "I am not sure what I feel, but I sure feel it . . ." He might call it "that funny feeling I get when . . . ," or "this knot in my stomach," or he might use some other such phrase which in itself cannot convey any specific feeling. Yet it is clear that the patient uses the phrase in order to hold on to the specific feeling or sense he has. We recognize this as the relation between experiencing and statement that we earlier termed "direct reference."

Direct reference (along with statements or with a pointing attention such as Hadamard's [14]) is likely to affect the experience. If the patient will keep referring directly (and this may be somewhat difficult to do), specific aspects of this feeling will form, and although this, of course, is a major change, he will say that he now has his feeling more clearly. Perhaps he now can say it. The words he fashions are usually metaphoric, but designed to convey the specific aspect to which he directly refers (we called it *Comprehension*).

Quite often the process is not so swift. Both patient and therapist may make many true and trenchant statements valid in their own right, but without any felt effect. Psychotherapy can be defined as a search for the few statements—about five percent—that do have such a directly felt effect.

A statement which does have an immediately felt effect leads,

14. Hadamard, *Psychology of Invention in the Mathematical Field.*

as I have already said, to a further explicating of a somewhat changed texture of situational detail. Now the patient can say a more specific "this" and "that," usually in terms of situations—how he lives, feels, and acts in them. Such comprehension further shifts his experiencing. Unless the difficulty was resolved in one such step, which is rare, he soon feels again the incompleteness or difficulty he is working on—only the confusion he now feels differs from what it was before. He moves into his next step, where he may again stay for some time.

The steps in this process are like the steps in our example, which led from feeling "sort of tired" to not wanting to do the next task. Such a step, as we saw, often leads one to entirely different situational concerns from the ones thought to be relevant to the last step. Had we not gone on with the directly felt experience, we would have been stuck in long discussions about the considerations which seemed relevant at each step. We would have discussed how long the person was working, instead of what was hard about the next task. Or we would have discussed why that task is hard to perform, when at the next step the problem turned out to have nothing to do with its difficulty. We would have discussed how "they" will react and whether "they" are wise and fair or not, when again at the next step that would have turned out not to matter. Thus it is wise to return after each step to the directly felt experiencing of whatever difficulty is left, rather than engaging in statements not related to the direct experiencing of the moment.

A psychotherapy is phenomenological, according to my theoretical reformulation, if its words and vocabulary are used in relation to experiencing. Unfortunately many therapists of all persuasions prefer to argue with their patients, rather than constantly referring to their concretely-had experiencing, rather than foregoing each, however interesting, set of considerations for the revised interpretations of the next step.

Research

For many years, the leading research problem in psychotherapy has been the measurement of whether or not effective psychotherapy is taking place. In the past twenty-five years many cases have been tape-recorded, but the many attempts to define the differing problems that patients verbalize, or methods therapists use, have failed to show any relationship to outcome. Methods emphasizing different, supposedly "basic" psychological factors, show about the same degree of success. Different orientations of therapists concentrate respectively on sexual problems, infantile experiences, life styles, self-concepts, interpersonal relationships, or other kinds of "basic" contents. These differences do not seem to matter. Some therapies are successful and some fail, with or without any of these content areas. The resolution of this problem along phenomenological lines lies instead in studying *how* patient and therapist talk, rather than *what* they talk about.

The usual method in research was to give the patient psychological tests before the therapy began and after it ended, and then to establish whether or not change resulted. Sometimes it did, and as often it did not. But there was no way to study psychotherapy directly, and hence no accounting for why each method and emphasis sometimes succeeded and sometimes not.

Nor was it possible to measure the outcome of *psychotherapy,* since *psychotherapy* could not even be defined. One could measure the before-and-after change in a great number of cases and in different methods, but all that these cases had in common was that therapist and patient *intended* something undefined, called psychotherapy, to happen. It was clear that the ongoing process itself needed defining, but how to do so? Whenever those factors that most writers held to be basic were tested, it was found that they did not necessarily provide for a successful outcome. Interpretation, transference, discussions of supposedly basic contents did occur, but sometimes the outcome would be successful and sometimes not. About the only finding relating outcome to what occurred during psychotherapy was that those patients who later showed the most change made more positive statements about themselves in the later interviews than in the earlier ones, a finding that is clearly about the result and not the source of therapeutic change.

Using the relationships between experience and statement earlier cited, and the signposts of experiential explication they led to, it became possible to define and make operationally observable the kind of verbalizing that effective psychotherapy involves. The train of thought and steps of statement in effective psychotherapy clearly differ from narrative (and then this happened, and then that happened . . .) or logical deduction (and so it follows that such and such must be so). Instead, effective steps of verbalization are connected through relations to directly felt experiencing and, as we have seen, move in the kind of steps we defined. How such steps follow each other is understandable, but not by situational narrative, since the relevant situational considerations differ after each step of experiential explication. The steps are understandable, but not logically; in fact there is often a seeming flat contradiction and denial of what was affirmed earlier. One may see this, for example, in such transitions as the one from "I don't want to," to "I do want to, but . . ."

Working from signposts such as those already listed, and others, it was possible to devise an Experiencing Scale,[15] consisting of descriptions of specific aspects of verbalizations that can be observably noticed in tape-recorded psychotherapy. Using this scale independently, different individuals have arrived at measurably close scores.

A whole series of studies [16] has now shown that, indeed, those cases that score high on the Experiencing Scale during psychotherapy result in successful change. Successful outcome can be predicted from a surprisingly small number of short excerpts, in some studies merely from four, four-minute segments, so consistent, apparently, is the presence or absence of the experiential mode of doing psychotherapy in a given case.

As we have seen, the Experiencing Scale measures *how* the patient works in psychotherapy, not *what* he says, or what areas of concern he works on. He is successful to the extent that he refers directly to, and explicates, what he directly feels, and follows the steps through which experiential explication leads. He fails to the extent that he *only* explains or narrates (although everyone does some of these latter).

This measure is currently the only gauge which enables us to determine whether or not effective psychotherapy is currently taking place. The findings strongly imply that these experiential signposts are indicative of whatever makes therapy effective.

Possibilities for further research have also been greatly en-

15. M. Klein, P. Mathieu-Coughlan, D. Kiesler, E. T. Gendlin, *The Experiencing Scale Manual* (Madison, Wis.: Wisconsin Psychiatric Institute, 1969).

16. E. T. Gendlin et. al., "Focusing Ability in Psychotherapy, Personality and Creativity," in *Research in Psychotherapy*, ed. J. Schlien, Vol. III (Washington, D.C.: American Psychological Association, 1967).

larged, because we now no longer need to wait until the termination of therapy in order to measure individual cases. Previously, if an investigator wanted to test whether a given procedure or factor was related to a positive outcome, the tape recordings of completed cases had to be collected. Now one can test the effect of the factor by using the tape recordings of just a few interviews before and after the introduction of the procedure (or with, or without, the given factor); one can test swiftly whether or not the factor makes for an effective therapeutic process.

To further show what this scale measures, let me cite an example.

Low on the Scale

CLIENT: I'm trying to rewrite some of these papers, before I send them out with my Vita to find a job. It's only December, and it ought to be ok to spend two weeks rewriting them—nobody is going to give me a job over Christmas anyway. But I sit there and I can't let myself start. It seems like it's so urgent I ought to send them out today, right away. I can't work on them so I'll have to go and send them in the shape they're in.

THERAPIST: Well, maybe you could give yourself one week? Do they really need rewriting, or is it perfectionism?

CLIENT: No, I can't even give it a day. But there are some plain, obvious bad spots in the papers that I know how to fix. I just have no confidence at all that I can get a job. (*Long conversation lost in details of papers, time, and hiring policies.*)

High on the Scale

THERAPIST (*picking something that he wished the client would have an experiential sense of and go into*): Is the urgent feeling that you don't think you'll find a job?

CLIENT: Yeah. No. Well, something like that. (*Keeps quiet awhile.*) I'm so mad at myself.

THERAPIST (*thinking he's angry at himself for not being able to work and fix the papers*): It's urgent, and you're mad at yourself for being tied up.

CLIENT: No, I'm just mad. (*Long silence.*) It's like, I *should* send the papers out in bad shape, because that would serve me right. I didn't do them right and now it's too late. It's my father—

you didn't do it when you should have done it, so now go take your punishment. (*Shakes his head.*) Well, now I can work on them, but isn't that something?

THERAPIST: You've still got his kind of ethic in you—you didn't do it right, so suffer.

CLIENT: It has something to do with his dying last year, I would say it must have something to do with that.

THERAPIST (*not wanting to get off on the dying part, which seems extraneous*): It's a punishing, critical, go-suffer kind of angry.

CLIENT: Yes, it's him. (*Long silence.*) It's because he died.

THERAPIST (*understanding the connection now*): It's your way of hanging on to him.

CLIENT: No, he's hanging on to me. That's the only relationship he had to me.

THERAPIST: It's the bond between you.

CLIENT (*emphatically*): Yes, that's the way it feels. (*Long silence, then with mixed hate and love and slight tearfulness.*) You old sonofabitch, why you old sonofabitch.

This bit of psychotherapy illustrates the signposts that are a constant feature of *psychotherapy:* What is being worked on is an experiential "something," the nature and change of which takes surprising turns. Remaining on the initial level of attitudes and circumstances makes for no therapeutic change (though it can be valuable in other respects). The felt, directly-referred to, experiential sense of what is troubling the individual produces a series of steps whose verbal statements follow our signposts of explication. What seemed to be the subject matter changes, is even opposite to what had been thought—yet there is the continuity of a "same thing." The experiential process has steps which, in retrospect, have the peculiar "was" structure of explication (despite what I said then, what I say now is what it "was" all along).

The therapist, be it noted, is as often wrong as right, but the statements are used phenomenologically, to point to what is being experienced. Lengthy explanatory schemes could be introduced at every point, but these would only hold up psychotherapeutic movement and would not produce the next step.

It can be seen that the scale is interdenominational; it will fit any school of psychotherapy, whatever its vocabulary. Even "behavior therapy," which is usually contrasted to psychotherapy and uses behaviorist language in its theories and with patients, has been found similar on these indexes.[17]

There is one other area of psychological research to which the Experiencing Scale has been applied: old age. People in their seventies go through a process called "life review," wherein they attempt to cope with the meaning to them of all that has happened in their lives. Some ten years ago, in a major project at the University of Chicago, old-age-home residents were given five quite simple questions: "What is it like when you feel happy?" (sad, lonely, etc.). When their answers to this questionnaire were recently measured on the Experiencing Scale, it was found that those who were high on the scale had significantly more often survived into their eighties than those who were low on the scale. We interpret this to mean that "life review" is similar to psychotherapy, that both involve the same experiential process, that is to say, an organismic and bodily process whose manner affects life in a bodily concrete way.

Psychotherapy is not the only field in which the signposts of experientially related verbalization are important. We may want to measure the extent to which children in a classroom are engendered to think out their own experience of subject-matter they are encountering. We may want to know which kinds of children, fields, or methods of teaching maximize this process and which minimize it. Can the same indexes measure this? No, the actual measure has to be devised freshly for each new field and context, but the *kind* of indexes to be used are the same. Thus, in measuring the effectiveness of almost any activity, one may ask: Are there observable marks to indicate whether or not what is going on is experientially related and engenders experientially concrete steps? This form of question is likely to lead one to an effective research instrument through a shift from studying *what,* to studying *how,* a shift from an emphasis on the patterns of speech and action to an emphasis on what these patterns do or do not do in regard to concrete and ongoing experiencing.

For example, suppose we wanted to measure authenticity of choice and decision-making. It is unlikely that this can be done by studying what people choose, or what value-conclusions they

17. B. Weitzman, "Behavior Therapy and Psychotherapy," *Psychological Review,* 1967.

arrive at. It is likely that authenticity will become definable in terms of *how* an individual arrives at a value-conclusion, rather than what it is. Has the person experientially explicated various feelings and unclear commitments, loyalties, fears, and wants, and thus arrived at a value-conclusion? Was it taken over knowingly from some respected source, but without as yet relating to the person's own experiencing? Or has the person succumbed to a confusing and not clearly known pressure or wish to appear in certain ways to others? These three possibilities, if measured, would predict very different behavior and results, even though the value-conclusion itself might be the same.[18]

Creativity, an area that has been widely studied in psychology, also involves indexes of this type. What characterizes it is "how" it occurs. The uncreative individual has been characterized negatively as "stimulus-bound", i.e., not able to let go of the usual or given form of something so that a novel one may arise. There is now some experiential research that offers positive definitions of what one does do when one does not hold to an extant form. A person's own description of how he proceeded would reveal whether or not he referred directly to experiential aspects, and whether the first bits of structured form he obtained were or were not related to his experiencing in the ways I have defined. To measure this, one would need to devise specific indexes in accord with the range of comments people make about their own thinking. It is, however, already somewhat clear that those who are creative are able to focus their attention directly on what is being experienced but is not yet cognitively clear, just as the successful patient does in psychotherapy, and the successful phenomenologist does when he explicates.

Again I want to emphasize that specific signposts need to be formulated for each different process. I do not wish to say that the same process occurs in all these different settings. What is the same is the study of the *relationships* between what is structured, patterned, formulated, or explicit, and the ways in which experiencing is affected by these relationships. Such an approach, I find, is a more effective research approach than studying the patterns and contents as such. Either way, one studies formed and patterned observable data, but the marks or sign-

18. E. T. Gendlin, "Values and the Process of Experiencing," in *The Goals of Psychotherapy*, ed. Alvin R. Mahrer (New York: Appleton-Century-Crofts, 1967).

posts one seeks, the "variables" one defines and counts, differ. Advances in research do not usually come from merely relating already existing variables; new observations must first be defined and set up as demarcated variables. In this respect observation is at first as "implicit" as feeling. It has been fruitful to define observable variables by means of the philosophy of experiencing, which raises this type of question: How does whatever we seek to study differ observably when it is in certain relations to concrete experiencing, as against when it lacks these relations? This is a shift from *what* to *how*.

Other theoretical issues

In our discussion of the psychoanalytic views of "unconscious" and "interpretation," with direct reference to experiencing, instead of as part of an explanatory machinery, we have employed a shift in theoretical formulation.

How to conceive of the "unconscious" has long been a problem. One view is that it consists of unobservable ideas lying somewhere outside a person's thought. But these cannot be measured so that they might then be compared with what is later *said*, so that we may know if what is later said is what was unconscious before.

Phenomenology and empirical research are similiar in discarding merely imputed constructs which do not at any point lead to experience. Therefore, the concept of the unconscious has not been very useful in research, nor is it usually accepted by phenomenologists. But the method we have developed allows us to reformulate the unconscious theoretically. Instead of considering it in terms of a hidden place, or unthought ideas, we reformulate it according to relationships between statement and experience and steps of explication. In this way we define the specific observable differences which mark what a Freudian would call "something unconscious breaking through." For, while the unconscious may be unobservable, the signposts are observable: they distinguish from other statements those that now say what an earlier confused experience "was," and refer to or comprehend directly the experiential effect of such statements. I am sure that such statements can be mimicked even without experiential effect, but such mimicking is not usual and would require a good actor, poet, or seasoned patient. Theoretically, the implication is neither simply that there is no unconscious, nor that the unconscious consists of complete thoughts and experiences that happen outside of consciousness. Rather, experience can be understood as a process in itself and thus as capable of further structuring which has not yet occurred. The capacity of experience to be further structured (in thought and action) is "the unconscious"—the not indeterminate, but also not finally formed character of experience. Thus the unconscious includes bodily, evolutionary, cultural, verbal, situational, and personal aspects which have much to do with what can or cannot be further said and done but are not sayings and deeds.[19]

We should not allow phenomenology to be so shallow as to simply deny the unconscious. Phenomenology need not be limited to one-step descriptions of some experience;[20] however elaborate and interesting such descriptions can be in themselves, they take off from experience but do not return to it. The important criteria for phenomenology lie not only in beginning with experience, but also in returning constantly to it and allowing it to have the corrective force which the occurrence of experiential effects gives it. When one explicates a difficult text, it is not enough to take off from some line and spin an interesting interpretation; one must return to the text and see if the interpretation sheds light on other lines in the text, whether it solves or shifts difficulties. If it has no such effects, then the interpretation of the given line was simply a digression, interesting for its own sake perhaps, but not attributable to this text. Thus a phenomenological psychology need not be baffled by the very real problems to which the theory of the "unconscious" is such a poor answer. It need only concern itself with steps of explication, rather than remaining fixed at one point.[21]

Steps of explication and their signposts give criteria for the truth of the next statement, only in relation to the previous. But then neither are there final statemens in ordinary science. The next discovery may overturn previously well-established statements. Phenomenological explication steps have criteria which

19. E. T. Gendlin, "A Theory of Personality Change," in *Creative Developments*, ed. Alvin R. Mahrer (Cleveland: The Press of Case Western Reserve University, 1971).

20. E. T. Gendlin, "Expressive Meanings," in *Invitation to Phenomenology*, ed. James M. Edie (Chicago: Quadrangle, 1965).

21. E. T. Gendlin, "Experiential Explication and the Problem of Truth," *Journal of Existentialism*, VI, no. 22 (1966).

can be called criteria of continuity. The relationships I have outlined do not simply produce abrupt changes in what is experienced. On the contrary, despite change and despite contradictory statements, the individual will have the insistent sense that "this" is now "really" what that earlier experience "was." Thus there is continuity: there is neither flat identity nor an abrupt new thing. Experience has its own kind of order, different from logic and defined events. Experience can always be "carried further," but not in just any way, only in some ways. These ways may have to be found or invented, but until they occur, the explicative continuity does not exist.

Thus, it is possible to make some seemingly convenient statement, explication, or value-conclusion which might state what one feels or wishes or desires, but which lacks the signposts of experiential explication. In that case it is quite likely that much of what is felt (and thus much that is important in living in situations with others) has not been carried further. What one says is not continuous with the many considerations that are "unconscious." Actually one can feel many of these, with awareness if one wishes, but cognitively they are unclear and only later come to have specifiable aspects.

A phenomenological ethics, for example, cannot do without experiential explication and its signposts. It is both a methodological and a moral error to say that authentic choice is nothing more than individual choice. What matters is *how* one does it. One may base decision on "experience" in the sense in which it is already identified and defined (for instance, as a desire to do such and such). Or one might simply follow the strongest passion, speaking and acting in ways that have poorer grounding than if moral precepts were used, however insufficient these might be. It is better for speech and action to be based on "experience" than on thought alone—but only if they are "based" in such a way as to give us more than do formulated thoughts alone. This will be the case only if the thinking is explicating and continuing the experiencing. Without specific criteria to help us recognize when this is so, everything becomes arbitrary.

PART IV

Phenomenology
and Linguistics

Philosophy of Language as Phenomenology of Language and Logic

Ernst Wolfgang Orth

The Phenomenological Theme: Philosophy and Language

THE THEME phenomenology and linguistics signifies both the confrontation and the correlation of two distinct disciplines. It states, first, that problems in the study of language are to be examined and resolved by the methods of phenomenology. It is a question of a phenomenology of linguistics, whatever linguistics means. It is therefore necessary at the outset to establish what is meant by phenomenology, that is, what type of phenomenology is being referred to. In our case it is the so-called transcendental phenomenology as developed by Edmund Husserl. Phenomenology in this instance, then, is equivalent to philosophy, the working-out or unfolding of the phenomenological methods of investigation being nothing other than philosophy itself.[1] Now if we conceive of phenomenology as philosophy, then our confrontation of linguistics with phenomenology comprises a thoroughly traditional theme, namely, philosophy and language—the philosophy of language.

But what is meant by the philosophy of language? If we adhere to such analogous formulations as "the philosophy of his-

Translated from the German by William McKenna.
1. *Ideas I*, pp. 165 f.; cf. *CM*, pp. 83 ff.; *FTL*, pp. 267 ff., 271 ff.; *EPh*, II, 193–301. [Abbreviations are used throughout for referring to Husserl's works. A list of these will be found at the end of this essay, together with full publication data.—Trans.]

[323]

tory" or "the philosophy of nature," then the philosophy of language—at least according to a widely held opinion—would be nothing other than a comprehensive evaluation of everything which the individual sciences have to say about language. The criterion for such an evaluation is, of course, never accurately defined. One speaks of "the question of meaning," of "the reference back to man," of something that goes "beyond" mere scientific exploration. And the respective conceptions of the philosophy of language fluctuate between a constructive method that is subject to control and speculations that are no longer capable of being reexecuted. Occasionally the philosophy of language is not content merely to be an "overviewing" evaluation of the individual sciences of language; on the contrary, it tries to offer a consideration of language of its own which is somehow outside of, before, or this or that side of every possible individual science.[2] In my opinion, however, talk about the philosophy of language, the philosophy of history, and the like can be meaningful only if this philosophizing understands philosophy as the theory of science [*Wissenschaftstheorie*]. It is the task of the theory of science on its part to determine methodologically everything which is constitutive for the methods and object of a thematized field of investigation.[3] In a philosophy, and in particular in a philosophy of language so understood, it is not possible simply to divide the theme into two parts, namely, to say in one part what philosophy is and in the other what linguistics is. For the answer to the question, What is linguistics?, insofar as the question seeks to fix the theme and methods of this field of investigation, is itself a philosophical question. This means that the contrast between phenomenology and linguistics can

---

2. Cf. Hans Lipps, *Die Verbindlichkeit der Sprache*, 2d ed. (Frankfurt: Klostermann, 1958), pp. 107–20. In an essay from 1938, bearing the same title as the book, Lipps, following Heidegger, devalues the *logos semantikos* in favor of the *logos hermeneutikos*. This restriction to pre- or nonscientific language is also found in anti-Heideggerian authors such as Theodor W. Adorno and Max Horkheimer, *Dialektik der Aufklärung*, 2d ed. (Frankfurt: Fischer, 1969), esp. pp. 1 ff., 138 f., 173 ff., 231. See also Adorno, *Negative Dialektik* (Frankfurt: Suhrkamp, 1966; 2d ed., 1970), esp. the Introduction. On this conception in general, see Ernst W. Orth, *Bedeutung, Sinn, Gegenstand: Studien zur Sprachphilosophie E. Husserls und R. Hönigswalds* (Bonn: Bouvier, 1967), esp. pp. 18–32, 68 ff., 163 ff.
3. "Methodological" should be distinguished from "methodical" (in the sense of "technical"), although for the present this distinction is not carried out terminologically and still is in need of further clarification.

at most be understood as only provisional. It holds only at a certain level of reflection.

If one were to apply to the consideration of language the conception of philosophy described above, then the philosophy of language—as well as phenomenology of language—would have to discuss and specify the principal scientific forms of access to language as a theme of inquiry while at the same time defining that theme itself. It would have to explain, on the one hand, why there are such varied types of considerations or disciplines with respect to the phenomenon of language. On the other hand, it would be necessary to establish precisely wherein the identity of the theme and phenomenon of language consists. Before all else, that would involve refining a univocal terminology or at least explaining why there are different terminologies and how the different terminological types might be related to one another.

PHENOMENOLOGY AS THEORY OF SCIENCE

IF THIS TASK should be performed not simply by a philosophy of language but by a so-called phenomenology of language, then the advantage of phenomenology over other conceptions of philosophy should be made methodologically operative. The advantage of phenomenology in our opinion consists precisely in the fact that it is suited for developing a sufficiently wide but nonetheless exact concept of the theory of science. When in the first third of the twentieth century Husserl was working out his transcendental philosophy, the expression *Wissenschaftstheorie* (theory of science) was still not an established term. At this time it occurs only sporadically, often as synonymous with *Wissenschaftslehre*.[4] Today, as a result of the

4. The term *Wissenschaftslehre* emerges first in Fichte, as the title of his book on knowledge (1794), and then—in a thoroughly different sense —in Bolzano (1837). In Husserl the adjective *wissenschaftstheoretisch* occurs in context with *Wissenschaftslehre;* cf. *LI,* I, 67 ff. *CM,* p. 7, speaks of "logic as a theory of science." In Husserl the theory of science is also connected with *prima philosophia* (cf. *EPh,* II, 193 ff.). See, in addition, Richard Hönigswald, "Zur Wissenschaftstheorie und Systematik" (with reference to Rickert's "Kulturwissenschaft" and "Naturwissenschaft"), *Kant-Studien,* XVII (1912), 28–84, and Alfred Schutz, *The Phenomenology of the Social World,* trans. George Walsh and Frederick Lehnert (Evanston, Ill.: Northwestern University Press, 1967), pp. 6 f.

work of the Neo-Positivists, the term designates a branch of inquiry firmly inscribed in the framework of the concerns of formal logicians. For all that, it is still a somewhat fuzzy, fashionable expression.[5] Logically oriented authors understand by the theory of science "a theory of the methods of the experimental sciences";[6] it is essentially "normative" and therefore not empirical.[7] "The theory of definition," "the theory of axiomatization," "the methods for grounding hypotheses," and "the procedures for the explanation of facts" form its focal point. The concept of theory holds the central position,[8] theory being understood as a formal system of *statements*.[9] "Logic, mathematics, and the individual fields for the investigation of their foundations" belong to the theory of science,[10] although logic and mathematics—but only for historical and sociological reasons—are distinct from the theory of science.[11] The commitment to a formal mathematical concept of theory—or to one at least analogous to mathematics—exercises an important limiting function on the theory of science. In particular, it guarantees the controllability of its methods and results, and thus proves useful even when it falls into error or suffers from a certain one-sidedness. On the other hand, those authors who argue from certain hermeneutical or so-called "ideological-critical" viewpoints oriented toward practice [praxis] or, finally, those who insist on "social relevance" employ in connection with the term "theory of science"—which they obviously do not want to

5. This also holds for the term "logic" which still turns up in paralinguistic (Paul Lorenzen) and figurative uses in such formulas as "logic of the humanities" (Erich Rothacker) or "logic of poetry" (Käthe Hamburger). For a sharpening of the terminology in connection with the analysis of language see Kuno Lorenz, *Elemente der Sprachkritik: Eine Alternative zum Dogmatismus und Skeptizismus in der analytischen Philosophie* (Frankfurt: Suhrkamp, 1970), esp. pp. 98 ff.

6. Wilhelm Essler, *Wissenschaftstheorie I* (Freiburg and Munich: Alber-Kolleg Philosophie, 1970), p. 18.

7. *Ibid.*, p. 14.

8. *Ibid.*, p. 16.

9. There is, of course, an ambiguity in the term "statement" [*Aussage*] that calls for attention and clarification (for a similar ambiguity in regard to "judgment," see *FTL*, pp. 134 f.). The wider use of the term "statement" embraces both logic in the narrow sense of mathematical logic [*Quantorenlogik*] and statement-logic.

10. *Ibid.*, p. 18.

11. *Ibid.*, pp. 15, 18. Husserl speaks of a "division of labor" of the philosopher and the mathematician (*LI*, I, 243; cf., on the "logic of the mathematician," *LI*, II, 518, 527 f.).

give up—a concept of theory which is not formal (in a defined sense) but which simply signifies a sum of meaning-forms.[12] They refer mostly to "insights" or "interests" or "concerns" whose evaluations are often interesting and do contain the rudiments of corrigibility. Nonetheless, they are for the most part methodologically uncontrollable, especially because the use of such expressions is not free from (unnoticed) equivocation.[13] If the logical, analytical theory of science has a close relation to formal and mathematical logic, the hermeneutical and ideologizing theory of science employs the method of dialectic (so named since Hegel).[14] The recent confrontation of the two approaches in the so-called controversy over positivism is well documented.[15] In my opinion, the real objections which from a philosophical standpoint could be brought against the foreshortening of the problem that is characteristic of the logico-analytical theory of science are generally not well represented in the arguments of the dialectical authors of hermeneutical or ideologizing persuasion. What the formal, logico-analytical theory of science lacks most is a clarification of its presuppositions, both the epistemological and those related to the theory of consciousness.[16] Among these presuppositions is the meaning of such basic concepts as "formal," "form," "extension," and "quantification," which guide the logical analysis. It is perfectly clear that such crucial but often ambiguously employed basic concepts are not clarified by evoking them as hermeneutical or ideological preunderstandings [Vorverständnisse]. This can only be done through a construc-

12. This concept of theory can be understood in conjunction with the theory of consciousness or—in a sense which is at bottom psychologistic and sociologistic—in conjunction with the criticism of ideologies.

13. Alongside equivocations of a logical and linguistic nature there are those of a historical nature, which manifest themselves in a very free understanding of traditional concepts and their respective definitions. That is, the historical and social understanding of concepts is often not promoted by the very men who, as practitioners of hermeneutics or as social scientists criticizing ideologies, make this their proper theme.

14. Dialectic is a procedural concept which is found not merely in professed Hegelians and Marxists, and which, beyond its initial plausibility, still has not found a proper logical form.

15. "Der Positivismusstreit in der deutschen Soziologie," *Soziologische Texte* Vol. LVIII (Neuwied and Berlin: Luchterhand, 1969).

16. This may be the reason why, occasionally at least, an attempt is made to treat the theory of science and epistemology together, as in Werner Leinfellner, *Einführung in die Erkenntnis- und Wissenschaftstheorie.* (Mannheim: B-I Taschenbuch, 1967).

tive analysis of clarification.[17] One might reproach the formal-logical theoreticians of science for treating only one part of their discipline, the (mathematically defined) theory. However, what knowing [*Wissen*]—in science [*Wissenschaft*] and theory of science [*Wissenschaftstheorie*]—is or means they fail to consider. If one calls the discipline which should intervene here the theory of knowledge and consciousness, then one must reckon with the reproach that one is dealing with judgment, knowledge, and consciousness but not with theory, which nonetheless also belongs to the theory of knowledge and the theory of consciousness.

It is precisely on this point that the relevance of Husserl's transcendental phenomenology for the theory of science manifests itself. For transcendental phenomenology attempts to combine research in the theory of consciousness with research in the theory of formal logic while it avoids furthering one at the expense of the other. The program of the *Logical Investigations* of 1900–1901 and the *Formal and Transcendental Logic* of 1929 clearly shows this, although we cannot present it in detail here.[18]

HUSSERL'S POINT OF DEPARTURE (IN *LI*) IN LOGIC AND IN THE INVESTIGATION OF CONSCIOUSNESS

THE ATTEMPT TO COMBINE logical research with the theory of consciousness is already present in Husserl at the stage of the merely phenomenological (descriptive psychological) and not yet transcendental-phenomenological *Logical Investigations*. As is well known, this has contributed not a little to confusing interpreters who never rightly understood what was supposed to be the theme of the *Logical Investigations*. Is it logic? And, if logic, then what logic, or logic in what respect? Or is it a

17. A constructive but nonepistemological attempt at clarification from the Lorenzen school can be found in Friedrich Kambartel, "Zur Rede von 'formal' und 'Form,'" *Neue Hefte für Philosophie*, no. 1: *Phänomenologie und Sprachanalyse*, ed. Rüdiger Bubner et al. (Göttingen: Vandenhoeck & Ruprecht, 1971), pp. 51–67.

18. Husserl is one of the few knowledge-theorists and transcendental philosophers who maintain a positive relationship to the tradition of formal and mathematical logic. For the development of his philosophy see Walter Biemel, "Die entscheidenden Phasen der Entfaltung von Husserls Phänomenologie," *Zeitschrift für philosophische Forschung*, XIII (1959), 187–213.

question of epistemology or merely psychology? Or, in the end, are epistemology and logic the same thing? The Sixth Logical Investigation is a special source of difficulties. Talk about reverting to psychologism has its foundation right here in the perplexity over what is the theme of the investigation.[19] And, finally, the consideration of language must be added as a third theme.[20] Although this work still has not reached the level of transcendental reflection but rather represents a (first) breakthrough to phenomenology on the theme of logic,[21] it contains all the fundamental problem headings of the later transcendental-phenomenological program. It is also basic for the later terminology.[22] Because of Husserl's intention—which we should view as fundamental for the *Logical Investigations*—to understand logic and the logical, he does not start from established values, such as "concepts" and "judgments" and the like, but from the manner of their givenness, that is, from the type of their phenomenological emergence in the living act of knowing. Such emergences are "statements" in the form of certain expressions, and these are primarily linguistic. They are meanings, meanings in the widest sense. Thus it is not the "concept" which is, first of all, the theme of the *Logical Investigations*, but "meaning,"[23] and meaning simply, and, therefore, not yet fixed logical meaning as ideal species. This character of meaning as ideal species and thus as logical element must first be shown (cf. *FTL*, p. 67). Thus:

Linguistic discussions are certainly [24] among the philosophically indispensable preparations for the building of pure logic: only by

19. For that—with the corresponding references to Paul Natorp—see Orth, *Bedeutung*, esp. pp. 240 ff.

20. Cf. Orth, *Bedeutung*, along with a treatment of the pertinent secondary literature, esp. pp. 243 ff.; see also Orth, "Grundlagen- und Methodenprobleme der Sprachwissenschaft vom Standpunkt der Transzendentalphänomenologie," *Linguistische Berichte*, no. 5 (1970), pp. 1–25.

21. Cf. Johannes Thyssen, "Husserls Lehre von den 'Bedeutungen' und die Begriffsproblem," *Zeitschrift für philosophische Forschung*, XIII (1959), 163–86, 438–58.

22. Theodorus de Boer, "Das Verhältnis zwischen dem ersten und dem zweiten Teil der *Logischen Untersuchungen* E. Husserls," *Saggi filosofici*, no. 27 (Turin, 1967), p. 9, justly warns against interpreting the *Logical Investigations* from the point of view of the later work.

23. Thyssen, "Husserls Lehre," p. 168.

24. It is important to observe the limitation of the aspect from which language is considered here.

their aid can the true *objects* of logical research—and, following thereon, the essential species and differentiae of such objects—be refined to a clarity that excludes all misunderstanding. We are not here concerned with grammatical discussions, empirically conceived and related to some historically given language: we are concerned with discussions of a most general sort which cover the wider sphere of an objective *theory of knowledge* and, closely linked with this last, the *pure phenomenology of the experiences of thinking and knowing* (*LI*, I, 249).

All theoretical research, though by no means solely conducted in acts [25] of verbal expression or complete statement, none the less terminates in such statement (*LI*, I, 250).

Also, it is made perfectly clear here that researches conducted under the title "pure phenomenology" are "neutral," that is, they are not designed for logic or at least not only for logic (*LI*, I, 249 f.). In the *Logical Investigations*, then, three motifs are to be observed: the epistemological, the logical, and the linguistic.

The theory of knowledge as investigation of consciousness

The *theory of knowledge* is what Husserl calls "pure phenomenology" (*LI*, I, 249; he also speaks of "epistemological or phenomenological groundwork" [p. 250]) or, as in the *Logical Investigations* in particular, "descriptive psychology" (*LI*, I, 262, and, in the first [German] edition, p. 10). Thus his considerations are directed entirely to the "side of the subject." It is an "analysis, so to speak, of the subject of language," [26] but certainly not of this alone. Phenomenology wants to exhibit the "sources" (*LI*, I, 249)—for example, of logic. And similarly, the call to the "things themselves" (*LI*, I, 252)—very likely misunderstood in the direction of positivism or realism—could be interpreted as a call *ad fontes*. "Even if phenomenological analysis of concrete thought-experiences does not fall within the true home-ground of pure logic" (*LI*, I, 251), nonetheless, recourse to consciousness is indispensable even for the formal (pure) logician whose proper concern admittedly is idealities and theories. For

25. This recalls *FTL*, p. 287: "not every evidence has the form, specific *Ego-act*."
26. Thyssen, "Husserls Lehre," p. 168.

logical concepts, as valid thought-unities, must have their origin in intuition: they must arise out of an ideational abstraction [*"ideierend"* is lacking in the first German edition, p. 7] founded on certain experiences, and must admit of indefinite reconfirmation, and of recognition of their self-identity, on the reperformance of such abstraction (*LI* I, 251 f.).[27]

One can see from the cited passage how Husserl's concept of idea is linked to the concept of possible and enduring identity.[28] To "meaning" as the meaning of a word there clearly belongs a mediating function between "concept," "pure law," or formal theory, on the one side, and living, presenting "evidence," on the other side (cf. *LI*, I, 251). For, "Such self-evidence [of the logical] . . . depends on the verbal meanings which come alive in the actual passing of the judgment regarding the law" (*LI*, I, 251). However, Husserl does not want to occupy himself with " 'mere words,' i.e., with a merely symbolic understanding of words" (*LI*, I, 252). "Nor does one exceed one's prescribed limits if one starts, e.g., from existent languages" (*LI*, I, 266).[29] The premature construction of theories and concepts in a vacuum, so to speak, is renounced in favor of a return to "intuition," i.e., to concrete experiences.[30] Consequently, according to Hus-

27. This presupposes that most basic reflection: retaining and re-positing the same thing. Alfred Schutz (*Phenomenology of the Social World*, pp. 45–96) has already (1932) carefully analyzed its polythetic and monothetic forms of development and the different types of representation connected with it in reference to the performance and judgment of act and action.

28. To this factor of identity Husserl also links the possibility of clearing up equivocation (*LI*, I, 252), which he will later characterize as "shifting intentionality" (*FTL*, p. 176).

29. The eminent linguist Ferdinand de Saussure also starts with language as an objective phenomenon in his *Cours de linguistique générale* (Paris: Payot, 1916; English translation by Wade Baskin, *Course in General Linguistics* [New York: Philosophical Library, 1959]), which remains one of the basic books in the science of language (see the new edition by Payot [Paris, 1971], esp. pp. 22–43; ET, pp. 7–20). Saussure's distinction between *langue, langage,* and *parole* and that between synchrony and diachrony show that the fact of language is not present simply as a *factum brutum* but that its grasp requires preliminary methodological discussions and conceptions.

30. For Husserl's peculiar concept of "intuition" [*Anschauung*], which does not simply mean empirical intuition in the traditional sense (*Ideas I*, p. 83), cf. Hermann Asemissen, "Strukturanalytische Probleme der Wahrnehmung in der Phänomenologie Husserls," *Kant-Studien*, Supplement no. 73 (Cologne: The University Press, 1957); Hans Ulrich Hoche, *Nichtempirische Erkenntnis: Analytische und synthetische Urteil a priori*

serl's conception, such a theory of knowledge is "properly . . . no theory"; it is not

> science in the pointed sense of an explanatorily unified theoretical whole [where] *theoretical explanation* means an ever increasing rendering intelligible of singular facts through general laws, and an ever increasing rendering intelligible of general laws through some fundamental law (*LI*, I, 264).[31]

Thus, pure phenomenology as research into sources precedes all theory. The theory of knowledge as pure phenomenology does not want "*to explain*" but "*to shed light* on the Idea of knowledge in its constituent elements and laws" and "*to understand*" (*LI*, I, 265).[32] Such research into sources can also be understood as the investigation of meaning (*LI*, I, 263 f.) insofar as the meaning-experience, consciousness in its meaning and its meanings, is the source of all presentations, statements, predications, judgments, and theories, of all meant and supposed being, outside of which absolutely nothing is given to us.[33]

In this field of pure phenomenology, pretheoretical in the strict sense, where "*primitive* concepts" are obtained and assigned their logic (*LI*, I, 236 ff.), certain articulations are possible; i.e., it is possible to grasp as essence in an "ideational abstraction" (*LI*, I, 226; "*ideierende Abstraktion*" is lacking in the first German edition; see also *LI*, I, 252: "an intuitive carrying out of our abstraction"; p. 262: "ideational universality"; see also pp. 264 f.). It is because such ideational abstractions are per-

---

bei Kant und Husserl (Meisenheim: Hain, 1964). The so-called problem of evidence is also connected with this question. Starting from the question whether evidence is to be led back to truth (as in *LI*) or whether truth is to be led back to evidence (as in *Ideas I*), cf. Günther Patzig, "Kritische Bemerkungen zu Husserls Thesen über das Verhältnis von Wahrheit und Evidenz," *Neue Hefte für Philosophie*, no. 1, *Phänomenologie und Sprachanalyse* (1971), pp. 14–32.

31. Cf. *LI*, I, 265, and §§ 69 ff. Connecting the pure concept of theory with the term "objective" rather than "subjective" reminds one of Kant.

32. This must be kept strictly separate from Dilthey's distinction between explanation and understanding, as also from that of the hermeneutical movement up to Heidegger.

33. Cf. Günther Patzig's citation ("Kritische Bemerkungen," p. 31, n. 11) from the Husserl Archives: "The being of nature 'unknots' itself in consciousness" (from 1908). Patzig's penetrating contribution, which illuminates the development of the problems from *LI* to *Ideas I* quite well, proceeds in our opinion from a too one-sided alternation of evidence and truth.

formed in the pretheoretical field that they are able to provide knowledge with its ultimate ground. The foundation of such comprehension is the evident intuition which is directly given and which can and must be raised to the level of distinctness and clarity (*LI*, I, 251 f.).[34] This conception of pure phenomenology points ahead to later statements of Husserl in the essay "Philosophy as Rigorous Science" and to *Ideas I*, in particular to the "principle of all principles." [35]

Logic and the theory of science

Over against the theory of knowledge or pure phenomenology, the task of logic is "to give firm clarity to notions and laws on which the objective meaning and theoretical unity of all knowledge is dependent" (*LI*, I, 250). Husserl refers here expressly to his comments in the *Prolegomena*, § 66 (see also § 62), where, of course, this objective-theoretical side of the question was more clearly recognizable. There psychologism was under attack, and a warning against a false preoccupation with the subjective side of knowledge was delivered with the help of a historical scrutiny of psychologistic theories.[36] Now, in conjunction with the task of logic just cited, a difficulty arises which consists in the repeated confusion of the boundaries between logic and epistemology. If it is the task of pure logic to give "firm clarity to notions and laws" on which objective-theoretical knowledge depends, then it is necessary to ask: Was it not precisely the task of pure phenomenology to provide such a foundation? Here logic first precedes epistemology (i.e., pure phenomenology) and then coincides with it. In fact, the formulation here is not exact, and there are plenty of examples of such inexact or wide use of the term logic in Husserl's later

---

34. On distinctness and clarity see *FTL*. Husserl reverses the traditional sequence of these terms. "Distinctness" for him signifies the so-to-speak external graspability of a concept, "clarity" its ultimate truthful tenability (a distinct concept can be "absurd" but not "nonsensical," e.g., "round square"). Cf., on the other hand, Christian Wolff, *Vernünfftige Gedancken von den Kräfften des menschlichen Verstandes. . .* , 3d ed. (Halle, 1722), pp. 18–32.
35. *PRS*, p. 109; *Ideas I*, § 24.
36. In spite of this, John Stuart Mill is also cited in a positive vein (*LI*, I, 248 f.). On "false anxiety" with respect to psychologism see *FTL*, pp. 151 ff., 173 ff.

works also.[37] But it is inexact for an important reason. More-over, the logic being treated in the present context and under-stood as formal emerges later alongside a transcendental and, eventually, a prepredicative logic. If one remembers the reference which Husserl makes in the present context to the corresponding places in the *Prolegomena,* then some clarification is possible. The essence of logic is objective ideal theory in general, i.e., the lawfulness of possible scientific fields as "objective or ideal interconnection" (*LI,* I, 225; see also *FTL,* pp. 83, 88; *FTL,* p. 243, speaks of the "idealized sense" of formal logic). Possible objectivity consequently is bound to the possibility of ideality (identification). And logic is "the science of science . . . which could therefore be most pointedly called *Wissenschafts-lerhe* or theory of science" (*LI,* I, 60; cf. §§ 4–11).[38] Here, however, it is not a question of acts of thought and their interconnections as such (*LI,* I, 225) but of a unitary objective relevance in the "unity" and "ideal validity" of this objectivity. "Pure logic has as its thematic sphere ideal formations . . . ideal objectivities" (*FTL,* p. 258). This objectivity is to be understood in the wide sense as "anything whatever," be it fact, thing, process, real, ideal, etc. (*LI,* I, 226). And so an ideal object is just one object among other objects. Husserl also uses the expression "self-subsistent being [*Sein an sich*]" (*LI,* I, 226), which, as one can readily see, has nothing to do with any "thing in itself [*Ding an sich*]." In this connection one should recall, rather, Bolzano's "sentences in themselves." The "objective-ideal"—be-cause existing essentially—interconnection of such things [*Sachen*] is theoretical, i.e., logical. This is the meaning of "truth in itself." Being as the essence of possible things is always deter-mined in some way, and it is in this determination that ideal validity, the truth, consists (*LI,* I, 225 f.). Truth is determi-nateness. Self-subsistent being and truth in itself are correlates connected a priori (*LI,* I, 255 f.).[39] Thought-experiences are "in-

37. This is especially true in *EPh,* II, 193 ff. and *EU.*
38. Here the identification of *Wissenschaftslehre* with *Wissenschafts-theorie* and *Metatheorie* appears justified. [Note: Although the author makes a point of the difference between *Wissenschaftslehre* and *Wissen-schaftstheorie* (cf. above, pp. 325 f. and n. 4), there does not seem to be any way to render that difference in English.—Trans.]
39. At first this is given only "abstractly" and has to be transformed into an "original" [*originär*] given (*LI,* I, 226). For the "universal a priori of correlation," see *Crisis,* pp. 159 f., and *FTL* in its entirety.

tentionally" related to such interconnections as obtain among things and, correlatively, among truths (*LI*, I, 225). This means that the unity of objects (or objectivities) and that of truths— which are distinguished only "abstractly"—are both given in knowledge insofar as "we perform an act of cognition" or "live in it." Intentionality, then, is a third realm alongside the "realm of things" and the "realm of truth." Pure logic is not interested in intentionality as such—as "individualized in experience" (*LI*, I, 226)—but with the universal interconnection within the intended object and, correlatively, within the truth. Through reflection and ideational abstraction it [40] apprehends "the truth as the ideal correlate of the transient subjective act of knowledge" (*LI*, I, 226 f.). It is precisely here that it becomes clear how closely epistemology (pure phenomenology) and logic are bound together. For without the giving act of experience in which the "object is given in primal fashion [originär]" (*LI*, I, 226; the first German edition does not have the term *originär*), pure logic as the most universal theory and theory of science would not be possible. But mere experience as such, as an actual performance, does not constitute science (*LI*, I, 60 ff.; cf. *FTL*, p. 267).[41] Science calls for "*systematic coherence in the theoretical sense. . . . The essence of science . . . involves unity in the whole system of grounded validation*" (*LI*, I, 62).[42] It goes without saying that this system does not spring from architectonic play but is present—as Husserl says in a manner not entirely free from misunderstanding—"in the things [*Sachen*]" (*LI*, I, 62) to which the "realm of truth" is correlative. The necessity of proceeding step by step in the conduct of a proof in order to arrive at the truth furnishes Husserl with the "idea of science as system" (*LI*, I, 62 f.). "The realm of truth is no . . . chaos" (*LI*, I, 62). It has a "teleological meaning" (*LI*, I, 70).[43] "That we need grounded validation in order to pass beyond what, in knowledge,

40. Here one can ask: Which? Logic or epistemology?
41. Therefore, in spite of evident givens, there is need of methods which lead beyond the trivial as well as a means for distinguishing between "meaning" and "knowing."
42. Cf. *FTL*, pp. 218, 232; *CM*, esp. pp. 41–55. For this idea of system see Descartes's *Regulae* (esp. n. 1).
43. "But, after all, we do have de facto cognition" (*FTL*, p. 198). The term "teleological" in the sense of the lawfulness of consciousness plays an important role in Husserl's transcendental philosophy (*Ideas I, EPh, FTL, CM, Crisis*) and deserves an investigation of its own.

is immediately and therefore trivially evident, not only makes the sciences possible and necessary, but with these also a *theory of science,* a *logic*" (*LI,* I, 63). Thus from the idea of science there follows the possibility and necessity of the theory of science or *Wissenschaftslehre* and logic. That the possibility and necessity here are merely hypothetical, that is, they are *required* if science is to function as the search for truth, seems obvious. Nothing is said about whether science will in fact become actual. There would appear to be a very unphenomenological Neo-Kantianism in the notion of an idea of science as the condition of possibility of a theory of science and of a pure logic (this notion must also be formulated in reverse: namely, the theory of science as the condition of possibility of science) in the sense of a hypothetical requirement. For it must be asked whether this intuitively posited idea of science—as phenomenology means it—is also intuitively given and can in its essential lineaments be observed.[44] It is necessary to add that here something is being built, as it were, on an unfulfilled hope, namely, that in the living act of knowing, pure essences and essential relations can actually be observed, i.e., that there are in general such essential relations and not, rather, disorder. The idea of science in Husserl appears to be pregiven in inadequate but apodictic evidence.[45]

The amalgamation of logic with theory of knowledge

It may be possible to separate logic and epistemology (as theory of knowledge) in the abstract; actually, the one does not appear to be possible without the other. And this is the source of the thematic difficulties of the *Logical Investigations* (including the closely connected problem of psychologism). For the validation of logic, one must reach back to the phenomenological. Conversely, logic, theory, and essential reflection are already in play when phenomenology is made the foundation of logic, as the discussions over the possibility of a pure theory of science showed (*LI,* I, 63; see also *FTL,* pp. 228 ff.). The reciprocal influencing and intertwining of logic and phenomenology become clear in a characteristic change between the first and second editions of the *Logical Investigations.* On the occasion of clari-

44. For this see *CM,* pp. 7–26, 56–64, and the problem of evidence discussed there.
45. Cf. *Ideas I,* pp. 382 ff.; *CM,* pp. 7 f.

fying what is meant by the investigation of the "origin" of concepts, Husserl explained that it is a matter, not of the psychological question as to the origin of conceptual presentations, but of their "*logical origin*" or, even better, of "insight into the essence of the concepts" (*Prolegomena*, 1st German ed., p. 245). In the second edition, on the other hand, Husserl says it is a matter of their "*phenomenological origin*" (*LI*, I, 238). This is not a change which can be satisfactorily explained by the well-known change of outlook from 1900 to 1913. For the depreciation of psychology or psychologism, attacked on both of these occasions, is retained; and in the first as well as the second edition, phenomenology as "descriptive psychology" is distinguished from "genetic psychology." [46] The change from "logical" to "phenomenological," then, has nothing to do with any relapse into psychologism. Similarly, talk about the principle of the presuppositionlessness of epistemological investigations (*LI*, I, 263) retains its limits. Only such statements should be cited which "permit of a comprehensive *phenomenological* realization" (*LI*, I, 263). And yet, at the same time, "theory" is striven for. On the "exemplary basis of actually *given* experiences of thinking and knowing" [47] "an intuition of essences is performed" "as a thinking over, a coming to an evident understanding of, thinking and knowing as such, in their pure generic essence" (*LI*, I, 263 f.). The term "generic" signals an explicit reference to the elements of traditional logic. One might say: none of these phenomenological (pretheoretical) validations would be possible if the logical—namely, ideal essential relations—were not already present in the thought-acts—which thought-acts we can get hold of in their "reperformance" (*LI*, I, 252, 255; *Ideas I*, p. 286) relations.

Even if phenomenological analysis of concrete thought-experience *does not fall within the true home-ground of pure logic*,[48] it none the less is indispensable to the advance of purely logical research. For all that is logical must be given in fully concrete fashion, if, as an object of research, it is to be made our own, and if we

---

46. The term "genetic," which is used here in Brentano's sense, has to be distinguished from the transcendental use of "genesis," especially in such works as *FTL, CM*, and *Crisis*.

47. Cf. *FTL*, pp. 62, 198; the later concept of the "guiding principle" [*Leitfaden*] is already sketched out here.

48. Italics added.

are to be able to bring to self-evidence the *a priori* laws which have their roots in it (*LI*, I, 251; so also the first German edition, p. 6. See also *FTL*, p. 203).

Thus, what is given in concrete phenomenological fullness is logical, i.e., capable of logical structuring. Moreover, the performance of acts of a higher level are involved in instituting epistemological reflections. Much, then, is already presupposed which is to be clarified and understood in what follows. Husserl is well aware that this task belongs to works still to come (*LI*, I, 256; *Prolegomena*, p. 63). He is also aware of the special difficulties of his own undertaking, which can be clarified only in the course of the research—for example, the difficulty that acts are directed to other acts and that the former contain the latter (*LI*, I, 255; *Ideas I*, pp. 286 f.). And there is, according to Husserl, the further complication that laying down "the phenomenological founding of logic involves the difficulty that we must, in our exposition, make use of all the concepts [i.e., logical concepts] we are trying to clarify" (*LI*, I, 260). Therefore, the investigation must "move, as it were, in a *zigzag* fashion" (*LI*, I, 261). Later Husserl also speaks of "a *zigzag* judging, so to speak" (*FTL*, p. 125). Similarly, one reads in *Ideas I* that

> in the beginnings of phenomenology all concepts or terms must in a certain sense remain fluid, always prepared to refine upon their previous meanings in sympathy with the progress made in the analysis of consciousness and the knowledge of new phenomenological stratifications, and to recognize differences in what at first to our best insight appeared an undifferentiated unity (§ 84, p. 244; see also *FTL*, pp. 174 f.).

The problem of the beginning, then, is clearly posed. We begin with thought-experiences. But that in general something meaningful and lawful can be found here is at the outset only "given" or "pregiven" with the "idea of science" (*EU*, p. 3). Thus in Husserl, in view of his correlation principle,[49] it is necessary to consider the structuring not only of what is comprehended by consciousness but of the comprehending itself (cf. *FTL*, pp. 166, 185, 246). To be sure, no ready-made science is presupposed, but only the idea of a possible science. And it is given as a mean-

49. Cf. n. 39.

ingful question and as part of our historical stock.[50] At this stage more cannot be said. Only the relation of acts to the theoretical and essential relationships manifest in them—if they are manifest at all—can be certain at the beginning. Everything else must wait upon the actual carrying-out of the analysis. This relation itself is, furthermore, an essential relation, an idea (see *LI*, I, 225–27; cf. *Ideas I*, pp. 286 f.; *FTL*, p. 250; and *CM* in general).

Just as we were able, above, to establish an interchangeability of the terms "logical" and "phenomenological," so in concepts like "constitutive," "constituting," and "constitution" more layers of meaning can be ascertained.[51] "Intuition," i.e., concrete experience with its self-evidence, out of which concepts "arise," is the primal "origin" of logical "concepts" (*LI*, I, 249). If one asks for the sources (and of course not in the psychological sense of genesis) of a concept as a basic logical element, they are the "experiences in which such objects become constituted for consciousness" (*LI*, I, 255 f.). Everything is still on the phenomenological level. But an ideal theory is no more given with *one* concept than with a *concept*. There is then a use of the term "constitution," which, though not explicitly and terminologically so characterized by Husserl, can mean logical constitution instead of phenomenological constitution. However, the same word is always employed. And the separability of "phenomenological constitution" (as the place of origin) from "logical constitution" manifests itself as only apparent. Concepts constitute themselves in experience; similarly, the various networks of concepts, essential *relations*, theories, the theory of theories, laws, and theory in general "constitute" themselves out of concepts (*LI*, I, 234 f.). All the various networks of concepts on their part can be viewed as concepts of a higher type (law concepts, theory concepts, etc.). Although one may speak here also of an experiential side to such conceptual networks, nonetheless at this level it appears irrelevant to the actual dis-

---

50. Cf. *FTL*, p. 245 ("sedimented history"). Husserl developed an authentic concept of a history of constitution in the sense of a genetic rather than a static constitution (see also "monad" and the "genesis of habitualities" in *CM*), which he also employed for a critical history of science (*Crisis*, pp. 21 ff., 353 ff.).

51. It is not rare for the term to be used analogously. See Eugen Fink, "Operative Begriffe in Husserls Phänomenologie," *Zeitschrift für philosophische Forschung*, XI (1957), 321–37.

cussion of the logical questions awaiting an answer. If *"primitive* concepts" are "laid down" (*LI*, I, 236 f.), i.e., made evident and present through the process of reconstitution, and their *"elementary connective forms"* are obtained, then these become "constitutive" for all further logical theories and for logical theory in general. It is necessary here to add a relationship of the dependent stages of constitution, and, what is more, in the sense of linear reflexive or reciprocal relations. Later higher-level complexes then refer back to earlier and more primitive ones, interpreting them more exactly.[52] Constitution now is a matter of (categorial) concepts and contents of knowledge and what they contain by way of complexes, possibilities, and variations. These concepts and contents contain no reference to "knowledge as an act of a knowing subject" (*LI*, I, 234). Insofar as phenomenology deals with the investigation of concrete experience, these relations are not phenomenological but logical. The higher-level logical structures, accordingly, are "not *made up of acts* but of purely *ideal* elements [elements which on their part, of course, are constituted by acts], of *truths*, and that in purely ideal forms, those of *ground and consequent*" (*LI*, I, 234; see also *FTL*, p. 88, where §§ 64 and 67 of the *Prolegomena* are referred to). Here the logical appears to have been separated completely from the phenomenological. The concepts, the idealities, are related among themselves, and one can view on different levels, almost like a spectator, the possible combinations permitted them in various meaningful "modifications" (*LI*, I, 235). All these complexes and modifications are nonetheless objectively ideal and independent of the individual knowing subject, i.e., they possess self-subsistent being. Husserl addresses himself later, in the *Formal and Transcendental Logic* (see pp. 62 f.; also p. 33), to these a priori possibilities with which pure logic has to deal. They hold for the subject (of knowledge), but "not in so far as we have insight into them; . . . we can only have insight into them in so far as they hold. [Thus,] they must be regarded as objective or [!] ideal conditions of the possibility of our knowledge of them"

52. Here Husserl's concept of founding, which he developed in the Third Logical Investigation, "On the Theory of Wholes and Parts" (*LI*, II, 436 ff., 463 ff.), is important. It is not to be confused with formal derivation or formal grounding, which it includes. Independent/nonindependent = concrete/abstract.

(*LI*, I, 233). Now the basic idea of phenomenology, the idea that every conceivable being and the condition of its possibility are to be sought in consciousness, emerges in reverse: "Plainly we are here concerned with *a priori* conditions of knowledge, which can be discussed and investigated apart from all relation to the thinking subject and to the Idea of Subjectivity in science" (*LI*, I, 233). They are conditions which are "grounded purely in the 'content' of our knowledge" (*LI*, I, 233). In place of "content" we may say "object" or "anything whatever" (cf. *FTL*, pp. 265 f.).[53] On the other hand, it is necessary to maintain that such conditions of knowledge are to be obtained according to their *"phenomenological origin"* (the first German edition has *"logical origin"*) or—in order to avoid "unsuitable talk of origins, only bred in confusion"—from *"insight into the essence* of the concepts involved, looking methodologically to the fixation of unambiguous, sharply distinct verbal meanings" (*LI*, I, 238). Here it is a question of an "intuitive representation of the essence in adequate ideation" (*LI*, I, 238; the term "adequate ideation" is lacking in the first German edition, as is the concept "intuitive"). Thus we find ourselves again in the phenomenological sphere, i.e., the sphere of consciousness. The ideal logical essences must become self-evident, and "self-evidence is indeed nothing other than the character of knowledge as such" (*LI*, I, 232, n. 1). And so Husserl distinguishes, in "The question as to the ideal conditions of the possibility of science and of theory in general" (the title of § 65 of the *Prolegomena*), "A. The question as it relates to actual knowledge" and "B. The question as it relates to the content of knowledge" (*Prolegomena*, § 66). He also calls these conditions "noetic" conditions, on the one hand, and "logically objective" conditions, on the other. Both belong to the "ideal conditions of knowledge" (*LI*, I, 233). The noetic conditions as subjective allow themselves to be subdivided into conditions which once again are ideal and real. The latter (the real) conditions are psychological in the narrow sense and can be passed over in this context (*LI*, I, 232). It is essential to note that, according to Husserl, the logical laws "obviously" may undergo a "self-evident transformation" through an express "relation to the knowing subject." Indeed,

53. "Content" here is *form* of content.

The ideal conditions of knowledge which we have called "noetic" [54] as opposed to those which are logically objective, are, basically, no more than such modifications of the insights, the laws which pertain to the pure content of knowledge, as render them fruitful for the criticism of knowledge, and, by further modifications, for practical, logical normativity (*LI, I*, 233 f.).

According to this text, the noetic conditions of knowledge appear in the last instance to be epistemological. But already through conclusions drawn in the next section (§ 66) this conception is once again restricted considerably. For:

> Our treatment has shown that questions as to the ideal conditions of the possibility of *knowledge* in general, and of theoretical knowledge in particular, ultimately lead us back to certain *laws*, whose roots are to be found purely in the content of knowledge, or of the categorial concepts that it falls under, and which are so abstract that they contain no reference to knowledge as an act of a knowing subject. These laws (or the categorial concepts which enter into them) are what are to be understood as constituting the conditions of the possibility of *theory* in general, in the objectively ideal sense (*LI, I*, 234).

The role of language

On the level of logical and epistemological reflection which has been presented so far, language has become important in a twofold respect: once as a system of "meanings" and again as a so-called "pure logical grammar." The one could be called Husserl's contribution to semantics, the other his contribution to syntax. Neither contribution arose in conjunction with a concern for the science of language. Rather, they serve questions of philosophical epistemology and logic, i.e., the theory of science. The results which are interesting for the study of language are—even if very important and fruitful—by-products. In addition, the two contributions must be sharply distinguished. Husserl's most important finding for the theory of meaning is that he acknowledges an ideality in meanings which raises them above the merely experienced performance of an act of knowing. [55]

54. This term is not to be identified with "noetic" and "noesis" in *Ideas I*.

55. This leads to Husserl's theory of time and history, which, in opposition to existentialism and the philosophy of existence, is concerned

Meanings are meanings as stabilized identities. As a result, the fluctuation of meanings is in reality a fluctuation of the act of meaning (*LI*, I, 312 ff.), while the meanings themselves maintain their strict identity and ideality. This ideality is "not normative," a point which is especially important for the philologically and historically oriented linguistic scientist, who is reluctant to accept the notion that a word should be an idea. A word is an idea insofar as it is a *nomen appellativum* (*LI*, I, 331, §32).[56] Accordingly, meaning and concept cannot simply coincide. For in spite of the fact that meanings are "universal objects," they can, with respect to the objects to which they refer, be individual or special, e.g., the concept of the number "four" as "the second even number in the number series," or as 2^2 (*LI*, I, 331 f.). These differences are all the more important since in the normal performance of a "unitary act of meaning" we refer to the object meant in the act and not the meaning itself. Verbal meaning and propositional meaning are likewise to be distinguished (*LI*, I, 332 f.). With the example of the endless number series, Husserl illustrates the difference between what he calls "meanings 'in themselves'" and "meanings of expressions." Numbers—in the ideal sense that arithmetic presupposes—do not spring forth and vanish with the act of enumeration but represent an "objectively fixed set of general objects, sharply delimited by an ideal law." It is the same with the "ideal unities of pure logic," to which "being thought or being expressed are alike contingent." There are then meanings in the sense of "possible meanings" which could be "realized" if necessary—as perhaps in the case of "concept formation" (*LI*, I, 333, § 35). With this observation —which Husserl makes chiefly with logic in mind—it seems to me that a motif of modern, so-called generative and transformational grammar has already been grasped.[57] Obviously there are words which we do not possess as handy expressions

---

with structuring the processes of living, acting, and interacting with a view to providing a foundation for the possibility of knowledge and rational praxis. Similarly, the Saussurean structuralism tries to secure language as an objective phenomenon.

56. Of course, every meaningful sign exercises this function. Cf. Saussure, *Linguistique générale*, pp. 32 ff., 97 ff. (ET, pp. 15 ff., 65 ff.); Andre Martinet, *Eléments de linguistique générale* (Paris: Colin, 1960), speaks of a "moneme."

57. Noam Chomsky, *Aspects of a Theory of Syntax* (Cambridge, Mass.: M.I.T. Press, 1965).

in our vocabulary and which nonetheless we actually—indeed, effortlessly—could both actively form and passively understand. And that although we have never heard them. This holds, for example, of large numbers in the number series. Thus, if I have not yet heard or even formed the number two hundred seventy-three million, six hundred seventy-nine thousand, eight hundred seventy-nine (273,679,879), I can form it effortlessly and understand it at first hearing. In conjunction with the ideality of meanings, Husserl also elaborated on the ideality of the expression, i.e., the ideality of the mere sign. Of course, here, at the stage of the *Logical Investigations,* no fully unambiguous interpretation can be given (*LI,* I, 284, § 11). But Husserl already specifies: "We only call significant signs expressions" (*LI,* II, 501). It is only through the subtle investigations of *Ideas I* that something like the "ideality of the sensible" itself is worked out and afterward given clear expression in the *Formal and Transcendental Logic.*[58]

The elaboration of the distinction between "essentially occasional expressions" and "objective expressions" (and between occasional and objective meanings) is important for the study of both language and philosophy. An "objective expression" is one which pins down its "meaning" by its "manifest, auditory pattern"[59] and therefore does not require a reference "to the person uttering it, or to the circumstances of the utterance" (*LI,* I, 314). An expression is *"essentially occasional"* if it belongs to "a conceptually unified group of possible meanings, in whose case it is essential to orient actual meaning to the occasion, the speaker and the situation." It is necessary, then, to "look to the actual circumstances of utterance" if the specific meaning intended is to be successfully grasped (*LI,* I, 315). To the class of such expressions there belong, in particular, personal pronouns, those expressions "which serve the practical needs of ordinary life" (*LI,* I, p. 315), and expressions which indicate such "subject-bound determinations" as "here," "now," and the like,

58. *FTL,* pp. 20 ff., 165 ff. (*LI,* I, 284, speaks of "the ideality of the relationship between expression and meaning"). It is to Saussure's great credit that he had already preserved this "ideality" from a purely linguistic point of view through his concepts of phonology and phoneme (*Linguistique générale,* pp. 55 ff., 63–95; ET, pp. 32 ff., 38–62).

59. Cf. Saussure's *image acoustique* (*Linguistique générale,* p. 98), *valeur idéographique* (p. 57), and his definition of the phoneme (p. 65). (ET, pp. 66, 34, 38.)

i.e., time and place words. It is a matter then of the "intuitive, believing presentation" of a person and his place (*LI*, I, 317),[60] including cases "where the speaker gives normal expression to something concerning himself, or which is thought of in relation to himself" (*LI*, I, 318). Husserl treated occasional meaning and expressions in conjunction with his attempt to point out and avoid equivocations harmful to logic and epistemology alike. He distinguishes occasional expressions as equivocations from other equivocations, because occasional equivocations clearly cannot be corrected by means of objective expressions, but only through taking into account the particular situation and perspective or "attitude" [*Einstellung*] of the speaker. If one accepts the last term, attitude—which of course does not occur in this context in the *Logical Investigations*—then the treatment of occasional meaning acquires immense importance for phenomenological philosophy in general and for the problem of access to the object of inquiry, i.e., method, in particular. For what is called the "phenomenological attitude" characterizes one such perspectival and occasional situation of the investigator, one which should play an important role in the determination of both the "transcendental" realm and the "life-world." At the same time—and therefore in conjunction—Husserl treats under the title "occasional expressions and meanings" problems which elsewhere are designated as metalinguistic in contrast to problems in object-language.[61]

Alongside these semantic discussions, which could have a direct function for the science of concrete languages, there are some very basic considerations relative to a possible (logical) "syntax." Although the last term does occur in Husserl—he speaks of "syntactic forms" which arise out of "formal logical" and "formal ontological categories" (*LI*, II, 455; cf. *LI*, I, *Prolegomena*, Chap. 11; *FTL*, pp. 106 ff., 294 ff., 334 ff.)—it is

60, Husserl refers here to the scholar of the German language, Hermann Paul, *Prinzipien der Sprachgeschichte*, 3d ed. (1898))*LI*, I, 318). Included here is the later pragmatic aspect of language (Morris and Carnap).

61. This is not noticed by Gilbert Ryle (who himself refers to Ludwig Wittgenstein) in a very abstract essay which touches upon the Husserlian text: "Phenomenology and Linguistic Analysis," *Neue Hefte für Philosophie*, no. 1, *Phänomenologie und Sprachanalyse* (1971), pp. 3–11. There is a connection between Husserl's theory of "occasional meanings" and the later ordinary language philosophy.

necessary to keep in mind that the term "syntax" in Husserl does not serve as the title of a leading investigation. Nonetheless, its peculiar instructive importance does stand in the foreground. It is the concept of the so-called "nonindependent meanings" which leads Husserl, in connection with his theory of founding relative to the relation of whole and part, to the idea of a pure grammar as a theory of the formal relations of statements— which relations constitute an essential part of formal logic. Now it is the task of "analytic phenomenology" (*LI*, I, 257; cf. *LI*, II, 437 f.) to work out, as such a "syntax," a "universal pure grammar." Starting with Anton Marty's distinction between "categorematic" and "syncategorematic expressions," Husserl discovers that in conjunction with such expressions there must be corresponding meanings, which he conceives as independent and nonindependent meanings (*LI*, II, 500 ff.). The formal types of combination for statements and systems of statements manifest themselves in the nonindependent meanings. For Husserl it is important—in spite of a "certain parallelism between thinking and speaking," in spite of the importance of "traditional grammatical analyses" (*LI*, I, 257), and in spite of the detachment of ideally objective essential relations "from their psychological and grammatical connections" (*LI*, I, 322 f.)—to separate his idea of a universal pure grammar as logical syntax from what is called grammar in the linguistic sense. It should be noted that "grammatical differences need not coincide with logical ones" (*LI*, I, 258). Pure logical grammar formulates the "formal laws of meaning which, on the basis of the (nonindependent) categories of meaning—apart from any objective (or ontological or formal-ontological) consideration—provide for the avoidance of "nonsense" and "absurdity" (*LI*, II, 522). This is not to deny that certain "equivalences" do hold sway between the categories of meaning (and their complexes) and the categories of objects (and their complexes) (*LI*, II, 524). The result is that there can be talk of a "pure logical grammar" only "in an analogous sense" (relative to a general science of language).[62] The task of this pure logical grammar is not and cannot

62. Ryle, "Phenomenology," p. 11, says "metaphorical" instead of "analogous." He opposes—without appreciating the text—logical grammar to meaning-theory. Chomsky speaks of "universal grammar" which embraces the individual languages from the creative aspect of language itself (*Aspects*, pp. 6 ff.). He wants to employ the terms "grammar" and "theory" in a systematically ambiguous sense."

be to comprehend in itself "all the particular grammars [of linguistics] as contingent specifications" (*LI*, II, 527). Still, every concrete language is determined by the pure form of the statement, the pure logical a priori, for "the foundations of speech are not only to be found in physiology, psychology, and the history of culture, but also in the *a priori*" (*LI*, II, 525). It is, of course, necessary to note at this juncture a lack of precision or clarity in Husserl's manner of expressing himself in comparison with his later conceptions. For not only are the elaborated basic structures of pure logic a priori, but one has to reckon with a physiological, a psychological, and a cultural a priori.[63] Here we find the motive which occasioned Husserl in the *Formal and Transcendental Logic*—in accord with his analyses since *Ideas I* —to modify his conception of pure logic. This of course does not mean that he abandoned the idea of a pure formal logic, but rather that he extended it.

PHENOMENOLOGY AND TRANSCENDENTAL LOGIC

THE GENERAL MOTIVE for this modification consists in the endeavor to understand more accurately the meaning and the concept of the "formal" and the "a priori," and it leads to the elaboration of a theory of consciousness. In the *Formal and Transcendental Logic*—whose title indicates a twofold division— Husserl carries out a threefold division of logic. First, there is the formal-analytic "apophantic," i.e., a formal theory of statements. Second, there is a formal theory of manifolds as formal ontology. Together the two constitute the new, extended idea of formal analytics (cf. *FTL*, §§ 22–37). Formal apophantics is formal inasmuch as it elaborates the ideality of meanings in general—in the sense of an eidetics. It includes, in addition to the nonindependent meanings, the combinations in judgment and the complexes of judgmental forms and relationships. Formal ontology is formal in the sense of containing a reference to the universal empty form "anything whatever" (*FTL*, p. 77).

63. For the "physiological," "biological," and "bodily a priori," for the necessary "localization" of the pure ego, and for the "life-world a priori," see *Ideas II*, p. 153, and *Ideas III*, pp. 5, 109, 114 (*Ideas II* and *III* are concerned in particular with the theory of cultural forms). See also *PPsych*, pp. 108, 197 ff., 326; and *Crisis*, pp. 103–89 and (only in the German edition) Beilage 23 to § 65, p. 482.

These two fields, which must be distinguished from each other on account of their different themes, are at the same time related to each other. They are related because there can be no formal apophantics which for its part is not related to the objective in general, and there can be no formal ontology which, on the other hand, does not emerge in judgments (*FTL*, p. 78). One can also add that even statements themselves—apart from the fact that they are statements about something—belong to the province of "anything whatever" and therefore to formal objective *mathēsis*. Both forms of logic—the analytics of judgments as well as the logic of statements—are "taken as pure of any thematizing activity directed to the subjective" (*FTL*, p. 78).

The defining of languages as systems of intentionality

Now a new thematic—free from all psychologism—directed to the subjective constitutes the third division of logic, namely, transcendental logic. One cannot simply separate formal from transcendental logic. Rather, so-called formal logic is included in transcendental logic (in the appropriate attitude). Transcendental logic merely provides, in terms of a theory of consciousness, the ultimate understanding and meaningful [64] foundation of any logic. It contains, in addition to the purely formal a priori, the so-called *"contingent Apriori"* (*FTL*, pp. 29 ff.). It is now permissible (which was not entirely clear in the *Logical Investigations*) to maintain "the universality of the coincidence between speech and thinking" (*FTL*, p. 24) without falsely— in the psychologistic sense—characterizing logic as a mere theory of thinking. For now "reason itself, including theoretical reason in particular," is conceived as a "form-concept" in an a priori sense (*FTL*, pp. 29 ff.). It is from the point of view of the transcendentality of reason, to which not only the purely formal but also the contingent a priori belong, that the relation of parallelism—indicated above and expressed in the common idea of analytics—between formal apophantics and formal ontology can be transcendentally and phenomenologically clarified. Such a clarification is the result of an exhibition, in terms of a theory or

64. For the term "meaning" [*Sinn*] in Husserl cf. Schutz, *Phenomenology of the Social World*, pp. 15 ff., 53 ff., 69 ff., 126 ff.

phenomenology of consciousness, of the structures and lawful-ness of the act of knowing in the sense of opinion. Husserl lays out this exhibition generally—while at the same time carrying out detailed analyses from different perspectives—under the title of intentionality. This intentionality of consciousness is itself—and this it shares with the intentionality of formal (apo-phantic) analytics and formal ontology—a form-concept ob-tained through a reduction: the form-concept manifest in the basic and regulative structure of the *ego-cogito-cogitatum*, be-yond which one cannot question further, for every further ques-tioning runs into the same structural form. And so this structural form may not be hypostatized.[65] Consciousness, concen-trated in the ego, constitutes by means of definite *cogitationes* certain identifiable *cogitata*. The *cogitationes* are also called *noeses,* the *cogitata, noemata.* The noeses are performed on the foundation of real [*reell*] hyletic data belonging to them and in the medium of immanent temporality (passive synthesis). Hus-serl's here-developed concept of "noematic intentionality" (cf. *Ideas I*, pp. 290 ff., esp. 294 ff.; see also pp. 241 ff., 359 ff., 268 ff.) also serves to clarify what language and logic have in common as well as what distinguishes them. Identifying and synthesizing the cogitationes or noeses constitute definite cog-itata, e.g., sense perceptions. These cogitata or noemata (sense perceptions, for example) are identical ideal (meaningful) uni-ties. This is what we call the "ideality of the sensible" (cf. *FTL,* pp. 20 f., 165 f.).[66] These ideal noematic unities are now em-ployed in turn to bring other things to expression. To bring the already meant to an identifying noematic expression once again is the foundation of both language and (apophantic) logic (*Ideas I*, pp. 345 ff.). This making something express and re-peatedly identifying it has at the same time the character of a reflection (cf. *Ideas I*, pp. 215 ff.). The theory of meaning and

65. Orth, *Bedeutung,* pp. 245 ff., and "Grundlagen," p. 11; cf. n. 72, below.

66. The real hyletic data immanent in consciousness are already identifiable and therefore irreal and ideal (*Ideas I*, pp. 246 ff.). For the "stuff a priori" see *FTL,* pp. 294 ff. and 313 ff. The sensible thing is a "sign *for itself*" (*Ideas I*, p. 161; cf. "unity of the prelinguistic" in the Textkritische Anmerkungen of the new German edition of *Ideen I*, edited by Walter Biemel [*Husserliana III*] [The Hague: Martinus Nijhoff, 1950], p. 476); cf. *PPsych,* pp. 397 f.; *EPh,* I, 98: "the so-called word" as a "sharply distinguishable sensible idea." See also Orth, *Bedeutung,* pp. 121–28.

the theory of (immanent) time have this in common: they both uncover and employ structural stabilities in the stream of experience and the stream of constitution, which stabilities first and foremost make the appearance of knowledge possible. The effective "ability" in the flow of immanent time and the flow of constitution "to recollect" is fundamental to knowledge (*FTL*, p. 285).[67]

Languages are accordingly, complex noematic systems of intentionality which share with logic the capacity for repeated expression and identifying ideality. The effect of this logicality of language is that language, in order to be and to remain language, cannot go below a certain minimum in rule-determined structure. What distinguishes language from logic is of course the fact that it manifests the idea of the formal and of formal types of combination only imperfectly. It might perhaps be considered as converging toward this idea. The positive reason for this is that language is or can be linked to yet another (e.g., the contingent) a priori.[68]

Language and transcendental consciousness

The distinction between language and transcendental consciousness is more difficult to draw than that between language and logic. The reason for this is that, in addition to the already mentioned logical formality, still other moments characteristic of consciousness are discernible in language. This occasioned Husserl, in conjunction with the discussion of the principles of his concept of consciousness, to engage directly in linguistic analysis and make use of it for philosophy. At the point where he

---

67. This is the reason why Husserl's posing of the task of formal logic, to which *FTL* is only a kind of programmatic introduction, appears to lapse into mere reflections on the phenomenology of consciousness. Cf. *PIT*, as well as *APS*, and the introductions by Boehm and Fleischer, respectively. The questions of both formal logic and formal quantification are taken up here, because it is characteristic of immanent temporality and its hyletic fields that they offer the first forms of quantification. In the "retention-now-protention" structured flow of time, the hyletic data are identified in passive syntheses and distinguished according to their position or sequence in the temporal flow. The completely empty form of this distinction is the origin of number and of the concept of number as the prototype of formal quantification, which thus rests ultimately on identification and distinction.

68. Cf. n. 63, above. The ultimate contingency is temporality.

formulates as the methodological foundation of this theory of consciousness the "principle of all principles," the text reads:

> Every statement which does nothing more than give expression to such data through merely unfolding their meaning and adjusting it accurately is thus really, . . . an *absolute beginning,* called in a genuine sense to provide foundations, a *principium (Ideas I,* p. 92).

Correspondingly, in Husserl's programmatic essay of 1910–11, the text reads:

> All statements that describe the phenomena in direct concepts do so, to the degree that they are valid, by means of concepts of essence, that is, by conceptual significations of words that must permit of being redeemed in an essential intuition.
>
> . . . all that [the phenomena] bears the title "consciousness-of" and "has" a "meaning" and "means" something "objective." [69]

It is easy now to make the transcendental-phenomenological (reduction) formula *ego-cogito-cogitatum* equivalent to the parallel formula *ego-dico-dictum* and thus identify the constitution of language and the constitution of consciousness, or language and consciousness. There are, however, two errors in such a line of argumentation:

a) If language is characterized in this way as a basic transcendental structure, then as a rule at least one thesis about what language is is already anticipated—and, indeed, a thesis which is not transcendentally meant but derives, rather, from definite empirical observations and generalizations. It proposes that the concept of language which a man has at the beginning of the investigation of language is completely different from the one which he has at the end of the investigation. Here it is a matter of an equivocation which confuses the concept of language in the Saussurean sense of *la langue* with linguisticality, i.e., identifiability in an act of meaning in general. This confusion or equivocation can be resolved or avoided only through considera-

---

69. *PRS,* pp. 109 f. The "principle of all principles" does not demand a naïve intuitionism in the realms of consciousness and language, for the phenomenally given is indeed to be accepted *"as it gives itself out to be, though only within the limits in which it then presents itself"* (*Ideas I,* p. 92). These limits indicate the idea of the reduction that is also present in the "principle" which virtually establishes the inescapability of the egological starting point. Thus, according to *EPh,* II 42, "The sentence 'I am' [must be] the true principle of all principles."

tion of what Husserl calls the concept of the *"guiding principle"* [*Leitfaden*]. The guiding-principle concept is not a concept which results from the analysis of language as such; rather, it is a concept of the analysis of consciousness.

b) Two instances of transcendental validation can concur with each other as two different instances of constitution without a third instance—a methodological and systematic demand—being specified to legitimate the unity of the validating constitution. If one holds to Husserl's concept of the guiding principle, then two principal points of view are to be distinguished. First, the guiding principle proves itself after the general structure of experience and knowing has been exhibited in the formula ego-cogito-cogitatum through the transcendental-phenomenological reduction. Thus, an attitude must already be present which has grasped this formula. This means that, prior to every conscious research directed by a guiding principle, there is an explicit presumption which justifies itself, on the one hand, by referring to the principle of all principles, its comprehensibility, and the possibility of the discursive and orderly research proceeding from it. On the other hand, such a research is still employing at the beginning an indefinite and unclarified guiding principle. Second, it should be pointed out that in Husserl there is a ranking type of guiding principle, namely, the relation of the cogitatum to the ego-cogito.[70] To follow the guiding principle, then, means to hold to an intentional system of constitution against the background of the knowledge of the universal structural type (ego-cogito-cogitatum).

Cogitative types

There are, in addition, other completely different constitutional or intentional types to be distinguished. It is necessary to observe, however, that all these types must be related to one another if they are ultimately to be comprehended under a universal concept of constitution. Furthermore, within the constitu-

70. *CM*, pp. 50 ff. It is necessary, of course, to observe the relativity of the concept *cogitatum*. For absolutely everything—even the universal structure of consciousness itself—can be made into a cogitatum; cf. Orth, "Grundlagen," p. 11. The reductive "attitude," which does not posit the cogitatum absolutely, also guarantees that after the reduction "we can even continue undisturbed to speak as in our capacity as natural human beings we have to speak" (*Ideas I*, p. 189).

tional types—in accord with the method of analysis and the theme of the research—different important type-schemata are to be observed. Husserl calls them cogitative types.[71] The specific interest of the research, especially the concern in such a case to get a precise grasp of the thematized phenomenality, whatever it might be, determines whether such individual cogitative types are threshed out. "Description" and the different types of "abstraction" and "reduction" are the names of the various methods by which such cogitative types might be obtained.[72]

The cogitative types mentioned by us—ego-cogito-cogitatum and ego-dico-dictum—are such distinguished and universal (names for) types that their distinction is meaningful only if one takes into account all the attitudes habitually linked to them, i.e., if their concrete cognitive and operative working is made conscious. The first-named structure describes the most universal result of the so-called transcendental-phenomenological reduction, which provides the basic schema for cogitative types in general. The second-named structure is a thoroughly universal and reductive description of the constitution of language. One could characterize the relationship between the two types as one of genus and species. Husserl characterizes the relationship between the two—primarily from a logical interest—in the following epistemological manner: The constitution of language according to the schema ego-dico-dictum runs parallel to the universal constitution of consciousness, ego-cogito-cogitatum. It adds nothing new in principle. Its function is simply to nominalize, to bring to expression and make reflectively conscious, what consciousness performs. This means that linguistic constitution has certain principal traits in common with the constitution of consciousness, but—let it be marked—only these principal traits. What distinguishes the two from each other is that linguistic constitution brings with it modifications of the constitution of consciousness. These modifications must, with respect to their properties, be clearly distinguished from the constitution of consciousness so that their relation to the constitu-

71. Cf. *CM*, pp. 50 ff., 74; cf. "modification," "variation," *PPsych*, pp. 72 ff. One can also speak of "experiential types" [*Erlebnistypen*].

72. Obtaining a cogitative type always occurs across the path of abstraction and ideation. But one must distinguish abstract-nonindependent types from concrete-independent ones, or factually possible types from abstractly possible ones.

tion of consciousness can be made transparent. If one tries to represent the schema and the relations of the schemata by way of examples and paradigms, there is the danger that the structures of transcendental consciousness will be confused with the special structures of the paradigms. This confusion is all the more a source of error since the transcendental structures of consciousness on their part are supposed to be effective in the paradigms (which function then as the guiding principles), and the structures of the paradigms in turn claim a transcendental relation.

Constitution of consciousness and constitution of language

The terms *constitution of consciousness* and *constitution of language* can be made more precise. Constitution of language can be understood as a subjective genitive and as an objective genitive, i.e., first, as constitution by means of language (thus, the constitution of the world by means of language), and, second, as the constitution of language (in the sense of the question: What are the constituents of language[s] itself?). If one holds to the first sense and restricts the concept of constitution to it alone, this means that a scientific and theoretical preeminence is granted not only to the study of language but to language itself: all constitution of the world would prove to be constitution by means of language, all knowledge, knowledge of language. In the second sense, this question would remain open, and there would be the beginning of a scientific clarification of the concept of language itself in the sense of a theory of science [*Wissenschaftstheorie*]. Above all, in the first case the concept of what is usually called language would have to be extended, with the result that a precise understanding of the phenomenon of language in the stricter sense would be excluded, the phenomenon of the linguistic having been stretched to the point of indeterminability.

The constitution of consciousness can also be understood in the sense of an objective or a subjective genitive. However, a crucial distinction manifests itself, between the concept of the constitution of consciousness and the concept of the constitution of language, through which their parallelism is decidedly reduced and at the same time undergoes a methodological specification. This distinction consists in the following points:

a) The constitution of consciousness in the last instance of constitution always leads back to consciousness itself.

b) The constitution of language (in its twofold form as self-constitution and world-constitution) on the contrary leads back in the last instance to consciousness rather than to language.

c) Every constitution of language is also a case of constitution of consciousness, but not every constitution of consciousness is a case of constitution of language. In a formally superficial sense the relationship of consciousness (constitution of consciousness) and language (constitution of language) could be characterized as the relationship of genus and species. However, this can merely serve as an abstract orientation. Indeed, it is even false if it claims to be the last word on the relationship, leaving certain concrete features of the problem untreated. According to Husserl, consciousness is not sufficiently defined when it is characterized as the highest genus, for consciousness is concrete, absolute being.[73] According to this account, it becomes clear that the thesis "What language is manifests itself in speaking, and from the linguistic performance one may argue back directly to the type of constitution," is thoroughly imprecise and may well cause us to miss (scientifically) the phenomenon of language. Recently Noam Chomsky has quite correctly pointed out that, while it is true that the linguistic competence of the speaker-hearer must be the ultimate norm for determining the accuracy of any theory of language, still, this intuitive understanding of language on the part of the user and producer of language does not lead immediately to a scientific explanation of what language is.[74]

The concretization of the formula of transcendental consciousness by language

The formula ego-cogito-cogitatum, which, considered in itself, is abstract, must now undergo some modifications with regard to the formula ego-dico-dictum. Speaking figuratively, one could say that ego-cogito-cogitatum represents a horizontal structural organization which must be supplemented by a vertical organiza-

---

73. *Ideas I*, pp. 150 ff., 168 ff.; *FTL* and *CM* in their entirety. It is necessary to distinguish in Husserl two concepts of the concrete—the independent individual and the independent as a totality (the latter holds for transcendental concretion). One should not confuse the abstract names for something concrete with the concrete thing itself, not even if they signify the transcendental.
74. Cf. Orth, *Bedeutung*, pp. 70 ff.

tion. Consequently, there is not only the transverse relation from ego to cogito and to cogitatum (or, better, from cogitatio to ego to cogitatum), but the individual "elements" themselves have a genesis and a structural lawfulness as well as discernible "layers" or foundations. If we start from the cogito (or the cogitatio), it is because this is first of all "immanent temporality," the stream of consciousness; and the hyletic data and fields in it are "real" [*reell*]. This hyletic material is processed by the various noeses, with their different but regulated interrelationships depending on the different types of performances. (The structures of the noema or cogitatum correspond to the interrelationships among the noeses.) The performed passive and active constitutions have a habitualizing effect on the ego, which no longer remains a mere ego-pole but becomes a "monad" in the Husserlian sense, i.e., a concrete ego as the substrate of habitualities (*CM*, pp. 66 ff.). The ego must also undergo a bodily localization (cf. bodily a priori, localization a priori) if the hyletic data and fields emerging in the cogitatio are to be organized. Bodiliness, "bodily intentionality," is involved in sensibility (*PPsych*, pp. 108, 197 ff., 326). The body plays a distinct role in language, for language consists in constant identifying repetition by means of sensible expressions (whichever field of sensibility man may employ). The ego in ego-dico-dictum thus brings an ego as monad and system of sense organs into account.

With bodiliness, the ego as alter ego is also implied and thus intersubjectivity,[75] whose chief function in our context is the stabilization of the intentional and constitutional systems.

This is the place to point out the twofold use of the term "objective" (-ideal) in Husserl. On one occasion "objective" (-ideal) signifies the identification and thus ideal positing of objects in egological consciousness (*FTL*, § 62). In the *Logical Investigations* it plays an important role in the context of the act of meaning. At other times objectivity is defined through intersubjectivity, that is, it is proved trustworthy (*CM*, pp. 120 ff.). However, there is no contradiction here. The idea of the objective

---

75. Cf. *CM* (Fifth Meditation), pp. 89–151. There is no empathy. It is necessary to hold to the absolute separateness of individual consciousnesses if one wants to understand the fundamental theoretical and practical significance of the social and the social implications of the individual subject. One could say, construing Leibniz freely: *nihil in intellectu, quod non fuit antea in societate—nisi intellectus ipse.*

in the identifying and synthesizing function of egological consciousness is already manifest in the field of immanent temporality. Without such identification the appresentation of the alien experience of the alter ego could not be performed. The constitution—in acts not expressly conscious—of intersubjectivity then guarantees the objectivity of anything in that it makes a test, so to speak, of the purported instance. It has also undertaken the function of objectifying temporality and thus grounds history,[76] social history, tradition, and projection and serves as a stable point of orientation for social interaction and institutions (*Ideas II*, Pt. II; *Crisis*). Precisely these intersubjective functions must be present if we are to comprehend the full meaning of the phenomenon of language [77] and how, inversely, language is *the* case of intersubjectivity.

There is one last thing that has to be nailed down, and that is that a so-called methodological solipsism is unavoidable. For none of these explanations—in the sense of the articulation (analysis) of systems of intentionality—is possible if I cannot perform it in "my" consciousness, however socially and historically conditioned my consciousness may prove to be.[78] It is to the great credit of Alfred Schutz, who was the first to develop a theory of the social sciences (or sociology), that, while underscoring Husserl's theory of intersubjectivity, he held to the methodological priority of the analysis of consciousness. Thus he has become the initiator of a sociology of knowledge capable of yet further development.[79]

76. In addition to objective historical time it is necessary to consider natural time, which has an effect upon the former.

77. In Saussure (*Linguistique générale*, p. 110; ET, p. 76) signs and languages are labeled "very special institutions." Dialogistic logic speaks of a "schema of action"; cf. Wilhelm Kamlah and Paul Lorenzen, *Logische Propädeutik*. (Mannheim: B-I, 1967), p. 62.

78. Karl-Otto Apel's objection against methodological solipsism in "Die Kommunikationsgemeinschaft als transzendentale Voraussetzung der Sozialwissenschaften," *Neue Hefte für Philosophie*, nos. 2/3, *Dialog als Methode* (1972), 1–40, esp. p. 13, does not hold good.

79. Cf. the works of Alfred Schutz in the series *Phänomenologica*, Volumes XI, XV, and XXII (The Hague: Martinus Nijhoff): *Collected Papers*, Vol. I, ed. Maurice Natanson (1962); Vol. II, ed. Arvid Brodersen (1964); Vol. III, ed. Ilse Schutz, with an introduction by Aron Gurwitsch (1966).

LIST OF ABBREVIATIONS

THE FOLLOWING is a list of the abbreviations of Husserl's works employed in the essay. It should be noted that, where possible, the references will be to the available English translations only.—Translator.

APS *Analysen zur passiven Synthesis.* Edited by Margot Fleischer (*Husserliana XI*). The Hague: Martinus Nijhoff, 1971.

CM *Cartesianische Meditationen und Pariser Vorträge.* Edited by Stephan Strasser (*Husserliana I*). The Hague: Martinus Nijhoff, 1959. *Cartesian Meditations.* Translated by Dorion Cairns. The Hague: Martinus Nijhoff, 1960.

Crisis *Die Krisis der europäischen Wissenschaften und die transzendentale Phänomenologie.* Edited by Walter Biemel (*Husserliana VI*). The Hague: Martinus Nijhoff, 1954. *The Crisis of European Sciences and Transcendental Phenomenology.* Translated by David Carr. Evanston: Northwestern University Press, 1970.

EPh *Erste Philosophie.* 2 vols. Edited by Rudolf Boehm (*Husserliana VII and VIII*). The Hague: Martinus Nijhoff, 1956, 1959.

EU *Erfahrung und Urteil.* Edited by Ludwig Landgrebe. Hamburg: Claassen, 1954. (New edition forthcoming from Felix Meiner Verlag, Hamburg.) *Experience and Judgment.* Translated by James S. Churchill and Karl Ameriks. Evanston: Northwestern University Press, 1973.

FTL *Formale und transzendentale Logik.* Halle a.S.: Max Niemeyer, 1929. *Formal and Transcendental Logic.* Translated by Dorion Cairns. The Hague: Martinus Nijhoff, 1969.

Ideas *Ideen zu einer reinen Phänomenologie und phänomenologischen Philosophie.* Volume I. Edited by Walter Biemel (*Husserliana III*). The Hague: Martinus Nijhoff, 1950. (This is a new and expanded edition based on the hand-written notes of the author. W. R Boyce Gibson's English translation, *Ideas: General Introduction to Pure Phenomenology* [London: Unwin & Allen, 1931], is based on the original edition as it first appeared in *Jahrbuch für Philosophie und phänomenologische Forschung*, I [1913], and was twice reprinted in 1922 and 1928.) Volumes II and III. Edited by Marly Biemel (*Husserliana* IV and V). The Hague: Martinus Nijhoff, 1952.

LI *Logische Untersuchungen. Erster Band: Prolegomena zur reinen Logik.* Halle a.S.: Max Niemeyer, 1900. 2d rev. ed.: Halle a.S.: Max Niemeyer, 1913. *Zweiter Band: Untersuchungen zur Phänomenologie und Theorie der Erkenntnis.* Halle a.S.: Max Niemeyer, 1901. 2d rev. ed. in two parts, with the following subtitles: *Zweiter Band: Untersuchungen zur Phänomenologie und Theorie der Erkenntnis, I Teil.* Halle a.S.: Max Niemeyer, 1913. *Zweiter Band: Elemente einer phänomenologischen Aufklärung der Erkenntnis, II Teil.* Halle a.S.: Max Niemeyer, 1921. *Logical Investigations,* 2 vols. Translated by J. N. Findlay. New York: Humanities Press, 1970. (Note: Findlay's division into two volumes does not correspond to the division of the German text. His first volume includes the *Prolegomena* and the first two investigations of the *Zweiter Band.* The second volume contains the remaining four investigations. Since for reasons of economy in citations we are, where possible, limiting ourselves to the English translation, we will follow Findlay's division of the text.)

PIT *Zur Phänomenologie des inneren Zeitbewusstseins.* Edited by Rudolf Boehm (*Husserliana* X). The Hague: Martinus Nijhoff, 1966. This contains the *Vorlesungen zur Phänomenologie des inneren Zeitbewusstseins* from 1905, edited by Martin Heidegger (Halle a.S.: Max Niemeyer, 1928), the English translation of which by James S. Churchill is entitled *The Phenomenology of Internal Time-Consciousness.* Bloomington: Indiana University Press, 1964.

PPsych *Phänomenologische Psychologie.* Edited by Walter Biemel (*Husserliana* IX). The Hague: Martinus Nijhoff, 1962.

PRS "Philosophie als strenge Wissenschaft," *Logos,* I (1910–11), 289–341. "Philosophy as Rigorous Science." Translated by Quentin Lauer in *Phenomenology and the Crisis of Philosophy.* New York: Harper & Row, 1965.

Phenomenology and
Present-Day Linguistics

John W. M. Verhaar

Introduction; and Some Basic Concepts

The purpose of this paper [1] is somewhat unconventional, especially in linguistics, a little less so in philosophy—both of which disciplines are, each in its own way, relevant to the following discussions. A misunderstanding concerning the unconventional element of the purpose is likely to trigger confusion concerning the topic. Therefore, let me first say, somewhat loosely and provisionally, what the topic is: a consideration of phenomenology as holding potential for an approach in linguistic science alternative to both behaviorism and mentalism as commonly understood in that discipline. Presented this way, the topic itself has something unconventional about it also. What is it, the reader may demand, that behaviorism and mentalism have in common such that, if that common element were to be found objectionable, an alternative might be needed for curing the ills of both? It would seem, at first sight, that behaviorism and mentalism are mutually exclusive and that any elements common to both would have to be trivial.

At this point it may be fruitful to return to the purpose of this

1. As far as the over-all approach is concerned, the present paper supersedes my "Method, Theory, and Phenomenology," composed in 1966, which appeared in Paul L. Garvin, ed., *Method and Theory in Linguistics* (New York: Humanities Press, 1971), pp. 42–91. In particular, I have, in the past six years, developed more and greater objections against transformational grammar, which appears in a comparatively favorable light in the earlier paper.

study. This, again, formulated somewhat loosely and provisionally, is to expose, beneath a great many discussions in current and recent linguistic theory, a certain nonexplicit mode of thinking. This mode of thinking, faced explicitly, does not appear obvious at all, though it may well look obvious so long as the underlying assumptions are *not* faced. The mode of thinking referred to amounts to such underlying assumptions, and it may be compared to an "attitude" (as this is understood in ordinary language), or, somewhat more sophisticatedly, it may be determined as a "frame of reference." I follow earlier expositions by distinguishing such a "frame of reference" from a "framework"; while the former is (largely) implicit, the latter is (largely) explicit.[2] A framework, therefore, amounts to what is often called (and what I shall now understand by) a "theory." A theory in this sense is explicit: persuasions are explicit and systematized, and they are argued. On the other hand, no theory is entirely explicit; and, to the extent that there are always implicit elements, the theory, or framework, is based on a "frame of reference." Note that a theorist is not necessarily aware of the nature and/or extent of his frame of reference. It may serve as a very first introductory remark on phenomenology that for any theorist to desire to become aware of his frame of reference is to incline toward phenomenological research. The framework sums up what a man thinks; the frame of reference is about why he thinks the way he does. This "why" is largely traceable to elements of a cultural nature; and the cultural context becomes understandable (and explicit), among other things, in a historical perspective. These elements will be taken up again in due course.

Besides topic and purpose, there is the material subjected to analysis. By this I simply mean that it is no use discussing behaviorism without reference to actual behavioristic theories, or mentalism without reference to actual mentalistic theories. On the other hand, what follows here is not, and indeed could hardly be, a full overview of all, or most, theories in the two trends. More important, this will not be necessary. For in order to unearth a

2. For the "framework"/"frame of reference" distinction see my "Phenomenology as an Attitude," *Bijdragen,* XXVIII (1967), 399–421; it appears also in my "Dewart and the New Neo-Thomism," *Continuum,* V (1968), 634–42; "Some Notes on Language and Theology," *Bijdragen,* XXX (1969), 39–65 (reprinted under the title "Language and Theology" in *Continuum,* VII [1969], 3–29); and "Philosophy and Linguistic Theory," *Language Sciences,* no. 14 (1971), 1–11.

frame of reference, exhaustive description of theory is not called for, and samples will do. To put it another way: theories are only derivatively the object of study in the present paper. If this is not adequately understood, I may seem to be lumping together a number of disparate versions of what may at best have been one uniquely identifiable theory only at first. More clearly, I may seem to be setting up a straw man just to knock him down later. But I am not concerned with actual theories for their own sake but rather with their underlying "frames of reference." This word of caution applies especially to my discussions of the mentalistic frame of reference; behaviorism is not so popular any more, and I can afford to be briefer about that trend. As far as transformational grammar (henceforth: TG) is concerned, I shall confine myself for the most part to certain aspects of Chomsky's thought, as Chomsky is one of those very few TG linguists who has also moved professionally in the field of philosophy, including the history of philosophy, which, as just noted, is of importance for the uncovering of the frame of reference. But some of his assumptions are readily enough recognizable also in competitive forms of TG, to which, therefore, I shall also make occasional reference.

I have said that phenomenology serves here as an alternative to the frame of reference underlying (in part) both behaviorism and mentalism. I wish to note that "phenomenology" here refers also to a frame of reference rather than to one particular framework. One reason for this is obvious: phenomenology counts as part of its task attention to its own frame of reference. More practically, there are many phenomenological theories (just as there are also many different theories in [say] metaphysics, positivism, hermeneutics, Oxonian language analysis), none of which I shall bother to discuss in detail for its own sake. No phenomenologist, therefore, should expect full evaluation of his particular theory in the present paper; and I shall consider my sketch of some principal features of phenomenology successful if most phenomenologists would affirm that those features do indeed identify phenomenology in a wider sense, even though many might want to challenge some particular feature wholly or in part. Such recognition is more likely to be forthcoming than a comparable recognition of the (behavioristic/) mentalistic frame of reference on the part of theoretical linguists, for a reason already mentioned: phenomenology is interested in digging up its own foundations; behaviorism and mentalism are not (to the same extent), and in this manner I have already made a beginning, though as yet somewhat superficial, of the way in which phenomenology may be an alternative to mentalism and behaviorism alike. What this means from the point of view of theory formation must now be briefly explained.

For the moment I understand "theory," in deference to present-day usage, as an explicit system (and therefore a framework in terms of this study) somehow "explaining" how the raw data in any pursuit of knowledge have to be organized and thus made available for deeper insight. A theory, under the current majority understanding of that term, is conceived a priori; that is, it is an independent construction of the human mind, and its value consists solely in the power with which it may handle the data in a consistent (contradiction-free) and insightful manner. As to the epistemological way in which a theory is conceived, this is usually recognized as related to the data in obscure ways and in part only; for the most part it is precisely *not* due to discovery procedures but rather to a priori insights, which, as stated, become valuable only on being shown to be adequate, empirically speaking. Theories are therefore not random, hit-or-miss attempts of the mind, for there is true intuition behind the ways theories may emerge; on the other hand, theories conceived that way may be wrong, and they are accounted to be valid only when they can be shown to accommodate the data along lines of empirical verification.

If "theory" is understood this way, I think it is highly questionable. First, there is the (psychological) circumstance that in the pursuit of knowledge we are somewhat notoriously apt to invest much more in theories than provisional forms of intuition whose contents we grant may be doubtful; apparently the underlying frame of reference has to do with much more than just the desire to explain (say) the lingual "data." Equally notoriously, these "data," precisely because they are "raw" and may be molded into more than one form, have a way of accommodating themselves to theories which exposes the credit given to one particular theory rather than to other theories supposedly not firmly founded; this reflects adversely on both the explanatory power of any one particular theory and on the intuitive grasps underlying that theory. In fact, if a theory is changeable on principle, then a theory resembles what is usually meant by a "hypothesis," which is widely supposed to be more easily replaceable by an alternative hypothesis as soon as even the slightest need for this presents itself. That is to say, a hypothesis is much less a matter of principle, and of invested underlying persuasions, than is a theory. In fact, one gets the impression that "theory" is the more easily replaced by "hypothesis" in proportion as the scientist concerned cares less about the philosophical implications of the theory/hypothesis. The man in favor of a theory is more easily inclined to say to those contesting his claims: Prove me wrong. Indeed, the "burden of proof" seems to be the more easily shifted to the opponent and his alternative views in proportion as the original theory is supposed to be more eminent in the eyes of its proponent. The one holding a hypothesis, however, is more easily inclined to find ways of proving *himself* wrong while hoping to be right in the end.

However, such a comparison of the notions of theory and of hypothesis is one of extremes rather than of mutual likenesses. In actual fact, even present-day understanding of the notion of theory works with the kind of verification that may be called "operational," in the sense that this word would apply to verification of a hypothesis. Not that the theorist is an opportunist in the matter of truth; but he feels, perhaps (and more than someone advancing a hypothesis), that truth is, already in large part, guaranteed by the intuitions guiding theory formation. If he requires verification, this is with a view to obtaining consistency as much as truth, properly speaking. If the theory "works," that to him is already much. Meantime, he never goes far in questioning, let alone developing explicitly, the underlying assumptions of his intuitive sources. In that sense his theory has a low level of explicitness. Though he may speak about explicitness a great deal, that refers for the most part to his methods of verification and his formulations in the service of consistency and very little to his search for the nature, and justifiability, of the assumptions underlying his intuitions; to put it another way, his requirement of explicitness concerns the "how" rather than the "why." As a mentalist, he is a mechanic of the mind, ultimately, because he has the mind of a mechanic: here is one respect in which mentalistic linguistics is still far from having overcome the heritage of behaviorism. This is, I suggest, the underlying element which explains why a mentalistic linguist can speak so unproblematically of his object (mostly a "grammar") as a "machine" or a "device"; this is also why his notion of "creativity" is bound to be "rule-governed" (= in part mechanically determinable), while "rule-changing" "creativity" must be outside his scope as not fully belonging, supposedly, to natural language. For the moment this must suffice as an initial illustration.

Thus I would see a certain need for redefining "theory." A theory has to be explicit to a very high degree, not with the explicitness of method alone, but with that of the theory itself. Not that there is in principle an end to such explication of a theory as its justification. There is even one aspect of such an explication which depends upon saying what one means by certain terms and expressions; but this would, at least ideally, entail explaining what one means by the words and expressions used to clarify the original terms and expressions, and so forth *in indefinitum*. However, there is a certain foundation where one may reasonably stop. At this early point in this paper one example must suffice. If language is considered to be uniquely characteristic of man, and if, then, one probes into the unicity of man, one may (for example) go back to the point where one finds "selfhood" as characteristic of man. Now, "selfhood" is hardly a clear notion; yet it has something convincingly intuitive about it, at least for anyone not stubbornly refusing to emerge from an uncompromisingly nominalistic position. But such a refusal would be somewhat unreasonable, seeing that the notion of "self" is firmly embedded in natural language, does not share in the elusive abstractness of mere *terms* (toward which, as is otherwise generally recognized in theory formation nowadays, a nominalistic attitude is much more reasonable and indeed scientifically prudent), and, even though admittedly vague, has something of rock-bottom solidity about it also. If, however, the unicity of man is sought in the theory that he supposedly has "innate ideas," that, it must be admitted, may be an unambiguously clear notion in at least several of its features; yet it cannot seem to find any support in unreflective common-sense certainties, and if *that* is taken as a basis, little value appears to be attached to the clarity, or potential clarity, of such a concept as that of "innate ideas." *Then* the question arises, as reasonably as it does spontaneously: What, if anything, are "innate ideas" anyway?

As far as those "innate ideas" are concerned, Chomsky has at least done his best to go into them to some depth. As is well enough known, he has done this by tracing them back to earlier traditions in European thought.[3] Hence the new popularity of the "history of linguistics" (which is actually, for the most part, a history of the philosophy of language); but Chomsky has appealed to history mainly to prove that he is in good company. What he has not done is to challenge the cultural one-sidedness of that history or to investigate where that history has become discontinuous with itself, especially in the underlying problematic of body-soul, or body-mind.

All of these missing elements, i.e., discontinuity, explication of underlying assumptions, determination of cultural limitations, are found, although hardly with unchallengeable perfection, in phenomenology. Its frame of reference is the scientific and philosophical requirement to be aware of one's frame of reference. The more detailed exposition of these and other properties of phenomenology is the business of the following section; mention of them here merely serves the purposes of this introduction, which I must now conclude with a few additional remarks on theories.

The notion of "theory" as I have just redefined it excludes one sense of "theory" as used by Chomsky, that is, in the sense of some dispositional ability (innate or not; innate in the sense of Chomsky). In Chomsky's words: "The child who learns a language has in some sense constructed a grammar for himself [and] has succeeded in carrying out what, from a formal point of view, at least, seems to be a remarkable type of theory construction." [4] The "theory" here is, of course, implicit, not only in a sense in which a frame of reference is not, but it even defies explication in the form of conscious awareness (in the case of the child, or even in an adult native speaker) to any significant degree. The qualification "from a formal point of view" is telling; it amounts to saying that the *descriptive counterpart* of (in this case) the child's achievement in learning a language amounts to a theory; the suggestion is that data and the theory explaining

3. Noam Chomsky, *Current Issues in Linguistic Theory* (New York: Humanities Press, 1964), pp. 15–25; *Aspects of the Theory of Syntax* (Cambridge, Mass.: M.I.T. Press, 1965), pp. 47–52; *Cartesian Linguistics* (New York: Harper & Row, 1966); and *Language and Mind* (New York: Harcourt, Brace & World, 1968), *passim*.

4. Chomsky, review of B. F. Skinner, *Verbal Behavior*, in *Language*, XXXV (1959), 26–58; cf. Chomsky, *Language and Mind*, p. 77.

them are isomorphic. To the theory, the data appear as "facts," [5] which are repeatedly characterized as "abstract," no doubt because of the isomorphism that appears to be claimed. One would think, however, that the isomorphism is not, after all, enough by way of explanation, because, obviously, its justification would have to be traced back to the data and thus to discovery procedures. Therefore, as linguistic descriptions are abstract, a "characterization of the abstract form" is necessary, and this, at least according to Katz and Fodor, is what we would call a "metatheory." [6]

Note that what a metatheory of this kind does is the inverse of the explicitness obtainable by explication of the underlying frame of reference. The metatheory is imposed from without; explication of the frame of reference is gained from within. The metatheory is a higher-level mode of thinking, not really there until it is introduced, while explication of the frame of reference is the explication of what has been there all the time by implication, even before the theory emerged. The metatheory, of course, is also rooted in a frame of reference, usually quite recognizably determined by its cultural context and historical sources, especially the philosophical ones; but its imposition upon the theory it is supposed to explain in more ultimate terms may not be clearly connected with the data the theory was meant to handle in the first place. Thus the body-mind problem as philosophically continuous in fairly clearly determinable lines in the West has served as a metatheory (though not necessarily by that name) for both behaviorism and mentalism, and *its* frame of reference is really the same for both, even though alternative explicit solutions have been mutually exclusive, at least in extreme forms. Metatheories are on the whole somewhat too easy to come by; they also "rationalize" what may be in part nonrational, and we shall have occasion to recognize many nonrational features in natural language. Phenomenologists are interested precisely in those nonrational elements, not only when founding their own descriptions, but also in exposing alien elements in nonphenom-

5. Chomsky, "Some Methodological Remarks on Generative Grammar," *Word*, XVII (1961), 219.

6. Jerrold J. Katz and Jerry A. Fodor, "The Structure of a Semantic Theory" (written in 1963), in Jerry A. Fodor and Jerrold J. Katz, eds., *The Structure of Language: Readings in the Philosophy of Language* (Englewood Cliffs, N.J.: Prentice-Hall, 1964), p. 479.

enological theories. Thus in taking rationalism (in the historical sense) as founding much in contemporary linguistic mentalism, the phenomenologist is not interested in the philosophical position implied in mentalism, because it follows, as soon as it becomes explicit (as it has in the thought of Chomsky), the mentalistic approach by way of a rather external justification. Rather, what the phenomenologist is interested in is in what precedes a theoretical position such as mentalism, not only temporally (Chomsky did not start out by being a rationalist in the philosophical sense), but also, and more especially, "genetically."

These considerations may in part answer the question why a phenomenological study like the present one cannot simply stick to elaboration of its principles and to their application without insisting on a confrontation with alternative frames of reference. Nor can it even keep such a confrontation within marginal limits. Indeed, not too long ago, I still thought that was the most feasible thing to do.[7] I have changed my mind for two reasons, a practical one and one of principle. The practical one is that in a study on linguistic theory one cannot well afford to bypass the trend that has, in the past ten years or so, been introduced on such a large scale: TG. I have found—somewhat to my concern—that there are now many good universities where training in linguistics consists almost exclusively of TG studies, and I feel that further criticism on the level of theory and method may be in place. The principle coming in here may be briefly indicated as follows. What is here considered to be the most important feature of phenomenology (from the point of view of the history of ideas) is its discontinuity with a metaphysical tradition which has almost uniquely determined that history—that is to say, the metaphysical tradition of the West. Now, although I will speak about that history briefly below, for the purposes of the present study it has seemed to me more fitting to set forth that discontinuity within the contemporary scene; and this is readily possible because of the roots of TG in metaphysical rationalism in European thought and also, though to a lesser extent, *mutatis mutandis,* because of the roots of behaviorism in the same tradition.

Meantime, phenomenology has been introduced in an initial and very general way. I must now devote two separate sections to this complicated notion.

7. See Verhaar, "Method, Theory, and Phenomenology."

PHENOMENOLOGY

JUST AS THERE IS NEVER any uniquely identifiable system in any major trend in philosophy, there is no such thing as "the" phenomenological system either. Phenomenology originated in Europe, and some of its highly remote, less down-to-earth analogues are found already in Hegel. The trend has largely been confined to the continental European scene.[8] In the United States, particularly, there are some phenomenological centers, some of them of central importance (such as Northwestern University), but phenomenology is not widespread, and in fact it is largely unknown. At present phenomenology is leading a somewhat frustrated existence even in Europe. Among the various reasons for this, and for the failure of phenomenology to get firmly established in other parts of the world, a few may be worth mentioning briefly. One is that phenomenology must be called particularly difficult. Reading Husserl, for example, is hardly a relaxing pastime, even for the devotee. Also, and more important, the vagueness of the term "phenomenology" has, among other things, been responsible for its confusion with other trends from which, at least in its original features, it is quite markedly distinct: to a certain extent with hermeneutics, but most especially with existentialism. Furthermore, phenomenology has been unduly popularized, and for the methodologically unscrupulous it has, occasionally, been reduced to "saying whatever occurs to you." This is in part due to the circumstance that the vague must never be eliminated from the object of analysis; but to hold this is one thing, and to indulge in a vague *method* is quite another. In part, also, the reason for vagueness has been an overlap—in itself purely interdisciplinary—with abnormal psychology, a field in which understanding is often achieved by empathically sharing the other person's experience; and since the problems of the emotionally disturbed are frequently quite close to human prob-

8. Phenomenology originated with Husserl's *Logische Untersuchungen,* 1901 (for complete bibliographical information, see the Bibliography, below). On Husserl, see especially Marvin Farber, *The Foundation of Phenomenology: Edmund Husserl and the Quest for a Science of Philosophy* (New York: Paine-Whitman, 1962). Further references occur later in this section.

lems discussed in existentialist philosophy, the transition has been almost inevitable.[9] One may even wonder—though I will not go into this question now—whether phenomenology has ever been able to disengage itself sufficiently from the rationalistic tradition to which it was really a reaction. Thus it would not be very hard to uncover in Husserl's writings points of view somewhat analogous to rationalism (especially in the emphasis on "essences" and "consciousness"), and it is, among other things, for this reason that Heidegger has criticized Husserl as not yet coming up fully to the ideals of phenomenology.[10] Inversely, Merleau-Ponty played down many technical details of Husserl's method, inclined with increasing exclusiveness toward the vaguely suggestive in his own analyses, and in fact ended up, in his later works, so close to existentialism that the difference seems hardly appreciable.[11] It is when vagueness of object spills over into analysis and method that rejection of phenomenological studies becomes quite understandable. Thus, a work like Kwant's *Phenomenology of Language* cannot be expected to shed any light on phenomenology as understood here.[12]

It is difficult to obtain a satisfactory overview of the entire range of phenomenology. Even a standard work like Spiegelberg's *The Phenomenological Movement* has the disadvantage of

9. On this, see Verhaar, "Phenomenology as an Attitude," pp. 410–12.

10. The somewhat rationalistic element appears clearly in a portion of the *Logische Untersuchungen* dealing with language, where "pure grammar" is discussed (II, 294–342; English translation by J. N. Findlay, *Logical Investigations*, 2 vols. [New York: Humanities Press, 1970], II, 493–529). (For a free English rendering see also Farber, *The Foundation of Phenomenology*, pp. 313–32). On this see also Yehoshua Bar-Hillel, "Husserl's Conception of a Purely Logical Grammar," *Philosophy and Phenomenological Research*, XVII (1957), 362–69. For Heidegger's critique of Husserl, see Herbert Spiegelberg, *The Phenomenological Movement*, 2 vols. (The Hague: Nijhoff, 1960), pp. 275–83.

11. For the "simplification" of Husserl's "reduction," see the Preface to Maurice Merleau-Ponty, *Phénoménologie de la perception* (Paris: Gallimard, 1945), pp. i–xv; English translation by Colin Smith, *Phenomenology of Perception* (New York: Humanities Press, 1962), pp. vii–xxi. The existentialist character of Merleau-Ponty's later work appears perhaps most clearly in his (posthumously published) *L'Oeil et l'esprit* (Paris: Gallimard, 1964); English translation by Carleton Dallery, "Eye and Mind," in Maurice Merleau-Ponty, *The Primacy of Perception and Other Essays*, ed. James M. Edie (Evanston, Ill.: Northwestern University Press, 1964), pp. 159–90.

12. R. C. Kwant, *Fenomenologie van de taal* (Utrecht: Het Spectrum, 1963); English translation by Henry J. Koren, *Phenomenology of Language* (Pittsburgh: Duquesne University Press, 1965).

including a good deal of existentialism in its excellent surveys; but it is hard to see what else the author could have done without confining phenomenology in a way not in keeping with the purposes of a historical work. Thus Heidegger claimed to be a phenomenologist [13] and to have improved upon the phenomenology of Husserl; but a more usual evaluation of his work is that it is existentialism. Marcel disclaimed being a phenomenologist *and* an existentialist and instead insisted on being a "Socratic philosopher." Even more confusingly, phenomenology has affinities with trends rarely associated with it, language analysis in the first place. As it has occasionally been pointed out before, the antimetaphysical (though yet not positivistic!) attitude of language analysis makes phenomenological and analytic texts very close to each other, most interestingly, for our purpose, precisely in the cognitive evaluation of language.[14] Elsewhere I have pointed out affinities at a deeper level (in the frame of reference, therefore) with other trends among contemporary nontraditional philosophies.[15] My purpose in mentioning this is more than just the interest of comparative reference. For I take "phenomenology" in a somewhat (but not drastically) wider sense than is the case with most phenomenologists, in that I wish to include some attainments of Oxonian language analysis itself. What I wish to borrow from those quarters is the kind of insistence on

13. In Spiegelberg, *The Phenomenological Movement*, pp. 265–91, the occurrence of "phenomenology" in Heidegger's works (and course announcements) has been carefully analysed; it appears that, as time went on, Heidegger became more inclined to drop the term "phenomenology," in part, perhaps, out of deference to Husserl, in view of the two men's growing philosophical estrangement. See also William J. Richardson, *Heidegger: Through Phenomenology to Thought* (New York: Humanities Press, 1963).

14. See J. F. Staal, *Euclides en Pāṇini* (Amsterdam: Polak & van Gennep, 1963), pp. 8–9 (not to be confused with a drastically revised version of this, "Euclid and Pāṇini," *Philosophy East and West*, XV [1965], 99–116, in which, also, no reference to the affinities concerned any longer occurs). See also C. A. van Peursen, "Edmund Husserl and Ludwig Wittgenstein," *Philosophy and Phenomenological Research*, XX (1959), 181–97, and, especially, his *Fenomenologie en analytische filosofie* (Hilversum and Amsterdam: W. de Haan and J. M. Meulenhoff, 1968). Also Spiegelberg, *The Phenomenological Movement*, p. 670, and his "A Phenomenological Approach to the Ego," *The Monist*, XLIX, no. 1 (1965), 1–17 (this entire issue of *The Monist* is devoted to the relations between phenomenology and Oxonian analysis). See also Verhaar, "Method, Theory, and Phenomenology," p. 47, note 10, and "Phenomenology as an Attitude," pp. 404–6.

15. "Phenomenology as an Attitude," pp. 406–12.

the analysis of *terms* (and therefore mainly at the methodological level) which suspects an entire metaphysical heritage behind
them, used somewhat naïvely, as if no Trojan horse were thereby
brought in. My reason for this rejection of elements of which
phenomenology has never been as critical as has language analysis of the British kind is that the analysis of what "precedes"
(in the genetic sense mentioned above) the fully accepted use of
such key terms is perhaps a *via regia* toward the underlying frame
of reference, which may well, after adequate analysis of all that is
involved, have to be rejected as vacuous or, to use a term Chomsky
has used with an only partially correct and therefore somewhat
misleading application, as "myth." Though I shall work out this
point in detail below, one example may be useful here. It is the
term "the world," or occasionally "the universe." This term is
used regularly, even though not very frequently, in TG literature
for making certain distinctions between what belongs to grammar and what does not. What does an expression like "our
knowledge of the (external) world" mean, once we analyse * it
carefully? It is opposed to, at least distinct from, speaking man;
on the other hand, it includes man, because human reality is
being talked about as much as is "the world." Actually, therefore,
the "world" stands for everything there is, understood as objective
reality; and it is more or less the (immense) object that the
"world," or "nature," still was for Newton and Newtonian physics.
That kind of objectivity has long since been abandoned in post-
Newtonian physics; also, it cannot be considered as coextensive
with "reality" in the conceptions of many people, to whom, for
example, it may be an "idea" in the sense of Kant. What else does
"the world" stand for in many contexts but a popularized sample
of a questionable and outdated metaphysics?

A few remarks on the *term* "phenomenology" may be in place
here. There are strong, mainly historical, reasons for sticking to
it, but it has a great many serious disadvantages which have to
be borne carefully in mind if the phenomenologist does not want
an unrecognized frame of reference to enter his own picture. In
particular, the implication that only "phenomena" in the sense
of "what appears" (to the senses) is involved is inadequate and
extremely unfortunate. The term also sounds forbiddingly esoteric, and I agree with Austin's sobering comment that it is "quite

* [Author's preferred spelling.—Ed.]

a mouthful," the more interesting seeing that this remark occurs in a passage sympathetic toward phenomenology.[16] Ideally, it would be good to replace it with some other term; but apart from the circumstance that this would be out of place in a volume like the present one, it would also be extremely difficult to come up with a suitable alternative.

After these brief comments, I now propose to outline some features of phenomenology in my conception of it. I will, in doing this, be led by three considerations. The first is that it must be reasonably well established that the following constitutes a set of principles which would be recognizable to the professional phenomenologist, even though he might disagree on details, especially as far as the overt framework is concerned; I am not, in other words, merely appropriating the term to cover uniquely personal views. This requirement will lead me to say a number of things which are either not directly relevant to linguistics as pursued in the phenomenological frame of reference or whose relevance to linguistics cannot be worked out in this paper. The second consideration is that I must concentrate on requirements for linguistics wherever possible. This is naturally a limiting element, but in line with the topic of this paper. The third consideration will lead me to contrast phenomenology with behaviorism and especially mentalism, a thing not normally done in expositions of phenomenology.[17]

SOME FEATURES OF PHENOMENOLOGY

1. PHENOMENOLOGY, as this present work amply proves, is interdisciplinary. This appears, first, simply de facto. There are phenomenological trends in psychology, sociology, and linguistics, readily identifiable as such. Phenomenologists would also recognize much they might consider theirs in trends not usually labeled "phenomenology," such as certain trends in anthropological linguistics and sociolinguistics. In general it may be said that phenomenological inspiration in empirical sciences is

16. J. L. Austin, "A Plea for Excuses," in J. O. Urmson and G. J. Warnock, eds., *J. L. Austin: Philosophical Papers* (London: Clarendon Press [Oxford University Press], 1961), p. 130.
17. An interesting exception is T. W. Wann, ed., *Psychology: Contrasting Bases for Behaviorism and Phenomenology* (Chicago: University of Chicago Press, 1964).

recognized as philosophical in origin; and, indeed, it was in philosophy that it originated. Phenomenology, therefore, is interdisciplinary in at least two ways: it belongs in more than one empirical science, and it belongs in both empirical science and philosophy. (It also characterizes certain trends in theology, but that is of no consequence for our topic.)

Phenomenology is also interdisciplinary de jure. It is not coincidental that Husserl called phenomenology a "rigorous science" (*strenge Wissenschaft;* English emphasis mine),[18] even though he did not mean to say that phenomenology is an empirical science as distinct from philosophy; rather, *Wissenschaft,* though still philosophical, may as such be considered as distinct from philosophy as "wisdom," a conception deriving from Plato and, until quite recently, far more typical of traditional metaphysics in the West than philosophy as "knowledge."[19]

This feature, among others, shows phenomenology to be quite sharply discontinuous with traditional philosophy. It would therefore not be correct to say that phenomenology has caused empirical science to lose its autonomous status with regard to philosophy. To bear this in mind is crucial for what I shall say later about TG, which trend in linguistics I shall criticize for having allowed an empirical science to be assimilated into philosophy, that is, to be remetaphysicalized. More clearly: even if one were to say that empirical sciences basing themselves on the phenomenological frame of reference have allowed themselves to be influenced by philosophy, that, whatever it means (and that involves statements of principle about what philosophy is or must be), does *not* mean that such empirical sciences have been (re)metaphysicalized. In fact, remetaphysicalization of empirical science as found in TG (mainly in Chomsky's version of it) has led (and by Chomsky's own admission) to the identification of (rationalistic) philosophy of language with linguistics (as well as with cognitive psychology). It follows that, on this view, it would be meaningless to speak about interdisciplinary research, as the "disciplines" concerned are supposed to be one and the

18. Edmund Husserl, "Philosophie als strenge Wissenschaft," *Logos,* I (1910), 289–314; English translation by Quentin Lauer, "Philosophy as Rigorous Science," in Quentin Lauer, ed., *Phenomenology and the Crisis of Philosophy* (New York: Harper & Row, 1965), pp. 69–147.

19. On philosophy as "wisdom" versus "knowledge," see Verhaar, "Some Notes on Language and Theology," pp. 45–47 and *passim,* and "Philosophy and Linguistic Theory," pp. 2–3 and *passim.*

same field. In phenomenology, in contrast, different disciplines do not cease to be different just because their underlying frame of reference is characterized by a basic identity.

2. In traditional European metaphysics, rationalism may perhaps be called the epistemological counterpart to essentialism as its ontological basis. My "perhaps" refers only to the feasibility of this particular formula, for the feature indicated by it is too well known in the history of philosophy to need justification. Thus, to confine myself to recent philosophy for the moment, the reason why Heidegger called himself a phenomenologist rather than an existentialist was his opposition to Husserlian essentialism, and, as already briefly indicated above, not without ground; whether Heidegger's own version of phenomenology was any more convincing need not detain us here. His reaction mirrors a long line of of similar protests in earlier periods, albeit in different forms: existence (not as a logical but as an ontological notion) versus essence, or, more appropriately, *esse* versus essence in the thought of Thomas Aquinas, or "mystery" versus "problem" (Marcel), and sometimes in one and the same philosopher, for example in Pascal, in whom there was the never resolved conflict between Augustinianism and Cartesianism.[20] The trend rejected by Chomsky as "romantic" in the history of the philosophy of language and of linguistics is another version, in terms of frame of reference, of the antiessentialist protest.[21] Now, what phenomenology does, among other things, is to give methodological recognition to this protest (which explains the occasional overlaps of some forms of phenomenology with existentialism, as noted above). Its task is not an easy one: to stay out of existentialism and essentialism alike—or, in terms of the present paper, to reject "rationalism" without becoming "romantic"— and to analyse the vague without having the analysis become methodologically shaky. We shall see, further, that this involves quite concrete tasks, about whose circumscription there need be no vagueness at all—tasks such as involving, in certain ways, the speech situation in the analysis of lingual structure and distrusting, as briefly indicated earlier, metatheories as justifica-

---

20. Heidegger's charge that the history of philosophy in the West has been characterized by "forgetfulness of being" illustrates the same point. On Pascal, see the "Postscript" to Verhaar, "Philosophy and Linguistic Theory," p. 10.
21. See, e.g., Chomsky, *Cartesian Linguistics, passim.*

tions, including certain appeals to logic in the analysis of natural language.

3. Phenomenology has the mark of totality in one fairly clearly definable respect. Let the object to be analysed be x (an example: perception). It is phenomenologically necessary to place x in a larger context, because the way x is related to more comprehensive wholes is taken to be characteristic of x. In fact, if the larger totality, to be called y, is not *deliberately* selected, it will be selected anyway, perhaps unconsciously. For perception (for example) already takes a certain place in the view of the analyst, even before the analysis begins, perhaps (to mention only one approach, and one which would be incorrect) positivistically and behavioristically (the senses are "hit" by some "outward" "datum," etc.). To prevent y from being unconsciously chosen, any selection must be explicated. Thus, in certain body-soul theories perception might be taken to be "distinct" from "intellectual" activity as well as "one" with it (whatever, in turn, this activity is supposed to be, and that has to be explicated also), in such a way (for example) that the intellect is supposed to "abstract" the "universal" from the "particular" captured by the senses. Phenomenologically, what is important is that y should be defined by x, and not inversely; for, if inversely, preconceived views of y will impose themselves on the analysis of x as a possibly alien metatheory. Indeed, one might even have recourse to an even more comprehensive totality z, in order the better to situate y, ultimately to have a supposedly better view of x. It is in this respect that phenomenology will differ radically from metaphysics, in which the trend will precisely be for z to determine y and for y to determine x, at least in extreme cases (such as found in the dialectics of Hegel), on the view that "the whole is the true." As y is likely to be more abstract (in some sense) than x, and z more abstract than y, the tendency to abstractness will tend to be dominant. As one may imagine, abstractness does not promote attention to the nonrational, the imponderable, the vague, and the "down-to-earth," and rationalization is then inevitably in the picture. What this entails for linguistics is of great importance. The content of what we say is too easily "explained" in terms of a semantics of what is rationally ("clearly") determinable; more particularly, the neglect of the speech *situation*, as too complicated to be clarificatory and therefore left out as supposedly "extralinguistic," follows almost as a matter of course.

The exclusion of the situation is, admittedly, not typical of TG alone but of behaviorism as well and, indeed, of nearly all of "structuralism," beginning with the exclusion of the situation by Saussure himself.

4. The totality mentioned in paragraph 3 is taken to be already there—previous to and independent of the phenomenologist's analyses—in ways indicated (in different trends in phenomenology) by terms like "nonthematic," "antepredicative," "prereflective," and, whenever analysis is pursued philosophically only, "prephilosophical." The phenomenologist, therefore, does not seek to *establish* unity but to analyse a unity *already there* previous to even the first thought he gives to his object, even though (see paragraph 5) this unity is integrated with his experience. This shows that analysis in the phenomenological sense is quite distinct from analysis in the atomistic sense. Because of the experience aspect, the analysis, or description (see paragraph 6), can never be a counterpart of the object of analysis (unless in some trivial sense); the phenomenologist's description is in that sense isomorphic with the object. It is clear that any theory distrusting a totality preanalytically given (such as behaviorism), or accepting such a totality but in the form of a metatheory fully determining the object in its essential traits (for example, in a theory of the mind with "innate ideas," as in Chomsky's version of TG), must be irreconcilable with the phenomenological approach.

5. It has been stated that the "experience" side is basic. One might call this "subjective," but not as this term is understood within a larger totality characterized by a subject-object split overriding the original (phenomenologically rather: originary) unity of both; let alone "subjective" in the sense of "arbitrary," "unverifiable." What is behind this insistence on experience rather than knowledge is that phenomenologically the position of knowledge is derivative with regard to experience—often through the intermediate stage of awareness, or consciousness. The assumption here is that intellectual knowledge is more easily prejudiced when given priority over experience; it is also assumed that, whatever prejudices, or inconsistencies more generally, are present in intellectual representations (and precisely because they are *representations!*), we have little more than "logic" with which to discover them. Experience, though no doubt vaguer, is both wider and more basic. What the phenomenologist does,

therefore, may be described as placing himself in a position of experiencing but not knowing.[22]

In linguistics, an example illustrating this principle is found in speaking about a "word," or a "sentence," as already *in*cluding the semantic content of that word or that sentence. The example is crucial in at least two ways: phenomenological linguistics is "mentalistic," but not "mentalistic" in ways already determined by preconceived (nonlinguistic) theories of the human mind, as in some forms of TG, a determination which violates feature 3, above. Further, as "experience" necessarily introduces the vague, the rationally not clearly determinable, it is again the (speech) situation which proves to be highly relevant. Another property of "experience" as a central datum makes it inappropriate to speak about the "interpretation" of sentences or to have a brand of semantics which is "interpretative": we do not "interpret" sentences (necessarily a roundabout, indirect process), we *understand* them in the very act of producing or hearing them. We do not even "interpret" ambiguous sentences, because our understanding of them reveals them as two (or more) sentences. The expression "an ambiguous sentence" is a behavioristic expression, unless it is used to refer to cases in which, for quite coincidental reasons, understanding in one or more directions is momentarily blocked.[23]

6. Phenomenology cannot be identified with either induction or deduction (the first, therefore, with emphasis on discovery procedures, the second with emphasis on a priori insights), or, indeed, with Peirce's "induction" (the *terminus ad quem*, if I understand it correctly, is again too rational for dealing with natural language adequately); nor can phenomenology be identified with a posteriori or a priori as bases.[24] Instead, it proceeds analytically, or descriptively, by way of explicitation or explication: that is to say, both by recognizing the originary unity of objects and their totality as unity (as stated in 3) and by refusing to split up the unity of object and experience (as indicated in 4

22. This is the apt formulation of Peter Caws, *The Philosophy of Science: A Systematic Account* (Princeton, N.J.: D. Van Nostrand, 1965), p. 18.

23. For more on ambiguity, see below, at the end of the section on "Idealization and Rationalism"; see also Verhaar, "Method, Theory, and Phenomenology," pp. 59–61.

24. See Chomsky, *Language and Mind*, pp. 78–79.

and 5). I prefer, and have therefore used in previous passages, "explication" as a term, as it can mean "explanation" (which is what it is) and "unfolding" (which is what it is also). It is by reason of the isomorphism, already touched upon, that the two are one and the same and are also identical with analysis or description. Both deduction and induction are based on the unwarranted assumption (thus leading to pseudoproblems) that something already known ("general principles" and "facts," respectively) leads to something not directly accessible (the particular and the universal, respectively). Both entail the imposition of a totality from without, a reduced reality in the case of induction, an expanded but unduly dominating and abstract one in the case of deduction. This would offend 3, above, and 7, below.

At this point the following question is bound to come up. Does the phenomenologist accept the possibility of "new" knowledge arising from his analyses? A reply would point out the following. Results are "new" in that descriptions explicate, i.e., explain by "unfolding," elements so far implicit and below the level of awareness or consciousness, though yet within experience; but since such explications are also accompanied by a certain amount of recognition (at least to the extent that alternative frames of reference are not too predominating, i.e., if there is enough scope for implementation of 7, below), thematically, of the nonthematic, results are accordingly only comparatively "new." However, this is not to say that there can be nothing new in the way of *information,* or of new data, in phenomenological research, but those new elements would be contingent to the process of explication. Thus when I study a new language, certain (or, if I am a beginner, all) elements are new to me, which, however, is contingent in the sense that they are not new to native speakers; and in fact my analysis of such a language cannot start adequately until I have attained a reasonably adequate native command of the language. As complete command of the *lexicon* is not the privilege of even native speakers, there is a wider margin of new information even for them, something characteristically not the case with the native command of grammar.[25] Finally, insofar as what is altogether new is not con-

25. What has been said here explains why field methods need an approach that looks quite behavioristic in the beginning; later the field worker, as he becomes more familiar with the new language, can progressively rely on native intuition; by that time the behavioristic approach has

tingent but in part essential (such as is in part the case in the natural sciences), phenomenology will accordingly have only partial relevance,[26] but I cannot go into these problems in the present paper.

7. Stepping back from prejudice (so that, as Merleau-Ponty has it, all the threads of intentionality can be unraveled), or, in the expression of Husserl, from the "natural" attitude, likely to be fraught with preconceptions without any basis, is a primary preoccupation of phenomenology.[27] The suggestion is not, of course, that nonphenomenologists are particularly prone to prejudice but that phenomenology has a methodological precaution against it. In terms of this paper, what the phenomenologist wants to avoid at all costs is the adoption of an alien frame of reference. Certain frames of reference may be widely accepted, but they are likely to be historically and culturally conditioned. To illustrate this, almost any concept would do; but I will select an example crucial for the confrontation with "mentalism" in this paper, i.e., the concept of "mind." What the phenomenologist does not doubt is that there is an aspect to human experience called "cognition"; nor does he doubt that there is an acceptable meaning of "mental" and "mind" in which that cognitive aspect may be called "mental" and referred to the "mind." What he does question is a superimposed notion of mind and of the mental, however "natural" such a notion may be in a certain historical tradition or in a certain cultural environment. The phenomenologist knows, of course, that he cannot, any more than anyone else, start from scratch; but he wishes to begin at a point at which as little as possible is taken for granted, and he wants to check even that "early" point for the possibly unfounded implications that may be

---

become meaningless. We may reverse Caws's formula, cited above, when we apply it to the field worker setting out to describe a language that is new to him: he must necessarily place himself in the position of knowing without experiencing.

26. See H. C. van de Hulst and C. A. van Peursen, *Phaenomenologie en natuurwetenschap* (Utrecht: Bijleveld, 1953); see also van Peursen's further development, as reflected in his *Wetenschappen en werkelijkheid* (Kampen: Kok, 1969), in which phenomenology has a less central place.

27. Merleau-Ponty, Introduction to *Phenomenology of Perception;* Edmund Husserl, *Ideen zu einer reinen Phänomenologie, Erstes Buch,* ed. Walter Biemel (The Hague: Nijhoff, 1950), pp. 220–27 (published originally in 1913); English translation by W. R. Boyce Gibson, *Ideas: General Introduction to Pure Phenomenology* (New York: Humanities Press, 1931), pp. 258–66; paperback ed. (New York: Collier Books, 1962), pp. 238–46.

contained in his own "natural" conception of it. What makes such a point "early" is, among other things, something concrete in the sense of more easily communicable; thus a phenomenology of the mind (supposing that is a phenomenologist's object of analysis), since any conception of the mind is likely to be fairly abstract, is hardly a beginner's object of analysis, while a phenomenology of language would be less hazardous in this respect, as human language is more "concrete," more easily communicable among philosophers and scientists, more "down to earth" in a sense already noted above. Meantime, the phenomenologist of language will have to reject any basis in a phenomenology of the mind, however good that may be in itself, in order not to have his *x* dominated by *y*, or *y* by *z* in the sense explained in 3, above; and most certainly he must reject any metaphysical-rationalistic notion of mind. I will illustrate this latter point in the following section. Here let me take, as an example of the "stepping-back" mentioned above, Merleau-Ponty's rejection of "intellectualism" (of which "rationalism," in Chomsky's sense, is one important variety), on the ground that the notion of an autonomous mind, with its supposed potential for an overview of reality and privileged insights, is self-defeating.[28] Little familiarity with the work of Ryle is needed for recognizing that what Ryle has done with the notion of mind language-analytically has important affinities with the stepping-back from prejudice in the phenomenological sense.[29]

As a last example I wish to mention contemporary insistence on "logic" as supposedly indispensable for any coherent discourse. The phenomenologist will, of course, give due credit to logic for its potential for unraveling a number of things whose expression in natural language is either too cumbersome or is misleading even where not cumbersome; and he will also readily concede that logic can do many other things for which he does not appear to have any immediate use. What he will not accept is that logic, as a derivative (ultimately) of natural language, can guarantee the kind of coherence which *he* must value above all else: the foundation of his crucial concepts in a frame of reference that will stand further analytic explication. Note that if "logic" is taken to mean, not the highly technical subject matter known as "symbolic

28. Merleau-Ponty, *Phenomenology of Perception*.
29. See, especially, Gilbert Ryle, *The Concept of Mind* (London: Hutchinson, 1949).

logic," but, more widely, some coherent epistemology, similar suspicions are bound to arise in the phenomenologist's mind. A good example is perhaps the notion of "presupposition," now so popular in TG. Its problematic nature consists in this: that at the surface level presuppositions appear only in implied forms; and they must, therefore, become explicit in the deep structure. This actually might even sound reassuring to the phenomenologist initially, at least if he is for a moment misled by the "depth" metaphor in the expression "deep structure." In TG theory, however, and in its mixed-metaphor terminology, "deep" does not in any way stand for what is closer to immediate "uninterpreted" experience, but, inversely and unfortunately, for a "meta"-element in the sense that "meta" has in "metatheory." But that may imply, in many cases, that something "earlier" in experience is the same as something "earlier" in the cognitive order; however, this is not so, even in the metaphysical tradition of the West (as any student of the "ontological argument" knows), and in fact it is thus seen that the imposition of an alien frame of reference (in the form, often, of a metatheory) may amount not only to a failure to identify what belongs to one's object of analysis and what does not but to distortion even of an object that has been adequately identified for analysis. To return to "presuppositions" in the TG sense, it is especially when certain relations to the speech situation (as in metaphorical word use) complicate the rationally determinable content of what we say when making an utterance that that notion becomes untenable as a deep-structure constituent; he who resorts to it, and thus reduces experiential components of speech, as manipulation of a certain speech setting, to cognitive features, mistakes altogether the nature of natural language. He has, once more, been tripped up by his resistance to the vague and the imponderable.

8. One of the prejudices that may affect analysis of any kind is a prejudice about its object. First, of course, when speaking about an "object" of phenomenological analysis, we must bear in mind that its frequent connotations of what is "thing-like," or even "material" (whatever that means) must be banned from the analysis: "object" in this sense implies no ontological evaluation. What I wish to emphasize, as feature 8, is something to which Husserl also paid a good deal of attention: that an ontological evaluation of the object which concentrates on whether the object is, or is not, a "fact" must be carefully kept outside the

phenomenologist's task. To assume anything about the "factual" or "nonfactual" status of the object is, according to Husserl, typical of the natural attitude. Note that what Husserl rejects is not an analysis of "fact"; what he rejects is the supposed necessity of associating "fact" with the notion of "object." When such an association takes place, it will be ultimately reducible to an ontological evaluation, which, being metaphysical, introduces unwarranted assumptions. However, the point is not to deny that there may be "common-sense" evaluations of "fact," not (necessarily) aligned with frames of reference deriving from ontological systems. The point is rather that such evaluations must remain contingent to the "object" as an "object" and that, if there at all, they must be conditioned by different factors. To understand this adequately, note that an "object" cannot, for the reasons explained, be reduced to what one might call a "psychological fact"; for psychological facts are facts as much as other facts. The notion of "fact" should simply stay out of the notion of "object." [30]

This methodological precaution is known as "bracketing." The object is "bracketed," that is, ontological evaluation of it is left out of consideration; "bracketing," therefore, entails removing not only the evaluation of "fact" but also what is expressed as "not a fact." The "bracketing" principle has actually not been stated entirely accurately here as a rendering of Husserl's position, with which there have been problems in Husserl's later development; according to some specialists, this principle has moved Husserl to a metaphysical position after all: that of (semi-)idealism. But I would leave this historical problem for what it is, also because the "bracketing" principle has special consequences for the study of language, of a kind Husserl never considered fully. At this point I merely mention the "linguistic relativity principle" as applying especially to lexical use in different languages: there is no one-to-one correspondence between lexical items, on the one hand, and "facts" (in any reasonable sense) in the speech situation, on the other. Perhaps more importantly, in language we speak not only about what is "factual" (this time in whatever preanalytically reasonable sense) but also

---

30. Husserl, *Ideen I*, pp. 220–27; *Ideas I*, pp. 258–66; paperback ed., pp. 238–46. See also *Erste Philosophie, Erster Teil: Kritische Ideengeschichte*, 2 vols., ed. Rudolf Boehm (The Hague: Nijhoff, 1956), I, 53 (originally composed in 1923).

about the conditional, the imaginary, the nonexistent, the future, and the past, and so forth. Finally, as I shall work out in detail later, the failure to "bracket" has led, in both behavioristic and mentalistic linguistics, to the tendency to equate objective information with semantic content, a potent factor also in the tendency to assimilate lexical use into grammaticalness and grammaticalness into some superstructure of "thinking."

Note that the "object" (which Husserl calls *noema*) is the intentional other pole of consciousness (called *noesis*) in a manner which is defining for the *noesis*. In other words: consciousness, or *noema*, is necessarily (or essentially) *intentional*. Inversely, the *noema* cannot be taken to enjoy a status (factually or in any other way) divorced from the *noesis*. As consciousness is by definition, i.e., essentially, consciousness-*of*, so also is the *noema* necessarily affected by the way it appears in consciousness (and this is only one reason for the "bracketing" device). In this sense it is often said that the object is "constituted" by consciousness; but it is (again) unfortunately possible to think this through in an idealistic direction, and I wish here to prescind once more from the problem of how far this has been the case with Husserl himself. However, "constitution" need not be understood in relation to idealism at all: all it should mean (at least to this writer) is that the being-constituted of the object bypasses as irrelevant any autonomy it might be considered to have with regard to consciousness, since such an autonomy will almost inevitably connotate *ontological* autonomy; and this in its turn may lead to naïve realism.

Whatever the feasibility of these expressions as almost necessarily deriving from the confrontation of phenomenology with metaphysical systems, the "bracketing" principle (apart from the name) is hardly a novelty typical of phenomenology alone. I have already mentioned the linguistic-relativity principle, but that principle has analogues in post-Newtonian physics, in which scientists will shy away from determining their objects as "real" or as "facts," or, more in line with attendant changes in the philosophy of science, in the rejection of the traditional notion of "substance." [31]

9. Phenomenology traditionally looks for "structures." [32] This

31. See Verhaar, "Phenomenology as an Attitude," pp. 406–10.
32. I am not concerned with the thematic nature of the term "structure" in Husserl's *oeuvre*, and I have not analysed its use beyond finding

feature would almost as a matter of course be associated with "structuralism," at least in its meaning in linguistics. But that could be misleading, since, among other things, TG is not generally identified with "structuralism" (from which it is invariably distinguished as being superior to it), even though expressions like "structure," "structural description," etc., abound in TG. In general it must be recognized that there *is* an analogy between linguistic "structuralism" and the quest for "structures" in phenomenology. The Saussurean (and Hjelmslevian) principle "not substance but form" [33] is, up to a certain extent, comparable to the "bracketing" principle of phenomenology; in both approaches what is considered relevant is not what "is," in some sense, but how elements are interconnected. I do not know that anyone has ever completely uncovered the frame of reference underlying this element, which is common to phenomenology and the linguistic "diacritical" approach, and I shall not attempt that task here; but it would, I think, be an important piece of research in contemporary thought, to which possibly the more general tendency toward formalization, in not a few disciplines, is also relevant. Merleau-Ponty once, after reading Saussure, attempted to explain why the *valeur* aspect of the lingual sign as diacritical is basically phenomenological, seeing that thus the way is open to a "lending of sense" not naïvely associated with the "substance" in language form; but I fear that Merleau-Ponty's interdisciplinary venture reads things into Saussure which that linguist cannot have intended to convey.[34] However that may be, if it is the *differences* between phenomenological and linguistic "structures" that are important right now, where does the analogy break down?

The "structuralism" of phenomenology (in its *-ism* form the term is not usual) is open-ended in a way that linguistic "struc-

___

that it recurs. "Structure," as what analysis is aiming at, however, functions here as an indication of just one of the consequences of the "bracketing" principle.

33. Ferdinand de Saussure, *Cours de linguistique générale*, ed. Charles Bally, Albert Sechehaye, and Albert Riedlinger, 2d ed. (Paris: Payot, 1949), p. 157; English translation by Wade Baskin, *Course in General Linguistics* (New York: Philosophical Library, 1959), p. 113.

34. Merleau-Ponty, "Le Langage indirect et les voix du silence," in *Signes* (Paris: Gallimard, 1960) (originally published in 1952 in *Les Temps Modernes*, Vol. LXXX), pp. 49–51; English translation by Richard C. McCleary, "Indirect Language and the Voices of Silence," *Signs* (Evanston, Ill.: Northwestern University Press, 1964), pp. 39–41.

turalism" is not. This is already clear from Saussure's exclusion of situational elements to which we are related when making utterances. Saussure did explain that the *signe linguistique* consists of two elements and that neither coincides with (what we now call) the referent; [35] but then that referent moves out of the theoretical linguist's vision for good. In a similar way (using different terms) Hjelmslev built up *his* theory.[36] The open-ended part of linguistic structuralism is certainly not at the situation side. In Saussure it was on the "mental" side that further expansion of theory becomes possible; we can make a long story short by saying that not until Chomsky was this mental side brought fully into the picture—too fully, in fact, though in philosophical quarters this has been hailed as an accomplishment in the history of "structuralism." [37] It is therefore in the *idealizing* direction that structuralism in linguistics may be said to be open-ended. It was precisely this open-endedness which came into doubt in the Bloomfieldian tradition; for, obviously, it would entail considering meaning. Linguistic behaviorism, therefore, is not only not open-ended on the mental side, but it is not open-ended on the situational side either. It is this latter closedness which has been continued almost unchanged in linguistic mentalism.

Phenomenologically, the structures in natural language cannot be adequately examined without open-endedness on *both* the mental and the situational sides, but with important reservations. First, in line with feature 3 of phenomenology, above, the aspects in which the structures should be open-ended, i.e., both the "mental" side and the "situational" side, must not be allowed to determine the structures of our utterances, but, inversely, these sides should be determined by those structures. The structures "expand" *themselves*, or there is no expansion, or open-endedness, at all. Second, the "form, not substance" principle is misleading; it may be true (i.e., depending upon how it is explained) for sublexical structures, such as phonemic structure; but lexical items are "substantial" in that they derive, in the *experience* of the *native* speaker (or of the speaker who has acquired native

---

35. Saussure, *Cours de linguistique générale*, pp. 99, 97; English translation, pp. 67, 65.

36. See B. Siertsema, *A Study of Glossematics: Critical Survey of Its Fundamental Concepts*, 2d ed. (The Hague: Nijhoff, 1965), pp. 156–63.

37. H. Berger, "Van de Saussure tot Chomsky," *Tijdschrift voor Filosofie*, XXXII (1970), 175–96.

command of a second language), not from a "conventional," "arbitrary," "oppositive" system of manipulating situational elements, but from a *directly experienced* and spontaneous, and fully "motivated," unity between lexical item and situational element (apart from "implied meanings," as discussed later in this paper).[38] It is of course possible to prescind from this direct experience and ask "why," just as one may ask "why" one uses certain muscles for breathing or "why" one changes the position of one's lips when smiling. This questioning approach seems called for when we *compare* languages, at least one of which is not native to us (especially in adult acquisition); and, further, it may occur when we give in to the semantic blindness that may come over us in great fatigue (for example, after a long discussion at cross-purposes with someone else, especially when matters of principle are involved). The first, however, is not an analysis of originary experience, while the second, to the extent that it tends to become characteristic, is pathological.[39] In short, if "structuralism" is taken in the Geneva-Copenhagen "diacritical" sense, it is erroneous for at least certain levels of the structure of our utterances, one of which is the lexical level. It must be emphasized here that, to the extent that linguistic "structuralism" entails the thesis that *valeur* is not *in* but *between* lexical items, and is then applied to lexical semantics, TG has not made any mistake in this respect; however, the notion of "interpretation," even with the "lexicalists," is unphenomenological, i.e., it is outside the immediate experience of the language-user and is perhaps also in part to be reduced to the *arbitraire du signe* hypothesis.

10. As we have already indicated several times in the above expositions, of paramount importance to phenomenological analysis of the structures of utterances is the "situation." This is, within the contrast of the two frames of reference determining phenomenology on the one hand and behaviorism/mentalism on the other, perhaps the most weighty single feature to be developed further. It will take such a prominent place in the rest of this essay, in both the confrontation with TG and the pro-

---

38. In the 1930s there was a group of linguists and psychologists attacking the thesis of *l'arbitraire du signe;* for bibliographical data, see Verhaar, *Some Relations between Perception, Speech, and Thought* (Assen: van Gorcum, 1963), p. 47, note 1.

39. See *ibid.*, pp. 148–54.

visional sketch of a phenomenological approach to language, that I will not at this point develop it any further. Only one terminological clarification may be useful. I distinguish "situation" from "setting." By "situation" I mean the totality of elements to which the language-user is related in actual language use; by "setting" I mean the totality within which the speech act takes place. It is obvious that the latter is more comprehensive than the former. To take a clear example (and I do not care to state that it is also invariably a representative case), the "setting" entails many things which account for discourse relations between sentences, i.e., discourse relations that cannot be captured under the heading of lingual structure; [40] the "situation" consists only of elements appearing, in one way or another, in the actual utterances. The setting, to put it in another way, will also comprise what I shall later call the "mental component" of the speech act; the situation is the point of reference the relatedness to which, on the part of the actual utterances, determines what I shall call the "situational component." What belongs to the situation necessarily belongs to the setting also, but the reverse is not true. This terminological clarification is no more than a warning; the exposition will follow in its proper place.

I must now address myself to the last task preceding an exposition of what a phenomenological analysis of language would look like: a confrontation of this phenomenological approach with the alternative frame for both behaviorism and mentalism. I shall do this in two parts: first, I will make a few brief remarks about the historical background of that frame of reference in the history of ideas in the West; second, I will develop some specific objections that phenomenologists are likely to make against what is today the most topical realization of that frame of reference: the idealization inherent in TG.

40. Throughout the present essay (as in most of my earlier work) I distinguish between "lingual" and "linguistic." "Lingual" shall mean "pertaining to language," and "linguistic" "pertaining to linguistic science." My reason for so distinguishing these terms is that "linguistic" for "lingual" amounts to a misleading kind of idealization; see Verhaar, "Phenomenology as an Attitude," pp. 419–20. I introduced the distinction in *Some Relations between Perception, Speech and Thought* (1963), and it was only much later that I found that Pap had already made it in 1951; see Leo Pap, "A Note on *Lingual* vs. *Linguistic*," *General Linguistics*, II (1951), 42.

The Philosophy of Body and Mind in the West, and Some Notes on Empirical Science

Except for the very young, all linguists have seen the triumph of behaviorism, and they have seen its defeat. Chomsky reminisces that in his student days behaviorism defined the climate of research, and he adds that, though it hardly seemed promising for a more inspiring image of man, it did not, at the time, seem "unreasonable." [41] This author remembers how, about the same time, a number of students in his environment shrugged their shoulders about the Bloomfieldian tradition, finding it, in typical European fashion, "superficial." There were, and are, of course, many worthwhile things in the Bloomfieldian tradition, most of them hardly in harmony with the behavioristic opposition to meaning, as, for example, in Bloomfield's own chapter on syntax. [42] One may even wonder whether behaviorism became completely consistent before Harris' *Methods*. [43] It is the behavioristic frame of reference in that consistency that one cannot lay one's finger on, as it is so uncatchable, unobvious, and out of touch with anything that seems to matter. For that frame of reference, therefore, it is useful to inquire into its sources, which are in part contemporary, in part historical. I will be brief on the contemporary part, i.e., the rising success of natural science or perhaps, rather, of technology; that is, methodologically, the attractiveness, for research of predictability in areas in which free human initiative, in its *un*predictability, has long been supposed to reign supreme, and the fascination of mechanical consistency, the expansion of the machine concept (cybernetically, among other things), even now visible in the harnessing of creativity into a "rule-governed" one as supposedly the most interesting variety. [44] More generally, there was, perhaps, a growing awareness that the dividing line between the natural and the

41. Chomsky, *Language and Mind*, p. 2.
42. Leonard Bloomfield, *Language* (New York: Holt, 1933), pp. 184–206.
43. Zellig S. Harris, *Methods in Structural Linguistics* (Chicago: University of Chicago Press, 1951); see esp. page 7, note 4: "In principle, meaning need be involved only to the extent of determining what is repetition." Even this, of course, is not consistent.
44. Chomsky, *Current Issues in Linguistic Theory*, p. 23.

human sciences would recede obligingly for anyone determined enough to pursue the "objective" approach (with its physical and mechanical implications of harnessing the unpredictable) to its utmost limits. Chomsky describes this "euphoria" eloquently.[45] In fact, once one began to push this dividing line back, it seemed as though it could never again be recaptured, as though it had acquired the tendency to recede of its own accord, like some sort of horizon. The problem is well enough known in more than one discipline. Why talk to a mental patient if drugs will achieve the same, or better, results? Why eliminate an "inner" hindrance to spontaneous living by analyses hovering in mid-air if scheduled reinforcements will do the same job? Why appeal to a psychophysical parallelism if a merely neurological approach will do as well? Or why tell the neurophysiologist, as Katz did, not too long ago,[46] to find parallels for linguistic descriptions (suggesting to him, of course, that he not waste any time in doubting whether these are correct) on the neurophysiological level instead of, inversely, recommending to the linguist that he get his notions of recursiveness more down to empirical fact by modeling these on cybernetic principles in neurophysiological research (and, of course, not waste any time by wondering if *those* are correct)? There is, perhaps, in such reductionistic and/or dualistic approaches nothing more attractive than there is in following any heuristic lead in scientific research; but to get the imponderable under mechanistic control may be, on the other hand, too tempting not to pretend a priori, and gratuitously, that this is the only obvious thing to attempt in a scientific undertaking.

Historically, how did behaviorism originate? As Esper's informative study on the psychological backgrounds of Bloomfieldian linguistic theory has pointed out, Weiss's influence on Bloomfield certainly did not represent an extreme case of behaviorism, did not have any metaphysical axes to grind, and concentrated in fact on a behavioristic interpretation of *social* interaction.[47] It is where a kind of sudden (or gradual) "conversion" takes place that the reaction is more notable; to a mild

45. Chomsky, *Language and Mind*, p. 3.
46. Jerrold J. Katz, "Mentalism in Linguistics," *Language*, XL (1964), 136.
47. Erwin A. Esper, *Mentalism and Objectivism in Linguistics: The Sources of Leonard Bloomfield's Psychology of Language* (New York: American Elsevier, 1968).

degree this was the case with Bloomfield, whose earlier introduction to language study had been somewhat mentalistic, based as it was on Wundt's ideas.[48] On the other hand, Wundt's "mentalism" was not an extreme case either, and it is instructive to evaluate Reichling's objections to Wundt's theory on the ground that that theory was by no means free from behaviorism.[49] There are differences of degree between the two frames of reference, and the "conversion" I mentioned is perhaps in more than one sense the proper word for transitions from one extreme to the other. Interestingly, having "seen the light" can make converts rather intolerant, and what goes on in cases like that I do not understand, except that apparently there is much more at stake than adaptation of scientific method or alternation of theory alone. For some philosophical suggestions on intolerance, see my recent "Philosophy and Linguistic Theory."

An extreme case of behaviorism is found, not in Weiss, but in Watson. He is in fact known as the originator of behaviorism, and he opposed the "mentalist" MacDougall on very curious grounds. He claimed that postulating the notion of soul had been occasioned by religious motives. According to Watson, religious leaders, unable to use force to induce those entrusted to them to follow their directives, claimed to have a special hold on people's "souls." [50] The notion of soul, according to Watson, was not only of religious origin but had been thought up by religious leaders opportunistically. One may perhaps suspect too much suspicion here, but, undeniably, history does have a good supply of samples of this kind of religious leadership; on the other hand, to reduce the origin of the notion of soul, let alone that notion in its "secularized" form as "mind," to religious opportunism would be somewhat too simple; apart from this, the notion of soul is, as a matter of historical fact, indeed of religious origin, at least in Europe, and possibly universally.[51]

48. Leonard Bloomfield, *An Introduction to the Study of Language* (New York: Holt, 1914).

49. A. J. B. N. Reichling, *Het woord: Een studie omtrent de grondslag van taal en taalgebruik* (Zwolle: W. E. J. Tjeenk Willink, 1967; originally published in 1935), 83–88.

50. On this and following details, see Francis P. Dinneen, *An Introduction to General Linguistics* (New York: Holt, Rinehart & Winston, 1967), pp. 241–43; see also J. C. Flugel and D. J. West, *A Hundred Years of Psychology* (London: Methuen, 1964), pp. 215 ff., 228 ff.

51. See F. M. Cornford, *From Religion to Philosophy: A Study in the Origins of Western Speculation* (New York: Harper & Row, 1957), and

The first notion of an autonomous soul in philosophy, more properly so speaking in the West, with its epistemological corollary of the doctrine of innate ideas, is found in Plato; and that thinker's concept of soul is ultimately reducible to his conception of man as in part of transcendent origin [52] (a concept also found in many religions). When Aristotle, so much more empirical and down to earth than Plato, rejected the latter's higher level of reality of "forms" or (interestingly!) "ideas," invisible, yet supposedly more real than this world which we all observe, his notion of soul, which is still supposed to be some kind of "form" (in a systematic explanation known as "hylomorphism"),[53] spelled the death of the innate-ideas doctrine, replacing it by the *tabula rasa* theory: the mind is like a slate not yet written on, until the senses write their own data on it. Not that that was a solution either, as Aristotle realized when composing his *Ethics,* and especially, and thematically, in the third book of his work on the soul, *Peri psychēs.*

Since these first two clear European positions on the nature of the mind, the pendulum-swing between them has not stopped, even to the present day. If we take big strides (because for many centuries the issue of the soul was a theological one, in connection with the problem of immortality), we find Thomas Aquinas with a secularized notion of an autonomous soul (the argument, with him, being that the soul is "spiritual" as opposed to "material"), and, in the Middle Ages more generally, a veritable proliferation of *pluralitas formarum* theories, postulating more than one soul in man, only the "top" one of which was "spiritual." Aquinas himself posited the *prima principia intelligibilium,* not unlike the Platonic innate ideas, but perhaps more, if I may

Principium Sapientiae: A Study of the Origins of Greek Philosophical Thought (New York: Harper & Row, 1965). Especially the "group soul" notion is well enough known from anthropology and research in religion.

52. See any history of philosophy. Perhaps in some cases the better studies are those inspired by nonphilosophical specialization; two that I would mention are Eric A. Havelock, *Preface to Plato* (Cambridge: Harvard University Press, 1963), and E. R. Dodds, *The Greeks and the Irrational* (Berkeley: University of California Press, 1951).

53. The "form" is not, in hylomorphism, some "outer" shape, as the term might suggest to us now, but an inner principle of life and unity in all organisms and, as such, in fact, only a thinly disguised "secularization" of Platonic "Form" or "Idea." This history of the concept of "form" alone would (*mutatis mutandis,* of course, for one might accept an "inner" "form," as Aristotle did, and yet reject the innate ideas) exhibit a similar pendulum swing, as mentioned later in the text.

characterize it loosely now, midway between those "innate ideas," on the one hand, and the later Kantian "ideas" (and some "categories") a priori, on the other. But, before Kant, Descartes, as is now well enough known by linguists, had postulated the innate ideas again; and here we get to the philosopher who is at the origin of all that, according to Chomsky, is sound in the philosophy of mind (there are, in Chomsky's works, especially in *Language and Mind,* also references to Plato and Aristotle, but only in passing). Also, contemporary with the spread of Cartesian rationalism, Locke pushed the pendulum the other way again, calling the mind "white paper," reverting again to the Aristotelian *tabula rasa* position. It is interesting to note that one reason why Locke rejected the notion of an autonomous mind is quite similar to the argument later to be used by Watson *vs.* MacDougall: the tendency of those holding such a notion to be authoritarian in their presentation of what they consider to be truths; in other words, against the entailed possibilities of mentalistic control of other people's freedom of thought.[54] The "religious" argument brought forward somewhat crudely by Watson appears, therefore, to be much wider; in case one distrusts Mircea Eliade's term "crypto-religious" as applied to this problem, let us say, instead, "ideological." [55] In the religious dimension one might say that the human mind, or the intellect, as a source of privileged insights apparently not given to all mortals though granted to leaders, is a substitute for the divine, and I would even go farther and assume a correlation between the Greek roots of atheism in Western culture, on the one hand, and, on the other, the almost mythical, and at any rate counterfactual, exaltation of human reason, in varying degrees in different periods in the history of Western thought, in that same culture. The first would be easy to establish from the history of the theology of faith. The second must be my own responsibility, and my purpose in bringing it up here is to point out what the picture looks like if we substitute the ideological for the religious dimension; for then there is an extremely fruitful notion available, mentioned already a moment ago: that of myth.

As is well known, Chomsky has applied this notion to be-

54. Hans Aarsleff, "The History of Linguistics and Professor Chomsky," *Language,* XLVI (1970), 583.
55. Mircea Eliade, *The Sacred and the Profane: The Nature of Religion,* trans. Willard Trask (New York: Harper & Row, 1959).

haviorism,[56] and, in my opinion, we must agree with that characterization. Chomsky, it is true, does not use "myth" and "mythology" as technical terms but rather in passing, as a loose characterization; but there is a good technical meaning that would be in place here. I define "myth" here (more or less as Georges Gusdorf understands it,[57] but I will not go into the differences) as that element in metaphysical thought that resists further explication if the contents of such an explication are to remain systematically manageable. Thus, in behaviorism (which I consider metaphysical because of its over-all pretensions of explanation, even though the over-all character is attained reductionalistically), one would have to ask: what is "physical," or "mechanical"? It needs only a minimum of familiarity with problems of present-day (and all post-Newtonian) theories in physics to be aware that basic questions such as these land one in metaphors and "models" whose systematicity (though not necessarily methodology) are notoriously elusive.[58] Physicists and philosophers of science have in fact asked such questions and have acknowledged that their results relate not so much to an unproblematic "reality," objectively there and challenging merely in the vastness of the field, as to the *manner in which* the researcher grasps his object, with all the intermediary apparatus of his instruments (extensions, in certain ways, of human perception), his perceptual categories, and, above all, the metaphorical basis of his terminological arsenal. What, he will fruitlessly ask, is "matter"? Metaphysical systems, with their customary claims of systematic exhaustiveness, at least in principle, cannot admit that such epistemological problems run into the sand of the vague and the figurative; if they did so they would lose their identity as metaphysical *systems*. This is as true of reductionist dogmas like behaviorism as it is of nonreductionist systems. Therefore, behaviorism is indeed a "myth" in one truly technical sense. But if we consider the basic reasons for this correct contention, it appears that the same holds for "mentalism." What is "spirit" (unless nonmatter) or "mind" (unless nonsensation), and what are these "innate" qualities ascribed to it? How

56. *Cartesian Linguistics*, p. 104.
57. Georges Gusdorf, *Mythe et métaphysique* (Paris: Flammarion, 1953).
58. For further comments and a few references, see Verhaar, "Phenomenology as an Attitude," pp. 406–10.

does one systematically account for whatever they are without necessarily introducing the unsystematizable? If it is so hard to get rid of the inevitable centrality of concepts such as those of "mind," while in fact there appears to be so little that is quite obvious about that centrality, how are its nine, or ninety, lives to be explained?

It is here that the phenomenologist, interested as he is in the significance of vague backgrounds, wants to probe further. The history of philosophy is quite prompt to give him the key, for philosophers have, through more than two millennia in the West (though not in such other great cultures as the Semitic and Chinese), appealed to man's "spirituality," or to the autonomy of the "soul" or the "mind," as a symbol and the defining characteristic of the uniqueness of man. After all, animals do not think; neither (as many philosophers, especially rationalists, have remarked, and as Chomsky eagerly quotes from Descartes) do they speak. It is almost certainly, or so I would wish to suggest, this element that has made metaphysical thought a kind of "wisdom" rather than "knowledge," in a distinction metaphysicians have quoted from Plato throughout the centuries, esteeming, of course, the latter far inferior to the former and auguring, also since the beginning, many centuries of tension between philosophers and the predecessors of what we now distinguish from philosophy as empirical science.[59] It is this "wisdom" that made Locke decide against rationalism, and Watson against mentalism; and it is also this "wisdom" that went by the board in several nontraditional philosophies in our century, until the revival of rationalism in (among other things) Chomsky's philosophy of mind and of language. Human unicity, however important the topic, when considered against this intellectual background, has historically turned out to be ambivalent, beginning, perhaps, with Plato's *Republic,* with (typically) its philosopher-king as the ideal ruler, down to the astounding degree of flexibility of metaphysical systems when confronted with the truth values of their alternative claims, whereby (for example) Marx could turn Hegel's ontological hierarchy upside down with almost complete systematic impunity, simply because what is *un*systematic in it has been avoided at all costs; such things will happen when "insights" reign so unrestrainedly.

59. See Verhaar, "Philosophy and Linguistic Theory."

I have a special reason for mentioning the *motif* of human unicity in this section, as it is also a major theme of Chomsky's thought, including his views in the field of social ethics. I have discussed this aspect at some length elsewhere,[60] and here I merely want to summarize. In *Cartesian Linguistics* Chomsky points out that, in order to understand Wilhelm von Humboldt's views of language, which (apart from some unwarranted excursions into "romanticism") were those of rationalism, we should take note of his sociopolitical theories. These may be stated briefly as the requirement of freedom, on the part of individuals and groups, from interference by an authoritarian state. When Chomsky then goes on to appeal to Marx for views similar to those of von Humboldt, it appears to be irrelevant to Chomsky's principal thesis along rationalistic lines that Marx was a crass materialist, while in the case of Marx that philosopher's opposition to anything supposedly transcending man's bodily condition is, incidentally, readily comparable to and strikingly analogous with such protests as those voiced by Locke and Watson. If Chomsky, in appealing to thinkers so opposed to rationalism as Marx, derives from them arguments in favor of human unicity, then clearly there is no inherent necessity for this theme to be associated primarily with human reason as interpreted by rationalism and mentalism. Ultimately, that tradition gives a representation of man which is as "mythical" as any representation of man found in behaviorism or in positivism more generally.

What is wrong with the body-mind philosophy as briefly outlined here? If we grant, but only for the sake of argument, that man is definable in his unicity by recourse to the notions of matter (or the physical) and spirit (or the mental)—recourse either to both, or just to the physical, or just to the mental— then this definition will be valid only because the notion(s) selected is (are) supposed to represent a larger totality than what is really under analysis, i.e., man, and not a mechanism, a body, a soul, or a mind. This is what, among the features of phenomenology, has been characterized as the "metaphysical" approach (paragraph 3, above).[61] The clash of phenomenology with the metaphysical approach has nothing, or need have nothing, pro-

60. *Ibid.*, pp. 5–7.
61. For a more detailed argumentation of this, see *ibid.*, pp. 3–5.

grammatic about it; the two approaches are already irreconcilable in terms of "attitudes," of frames of reference, before the first polemic word has been uttered in their confrontation. No aspect of reality more comprehensive than man will tell us what man uniquely is.

Phenomenology has analysed the uniqueness of man in ways drastically discontinuous with the tradition just touched upon, especially with the rationalistic tradition. One of the best, though not the only, example is found in the philosophy of Merleau-Ponty (especially in *Phenomenology of Perception*). That philosopher rejected what he called "intellectualism" (any position attributing to the mind or soul an irreducible position) but also "empiricism" (any position that rejects human phenomena, i.e., places them in the realm of objects). Merleau-Ponty is in this respect so original that we would have to follow his thought more closely in this paper were it not for the fact that his approach to language (on which he has also philosophized) was so determined by his central conception of the body-subject (*corps-sujet*) that the latter dominated the former; Merleau-Ponty's philosophy in an over-all sense would not have been different if he had never philosophized about language at all. Merleau-Ponty is thus introduced here only within the general framework of the discontinuity of his thought with Western body-mind philosophy.

To the phenomenologist there is no body-soul problem, not even one that would differ irreducibly from the Western body-soul framework (such as, for example, found in the Judaeo-Christian Bible), that may legitimately form the background, or *encompassing* framework, for the empirical study of language. On the contrary, if philosophy is to avail itself of the attainments of empirical science (in what is currently known as "foundational research"), it must distrust first and foremost those "empirical" theories which are, basically, nothing but a secularized continuation of older metaphysical theories. It is, more particularly, somewhat disturbing to find that the two parties, the one from Plato to Aquinas to Descartes to MacDougall to Chomsky, and the other from Aristotle to Locke to Watson to Bloomfiield, continue, after twenty-five centuries, to push the pendulum at each other, ultimately because their frame of reference is the same, a different one is unavailable, and only their solutions differ. The phenomenologist wishes to analyse that frame of reference in the first place, finds that concerns alien to the empirical study of language (whether religious, metaphysical, or ideological) serve as motivations for sticking to that frame of reference, indeed, for failing to challenge it, and decides finally to unearth the mythical element and thus to expose the frame of reference for good.[62]

Admittedly, this sounds like a high ambition indeed; and too high it is, as an ambition. But ideals may be useful, even if unattainable within the foreseeable future, in that they may point in a direction one might otherwise lose sight of, i.e., in connection with the question of what, precisely, the difference is between an empirical science and philosophy. For when we talk

62. A further discussion of Chomsky's position would have to point out that the old body-soul problem in his case is actually in one important respect Cartesian, to the exclusion of pre-Cartesian theories: Chomsky's body theory is a machine theory. This is the more surprising seeing how poorly this harmonizes with Chomsky's rejection of mechanism. Especially in Chomsky's *Language and Mind,* what may have appeared more by implication in his earlier works becomes clear, i.e., that Chomsky's mentalism takes no position on the issue of physicalism. Thus Chomsky argues (pp. 83–84) that it is reasonable to expect that some day TG theory may find expression in neurophysiological terms, adding that the issue entailed is an issue only "for an uninteresting terminological reason," i.e., the exchangeability, in due course, of the terms "mental" and "physical" (p. 84); and Chomsky rejects the Cartesian notion of mind as a "second substance" (p. 83). What, then, will ultimately be left of the difference between mentalism and behaviorism? The difference to Chomsky is, apparently, that a physically expressed theory should be "free from stimulus control" (p. 11). However, what else is this but to substitute, for a precybernetic theory, a cybernetic one? Surely, behaviorists have long accepted cybernetic principles. Moreover, how this "physicalism" which is supposedly not behaviorism should be harmonized with Chomsky's appeals to a rationalistic tradition is hard to see, unless abstract expression (in which, incidentally, recursiveness would have obvious parallels with cybernetics), in a counter-commonsensical manner also found in modern physics (as Chomsky significantly points out, p. 84) in its investigations of neurophysiological processes, is, as a metatheory in that field, equated with a theory of the mind. But why should this be so? Unfortunately, no arguments in support of this position are forthcoming at all.

Considering all this, one cannot help wondering why Chomsky has not recognized that a nonmechanistic neurophysiological theory, insofar as that can be made to be consistent at all, fits the hylomorphistic theory (in which the body is *not* a machine) far better than the Cartesian image of man; for then the freedom from stimulus control finds a *positive* expression in the notion of "form" (reconcilable, in part, with the Humboldtian notion of "form" also!), and, since the Aristotelian version, with its *tabula rasa* theory, would be out of harmony with Chomsky's ideas more generally, Chomsky would have had to turn, not to Descartes, but to Aquinas. However, if he did, my objections against his resumption of the pendulum swing so culturally confined to the West would still stand.

about linguistic science we are talking about an empirical science; this principle has been upheld at least in theory for several generations in the case of linguistics. Only recently did Chomsky advance the claim that the so-called "autonomous" status of an empirical science was something rejectably novel.[63] A discussion like the present one cannot be reasonably complete without looking at this problem in some further detail.

I have elsewhere briefly touched upon the time-honored opposition between research in what we would now call natural sciences, on the one hand, and philosophy (especially of the Platonic "wisdom" type), on the other.[64] How much continuity there was, even long ago, between the two may appear from a remark made by de Santillana, who argues that in Hellenistic and Roman times the need for large-scale engineering caused interest in abstractions and pure logic to decline; Platonic "forms" were replaced by formulae, and mathematics by technology.[65] Perhaps it may plausibly be argued that much of the continuity there is must be ascribed to the fact that even abstract philosophy is somehow in touch with empirical reality, but I will not go into this further as far as the natural sciences are concerned. But whatever continuity there is between philosophy, on the one hand, and the sciences concerned with man, on the other, may not be wholly due to an empirical basis in previous philosophy of man. Nor is this particularly to be expected, as those disciplines are so much younger than some of the natural sciences. For linguistics, notwithstanding the present-day tendency to lump all Western philosophy of language together under the heading "history of linguistics," this seems clear enough. If we pass by nineteenth-century historical research (with its otherwise quite impressive attainments) as being, rather in the spirit of that era, bound up with the notion of evolution and its supposedly exceptionless rules almost along biological lines, we find a clear beginning only with the advent of (a changed) Ferdinand de Saussure. Yet the body-mind problem has never really ceased, throughout what we have already had of the twentieth century, to be the determining factor among the various competing linguistic theories. Linguistics cannot be said

63. Chomsky, *Cartesian Linguistics*, p. 76.
64. Verhaar, "Philosophy and Linguistic Theory," pp. 2–3.
65. Giorgio de Santillana, *The Origins of Scientific Thought* (Chicago: University of Chicago Press, 1961), p. 276.

to have emancipated itself from philosophy so long as its object, natural language, has not completely freed itself from metaphysical domination. If phenomenology is here resorted to as a cure, this is not to substitute a nonmetaphysical brand of philosophy for a metaphysical one but merely to derive one's inspiration from a trend that is free of hindrances to recognition of the uniqueness of the object. In this connection it is imperative to emphasize that a phenomenological philosophy of language would be different from a phenomenological approach in linguistic science; they would have to be distinguished as philosophy and empirical science, respectively. For the former the reader may be referred to an earlier work of mine, in which it is also explained that in a phenomenological philosophy of language the themes becoming central are those which need to be explicated only in part, in passing, and for methodological reasons in the work of a phenomenological linguist.[66] But I shall not allude further to this difference here.

The history of the transition from philosophy of man to the empirical sciences concerned with man has not yet been written. It seems certain that the material for such a history must be sought in those periods in which a "secularization" took place, e.g., from Plato to Aristotle. It appears that thematic awareness of the nature of such a secularization in philosophy itself did not fully come up until Auguste Comte's *Cours de philosophie positive*, published now more than four generations ago (1830–42). I have elsewhere discussed this work in greater detail.[67] It is now perhaps somewhat too easy to smile (or yawn) at Comte's "positivism," as the first tribute (rather romantic and almost "mythical," in Comte's own sense of "myth") to empirical science. But Comte appears to have greatly influenced the sciences concerned with man, especially through Emile Durkheim (with great influence on sociology), who was one of the determining influences on Saussure, especially on that linguist's distinction between *langue* and *parole*,[68] thus showing up a line, though not a straight one presumably, running right through to Chomsky's distinction between competence and performance. We need not,

66. Verhaar, *Some Relations between Perception, Speech, and Thought;* see, in particular, p. 14.
67. Verhaar, "Philosophy and Linguistic Theory."
68. See W. Doroszewski, "Quelques remarques sur les rapports de la sociologie et de la linguistique," *Journal de psychologie normale et pathologique,* XXX (1933), 82–91.

on hindsight, be now very much impressed with Durkheim's place in the pedigree from which science came forth: he was more of a rationalist than even modern mentalists would care to identify with.[69] We are, at any rate, still far removed from the point where empirical science of man has been completely emancipated from its philosophical origins in a remoter past.

Phenomenologically, the autonomy of an empirical science may be indicated by understanding "empirical" as "experiential," under conditions already worked out, in part, above. Experience is not clarified by any superstructure of a metatheoretical kind; and, as metatheories have a tendency to be rationalistic or atomistic (what they have in common being the urge for clarity), the necessarily vague in experience tends to be lost or considered unimportant. It will tend to come in again through the back door, in a form not allowing of further explication without damaging the essential systematicity; therefore, it comes in in the form of "myth," as we have defined "myth." I now wish to go into the problem of idealization attendant upon rationalistic approaches, first negatively, by analysing a few central assumptions of TG theory (in some of its forms), then positively, by showing how, phenomenologically, the danger of idealization can be avoided, in a way that sets it off not only against mentalism but against behaviorism as well.

IDEALIZATION IN RATIONALISM

IN TG THE MIND HAS BECOME the yardstick by which to measure human language. Among other things, this has two serious disadvantages. First, the structural aspect that I shall call the "situational component" is left out of consideration; second, whatever may be called "mental" in human language use—and, against the behavioristic position, an element which may be termed the "mental component" must be acknowledged— is analysed more completely according to its rationally clear determinability. The first may be caught in the issue of idealization; the second is due to the rationalistic element. For reasons already briefly touched on above, rationalism has always had an idealiz-

69. See Emile Durkheim, *Sociologie et philosophie* (Paris: Alcan, 1924); English translation by D. F. Pocock, *Sociology and Philosophy* (Glencoe, Ill.: The Free Press, 1953).

ing tendency; inversely, idealizations have always tended toward rationalism. Both go against the grain of the phenomenologist. The idealizing tendency leads linguistic science to pretend that language use is some outward form of thinking alone, while the rationalistic element prevents the linguist from fully recognizing how nonrational natural language can be and, indeed, quite frequently is. I wish to analyse both disadvantages somewhat more closely, following discussion of a few concepts basic to TG theory. My selection mainly serves the purposes of contrastive analysis; therefore the various issues have to be discussed fairly briefly, and I must bypass a number of details which could not legitimately be ignored if the purpose were to discuss overt TG theory rather than its underlying assumptions; it must be emphasized again at this point that, so long as this limitation upon the discussion is not carefully borne in mind, misunderstandings are bound to arise, and caution in this respect is the more imperative as this underlying frame of reference is hardly ever discussed in the literature.

First, we must be aware that TG "mentalism" is not the kind of "mentalism" that Bloomfield rejected but is rather in continuity with a more traditional rationalism. Furthermore, Chomsky does not think of the mind as a "second substance" in the Cartesian sense (see note 62, above), or at least so he claims. Actually, even if the mind were supposed to be some human property accessible to an analysis in which experience were to play some kind of role (to that extent, therefore, such an analysis would be phenomenological), that would have very little to do with the "mental" nature of Chomsky's "universal grammar," which seems to be completely unrelated to experience: "perhaps the most striking fact about human language," says Chomsky, is the "disparity between knowledge and experience." [70] In fact, Chomsky's "mind" seems to be little else but a highly abstract theory (or, rather, that to which such a highly abstract theory would correspond—but these two appear to be identical for Chomsky) of language, and "mental" precisely in that it is so abstract.

There is, however, another notion of "mental" which seems to be out of touch with such a conception of "mind" but which nevertheless plays an important role in Chomsky's theory. It

70. Chomsky, "The Formal Nature of Language," in Eric H. Lenneberg, ed., *Biological Foundations of Language* (New York: Wiley, 1967), p. 438.

consists in the grammaticalization of the lexicon. As the lexicon is quite substantially tied down—among other things in the way it fits into lingual structure—to the situational component (as that notion will be elaborated later in this essay), there seems to be nothing unexpected in the conclusion that sacrificing the situational component to abstractness entails a great deal more than merely redefining the mind in terms of abstract theory devised to elevate raw data into significant facts. I will return to the grammaticalization of the lexicon in a moment.

The first problem I select is that of "generation." Chomsky has repeatedly emphasized that generation is not to be understood as a psychological process, as psychological processes are subject to certain laws of performance that are irrelevant to laws of competence. So far this is substantially what has been claimed for *parole,* or rather certain features of it, over against *langue,* and, substantially, this part of it seems valid. But then, what is "generation"? All that has been said about it is that it accounts for the ("rule-governed") "creativity" of language, rather, therefore, a "creativity" on the part of language-users by reason of whatever it is that is supposedly "innate" in them and that amounts to a "source" to which all generativity has to be ultimately referred. But most of what has been said about "generation" belongs entirely within the system considered from a technical point of view. On the other hand, the question how generation relates to human experience has at least been clearly answered (that is, insofar as generativity implies principles of universal grammar): there is no such relation. Chomsky has also emphasized the overpowering limitations upon even a possible awareness of the nature of the generative rules that result in the very sentences he utters.[71] There *is* intuition into the well-formedness of these sentences, however; and since this is a point that most linguists will grant, it is perhaps from here as a common ground that one may start to go into Chomsky's theory of language. A first issue coming up here is the concept of "deep structure," and I shall attend to it in a moment. What should be noted here, however, is that there seems to be something wrong, apparently, with the intuitive judgments about well-formedness even among TG

71. Chomsky, *Aspects of the Theory of Syntax,* p. 21; "Topics in the Theory of Generative Grammar," p. 3, in Thomas A. Sebeok, ed., *Current Trends in Linguistics,* Vol. III, *Theoretical Foundations* (The Hague: Mouton, 1966).

linguists: everyone knows of the never ending "intuitive" disagreements in discussions (especially oral ones) as to whether
one can or cannot "say" a certain utterance, and these disagreements have, substantially, very little to do with dialectical and/or
idiolectical differences. What *does* play a considerable role, however, is the underlying disagreements as to whether one can, or
cannot, *think* (no quotes here, for that word is never actually
used) certain things. In a moment I shall return to that point
also; for now it is sufficient to note that to have one's intuitions as
to the well-formedness of utterances influenced by certain epistemological a prioris is a circumstance to be expected in a theory
relying on the "mind" as understood in the rationalistic tradition;
the grammaticalization of the lexicon, as part of the concept of
generativity, is just one factor in the ensuing one-sidedness.
When faced squarely, the domination of metaphysical rationalism in an empirical science is a load too heavy to carry and an
alien element in the study of language. Some TG linguists have
felt this very articulately: Fillmore's Ordinary Working Grammarian does not wish to be so burdened with philosophy; and,
whether one agrees or not that Fillmore has sufficiently rid himself of philosophy, and of metaphysics more particularly, the
principle itself is highly commendable.[72]

Let us now turn to the notion of deep structure. Generatively,
it is the level at which syntactic derivation and semantic interpretation diverge. This divergence, naturally, can be justified only
to the extent that syntax and semantics can be distinguished. No
wonder, then, that DS (deep structure) has come under fire from
generative semanticists' quarters, and in fact even Chomsky has
now departed from the principle that DS and SS (surface structure) must always be identical in meaning; but this deviation,
which is marginal and recent, I wish to leave unconsidered in
what follows, because I do not think that the frame of reference
is substantially affected by it. What I wish to discuss as the basic
drawback of the postulation of DS is its empirical, even more its
experiential, inaccessibility. I do not mean to say that the TG
linguist has unlimited freedom in postulating whatever DS's he
wants for certain sentences; for, after postulating DS's, he has to
show that certain transformational rules map the DS onto the

72. Charles H. Fillmore, "On Generativity," *Working Papers in Linguistics*, no. 6 (Columbus, Ohio: Ohio State University Computer and Information Science Research Center, 1970), pp. 1–19.

SS (I will now ignore phonological rules involved in obtaining terminal strings).

On the one hand, a fairly reliable native judgment as to the well-formedness of the resulting SS is possible, and also there is no juggling with transformational rules, which describe processes about which there can be no obscurity as such and which, in virtue of their explicitness, either work perfectly or not at all. On the other hand, the transformational rules are not only, as has been justly claimed, more powerful than rules of grammar in pre-TG theories; it must even be asked whether they are not too powerful. A good example triggering such doubts is a DS containing more constituents than the corresponding SS, for it is technically no problem at all to find the appropriate deletion rules. Therefore, as there is, also according to TG theory, nothing intuitive about the particular forms that transformational rules may take, nor indeed about the entire transformational component, nor, worse, about the adequacy of the DS concerned, the only experiential element available, i.e., native judgment about the well-formedness of the corresponding SS, relates exclusively to the *result* of the generative process. But how can one demonstrate the nature of traveling by merely demonstrating that, at the end, one arrived at the desired destination? Moreover, the assumption that transformational rules must be meaning-preserving makes the distinction between DS and SS merely one of form; since, however, the DS is supposed to be much closer to the essence of language and to language universals, the SS must be considered consistent only from the point of view of form, and meaning is in effect removed from SS to DS or is considered to be present in the SS only in an unimportantly derivative way. In a sense, seeing that the formal differences between DS and SS (or, perhaps, one should say, structural differences) are frequently considerable, one must say that a major violation has been perpetrated on the *experience* of the language-user, for whom form and meaning are *one*. Who feels that what matters semantically in what he says, or hears someone else say, goes on at some "abstract" and language-universally relevant level, and precisely not, or only arbitrarily derivatively, in the actual concrete sentences of which his language use consists? This shifting of all the semantic weight to an abstract and nonintuitive level of "deeper" structure is so surprising methodologically and so counterintuitive theoretically that one may have trouble believing that it is actually the case. However, it not only happens to be the case, but it is even explicitly acknowledged by Chomsky, who fully accepts offense to common sense (his analogy being one to theoretical physics).[73] And there has to be a different reason.

I think it would be too simple to look for that reason in rationalization and idealization alone, though these constitute a major factor; there is, I propose, also an element, in dealing with meaning, which may be called naïvely realistic. Rationalization replaces what one can "say" by what one can think (more or less apart from language, and certainly often quite apart from language particulars, and with undue emphasis on clear determinability of semantic content). Or, to phrase it somewhat loosely in an expression I have used before, it amounts not to readings of sentences but to mind-reading.[74] The question, then, is not so much what goes on in the speaker's utterances but what goes on in the speaker's mind as he utters the utterances. By those standards, for example, there will be no semantic difference between an active sentence and its passive, since both have an identical DS, in spite of the fact that the difference between the two sentences is that the one has an active and the other a passive meaning (and that the difference may be one of topicalization also). Thus the terseness of one-word sentences is taken out of them by referring them to pluriconstituent DS's. If the TG linguist sees no difference in meaning between DS and SS in such cases, this is hardly because such differences are easy to deny; it is rather because he has confused semantic content with objective information of some sort, and this is where the naïvely realistic element comes in: actually, what has been idealized in the end is not even semantic content but objective information harmonizing with that semantic content on an extralingual level. Thus, there appear to be two ways in which behaviorism has not been overcome in TG: a naïve realism serves as transition for idealization, and the DS is necessary ultimately because the actual utterance, the SS, has been reduced to its form as divorced from its meaning.

The tendencies we find implied in the notion of grammaticalness as used in TG go to confirm several of the elements explicated just now. On the TG view of grammaticalness, not only an ordinary sentence like *John comes tomorrow* is grammatical,

73. Chomsky, *Language and Mind*, p. 84.
74. See Verhaar, "Philosophy and Linguistic Theory," p. 8.

but this may also be the case, and by exactly the same standards, with a sentence 600 or 5,000,000 words long, provided, that is, that the (or a) correct grammar generates it. That sentences like these can have no place in natural language is of course readily conceded, but that circumstance is put down to limitations of memory, energy, life-span, etc. But it is strange to consider such limitations as immaterial to natural language and therefore as not really affecting the human condition as far as competence is concerned, the limitations being put down to inessentials of performance. Perhaps this is in effect to bow to the old metaphysical position that accords to the human mind an infinity of some sort; that notion, previously based on the "spiritual" nature of the soul, is now, at least explicitly, based on the mathematically infinite number of sentences that are possible in any language, even though not in any one person's lifetime or any people's history. Infinity (whatever it is from the viewpoint of an empirical science) has been replaced by infinitude; shall we say (in view of what we have seen above about "secularized" forms of old systems of thought) infinity "secularized"? This rhetorical question may be absurd from the mathematician's point of view, but to natural language there is more than what mathematics has to teach us. However, it is not necessary to press the infinity-infinitude argument. Grammaticalness has been severed from acceptability in as dualistic a way as the abstract DS's have been severed from their concrete SS realizations; there seems to be little justification for calling concrete, i.e., experienceable, phenomena a generative outcome, or rather ultimate form, of constructions which have nothing experienceable about them, and this holds for the abstractness of an infinity of sentences as much as for the abstractness of DS's. If, thus, standards of grammaticalness are subjected to wholly nonintuitive, mechanical ways of checking upon them, the same dualism emerges in its umpteenth form: on the one hand, the mind's irreducible capacities are determined (among other things, to be sure) by infinity; on the other hand, this infinity is one for which machines are, even if perhaps not capacious enough, at least more capacious than weak humans. If objections like these are made comparatively rarely, this may be in part because the implied vastness of the claims has been modified by such assertions as that merely an evaluation procedure is what is being aimed at, and in part also, I think, because a number of linguists are all too easily impressed by the powers of explicitness and by the potentialities of mechanical predictability of the otherwise unpredictable. There have been critiques of TG claiming that the inspiration of TG has essentially been interest in computerization and in translation machines. However mistaken these critiques have been in most, including decisive, ways, one cannot say that their only source lies in some monumental inability to cope with new theories; the basis for the objections raised in them has not been entirely chimerical.[75]

In this selective analysis of the TG frame of reference I wish to take as a next point, to be dealt with at some greater length, the treatment of the lexicon in TG, its assimilation into the concept of grammaticalness, and the consequent rationalization of the things we say in natural language into the epistemological field. Let our point of departure be an utterance like * *John sleep long* (not, of course, as a dependent constituent in, e.g., *The doctor suggested that John sleep long*), and compare this to (?*)*The bottles were jubilant,* or to (?*)*My desk drinks bread five gardens long.* The first is ungrammatical by the standards of any linguist, and for reasons too obvious to need explanation. But what about the other two sentences? No rule has been violated in the traditional, more restricted conception of grammar or, indeed, in Chomsky's conception of grammaticalness in his *Syntactic Structures.*[76] The question now is how this more restricted notion of grammar is to be expanded if the last two sentences are to be counted as ungrammatical. As is well enough known, this is done by the so-called subcategorization of lexical items (in a special form known as "selectional restrictions"). If we accept the traditional categorization (i.e., a *grammatical* classification) of lexical items such as Noun, Verb, Adverb, etc. (not asking, for the moment, whether these categories can be considered as language universals), what seems obvious is that *sub*categorization must be based on special arguments that it is— or rather, the subclasses are—really grammatical; for the very notion of grammar is at stake. Thus, to distinguish Masculine, Feminine, and Neuter as subcategories of Nouns makes sense

---

75. See Robert A. Hall, Jr., "Fact and Fiction in Grammatical Analysis," *Foundations of Language,* I (1965), 337–45; Yehoshua Bar-Hillel, "On a Misapprehension of the Status of Theories in Linguistics," *Foundations of Language,* II (1966), 394–99.

76. Chomsky, *Syntactic Structures* (New York: Humanities Press, 1957), p. 15.

only in languages in which these genders manifest themselves morphologically (for example, in concord) or by special selection (for example, of pronouns) in keeping with form distinctions already established as grammatical. But this means that subcategorization must be language-specific (as indeed is the case, though to a lesser degree, with categorization itself); however, dispute about these points among linguists is not likely to be widespread. A more stringent subcategorization would clearly be necessary in order to support the verdict "ungrammatical" with respect to the *bottle* and *desk* sentences above. For example, if *My desk drinks bread* is to be designated as ungrammatical, this must be done by limiting Nouns in Subject position (or, as immediately dominated by S) with Verbs of consumption of food to [+Animal] only; and the rule based on such subcategorizations of Nouns and Verbs would be violated because *desk* would not be in the subcategory mentioned; similarly, the rule having on its left side the Verb Phrase whose terminal form is *drinks bread* would specify that only Nouns with the feature [+Liquid] may follow the class to which *drink* belongs, etc.; which means that the grammar would never generate an S whose VP would look like *drinks bread* in the terminal string. It is hard to see, however, what else this is but the kind of reasoning which, once it is suitably explicated, would take the following form: one cannot drink bread, therefore one cannot think of bread being drunk by anyone, therefore sentences stating this are ungrammatical, so let us find rules (which, tautologically, are grammatical rules) preventing *My desk drinks bread* from being generated; this, obviously, calls for subclassifications of grammatical categories in certain ways, and since these subclassifications are supposedly grammatical, they amount to sub*categorizations*. This can be seen as a progression from naïve realism (bread is not something one can drink) to the idealized form thereof (one cannot think such a thing) to accommodation of grammar in consonance with such an idealization. Similarly, one might explicate the judgment that *The bottles were jubilant* is ungrammatical as emerging from the idea that bottles cannot be jubilant, that therefore one cannot think of them as such, and that therefore it is ungrammatical to utter anything reflecting such a manner of thinking. Perhaps this double-faced extralingual basis for the notion of grammaticalness (the naïvely realistic one and the epistemology-determined one) may in part adapt to language-specific features;

thus one may make rules in Indonesian ensuring that it is possible to say that someone "drinks" a cigarette or, in English, to ensure that it is possible to say that someone "drinks" soup from a cup, though hardly from a plate. This, however adequate it would look from the point of view of language particulars in this or that language, would obscure the basic issue, which is that both positivism (in its naïvely realistic aspect) and rationalism (in its form of idealization)—both of them extralingual elements too—intrude into the concept of grammaticalness. Thus, the judgment that one can, or cannot, "say" a certain utterance, far from being so unproblematically founded on a claim which in itself is otherwise true enough, i.e., that native speakers have intuitive judgments about grammaticalness, may be frustrated by theoretical preconceptions which have nothing to do with those intuitive judgments. Why must an English grammarian of TG persuasion find rules which would not admit *The bankrupt clouds sent their rain upwards*, though the same grammar would have to permit generation of *I dreamed that the bankrupt clouds sent their rain upwards* on the ground that I may dream that clouds do what in actual fact they cannot do?

The point made here is important enough to be gone into somewhat more deeply; and, as I am concerned with the over-all frame of reference, as crossing, in essential respects, the boundaries of divergent TG approaches, I wish to elaborate further by taking off from material close to problems discussed by Fillmore (without going into differences between his approach and the one followed here).[77] Consider the following four sentences: (*a*) *John made the table;* (*b*) *John repaired the table;* (*c*) *John painted the table;* (*d*) *What did John do to the table?* Now let us consider the suggestion that the *made* of (*a*) and the *repaired* of (*b*) be put in different Verbal *sub*categories, the first taking an "effective" and the second taking an "affective" Object; let us call these subcategories V_{eff} and V_{aff}, respectively. We assume that the distinction is intended as grammatical, as indeed appears already from the term sub*category*. Then (*d*) might be said to be a test case; for (*b*), but not (*a*), could be a reply to (*d*). In (*c*), however, we find ambiguity, and, supposedly, *grammatical* ambiguity; paraphrastically, the ambiguity might be conveyed as follows:

77. Charles H. Fillmore, "The Case for Case," in Emmon Bach and Robert T. Harms, eds., *Universals in Linguistic Theory* (New York: Holt, Rinehart & Winston, 1968).

(c_1) "John applied paint to the table" and (c_2) "John made an artistic painted representation of the table (on canvas)." The ambiguity could then be put down to the double Verbal subcategory, V_{aff} and V_{eff}, respectively.

No doubt (c) is ambiguous. The question is: lexically or grammatically? Note that the claim that the ambiguity in this case is lexical would amount to a claim that the notion of grammaticalness as subcategorizing into V_{aff} and V_{eff} in the case of *paint* takes grammaticalness in too wide a sense; as the expanded notion of grammar is here the issue, the counterchallenge would indeed have to consist in proof that either there is no lexical ambiguity here or that lexical ambiguity is linguistically irrelevant. But can either be proved? The TG linguist might point to (d) as a test case, for reasons already mentioned; and in the case of (c), as a reply to (d), (c) would be disambiguated, in favor of V_{aff}. But what is the source of this proof? It would be based upon the relation between (c) and (d); that, however, is (at best) a discourse relation. Now discourse relations are often notoriously not grammatical (and in many cases not even lexical). In the present case, however, as the TG position would depend upon proof that the discourse relation cannot be explained in merely lexical terms, it must be shown that such an explanation is impossible. However, it is eminently possible, for *do to* in (d) is, on lexical grounds alone, "affective" in regard to what follows (*the table*). Perhaps the lexical explanation may even be narrowed down to *to* in this case, but whatever one may think about this does not affect the principle illustrated here. (*Do*) *to*, then, in the present case, is lexically related to *paint* of (c).

TG has, as is well enough known, never insisted much on the function of the lexicon in the structure of language as distinct from the place of grammar in that structure. Consider another example (which I am advised derives from Lakoff's Ph.D. dissertation, to which, however, I have had no access; but the example will do, no matter what the source): I once heard a TG linguist claim that the sentence *He hardened the metal* is ambiguous—grammatically—on the ground that it may mean that the one doing the hardening made the metal *hard*, as well as that he made it *harder*. I do not know whether my source would make this case by actually insisting on the morphological and semantic difference between *hard* and *harder* (this would entail drawing evidence from paraphrastic clarification); however that may

be, the counterquestion here would be, again: why not *lexically*
ambiguous? But in a case like the present one we may even go
farther: why would the Verb *harden* be considered to be *even
lexically* ambiguous? If so, could that not be because of an empirical assumption that degrees of hardness as relevant to a
blacksmith's job are assimilated into language structure? And if
that is so, and if we assume that a smith has reasons of his own
for distinguishing five degrees of hardness, would that not mean,
if one is to be consistent, that *harden* might be five ways ambiguous? Admittedly, this is reducing an original question that
seems reasonable to its absurd basis, but we must do this if we
wish to find out whether the original claim was reasonable after
all. More generally, there seems to be a positive risk of equating
objective information with semantic content. Karttunen claims
that the sentence *All but one of the boys danced with all but one
of the girls* is ambiguous, seeing that there are different situational realizations corresponding to the contents of that sentence,
realizations which can be strictly demonstrated by having recourse to predicate calculus analysis.[78] But then the ambiguity
appears to consist in the circumstance that there is more than
one setting (not situation; see distinction above), in each of
which it is not exactly the same set of boy and girl who dance as
in the alternative setting covered by the sentence. Therefore,
given one "interpretation" of this sentence, there must always be
actual circumstances of more than one kind, under one of which
the "interpretation" would be true, while under another it would
be false. Truth-values, in cases like these, seem to constitute test
cases, even though Karttunen would not of course claim that
meaning equals truth; but the latter would be a test of the
former.[79] But such reasoning rests upon a fallacy. The meaning
of *all but one* is constant, even though its setting realization may
vary and may even be complicated (as in this case) by duplicate
occurrences of such a phrase in one and the same sentence. The
fallacy consists in the confusion of meaning and setting realization. By the same logic, a sentence like *He mixed Nescafe, sugar,*

78. Lauri Karttunen, "Definite Description with Crossing Coreference:
A Study of the Bach-Peters Paradox," *Foundations of Language*, VII
(1971), 157–82.
79. For a comparable case, see Chomsky, "The Formal Nature of
Language," in Eric H. Lenneberg, ed., *Biological Foundations of Language*,
p. 432.

cream, and hot water would be 24 ways ambiguous, as there are $4! = 24$ distinct orders in which these ingredients can be mixed, considering that (at least in English) the succession of enumeration does not necessarily reflect succession of the actual order. Also in the following case it would be useful to reduce this fallacy to its absurd consequences: *I like that book,* spoken in a library of 500 books, would be 500 ways ambiguous (and 2,000 ways in case the sentence is uttered by four different people). Here Bloomfieldian "semantics" is back again, in disguise, but recognizable enough once one gets right down to it.[80]

It appears, therefore, that the claim of grammatical ambiguity must first meet the challenge of the question: why not just lexically ambiguous? Even further, the claim of lexical ambiguity must eventually meet the challenge of the question: why not, simply, setting-realizable in more than one way? The first question keeps expansion of the notion of grammaticalness within bounds, and thus the assimilation not only of language into thinking but also of the lexicon into the grammar (apart from indubitable and genuine categorizations and subcategorizations as language particulars, especially in the case of *sub*categorizations); the second question prevents objective realizations from being assimilated into semantic content (lexical and grammatical); *both* questions oppose the idealizing trend that drags natural language out of its own sphere into some other sphere alien to it. The two questions embody forms of caution wholly ignored in TG studies; and they represent an approach that checks on theories and methods by explicating what would be entailed in them and thus leads to an assessment of what must be expected of linguistics as an empirical science.

I propose to conclude this analysis of the TG frame of reference with a few more remarks on ambiguity. We are now, in fact, in a better position to consider that concept than at an earlier stage of this analysis, because we can now, if we stipulate that ambiguity is concerned with meaning only, exclude from that concept more than one setting realization. Further, an utterance shall be considered ambiguous if more than one meaning matches an identical form. Therefore, one cannot have an adequate notion of ambiguity without clarifying the notion of form. Form shall here be confined to the form of the sentence;

80. See Bloomfield, *Language,* p. 27.

there is no reason not to expand the notion of form by applying
it to discourse stretches (under certain conditions, to be sure),
but I shall not consider such an expanded notion. I shall consider
the sentence as a unit of utterance which can be recognized intuitively. This is not wholly adequate, but it will do for the points
that must be dealt with now. Form shall further be kept apart
from indistinctness: if I do not quite catch what somebody said
indistinctly, in the sense that, for all I know, he may have uttered
any one of two, or more, sentences, which, if spoken distinctly,
would differ in form, then such a case shall not come under "ambiguity." [81] Further, it shall be considered irrelevant whether
orthographic representation would or would not make an utterance unambiguous, for orthographic form is a form derivative
from spoken form and as such is only secondarily an object
(though *as such* undoubtedly a genuine object) of linguistics.
Thus the utterance that is dually represented orthographically as
They went because of the sand which is there and *They went because of the sandwiches there* [82] shall be considered a case of
ambiguity; another example would be *You can do it* and *You cannot do it*, if the former has emphatic *can*, and (cumulatively) the
latter is American, not British, English; similarly *Some words
have no reference* and *Some words have no referents* (note that
this would not be a case of indistinctness; on the contrary, freedom from ambiguity in speaking this sentence could take place
only by hypercorrect pronunciation, itself actually based on orthographic awareness). Though all ambiguity entails identity of
form, and all identity of form involves phonetic identity, I shall
call a case of ambiguity "phonetic" if and only if the phonetic
identity is not matched by either morphological or lexical identity
or both. All other cases of ambiguity are either lexical or grammatical—lexical if the only source of ambiguity of an utterance
is ambiguity of a lexical item (as in *The bank is beautiful*),
grammatical if the source of ambiguity is either morphological
(as in what is orthographically set apart as *These are the student's*

81. On the other hand, truncated forms, as they follow certain definable rules (which I believe are due to Joos), should perhaps be considered as ambiguous; thus *You want a smoke* may stand for "You want a
smoke" and "Do you want a smoke?," in terms of paraphrase. But I will
not further attend to this special case.

82. This example I have borrowed from Paul M. Postal, review of
André Martinet, *Elements of General Linguistics*, in *Foundations of Language*, II (1966), 164.

books and *These are the students' books*) or syntactic (as in *Flying planes can be dangerous*). Lastly, metaphorical reference shall not give rise to ambiguity: in *That man is a fox*, in case *fox* is used metaphorically, the meaning of *fox* is constant; only its reference is particular (in a way to be discussed below).

A further comment on the notion of form is called for. I earlier used the expression "identity of form," but actually, as identity can only be between more than one, a more accurate expression would be "identity of forms." Now forms may differ qua forms or be distinct only in terms of distinct token occurrences. The distinct occurrences of identical forms are irrelevant here because no ambiguity arises from them. On the other hand, "identical forms," apart from distinct occurrences, is a meaningless expression; if the concept of multiplicity applies, that can be so only because multiple meaning gives rise to distinguishing more than one "form." Thus, though ambiguity requires inherently identity of form(s), the notion of multiple form is just another way of talking about multiple meaning; psychologically, multiple form can be talked about only because the device of paraphrase, used for avoiding ambiguity, does make one form multiple in terms of multiple occurrence. But paraphrases are at best a means of showing up ambiguity only to those whose understanding of an ambiguous utterance is blocked in some way or other; paraphrases rely either on a different construction of the utterance (on one understanding of it) or on contextual supplementation, which is really a supplementation in the area of discourse. At any rate, analysis of paraphrastic utterances may never take the place of the ambiguous utterance under consideration; and as the sole basis for providing paraphrases is to take away some block to understanding (which might also occur in the case of nonambiguous utterances), a block which does not in any revealing sense relate to language structure, paraphrases are just a means of clarification, almost didactically so, in explaining problems of ambiguity. I conclude from this that to speak about "identity of form" as "identity of forms" is (in the case of ambiguity) an empty expression, a mistaken way of speaking about identity of meaning; on the other hand, to speak about identity of meaning frustrates a reasonable understanding of "identity," seeing that only the "form" is "identical"—which throws us back on another empty expression. What is the source of this empty circle? Is it not the notion of ambiguity itself?

I have purposely spoken so far of the ambiguity of an utterance; I do not want to attach too much importance to my use of "utterance," except for one important motive I have for this use: that I do not wish to speak about an "ambiguous *sentence.*" Strictly speaking, "a" sentence cannot be called ambiguous, unless what is meant is that we have more than one sentence. Admittedly one can say, in some loose sense, that "the" sentence *Flying planes can be dangerous* "is" ambiguous. What, then, is "loose" about such an expression? The answer is that it is what I wish to call "ostensive" when it refers, for example, to this sequence of forms represented orthographically on paper, or when it is pronounced, characteristically not only out of context in terms of discourse but also, just as characteristically, in "mention" rather than "use" form; and I have borrowed the term "ostensive" from what in philosophical language analysis is known as "ostensive definition" (for example, defining "table" by pointing at a table). In both cases, then, i.e., in orthographic representation and in pronounced representation (and *here* the term "representation" is also *phenomenologically* adequate, for the "sentence" is no longer a human lingual activity but is merely an object of analysis, paralleled in linguistic activity only when there is a special need for it by reason of a blocking of [direct!] understanding, so that "interpretation," this time likewise also *phenomenologically,* becomes, exceptionally, necessary), it is possible, for reflectively analytic reasons (often simply didactic ones), to speak about "an" ambiguous "sentence"; but both "sentence" and "ambiguous" are then used in a distinctly ad hoc manner; and from that manner no help must be expected for a theoretical evaluation of the concept of ambiguity, unless it would be to argue, as I do now, that "ambiguity" is an empty concept. But if so, how could it arise at all?

In terms of TG theory, only SS's can be ambiguous, and not DS's. As the difference between DS and SS is not one of meaning but only one of form, "ambiguity" in TG theory can relate to form only, which is contradictory, since only meaning, but not form, can be "ambiguous"; but then, and here the vicious circle inexorably starts again, "a" (= one) meaning cannot, by definition, be ambiguous. Now, one can well see that a TG linguist would admit this much and would acknowledge that his notion of ambiguity is indeed (if he would care to adopt the above terms) only "ostensive," "didactic," etc. However, this would not end TG inconsistency, for one important argument for the distinction between SS and DS is precisely ambiguity: identical SS's may have to be referred to different DS's. However, why would anyone have to distinguish DS from SS? This is necessary only if SS is looked at from the point of view of *form* only—but that is precisely what Bloomfield did. I think Dik has reasonably argued that the reason why TG needs a DS at all is that its SS is still Bloomfieldian.[83] The separate identity of SS as distinct from DS is ultimately based on the occurrence of blocks to understanding; despite TG appeals to lingual intuition of the native speaker, the TG linguist is forced to assert by implication that we really do not (directly, experientially) *understand* the "terminal strings," which are the only thing that meets the eye (or ear). In this respect TG is Bloomfieldianism, only supplemented. This also appears from the favorite definition of "grammar" among TG linguists: combining sound and meaning; this, supposedly, is what the field is all about. However, what language as the object of linguistics is all about is not combining sounds and meaning but accounting for the fact that sounds and meaning *are already combined* before we ever reflect upon language in the first place.

THE STRUCTURE OF THE SPEECH ACT

AFTER THIS CONTRASTIVE characterization of what frame-of-reference phenomenology is as an alternative to both behaviorism and mentalism, the final portion of this paper will, provisionally and tentatively, describe what would be, in this writer's opinion, a feasible first approach to the empirical study of language. Needless to say, some of the details to follow are sufficiently known among linguists, and it cannot be expected that a comparatively unusual approach, like that of phenomenology, will produce a notable quantity of new material. Nevertheless, perhaps the *general approach* is sufficiently detached from what is usual in linguistics to merit further investigation and experiment.

While fairly detailed knowledge of what is generally accepted by linguists in one form or another is necessary, if only for communication, there is the added advantage that there is no

83. S. C. Dik, "Oppervlaktestruktuur en dieptestruktuur," *Forum der Letteren,* X (1969), 19–41.

need to start from scratch. Moreover, from a historical point of view a certain amount of continuity is desirable, even though application of the phenomenological principles discussed requires a suspension of judgment concerning what, precisely, may be continuous. I will confine myself to a few remarks about what continuity is likely to hang on in the first place, items of terminology. It will be useful, however, first to condense the phenomenological principles into just three, following in large part a similar summing-up found in an earlier publication.[84] These three major principles are the following: (*a*) Human experience should be the focus, experience understood as the cognitive and active aspects of selfhood (as appearing in language use); among other things this means that language entails, indeed is, one particular variety of what is ordinarily (and untechnically) called "thought." What "thought" might be taken to be when considered as apart from language, or even determinative of language, should be carefully kept at arm's length. (*b*) This "thought" is "intentional," i.e., it is directed toward a number of (what I shall call) "elements," the totality of which we call the "situation." That is, natural language is situation-related, and one cannot study it as if it were not. (*c*) In accordance with the limitations imposed upon the understanding of "thought," as in (*a*), the situation is equally carefully detached from whatever evaluations, in no matter what learned discipline other than linguistics or in no matter what popular belief, might be associated with the situation. The situation in the linguistic sense is entirely determined in terms of the speech act, or it is nonexistent. Thus we get the following principal components: a "mental" component (*a*), a "situational" component (*b*), while (*c*), the third component of the speech act, consists of the utterances themselves. The entire speech act of course belongs also in a wider setting, and often this is called the "situation"; but this would be confusing in the present terminology, and for this more comprehensive whole we use the term "setting."

A second set of comments is on terminology itself. The following distinction seems essential: between (1) technical terms in the strict sense, and (2) a "looser" kind of terms, taken from natural language rather than from the kind of jargon to which only the initiated have access. To (1) there would belong such

---

84. Verhaar, "Philosophy and Linguistic Theory," pp. 4–5.

terms as "subject," "predicate," "agent," "redundancy," "distribution," "neutralization," and the like; while (2) would contain such items as "meaning," "reference," "topic," "comment," or the one appearing in the above heading, "structure." The distinction is in part artificial, for some of those listed in (1) could, and do, occur as ordinary words also, while those in (2) can be used with great terminological sophistication by anyone defining them carefully enough. But those which may be used without this sophistication, while retaining their status of ordinary words also, must be exposed here as posing special methodological problems. With regard to most items of (1) the linguist may adopt a drastically nominalistic attitude; or he may fail to do so, and then his method may easily suffer from, or give rise to, the kind of controversial attitude which perhaps looks very substantial but quite often turns out to be merely terminological. This happens much less easily with items of (2); in these there is no doubt a certain degree of arbitrariness, depending upon definition or upon a meaning accruing to them from the method as a whole, but no appeal to the merely terminological will take away from them a certain underlying frame of reference not recognized by that method. In an earlier publication I have analysed the kind of prejudice that may stick to unanalysed use of such an apparently innocuous concept as that of "meaning." [85] More generally, there must be a limit to unambiguous definitions, for, if pursued too scrupulously, they would entail the need for the indefinite regress of defining terms used in the definitions, etc. The position taken here is that analysis in the phenomenological manner will expose in good time the need for special further explication. We shall presently run into a few cases where such a need is illustrated for certain terms. [86]

This understood, let me comment briefly on the speech act. We may do this by an analysis of what is known as *parole*. This term, however, is not clear enough. *Parole* is often used to in-

85. Verhaar, *Some Relations between Perception, Speech, and Thought*, pp. 77–80.

86. I doubt whether any *term*, properly speaking, as meant under (1), above, can ever be *merely* terminological and therefore open to *totally* nominalistic interpretation. For terms also have a *word* basis, while, inversely, ordinary words (as meant under [2], above) are hard to disengage from systems of thinking and (especially) belief, whereby they acquire something akin to terms. On such problems, which seem to bedevil the metalanguage of the linguist in curious ways, see *ibid.*, pp. 126–47.

dicate the coincidental, the nonessential, in language, such as all sorts of slips of speech, defects of certain speakers, or linguistically irrelevant features such as the sex, temperament, etc., of the actual language-user. This is not the content of *parole* as used here. Rather, *parole* stands for the actual use of language as preceding the study of *langue* in linguistic research. Without actual utterances to be studied, what can the linguist study? It is in this sense that I used the word "precede"; at the same time, one cannot analyse speech samples without somehow knowing what is essential and what is not, and this presupposes *langue* as (native) knowledge (of some sort) enabling the linguist to sample utterances as well-formed or deviant. Provided it is well understood, what Saussure said is therefore true: that we should take *langue* for our point of departure.[87] But there is more to it. Just as one may study speech samples with a background knowledge of *langue* for language-specific purposes, so one may also study speech samples, as part of the speech act, in order to discover the basic structure of that act, with a background awareness of what *langage* is and therefore with a view to finding language universals. It is this latter kind of analysis that I have in mind. Irrespective of what particular *langue* happens to be the medium in an actual occurrence of the speech act, one can analyse this speech act in a manner which is both more general (the target of explication is to answer, in part, the question: what is *langage*?) and more concrete, since one is then no longer bothered by questions whether samples do or do not deviate from the rules of this or that *langue*. The question, then, is: what goes on when language is actually and concretely used?

There is nothing original about the question itself. Innumerable answers to it have been attempted. To take the characterization that perhaps occurs most frequently: language, or rather the speech act, is supposed to be "social," or to be "communication." This is both true and irrelevant. If communication defines language, while communication is admittedly possible in a great variety of nonlingual ways, then the definition (or this element in it) subsumes language under some more comprehensive whole (which may be adequate in approaches in other disciplines) that is itself not characterized by language. To be sure, certain elements of communication will be of interest to the linguist,

87. *Cours de linguistique générale*, p. 25; English translation, p. 9.

first, naturally, as part of the setting of the speech act, and, more importantly, to the degree that the communicative dimension of speech (which is not the same as the lingual dimension of communication) may take on lingually determinable structures (for example, lexically or grammatically) in this or that language. But this is something language-specific, touching at best marginally the analysis of the speech act undertaken here. A less frequent but equally mistaken approach (for the linguist) would be to say that language is "expression" or even (in certain conceptions) "representation." What is wrong in all this is resorting to some "umbrella notion" under which to subsume the speech act.[88]

Extensive and multiaspectual analyses of the speech act are found in Reichling's *Het woord*. For our purposes now, it is sufficient to be aware that all language use involves "thought" as its "mental component" and involves as its "situational component" certain elements to which utterances, and some of their structural properties, are related. The utterances themselves (the third and last component of the speech act) cannot be adequately considered in themselves. Let me illustrate briefly what this entails for a (linguistic) understanding of "meaning." Meaning is not some mysterious property reflecting (and identifiable with) a "situation," as in Bloomfield (our "setting"), nor is there anything "arbitrary" about it, as claimed by Saussure and so many of his followers, nor is it just "natural," in the sense that gestures are (if they are), nor, again, is it some kind of objective "information." Meaning is what we "think" (to be understood from the

---

88. Reichling has demonstrated beyond any possibility of doubt that "communication" cannot be ultimately determinative of the nature of language (A. J. B. N. Reichling, *Het woord, passim*). The same holds for "expression" (*ibid., passim;* and Reichling, "Over het personaal aspect in het taalgebruik," *Bundel de Vooys* [Groningen: Wolters, 1940], 283–310). "Representation" is, according to Reichling, determinative of what language is (*Het woord*, pp. 35 ff., 305), but not as a *function* (*ibid.*, pp. 139–40). On the "functions" of language, there was a veritable spate of literature about a generation ago, foremost in it Karl Bühler's *Sprachtheorie: Die Darstellungsfunktion der Sprache* (Jena: Gustav Fischer, 1934) (see also copious references in Reichling, *Het woord*). We now also have advocates of the "communicative," or rather "social," nature of language; to Labov, for example, "sociolinguistics" is a strangely redundant term. However, Labov's sophistication makes the earlier theories sink far into the background. For a recent specimen of his work, see William Labov, "The Study of Language in Its Social Context," *Studium Generale*, XXIII (1970), 30–87.

angle of the mental component) "in," that is, not just "with," or "associated with," the sounds and their structures. It is of course possible (and linguistically vital) to determine this further, language-specifically and language-typologically and, perhaps, language-universally in the last analysis; but this is not just unproblematic induction in the way of the man who measures and counts; this "inductive" analytic process can never be detached from what can already be gleaned from the structure of the speech act without regard for language specificity and language typology. Therefore, behind a *langue* intuition (Chomsky's "competence") there is a *langage* intuition; only humans know preanalytically, and at first, of course, only implicitly, what it is to use human language. This has methodological priority. If one calls this *parole*-analysis, then *parole* comes first.

Further, it appears that *words* have a special status and function in the speech act, no matter what the *langue*. They stand out in the language-user's experience, as was already demonstrated by Sapir, noted by various other linguists, and treated most fully by Reichling in *Het woord*. How do they stand out? It appears that the word as a lexical item somehow "precedes" the structural whole we call "grammar" in such a way, perhaps, that the lexicon does not have its relative "autonomy" by being distinguished from grammar but by emerging in the analysis of the speech act even before grammar does. This appears in two ways, linearly and situationally. Sapir's argument is, essentially, the linear one. Native speakers requested to stop at certain points for a reason completely unrelated to syntactic structure, viz., the need to accommodate the slow rate of dictation, will stop *only* at the end of a word; however, they will stop at the end of *any* word. Since such behavior ignores syntactic structure but respects the morphological one, the reason for it must be, not that morphology itself dictates what pauses are made,[89] but that in an utterance there is no other way of segmenting lexical items but by the morphological form they happen to have; the ground, then, for the separation is the identity of the segments as lexical items. But the situational dimension is more important. To be sure, it has perhaps too often been naïvely supposed that all words refer to "objects" of some sort, and admittedly only certain classes of

89. Edward Sapir, *Language* (New York: Harcourt, Brace, 1921), pp. 33–34.

words do, while others do not. However, these classes are hardly exceptions in any language; and, moreover, all words have certain one-to-one relationships to situational elements in ways one can put one's finger on—something that is not the case with whatever relationships to the situation there (undoubtedly) are in grammatical, and especially in syntactic, structure. This is only a somewhat more sophisticated way of saying that, in speaking, we always speak *about something*. This may seem so obvious as to be trivial, but it is a major mistake in linguistic theory construction to prescind from this. Words are the most easily identifiable and most readily "manageable" instruments in which the language-speaking person relates to the elements of the situational component; and in fact, if the lexicon in any language is extensive, this is simply because the situational elements the language-user deals with (for the speech act is also an *activity* of some sort) are also numerous. Moreover, since these elements do not form a closed set, neither does the lexicon in any langauge. Specification of these multiple forms of the language-user's relatedness, socially determined and always exclusively within the same *langue*, to situational elements is what a dictionary attempts to specify paraphrastically. At this point it is not important to specify when these forms of relatedness may properly be called "reference," or whether the "elements" to which we relate, in the speech act, by means of lexical items are "objects," in any sense narrower than the widest possible one, or are, more problematically, "referents." All that needs to be explicated now is the fact that, by reason of their special situation-relatedness, words as lexical items stand out in the analysis of the speech act even before we have had much occasion to speak about those properties of the utterances which we traditionally ascribe to "grammar." Needless to say, whether one speaks about "objects" or about "elements" in analyses such as these, the "bracketing" principle should be kept carefully in mind: situation-relatedness in the speech act is in no way some kind of crude "ontology." [90]

Can we say, then, that the mental component of the speech act is the manner of "thought" appearing concretely in, and determined by, grammatical structures, while the situational com-

90. For both linear and situational foundation of the word, see Reichling, *Het woord, passim.* Reichling founds the situational aspect of word identity on the act of naming. Though this is adequate as far as it goes, it is not complete.

ponent must be treated concretely in, and as determined by, the lexicon? Clearly that cannot be the case. For words, too, are a manner of "thought" (as "thought" is understood here), if only by reason of the "bracketing" principle: in any *langue* the lexicon (though not the lexicon alone) imposes an interpretative grid on the situation (prescinding from language-particular articulation of it) in which language-users find themselves. In other words, though comparison of this "interpretation" with a supposedly uniquely objective view cannot (presumably) be found, what *can* be done is to compare the lexically determined interpretation found in the lexicon of any *langue* with any other view of the extralingual in the speech act; and then it will be found that the "linguistic relativity principle" is as sound as any theory in linguistics: the lexical "interpretation" decisive for the way speakers deal with concrete situations is unique to the *langue* concerned and to its lexicon—nothing more "basic" than that will be found to account for it. Otherwise, the notion of "interpretation" arises only in *comparing* languages; in native experience it is not found.

Inversely, there are also situation-related elements in the grammar, Fillmore's "cases" being perhaps the clearest level at which this is so; in a weaker and less easily recognizable manner this is also the case with categorization in grammar. Those topics will be taken up in a moment. At this point we must merely state that mental and situational components apparently overlap to such a degree that one cannot simply place the lexicon in the situational and the grammar in the mental component. Nevertheless, it remains true that words as lexical items derive their clearest determinability from the situational component and that the grammar derives *its* clearest determinability from the mental component. If that is so, it is within the structure of the speech act that the distinction between lexicon and grammar becomes initially apparent.

The analysis of the speech act involves a great deal more than what has just been said. The analyses conducted so far, however, suffice to bring us one step further in the present highly compendious approach. That next step consists in analysing somewhat more closely the distinction between grammar and lexicon.

GRAMMAR AND LEXICON

LET US DETERMINE grammar further, still highly provisionally, as the *internal* organization of the parts of utterances. By "internal" is meant, in part, what is technically known as "distributional," but prescinding from the tendencies to expand this term either behavioristically or mentalistically. What is truly "internal" about distribution is that at least some of its laws may be determined entirely within the linear dimension of the utterances; I do not care to say that this would exclude the mental component, but at least it does, possibly, exclude the situational component. "Organization" here indicates that there is nothing haphazard about grammatical structures; they are "rule-governed," if you will, although we will leave open how "rule" may be further interpreted (such an interpretation is not necessary for the purposes of the present paper). At this point I need not go into how "parts" of utterances can be isolated on grammatical grounds, except for one point: words can be so isolated, for the autonomous status of words as lexical items is reflected also grammatically, in the sense that the relationships among them are "distributionally" unique.

Apart from the unique status of words when looked at from the point of view of grammar, it is doubtful whether we can analyse grammatical universals out of such a largely *langage*-oriented whole as the structure of the speech act, except, perhaps, for some features which appear to be both intuitive and empirically general. As one such feature I would mention the possibility of analysing almost all sentences in any language (except for certain types of one-word sentences) as consisting of two parts recognized in a fairly straightforward manner, parts usually called Subject and Predicate, and legitimately so named as long as we refrain from interpretations, however plausible they may appear at first sight, such as that the Subject is always (or mostly) the Topic, that the Predicate accommodates significations of Action, etc. However, whether such an initial IC analysis would be indubitably the outcome of the analysis of the speech act only is perhaps hard to demonstrate. A better example of what analysis of the speech act yields for the field of grammar would be negative: the inappropriateness of a term like "redundancy." Whether some grammatical element is "redundant" or not entails considerations derived from a metalingual point of view or—what comes to the same thing methodologically—from standards obtaining in some different *langue*. Meaning cannot really be redundant; information can. If the manner of "thought" found in the utterances appears to be in some way repetitive, or duplicated in some other way which is not one of repetition, while it is otherwise in accord with grammatical rules, even where those are "optional," it must be asked what kind of *different* "thought" the linguist has in mind when he dubs certain features "redundant." It is true, of course, that only language-specific considerations will enable us to decide about concrete cases of alleged "redundancy"; [91] but whether or not we are going to consider "redundancy" as affecting not information but meaning—and this is obviously crucial—is a matter not to be solved by any language-specific consideration, because the distinction between meaning and information can be yielded only by a *langage*-oriented analysis of the speech act.

With the lexicon, things are considerably easier, for it must be assumed as true that all languages have entities called words. To be sure, no one has yet investigated all the world's languages, but the very structure of the speech act appears to require those items called words almost a priori, by reason of the situational component and the numerous elements found in it, and the necessity of all human speakers to deal with them. Apart from this, the specific way in which lexical items are interwoven with grammatical (especially morphological) structure in different languages is, as all linguists know, problematic enough (for example, in many languages no lexical items in certain categorial classes ever occur "unmarked"). These problems, however, do not affect the principle that the lexicon and the grammar should be kept distinct in any language. For further details of the analysis of the speech act the interested reader may be referred to Reichling's *Het woord*. We are now ready for a consideration of

---

91. An example: It is sometimes claimed that Indonesian *oleh,* "by" (Agentive), is optional and therefore redundant in Indonesian "passive" sentences (whatever it means to apply the notion of passivity in that language). *Oleh,* like any other form, is redundant only if it does not affect the meaning of the sentence concerned. I have grave suspicions that it is not redundant, and I suspect that such claims about "redundancy" are based on an assessment of information, not of meaning.

how the relation between grammar and lexicon may be structured in several levels.

THE CLINE FROM GRAMMAR TO LEXICON; SYNTAX

WITH THE WORD "CLINE" in the above heading I have committed myself to a structure characterized by two "poles"—or to a "hierarchical" view of "levels." On the one hand, this is hardly an innovation; many linguists accept structures which are "hierarchical." On the other hand, it would be hard to find discussions justifying, in any detailed way, the use of the metaphors involved. The reason is no doubt that metaphors do not carry an overtly terminological load, and that is true of the "framework" (as defined earlier); sometimes we even find mixed metaphors, as in TG, where "high" in certain senses relates to "deep," or even (both) to "early," as in "early rules." However, even though the framework is indeed hardly affected, the frame of reference is; and for that reason metaphors are not unimportant phenomenologically. I must therefore justify the metaphors implicit in my use of the terms "hierarchy" and the "poles" between which the hierarchical "levels" may be distinguished.

One way in which earlier controversies, no longer modern, articulated the hierarchical view was by speaking about "priority"; one of the two poles was supposed to have a "priority" of some kind, the poles being the word and the sentence. The later dispute, also no longer modern, about the "way up" and the "way down" in grammatical analysis is just another dimension of the same problem. TG, of course, is the latest option, and it is in favor of the sentence; and here the concept of "generation" has articulated also the older "priority" notion. Here I wish to point out that it is possible to accept a hierarchy without being immediately committed to one single "priority" of one of the poles (or without saying, as one may hear it rather lamely worded occasionally, that the poles have a "mutual priority," whatever that means); and this is at least a more neutral way of setting out in the description of the levels.

Why would the cline from grammar to lexicon be one from high to low? Why not from low to high? A further analysis in answer to this question would not easily get out of the metaphorical circle. It might be said that the lexicon, because of the one-to-one relationship of its items to situational elements, is more "basic" or, again, that the mental component, because of its considerably more abstract character, is "higher" in the sense that everything abstract is supposed to belong to some "higher" level. One might point out that the "inner" organization of structures called grammar presupposes a kind of "autonomy" it could not have if defined entirely in terms of an "outward" situation. All this is consistent enough in its own way. But perhaps vindication of the "high-low" structure of the various levels now to be discussed will appear from these levels themselves. The more detached grammar is from the situational component, with its fairly concrete determinability, the more "formal," as opposed to "substantial," is the structure characterizing it. If we pursue this still largely metaphorical characterization more concretely, we may do so in the proposal that at least one "priority" be accorded to the lexicon over against the grammar, i.e., that, though a lexicon without a grammar would seem to be possible (however primitive a language would thereby become), a grammar without a lexicon can in no way be imagined.

To demonstrate the latter point, let me play the devil's advocate and "prove" the opposite. Let us borrow (I forget my source) the sentence *The gostake distimmed the doshes.* All the lexical items in the sentence (except *the*—but then, we could of course say *Gostakes distim doshes*) are nonexistent in English; in terms of the situational component, at least as far as that is primarily determined by the lexicon, we do not know what the utterer of this sentence is talking about. Yet it would not be true to say that the sentence is without content altogether. For, if *the gostake distimmed the doshes,* at least we know that *the doshes were distimmed by the gostake.* As this alternative wording is paraphrastic, it cannot be entirely synonymous with the original, and sameness is obtained at best at the level of information. Yet it seems safe to say that information, even though it is distinct from semantic content, does have something (it is not now important precisely what) to do with that semantic content. Therefore, we do understand something by *the gostake distimmed the doshes.* This understanding, however, cannot be due to the lexicon, for the lexical items are fictitious. Therefore, grammar is possible without a lexicon. But this argumentation is inadequate. First of all, the syntactic and morphological understanding which indeed is there is based only upon the (experiential) supposition that the lexical items do exist, even though in fact this is not so. Second, there is also a convincing explanation why such a supposition is possible: the lexicon in any language is an open set. There is therefore, in the experience of the language-user, a basis for expansion of the lexicon. Someone who hears the cited sentence may conclude that he does not know what its lexical items mean, but what he will not spontaneously conclude is that the items used are nonexistent. In fact, there is no compelling reason why they could not be in use tomorrow in some definite meaning.

Is a lexicon possible without a grammar? That point is much easier to establish, not because actual languages are known to contain lexica and no grammars, but because at least one level of lingual experience leaves this possibility open. There is even a factual, empirical, aspect to this level: there are sentences consisting of one word only, and among one-word sentences there are even those without morphological marking(s). As we have already eliminated the explanation relying on a pluriconstituent deep structure, how should we analyse the experiential aspect of one-word sentences? If we bypass interjections, as they are very little representative of lingual structure, we may suggest that it is in fact the deictic character of many words that makes it possible for them to occur in isolation, at least in isolation from other constituents in the same sentence (there might still be discourse relations). Of course it might still be argued that it is possible to assign words occurring in sentences to certain word classes or *grammatical* categories, but such an assignment cannot readily be proven to be vital for the experience of a language-user uttering (or understanding) a one-word sentence; the only element involved in categorization, so far as categorization is situation-related, i.e., the deictic character of certain supercategories (Nominals, mainly), would not in itself be grammatical (to this point I shall return below). It is this deictic character which is important. The point is not to show that a language could conceivably do without a grammar but rather that there are certain self-contained lingual experiences—i.e., those of one-word sentences—which, though genuine utterances and specimens of language use, rely on deixis rather than on the "inner" organization of constituents called grammar. Deixis in this sense is only a limited (though not highly exceptional!) form of language use; but as such it is genuine and is, to a degree, representative—at least (and this is the point) to a degree that grammar without lexicon could never be. Perhaps it is in this experience that we must look for the almost unproblematic and recurring recourse linguists have had to hierarchical structures, in which at least one kind of "priority" is "basic" in the sense that it does not seem to be wholly dependent upon the other pole; nevertheless, that other pole may have some other kind of priority in that it, i.e., grammar, alone provides the possibility for the considerable sophistication of the "thought" we find in grammatical organization, a factor obviously missing in the lexicon alone.

Even though such analyses as these are fairly unconventional, and apart from the fact that others, insofar as they agree, might wish to phrase them differently, the material treated in them is not exactly novel. What is comparatively new about the over-all treatment here, however, is that the poles determining the cline, the hierarchical structure, are ultimately not determined by grammar and lexicon but by the mental and situational components of the speech act. It may be true that the mental component appears primarily (but not exclusively) in the grammar and that the situational component appears primarily (but not exclusively) in the lexicon; however, the reservation "not exclusively" is crucial in both cases. It is this consideration which enables us to articulate the multilevel structure of the cline. Beginning at the top, I take syntax first, for reasons which will become apparent. But within syntax itself we find more than one level.

The first level is what is traditionally known as the grammatical functions (I prefer: syntactic functions). No problem can initially be made about the terms Subject, Predicate (to which two I wish to confine myself), Object, etc.: we may continue to use them. It is also at this point irrelevant whether a linguist might have specific reasons (such as ordering of rules) to distinguish a tripartite rather than a twofold principal division. The question at this stage is rather: what, if anything, are those "functions" of which we distinguish two (or more) in a first IC analysis? Or, if we retain the old terms: what is a Subject and what is a Predicate?

Here we cannot expect to get all of the data from the analysis of the speech situation only. Empirical material from various languages, and especially from various language *types*, must be brought to bear. In the recent past, consideration of such material has led theorists to distinguish (say) the "psychological," the "logical," and the "grammatical" Subject. The first two kinds of Subject must be eliminated insofar as they derive from a view alien to the data provided by natural language alone. The "grammatical" Subject is frequently identifiable formally, by order of constituents, by markings (or unmarkedness), and possibly by other formal means. As the "thought" we analyse must never be looked for outside such overt features, even though overt features (which frequently allow of cross-classification) must not be the only data brought to bear, we must find a "field" where semantic and formal features harmonize. Since formal features are overt and do not pose problems of principle, it is the question what *meaning* makes a constituent a Subject that is the core of the problem. Concretely, this means that we must ask whether the Subject is (usually) perhaps the Agent, or the Topic, or the Starting-Point of what the Predicate means, etc. But this appears to differ from language to language and, most determinately, from type to type (structural or genetic). For example, there is a distinct preference for the Agent Subject in representative sentence types in Indo-European and for the Topic Subject in Malayo-Polynesian languages. This kind of research has, otherwise, only barely started. There is, notoriously, no single publication which lists with reasonable fullness the types of syntactic functions; Fillmore's recent attempts to look for a basis in (deep) Case are interesting and will contribute to further research of the same kind; but these attempts make a single choice, without giving an overview of the kind mentioned as desirable here. So far as the evidence now goes, it is perhaps best to describe the syntactic functions language-universally as "empty" and language-typologically as displaying distinct preference for a particular kind of semantic "filling" by what I shall, below, call "syntactic roles"; but this means that the semantic content belongs to those "roles" and not, properly speaking, to the syntactic functions. Let us then decide that the syntactic functions, though (frequently) formally marked, are empty; this, however, entails also "emptiness" *formally,* for formal "filling" belongs, as we shall see in a moment, to the syntactic categories. Therefore, syntactic functions are semantically empty and formally undetermined. In terms of the mental component, this means that the functions entail a purely inner organization. There seems to be no tie with the situational component that one can put one's finger on. Functions are in that sense purely "mental"—"purely" only by prescinding, of course, from formal and semantic "filling." Because of its purely "mental" features, syntactic functions must therefore rank highest along our cline; there appears to be no level higher than these functions.[92]

The next-lower level in syntax is that of the grammatical *categories*. We may again, provisionally and initially, borrow the traditional terms Noun, Verb, etc. How can these categories be further determined? Obviously, not necessarily by a renewed avowal of allegiance to the Stoic philosophy they originated from. A potentially important feature of syntactic categories is that, whatever the total of them in any language (and this is likely to differ from language to language), they allow of supercategorization, which perhaps makes them good candidates for language universals. One such supercategory is perhaps that of the Nominals, comprising such categories as Noun, Pronoun, Adjective. In these considerations I confine myself largely to these Nominals. What is syntactic about them? Presumably it would be correct to say that in a considerable number of languages (perhaps all) they may "fill" the Subject function as (if we follow tagmemic terminology) their "slot." But what is the nature of such "fillings"? In part it will be formal: Nominals, in quite many languages, are recognizable formally, either by syntactic order or morphologically. In part also it is semantic in a nonformal manner: Nominals are the kind of lexical items whose situation-relatedness easily (perhaps always) takes on the character of reference. Now reference is clearly an aspect belonging to the situational component. Therefore we have here the first level, in grammar, in which the situational component is relevant. To be sure, that relevance is still extremely remote because hardly anything is left of the one-to-one relationship between lingual elements and situational elements found most clearly in words as lexical items. In this sense of "remoteness" the relevance of the situational element in supercategories is still very abstract. Moreover, as such it is not exclusive; also Verbals—assuming that there is a basis for considering Verbals as a super-

92. Present-day theories of the functions (apart from textbook presentations, as in John Lyons, *Introduction to Theoretical Linguistics* [Cambridge: At the University Press, 1968], pp. 334–99), seem to move almost entirely within TG; see, for example, Chomsky, *Aspects of the Theory of Syntax*, pp. 68–74, and Fillmore's shift from function to role ("case") as more basic (Fillmore, "The Case for Case," in Bach and Harms, *Universals in Linguistic Theory*).

category, in some cases perhaps comprising certain classes of Adjectives—have a much more clearly "referential" character than is the case, say, with Adverbs of time or manner; on the other hand, the "reference" is then not to the kind of "objects" (keeping the "bracketing" principle in mind all the time!) that Nominals are referential to. Yet the similarity cannot be missed.

I do not wish to say much more about the syntactic categories here. Perhaps a final warning may be in order: though it would seem fairly straightforward to assign Verbs as "fillers" to the Predicate function as "slot," we must remember that there are many languages (Malayo-Polynesian, for example) in which prominent sentence types are ones with nonverbal Predicates. Perhaps we should even suspect that verbal Predicates in those languages are in some decisive manner distinct from verbal Predicates in (for instance) Indo-European languages; that is, if a Predicate may be filled by Nominals, this perhaps assigns to the Predicate (in those languages) a deictic character found also in the Subject (and Object) functions, in such a way that the Subject-Predicate relation would then be much more juxtapositional than in languages in which the Predicate must be verbal. Very little is known about such problems; but the linguist will have to cope with them, and perhaps in phenomenology this is more readily possible than in theories playing down language or type particulars in favor of language universals.[93]

As the next-lower level, still within syntax, I suggest the "syntactic roles," already alluded to briefly. They are those of Agent, Patient, Object, Goal, Beneficiary, and (in contrast to Fillmore's Case Grammar)[94] Action. In the present approach there would be no very obvious need for finding "case frames" for Verbs, for the notion of Verb itself belongs on the categorial

93. On categories, again an excellent textbook presentation is that of Lyons, *Introduction to Theoretical Linguistics,* pp. 270–333. On their Western history, see R. H. Robins, *Ancient and Mediaeval Grammatical Theory in Europe* (London: G. Bell & Sons, 1951), *passim,* and *General Linguistics: An Introductory Survey* (London: Longmans, 1964). Vital, also, is the 1967 volume of *Lingua,* which shows eloquently how little there still is of a widely enough accepted theory of word classes once one moves out of theories occurring only in other theories differently motivated. For TG, see Chomsky, *Aspects of the Theory of Syntax,* pp. 64–68. The status of categories is becoming increasingly more problematic in that trend; for a sample, see Emmon Bach, "Nouns and Noun Phrases," in Bach and Harms, *Universals in Linguistic Theory.*

94. Fillmore, "The Case for Case."

level, not on that of the "roles"; otherwise, verbal (and nonverbal predicative) roles will have to adapt to language-particular distinctions of "voice." As these notions are not naïvely objectifying ones (they could not be, by reason of the "bracketing" principle), it may be preferable to indicate their semantic content by means of the -ive terms (Agentive, Benefactive, etc.). Though Fillmore has breathed new life into the "roles," the problem itself has been known for a long time; for example, in Bloomfield's study of Tagalog (though his terms are different); [95] and the Malayo-Polynesian languages have been long known for their "verb focuses," which enable the Subject position (and other functions) to be "filled" by more roles than would in general be possible in Indo-European languages. What is new in Fillmore's studies is the accommodation of the roles to a transformational theory, as well as their treatment language-universally. He does this by assigning "deep cases" to deep structures, a position which, as I have explained, cannot be accepted in the present approach.

What makes the "roles" into a level lower down and therefore closer to the situational component? In any language, when what is spoken about is giving or taking, buying or selling, etc., the syntactic structure must come to terms with what is, in such cases, situationally universal: one who gives or sells, one who takes or buys, objects given/taken, sold/bought, and (in the case of buying and selling) other objects given in exchange. To be sure, these "situational universals" must not be thought of in a naïvely-realistically objective sense; that is, we must always be prepared to find, language- or type-specifically, situational elements which are invariable in the culture concerned but culturally/lingually not universal. They are, however, in their basic structures not lexically, but grammatically—more particularly, syntactically—semantic. Note also that the situational relatedness of the "roles" is determined in considerably more detail than is the case with the supercategories, the situation-relatedness of which I indicated above. But "more detailed" in fact means "more situational," or perhaps (but for the principle illustrated here it does not matter much) "more clearly situational"; that is, though roles do belong to the mental component also (and primarily), their greater adaptedness to the situation and to certain determinable elements therein as compared to the adaptedness of

95. Bloomfield, *Language*, p. 201.

supercategories to the situation entails greater limitations upon the mental component. Since the present approach to the roles has had no striking analogies in recent works dealing with syntax, and since Fillmore's approach has been quite different from the one favored here, these few remarks can form only a beginning. To point here to one or two problems only: morphological form may belie role function, as is the case in the deponent verbs in Latin, which, though morphologically passive, may be transitive, taking objects; also, perhaps new light may be shed on the Classical Greek middle voice. As regards "voice" more generally, the notion of the "passive" in Malayo-Polynesian languages should perhaps be changed for another one that does more justice to verb focuses and, more generally, to the function of the Verb (rather, of the "roles" suiting semantically what we call "Verb" categorically) in those languages.[96]

We may finally summarize the interrelatedness of the three syntactic levels: functions, categories, and roles. The functions are "empty" (language-universally); the categories fill them formally in the first place, and semantically only in some highly general and secondary way, while the roles also fill the functions, in the first place semantically, and formally only in a manner secondary to the semantic filling—all of this in different ways language-typologically and language-specifically. As such state-

96. In a number of languages in Indonesia (and Indonesian itself) the part played by the so-called "passive" and the distinction between Noun and Verb have been problems frequently debated by linguists. With them, one finds fairly regularly the suggestion that the "passive" is distinctly more "nominal" than the corresponding active forms in certain classes of verbs. This is not the place to adduce material and evidence. I merely wish to point out that such categorial distinctions as between Noun and Verb for a number of non-Indo-European languages (languages like Nootka and Kwakiutl are well enough known among linguists for this problem) pose problems linguists have not even begun to resolve and that other theoretical problems are closely connected with them. Not surprisingly, when such "passives" as occur in Indonesian languages have pronominal Agentives affixed to them, while pronominally there is no morphemic distinction between "personal" and "possessive," that fact invites comparisons with languages having a "genitive" Subject (as is apparently the case in certain Amerindian languages and, incidentally, also in substandard Dutch), and also the pronominal system would invite other comparisons, such as between affixations for alienable and inalienable possession. Admittedly, a number of linguists have given in to undue speculation (a few samples have recently been given by Fillmore in his "The Case for Case" and have been justly criticized by him), but the so-called "psychologistic" speculation of that kind has been led by genuine heuristic leads all too often overlooked by linguists of rationalistic persuasion.

ments cannot be analysed on the basis of the structure of the speech act, they amount to a hypothesis. They are not, however, merely hypothetical in a sense wholly out of touch with phenomenology, for the (few) arguments given for them here rely heavily on recognition of language particulars (type-specific in this case rather than language-specific, but at any rate not language-universal); and recognition of them is phenomenological in inspiration, because it can be based only on the experience of the language-user (which is at least for the greater part language-[type-] specific rather than universal).

FROM GRAMMAR TO LEXICON: MORPHOLOGY

IT IS HARDLY a coincidence that, just as the study of syntax became anemic under the behavioristic ascendancy, morphology has more recently suffered a comparable fate at the hands of the mentalists. Whatever the shortcomings of mentalism, at least it has in recent times become very clear that the study of morphology is not possible in complete divorce from syntax. I bypass the fact, well enough recognized also by non-TG linguists in *their* own theories, that syntactic structures have complicated consequences for morphology, in which they find, in part, formal realization. Also, it is sufficiently well known that morphological markings may have for their immediate constituents units more extensive than single morphemes or even than one single word. I merely mention a fact less widely known, i.e., that in some languages lexical status (which is normally marked by the "free" status of morphemes) may be retained in a morphologically bound form, under rules which are properly syntactic (as syntax is defined in the present essay).[97] Many

97. In Indonesian, pronominal Agents of first and second person (as well as certain third person forms of honorific address) are, linearly, inseparable from and irreversible with a following (say) "passive" form. Whenever the first and second person pronouns concerned are of the more "intimate" variety, they occur in truncated form. They have then, therefore, lost their morphologically "free" form and their syntactically "free" position, precisely the two features normally (and in many languages invariably) determining lexical status distributionally. If, however, we stick to the autonomy of lexical items in terms not of distribution alone but of the autonomy of the situational component in the first place, the distributional (in this case also grammatical) aspects become, as they should, coincidental to determination of lexical status. In other words, these trun-

more problems have not even begun to be investigated. Given enough time, energy, erudition, and interest, any linguist might fruitfully spend a long time solving what problems enter "unmarkedness" in a morphological paradigm, investigating, for example, the whole "nominative" theory in the West, theories on basic forms and roots, and solving cases where every member of a paradigmatic list is marked. A similar problem would be posed by morphemes which are not morphs.

Morphology is properly about all morphemes, bound and free, apart from the inventorying of free morphemes, which is the business of the lexicographer. A common area for the morphologist and the lexicographer would be the description of rules governing the use of productive bound morphemes. Merely for convenience in discussing a few points to follow, I shall call this productive affixation "derivation," and no other process, such as affixation by reason of concord or government, shall be so called (there are, of course, overlaps, depending on how widely "productivity" is taken to apply, but this problem is immaterial for the discussion to follow). Paradigms may then be defined as excluding derivation (though such a definition does not necessarily follow from what I have just said). One productive process which is morphological and yet not derivational (as defined) is that of compounds: composition. What I shall discuss about morphology is only that which is presumably relevant to the grammar-lexicon cline once this cline has been accepted; and what I want to suggest, tentatively, is that paradigmatic affixation, derivation, and composition follow the next-higher level of the syntactic roles in the scale, in that order. I have not yet been able to come up with counterevidence to this hypothesis; but since what I shall be doing is a comparatively novel attempt at structurally hierarchical description, some counterevidence is likely to be forthcoming on further analysis.

Of paradigmatic affixation, as coming first after the syntactic roles, I isolate the kind that must be referred to concord and government, even though exceptions (such as the vocative in many languages) are exciting enough to merit further treatment. Let an exception be third person singular present indicative -*s* in English (regular) verbs. It has no semantic content of its

cated forms simply retain lexical status. This phenomenon occurs also in other Malayo-Polynesian languages.

own, i.e., as compared with a derivational affix like *-less,* to be discussed in a moment. Yet there must be a meaning in some sense to *-s*, since denying this would stamp *-s* as "redundant" (which otherwise in certain cases it is not), a qualification whose drawbacks I have already discussed. It is not obviously vacuous to maintain that the meaning of *-s* is "grammatical," if only in the sense that it is decidedly not lexical and also bears no resemblance to lexical meaning, as do a number of derivational affixes. Its function, i.e., that of concord, may be rightly called a "function"(or, more cautiously, "functional"), as indeed a relation between syntactic functions is determined by it. I have said earlier that such a syntactic function is "empty" and that whatever semantic content is entailed holds between the functions mutually, needing a realization in form (of which morphological form is one important part), and one semantically, in terms of the "roles." If, then, relations between functions are, in addition, also indicated by affixation, such as by verbal *-s* in English, then naturally (i.e., in the experience, though not usually in the explicit awareness, of the language user) this *-s* "means" something. However this "meaning" is in no way rooted in the situational component. Therefore, it seems that in the first morphological level down our cline we face once more something found also in the syntactic functions: unrelatedness to the situational component, though this time with a certain "meaning." I do not know why this should be so (and at any rate it is not so language-universally), but the phenomenon is not confined to this particular example and others comparable to it. I merely add one "pointer": what to do with a problem like a singular verb form required by "concord" in Classical Greek whenever the Subject is plural neuter (it would not be hard to find other examples like it). With these few comments, I must leave discussion of this level.

Derivation is next down the ladder, because the affixes used for it have a meaning much more clearly recognizable in isolation, while, moreover, such affixes are not easily "plurifunctional" (i.e., *-s*, in English, is not only verbal but also nominal [plural and genitive]). A good example in English is *-less.* Though *-less* is a bound form, its meaning is, prescinding from grammatically different behavior, quite close to, if not identical with, the lexical item *without;* the same, *mutatis mutandis,* with *un-* (*in-, im-*), *-ful, -head, -ness,* etc. The semantic closeness of these affixes to lexical items makes their situation-relatedness a much more easily determinable one, i.e., in one-to-one correspondence with situational elements. To the extent that derivational suffixes are, at the same time, categorical markings, the more general situation-relatedness of supercategories, discussed above, must also be taken into account. On the other hand, in contrast to lexical items, derivational affixes are a matter of grammar only; apart from the quite different grammatical behavior of lexical items and derivational affixes, there is the important difference that the lexicon in any language is an open set (among other things by reason of the possibility of derivation), while the set of derivational affixes is (from a synchronic point of view) a closed set.[98]

The third morphological level is that of composition. Its mysteries have baffled many linguists, and TG has also found them to be a tough set of problems. The semantic relations between the components of compounds seem to defy whatever analogies there may be in the language with syntactic rules in word groups. On the other hand, these relations are sometimes so close to word-group rules of syntax that the distinction between compound and word group becomes problematic. The former, which, following Reichling,[99] I propose to call "compositions" (Reichling's *samenstellingen*), seem to allow of little more than extensive lists according to certain semantic considerations. ("Compositions" is to be distinguished from singular "composition" as the name of the morphological process accounting for *all* compounds.) They have an order of their component parts which is not possible syntactically in the language (the comparison is possible because the components may occur as free forms). The latter may be called "concatenations" (Reichling's *samenkoppelingen*), and they comprise those compounds whose component parts occur in an order also possible syntactically in word groups in the language. It is assumed here that compounds

---

98. The number of derivational affixes is astonishingly high in English, no doubt because of the many source languages, Germanic, Romance, and (neo-)Latin, tapped when *their* affixation system was still felt to be productive for English. See Hans Marchand, *The Categories and Types of Present-Day English Word-Formation*, 2d rev. ed. (Munich: Beck, 1969), which is the most extensive treatment of this field now available (also on the formation of compounds). Regrettably, Marchand's treatment of the word is entirely in linear terms, and very brief at that; Reichling's work is not found in its bibliography.

99. *Het woord*, pp. 380–82.

are words and behave like them in all respects, while the component parts do not—even though those that are "free," abstractly speaking (that is, in compounds they are not really "free")—and must be regarded as morphemes, not as words. A few examples of Reichling's two species of compounds may be useful. Compositions are exemplified, in English, by *bottleneck*, *street lamp*, *school committee*, etc.; examples of concatenations in English are *high school*, *jack-in-the-box*, etc. For obvious reasons, it is the concatenations that raise the problem of identity, i.e., of compound or word group. Thus, when *high school* means a school building of notable height, it is a word group; when it means an institution of secondary education, it is a compound— more particularly, a concatenation. The criterion of meaning here is too obvious to be missed, but relying on meaning alone must be accounted methodologically inadequate as long as formal checks are possible. Often they are. Thus *high* in the concatenation *high school* may not be modified by an adverb of degree: *a very high school* can be interpreted only as a word group; i.e., *high school*, in that phrase, cannot be a compound. Phonological criteria such as primary accent on *black* in *'blackbird* stamp it a compound, while *'black 'bird* is a word group. While this is well enough known,[100] more involved problems are found in English by reason of categorical conversion. For example, is *London streets* a compound? If we regard both segments as nouns, it must be, because it would constitute a composition, not a concatenation. But names of cities may be used adjectivally in English, which could make the example a candidate for identification as simply a word group. On the other hand, degree-modification is impossible: *the very London streets* is ungrammatical. Perhaps in cases such as these we have to appeal to semantic criteria alone: the difference between *London streets* and *Leicester Square* is that *London* in the former makes the speaker "think" *London* "in" the phrase, while *Leicester* cannot be said to be "thought" "in" *Leicester Square* in a comparable manner. Therefore, *Leicester Square* is a compound (and, more specifically, a composition, as *Leicester* need not be considered as an adjectival use of the Noun *Leicester*), while *London streets* is not. That in the latter case *very* cannot be added must simply be considered as a restraint on word-group formation. It would be

100. At least since Bloomfield, *Language*, p. 180.

worthwhile to investigate whether there may be formal checks on a case like this after all; for example, *the distinctly London streets* is grammatical, while *the distinctly high school* (where *high school* is a secondary school) is not.

However, working out these more detailed problems is not a specific task of the phenomenologist alone. Assignment of composition to the particular hierarchical level discussed here ultimately is. For compounds are much closer than any of the higher levels to the situational component. In fact, as lexical items, they simply belong to the lexicon, and not to grammar; it is the process of composition rather than the actual compounds that makes assignment of this process to grammar—more specifically to morphology—imperative. Therefore, though compounds belong to the lexicon, composition belongs to grammar. It follows derivation immediately down the cline because, like derivation, composition also is productive; *its* productivity, however, is much more adaptable to the situational component, seeing that the semantic relations obtaining between components of compounds absorb, even though in themselves they must be considered as grammatical, situational variability to a much greater extent than any grammatical process, morphological or syntactic, in any of the higher levels discussed so far.

In the hierarchy discussed here, composition is the lowest level that is still grammatical. For the rest we will have to turn to the use of words considered, not grammatically, but as lexical items.

Lexical Collocation; The Application of Meanings

I have argued earlier that assimilation of the lexicon into the grammar is inadequate, as it leads to idealization of the situational component and to distortions of the notion of grammaticality itself. In the light of the speech-act analysis, it must be recognized that grammaticalization of words as lexical items is the more serious, seeing that at no level is the importance of the situational component so great as it is in the lexicon. But all this is not to deny that in sentences of the type *Colorless green ideas sleep furiously* there is something strange. Let us call this strangeness "deviance." Therefore, a sentence like the one cited may be called "deviant," while yet it cannot be called ungrammatical. Once deviance has been divided into grammatical and ungrammatical (ungrammaticalness is of course also "deviant") what is the nature of nongrammatical deviance? Note that, although the grammaticalization of the lexicon has been motivated by rationalistic prejudices, it is still possible to be rationalistic about deviance in lexical semantics even after its nongrammatical nature has been recognized. Deviance (which henceforth shall mean only nongrammatical deviance) must not, in other words, be related to some epistemologically inspired conception of natural language. If so, what should it be related to?

To show what a full analysis of this problem would look like, I wish to go, for a moment, into related problems in philosophy. If deviance is related to what is "normal," and what is "normal" is related to something more comprehensive than merely the speech act within which sentences occur—sentences whose deviance is to be assessed—then that more comprehensive totality will take the form of a network of "semantics" wider than that of lingual semantics alone. In somewhat more traditional philosophical terms, we may identify that more comprehensive totality with what is referred to as a "universe of discourse." Philosophical language analysis of the Oxonian type is, in some of its forms, merely a lingual restatement of the relevance of that "universe of discourse." Thus the language of art or of religion has its own semantic laws, and the "meaning-is-use" principle is ultimately reducible to that principle. Note that, though a universe of discourse may have been systematically set up and established, this is not essential; popular beliefs exist without such substantiations, and even in natural language everyone instinctively appreciates the different rules holding for fairy tales, science fiction, a political harangue, or the language of the law. Philosophical analysis of the type just mentioned has, in the same spirit, mostly realized that the analysis of meaning not only precedes attachment of truth values but is in principle possible without such a following truth determination. Phenomenologically one might speak of "empathy"; thus one may explain to an atheist the meaning of a sentence like *God loves us as our Father* without committing him to a belief in the existence of God, let alone to an assent to the truth of the sentence. Thus the principle that meaning is in its use, which must be objected to if "use" is rooted in the "situation" (or even in the "setting"), may be assented to when taken in the language-game sense of Wittgenstein in his "second" period (but even then the principle might be better worded).

Where, then, does the linguist come in? On the one hand, some familiarity with the philosophical problematic just indicated might prove helpful; yet, on the other hand, a great many of the insights derived from it may be known intuitively, and such an intuition could perhaps be reduced to zero only by a set of strong rationalistic preconceptions about natural language. We all recognize what is often indicated as different "styles"— poetic, oratorical, allusive. But a refinement of such a recognition is necessary; otherwise the linguist might be tempted to consider (say) poetic language as sufficiently marginal even to natural language for it to be discounted. While this is in itself reasonable enough, it is also necessary to realize how counterrational natural language can be, and frequently is. In the final portion of this paper I shall discuss the counterrational factors operative in such style figures as metaphor and metonymy. The way, however, these factors appear concretely is in sentences. The sentences in which such style figures occur must naturally be assessed, not by focusing solely on the words being used metaphorically, but rather on the way those uses are combined with other words in the same sentence. Thus, what the linguist faces when he tries to lay down rules for the nondeviance of such sentences is the combinations of words calling for special analysis. A term already current in linguistics and well adapted to our purpose is that of "collocation." [101] This may, for all we know, entail recognition of a certain universe of discourse, but that would hardly be what the linguist begins with.

Since virtually no work has yet been done in this area, I may simply attempt a modest beginning. Though I will not consider it my task in this paper to work out collocational rules in detail, it is desirable to state in general what kind of rules they are. Negatively, they differ from selectional restrictions in that the latter are grammatical, while collocational rules are lexical. They are essentially about combinability of situational elements as reflected in word use. That this combinability must ultimately be founded in some universe of discourse has already been made clear. It will be good to bear in mind at this point that combining or not combining situational elements has nothing to do with

---

101. See, e.g., Robins, *General Linguistics*, pp. 67–70.

the "objective" (non)combinability of extralingual entities of whatever kind. By reason of the "bracketing" principle, situational elements are not extralingual. As most of them are determined by lexical items, their combinability may also be expressed in lexical terms. From this it follows, naturally, that the lexicon of any language—*langue* element as it is—goes far to determine also the combinability of situational elements. However, this functions more by way of a background, or a basic pattern; or, in other words—and in accordance with the "linguistic relativity principle"—the *langue* determines, in part, also the universe of discourse that is operative. But as each sentence is not only the environment in which lexical items actually occur but is at the same time the unit of the speech act in which lexical items are *used*, the combinability of situational elements also surpasses that basic pattern set by the lexicon as a *langue* aspect. This is where the creative use of the "style" figures comes in.

To say that in sentences words are *used* is to say that they or—what comes to the same thing—their meanings are *applied.* Applied to what? To situational elements. The clearest cases of the application of words (Reichling's *toepassing*) are the ones referentially determinable—in general, Nominals and Verbals. It is, then, not surprising that it is with Nominals and Verbals that application is freest. The use, or application, of word meanings is further to be analysed as an activity. Bloomfield already recognized that in speech there is something that takes the place of some nonlingual action; [102] when I ask you to hand me a certain book, my sentence replaces the alternative of ignoring potential help from you and getting the book myself. Whether just any sentence may be considered as replacing an act possible without it is a problem I do not wish to go into. I merely wish to emphasize that language use is an act. The application of lexical meanings is one outstanding form of this activity.[103]

102. Bloomfield, *Language*, p. 25.

103. The conception of the use of words as the application of their meanings, in the form it takes in the present discussion, is due to Reichling (*Het woord, passim;* see esp. Chap. VIII, pp. 319–61). Further, I rely heavily on Reichling's theory of metaphor as "disjunctive application," and the reference to *categorematica* and *syncategorematica* is also found in Reichling (p. 273), though in a less satisfactory context, in my opinion. For language as an activity, see *Het woord*, pp. 125–26 and *passim;* but see especially Reichling, "Het handelingskarakter van het woord," *Nieuwe Taalgids,* XXXI (1937), 308–21. Finally, I have also borrowed the notion of "proper" or "conjunctive application" from Reichling's *Het woord.* For

Note that this use of a dictionary item does not compare to that item itself as a *langue* item as token relates to type. For token and type (as these terms are usually understood) are not associated with presence or absence of situation-relatedness, respectively, and this is the distinction that is relevant in the analysis followed here. Granting that the token-type distinction may be useful for certain types of analysis or for clarifying certain forms of misunderstanding in scholarly discourse, that distinction, as applied to *parole-langue*, mistakes that latter distinction for one ultimately looking like "material"-"ideal," or "actual"-"abstract," or "concrete"-"abstract." While it is true that the speech act is "concrete" in a straightforward sense of that expression, much reservation is necessary in regard to the alleged "abstract" nature of (in this case) the lexicon. The lexicon is simply a group total of social relatedness to a more or less common type of situation; whether it is enlightening rather than misleading to call this "abstract" is a matter which may be doubted. Finally, situation-relatedness of language-users in their use of lexical items should not be confused with reference without more ado. Reference is merely one particular (and perhaps most concretely identifiable) form of a language-user's situation-relatedness. If it is true that it is especially Nominals and Verbals which are referential, more properly speaking, and that they offer greater scope to the language-user for applications other than (what will in a moment be called) "conjunctive," then perhaps the lexicon can be split up into two sublevels, roughly corresponding to the medieval *syncategorematica* and *categorematica*, respectively. The *syncategorematica* would still be situation-related, but in a manner closer to grammar while yet within the lexicon; but the *categorematica* would be so related referentially, therefore more clearly determinably in one-to-one correspondence with situational elements. In any case, the various modes of applying lexical meanings in the speech act will concern *categorematica* mainly; but I will not go into whatever implications this holds for a subdivision of the level called lexical.

The meaning of a word is, of course, itself a *langue* item. It can never be identified beyond all doubt; it can only be described (imperfectly) in terms of the native speaker's experience. Dic-

---

the rest, I alone must be responsible, as well as for the larger context within which the borrowings from Reichling function.

tionaries do this paraphrastically, and with such difficulty and lack of satisfactory results that it must be doubted whether any dictionary-maker would feel he could be committed, for the entire lexicon in a language, to the treatment of the lexicon found in Fodor and Katz,[104] and in subsequent versions of it in TG. First of all, paraphrases tend to change meaning; more seriously, they hardly ever seem to be complete. Admittedly, dictionaries have an evocative and catalytic function as much as a defining one, and learners of a language other than their own invariably find dictionaries more useful (especially in active use of the new language, as distinct from receptive use only) in proportion as they already know the language better: a dictionary helps in the way of an *"Aha"-Erlebnis* rather than by way of information. The essential vagueness of lexical meanings in natural language may be alleviated by ostensive definition, but this is possible only with names of concrete objects (the older dictionaries featuring pictures have been superseded by newer ones perhaps gratuitously lacking them); for other meanings contextual information and the situational "feel" will help, in the long run, to give the intuition necessary for adequate lexical identification. Not surprisingly, many good dictionaries give examples of sentences (or representative portions of them) to make at least the contextual catalysis possible.

Yet it would amount to a basic misunderstanding if it were to be supposed that lexical meanings do not have their own context-free content. To appreciate this point, let us (by way of a thought experiment) equate context with situation—not a totally unacceptable thing to do, as the structure of a situation is likely to be reflected in the context of sentences or discourse. Then we have a theoretical background for the evaluation of the slogan, used in philosophy as well as in linguistics (Wittgenstein and Firth, respectively), that "meaning is (in its) use." It is necessary to carry this thought experiment to its ultimate conclusion, i.e., that any sentence could (in principle) mean anything; but this is absurd. It is to the credit of TG to have exploded this conception, even though Reichling had refuted it, almost *avant la lettre*, before.[105] When we say (as we must) that lexical

---

104. Jerry A. Fodor and Jerrold J. Katz, eds., *The Structure of Language: Readings in the Philosophy of Language* (Englewood Cliffs, N.J.: Prentice-Hall, 1964).

105. In *Het woord*, first published in 1935.

meanings are in most cases *vague*, this means that complete descriptive equivalents of such meanings are impossible to come by. Now inadequate descriptions may lead to a lack of clarity, which may be confused with the experiential certainty with which native speakers handle the items so hard to describe. But the confusion of clarity (on the reflective level) with certainty (in the experiential sense) would itself be a mistake almost necessarily made by rationalistic, idealizing theories. The phenomenologist is unlikely to confuse them. Let us express the difference alluded to by saying that the meaning of any word (with the exception, perhaps, of interjections) is prereflectively stable and invariable (synchronically), displaying, moreover, an internal unity (as Reichling has extensively argued) which cannot be broken, while descriptive "equivalents" in their reflective characteristics tend to make us lose sight of this stability, invariability, and unity. It is therefore basic to the phenomenological approach to have many second thoughts about descriptive attempts to deal with meanings of individual lexical items. And this would naturally affect considerations of collocation also.

Following Reichling, we may describe lexical meaning, as far as constituted by the mental component, as what we think "in" a word; dictionary definitions may be considered as more or less successful descriptions of what the typical native speaker thinks "in" any word. As the "typical" native speaker represents the *langue*, *langue* is already implied before it is explicated, and this distinguishes what is thought "in" any word from what individual native speakers, on grounds not found in the *langue*, may think "with" a word (and that may be a great deal). Thus the word *church* in English entails quite different "with"-elements (which we might call "associative," provided this not be understood in the behavioristic tradition of associationism) for a pastor, a parishioner, a city-planner, an architect, an atheist, or the church committee's creditors. Psychologists know well what such "associative" elements may be, and linguists on the whole care little about them, although, as we shall see, they may be linguistically relevant. As such they do not, it is true, belong to the situation, but they may belong to the setting of the individual speech act. Otherwise the "with"-elements do not belong to the meaning of the word with which they are associated. Finally, it should be noted that the lexical meaning itself, in the case of each lexical entry in a language, usually also consists of certain elements, because what the typical native speaker thinks "in" any word normally consists of certain "parts," which can be distinguished and must be distinguished in certain varieties of the application of lexical meanings, as we shall see. Again, the *description* of these elements or parts raises not a few problems; however, to say that the description is problematic is not necessarily to say that what is being described is problematic for the same reasons. One problem of the description of parts constituting any individual lexical meaning is that it must necessarily be paraphrastic. Thus English *dog* will have parts which may paraphrastically be described as "four-legged," "mammal," "carnivore," "domesticated," and a number of other such parts. Here it should be remembered that we are describing natural language, so that a scientific description will presumably overlap to a great extent with the description of the parts of lexical meaning in the case of each word, but cannot be identified with it. Thus the meaning of *dog, chien, Hund,* etc., does not necessarily coincide fully with the description given by a zoologist; similarly, *water* is (mercifully!), so far as its meaning in English is concerned, more than just H_2O.

We must now take a closer look at what all this entails for the application of meanings. But a final terminological remark is in order. I have spoken about "elements" and "parts" thought "in" a word, and therefore belonging to its meaning, and about "elements" thought "with" a word. However, the use of "elements" in the present essay has already been preempted in the expression "situational elements," to which words as lexical items relate. It would therefore be confusing to use "element" also for "parts" of any individual lexical item's meaning. I shall therefore use the term "moment" for those elements. This is also done by Reichling (to whom the basic theory here employed is due), following Husserl. A "moment" is any part (phenomenologically) whose only *raison d'être* is in its "part" character with regard to the whole. I do not like the term, with its deceptive associations with the time concept and consequently its esoteric character; also, its Hegelian origin does not make it a very appropriate term in the present context. I will use it only to forestall the confusion that would arise if I used "element." But I wish to disengage myself from the esotericism and above all from the Hegelian origin of this term. For that reason I shall preserve scare quotes throughout.

Let us derive examples from English. When *fox* refers to a fox, *monkey* to a monkey, and *foot* to a foot, we speak of "proper application" of the meanings of those words. In proper application, all "moments" of the word's meaning are applied; this is not to say that the language-user is necessarily always aware of all these "moments," but, the application being a "proper" one, no "moment" necessarily applies to the referent more prominently than does any other "moment": the application is one single act, of which, moreover, the language-user need not otherwise be articulately aware. Though the expression "proper" has been used before, I adopt a term introduced by Reichling, one which is more precise in that it says something about the relations among the "moments": "conjunctive" application. That is, all "moments" making up the entire meaning apply "conjointly"; what we have in "proper" application is "conjunctive" application. This appears to be what we might call the "ordinary" or "proper" use of words, which is to say that use and meaning coincide.

Suppose, however, that *fox* is applied to a human, or *monkey* to a naughty little boy, or *foot* to the lower part of a mountain or hill. In such cases not all "moments" making up the whole of the meaning of each word are applied, but only some. In cases like these also, there is, again, the problem of the practical description, but the principle itself is clear enough. What makes a speaker apply *fox* to a human is (at least) the "moment" "wily" (as well as, perhaps, some others, such as "quiet"); application of *monkey* to a little boy may select the "moments" "amusing," "unpredictable," and "mischievous"; and similar selections will account for *foot* in an expression like *the foot of the hill*. It may, incidentally, be good to note that from this it appears that the "moments" of a lexical meaning are not in good hands with a scientist having the referents for his field of specialization: no zoologist will get "wily" into his definition of *fox* or "hilarious" into that of *monkey*. But back to the "moments." Certain ones are selected and applied to the referent. What about the other "moments" *not* applied? Do they, ad hoc, disappear from the lexical meaning of *fox, monkey*, etc.? This, however, is impossible, for the meaning of *fox* (etc.) remains intact as a whole; the "moments" *not* applied are nevertheless "thought" "in" that word. This is actually what gives a metaphor (for that is what it is) its provocative character (and the more so when a metaphor is original); as a human is not a fox, *fox* cannot apply to a human, simply as a matter of course. Or, though *fox* does apply, in metaphorical (or "improper") application, to something not a fox, yet *fox* in no way ceases to mean what it means.[106] To overlook this point is perhaps the principal error (at least potentially) in the slogan that "meaning is (in its) use." Reichling says, about the "moments" *not* applied, that these are nevertheless "actuated" (*geactueerd*) in the mind of the language-user. The "improper" application he calls "disjunctive" application: the "moments" applied apply disjointly. Of the moments *not* applied, Reichling says that they are "disjunctively relevant"; after the explanation given above, it is clear what is meant by this. (Perhaps the expression "disjunctively relevant" is not felicitous, because it amounts to a confusion in the use of "disjunctive"; however, in itself this is merely a terminological matter.)

A few words should be said on the function of the mental component in disjunctive application. I have remarked earlier that, although the use of lexical items is primarily to be referred to the situational component, the mental component is still relevant at the lexical level; for obviously the kind of "thought" going on in language, though it appears in a more exclusive manner in grammar, does not stop at the level where grammar goes over into the lexicon. This kind of "thought," I may also add, is very much socially determined: no speaker has a private lexicon. But all this holds most especially for conjunctive application of lexical items. In disjunctive application, the language-user, or rather his mental activity, goes beyond the specific features of lexical items, which, in their turn, no longer fulfill their nomenclatural function. Though there is still, in each case of lexical use in disjunctive application, a one-to-one correspondence between lexical item and the situational element to which it happens to be (metaphorically) applied, this is no longer based on parity of lexical item and situational element: meaning and referent (for in metaphorical denomination the situational element concerned is usually a referent properly so speaking) no longer coincide. A

106. The point is made clearly by Reichling, and it is perhaps one of the more powerful principles that may prevent lexical semantics from becoming the mess (or rationalistic distortion) it so easily can become. Otherwise, what has just been noted holds only synchronically; *diachronically* a word may have the features of its original metaphorical use assimilated into its meaning, which then comes to be applied only conjunctively and to be simply a metaphor. This point is due to Reichling, "Het handelingskarakter van het woord."

special mental activity (which, again, does not have to be such that the language-user is fully aware of it) is required for disjunctive application. On the one hand, it might seem as if what gives rise to metaphor is similarity between situational elements, so that what we may call a "referential crossover" becomes possible. However, if that were so, metaphor would be the business, not of the linguist, but at best of the psychologist, sociologist, or anthropologist. The very fact, however, that metaphor can be described as "disjunctive application" of *meanings* shows that the condition for the possibility of metaphor is found in (lexical) semantics; it could, moreover, hardly be otherwise, seeing that an evaluation of situational elements apart from the lexical items related to them would violate the "bracketing" principle, without which a consistent theory of lexical semantics would not be possible. Therefore, in disjunctive application the mental component in the speech act displays a creativity not found in conjunctive application, which follows, so to speak, the dictionary of the language. Another way of explaining that disjunctive application still belongs within the analysis of the structure of the speech act is to draw attention to the fact that the "referential crossover" still takes place within the situational component; only, the situational component is articulated in a more sophisticated manner, not only according to the structure it takes under mental organization through the lexicon as a whole, but also under distinctions which must be referred to the distinction of "moments" with the meanings of certain individual lexical items. In other words, to explain disjunctive application, we do not have to extend the boundaries of the situation to the point where it comprises the entire *setting* of the speech act. It will become clear in a moment how important that distinction is: in metonymical application, the basis is no longer the situation but the setting.

It is relevant to note at this point that the intentionality of the language-user in metaphorical use terminates at a "point" which still retains a great deal that is implicit. Descriptively, of course, we can isolate the "moments" applied from the entire meaning from which they have been selected, but we should not forget that an explicating description does not cause what is implicit in experience to become explicit therein; what remains even more implicit in metaphorical word use is the other "moments," *not* applied, but yet *actuated,* "thought along with," the "moments"

that *were* applied. Thus, in calling a naughty boy a *monkey*, the
"moment" "tail" is not applied, but it does contribute to the
imaginative aspects of the experience of such metaphorical word
use. We have, therefore, two species of implicitness in metaphor:
that of the "moments" applied, and that of those not applied. The
first can at least be reasoned about in some fashion, however
nonrational metaphor otherwise is, in the sense that a linguist
can argue about the possibility or impossibility of applying a
particular word metaphorically to a particular situational element; the second is beyond reasoning, or at least beyond the kind
of reasoning that belongs to linguistics: one cannot "justify" anything about them from the linguist's point of view. Otherwise it
is clear that the "reasoning" one can do about the first species of
implicitness proves the principle of rational determinability
wrong: metaphor is possible only because natural language is
essentially vague. For that reason, perhaps, concepts, as the
semantic content of learned *terms*, cannot be used metaphorically. The medieval adage which said that concepts are like
numbers already recognized this: just as, with a number, if you
isolate, disjunctively, one or more "moments" of a concept, you
have a different concept, so the semantic content loses its inner
unity when its "moments" (or, as the Scholastics had it, its
notae) are applicationally disengaged from it.[107] In natural language you and I can still talk, even though our evaluation of the
"moments" of the meaning of *table* or *bear* do not fully coincide
(*this*, too, is entailed in the vagueness of natural language); but
assuming that you and I are linguists and are talking about
(say) a phoneme or about redundancy, careful and detailed
definitions of *phoneme* and *redundancy* will have to be given if
all chances of confusion are to be excluded.

When all this is adequately understood, a few more comments are necessary on where collocation comes in. From the
preceding it is clear that the nature of disjunctive application can
be explained without overt reference to co-occurrence of other
lexical items in the sentence. But as any application is use, and
use occurs only in the concrete speech act and therefore in the
unit of speech, the sentence, collocation comes in necessarily.
Without collocational clues we do not know whether a word is
being used metaphorically or not. In the sentence *I saw a fox*

107. Reichling, "Het handelingskarakter van het woord."

yesterday, there is no way of telling whether *fox* is being used metaphorically or "properly." In *That man is a fox,* metaphorical use is clear.[108] That collocational clues must often be derived from discourse instead of from the sentence concerned does not affect the principle here illustrated. Here it may be asked whether the setting, and therefore not collocation, might not sometimes have to provide the clue. This would be hard to deny, and in one-word sentences with no discourse, or no collocational clues from discourse (as when I say to, or about, someone, *Fox!*), we would have a clear case. I do not know what to do with this problem except to point out that such cases are rare (in contrast to one-word sentences more generally). Perhaps a theory of setting-based ellipsis ought to account for them.

LEXICAL COLLOCATION; VARIETIES OF IMPLIED MEANING

I NOW WISH to bring together two features of the above analysis that so far are still unconnected in the argumentation. I have said that, in disjunctive application of words, what is peculiar about it is not the word's meaning (which remains unaffected) but its application. In that sense, the *meaning* of *fox* does not change in the sentence. *That man is a fox.* I have also said that the relevance of lexical use to the hierarchy we have been discussing is to be sought in lexical collocation, i.e., in the sentence (or in discourse). Now if we take these two together we can say that, although there is nothing peculiar about the *meaning* of *fox* even when applied metaphorically, as in the sentence just given, *the meaning of that sentence is indubitably affected.*

Reichling has argued that what is characteristic of the sentence *as sentence* is that it posits whatever there is of meaning in the sentence *as real.*[109] I do not agree with this, at least at face value, since it violates the "bracketing" principle. Otherwise, I think Reichling's statement can be salvaged insofar as even the *experience of* what constitutes reality can be analysed with the "bracketing" principle intact. However, the interpretation of

108. Of course, apart from discourse context, alternative understandings are possible. For example, *man* in this sentence may be "quotational" (in a sense to be explained below). But *if* there is a metaphor in the sentence, it cannot be *man;* it has to be *fox.*

109. Reichling, *Het woord,* p. 415.

Reichling's claim does not affect my own claim that there may be something like the *meaning of a sentence* in the sense indicated, and I have mentioned Reichling's claim merely because it is the only one known to me, about the nature of the sentence, that is combined with an elaborate linguistic theory. The sentence meaning I am referring to does not hold for every sentence. Our only material so far has been sentences with metaphor in them. I wish to determine sentence meaning (in such cases) as instances of what I propose to call "implied meaning." How should this be further analysed?

The variations of implied meaning are far too numerous to be reviewed here in reasonable detail. Intonation, to begin with, is often responsible for implied meaning. I wish to prescind here from the question whether it would be feasible, within the approach and terminology used here, to call the interrogative intonation in a sentence which is otherwise not marked for interrogation (*He went to the beach this morning?*) a case of implied meaning. But a certain case of implied meaning would be one in which the intonation is out of harmony with the "ordinary" meaning of the sentence. Thus, when a short-tempered man betrays his temper intonationally in a sentence whose meaning is totally unrelated to his agitation, that would be a case of implied meaning. Mere pitch (whether it enters intonation or not is immaterial for the point I am making), when used, for example, to mimic the conversation partner in irony, gives the sentence an implied meaning. The last two examples are certainly extralingual, just as other phonetic features manifesting age, sex, mood, temperament, etc., of speakers are ordinarily extralingual. We "imply" many things in the way we speak, with gestures, facial expression, or, for that matter, by not saying anything under circumstances in which we would naturally be expected to speak. The analysis of such implications is properly the business of whoever wishes to study communication (for example, the social psychologist) and the role of language in it. It is by no means always easy to determine whether or not such forms of behavior may in part belong to the analysis of the speech situation. One example of this may suffice. Suppose that I reply, affirmatively, to a question, not by saying *Yes*, but by repeating the entire question in the affirmative structure. The implied meaning of my reply may be that I think the question is superfluous, or clumsily worded, or a tactless one to ask. But is such an implied meaning properly the object of linguistics? If there is "quotation" in my reply (on which see below), it probably is, in part. Moreover, repetition in dialogue may carry implied meaning in one language and be necessary for discourse in another. These few remarks must suffice on "implied meaning" as a generic notion.

Implied meaning, then, whenever linguistic, is sentence meaning; and sentence meaning, whenever it occurs, must be implied. Our only example, so far, has been metaphor. Let us now consider metonymy. In metonymy, we observe a partial resemblance to what happens in metaphor. Certain "moments" are selected, applied, while others are not. But the difference from metaphor is that, this time, the "moments" applied are not "moments" belonging to the meaning of the word concerned, but only "moments" "associated" with it, *and in specific circumstances only*. The circumstances are determined, not by the situation, but by the setting. *Top hat,* in *"I do not like it," said the top hat* may refer to the person wearing the hat (I say "may," as top hats *can* speak—for example, in fairy tales). The setting in question has to be characteristic in the experience of the language-user (for example, because the person always wears the hat or because he looks ludicrous in it); otherwise the association of the hat with the person is not obvious enough to strike all participants in the speech setting. Nevertheless, the setting is specific: the metonym will be understandable only to those familiar with it. In this respect, metonymy also differs from metaphor, which, in order to be understandable, requires no familiarity with the specific setting that may give rise to it. Note that the basis for metonymy is no longer in the situation only, but has to be found likewise in the setting. That is, there is no basis for the associations made in the situation (which, as far as the lexicon is concerned, is articulated only with respect to itself, this articulation including, as we have seen, "moments" within each lexical meaning); and yet these associations are still linguistic, as they form the basis for a special manner of application.

For a third case of implied meaning I select what I will call "neutralization." An example is *This wall is only three feet high.* The source of the implied meaning is the use of *high.* There is, here, even some kind of contrast between the meaning of *high* (which is antonymous with *low*) and the referent itself, which, being three feet only, is low (for a wall). Neutralization consists in "objectifying" a relative quantity into an absolute one: *high,* though not low, may in fact apply to something low.[110] I include neutralization in implied meaning because otherwise there would be no collocational rules taking care of a perfectly nondeviant sentence like *A wall three feet high is not high.* It is, fairly obviously, the second occurrence of *high* which is the "regular" (or "conjunctive") use; therefore, its first occurrence must be a case of nonconjunctive application; it is this that gives to the sentence its implied meaning. Perhaps it may be said that the "moments" applied in that first occurrence of *high* are "associated" with the "ordinary" meaning of *high* in a manner which is due to abstraction: reduction to pure quantity. These few comments will have to suffice here for neutralization.

The obvious way of continuing the analyses, all of which are related to the traditional "figures of speech" or tropes as found in stylistics manuals, is to discuss other tropes as well. However, completeness of discussion of any specific problem is not the purpose of the present study. I shall therefore conclude with two more examples, to indicate the range to which this kind of analysis may be expanded. The first one is what I shall call "quotation." I will not include cases of mention versus use, simply because I do not think they constitute a case of implied meaning; perhaps the term "self-reference" (modeled after de Groot's term *zelfnoemfunctie*)[111] is more adequate, and its mysteries are, as yet, far from being wholly unraveled. There are, for one thing, so many cases of self-reference, e.g., to orthographic form (*Book has four letters*), to phonetic form (*Book ends with a stop*), to phonemic form (*Book consists of three phonemes*), to categorization (*Book is a Noun*), etc. (Further, self-reference is usually indicated orthographically, by the use of quotation marks or italicization.) Self-reference is most certainly an exceptional case of application, not because the mean-

---

110. I have treated this matter in "Method, Theory, and Phenomenology," but after completion of the manuscript (in 1966), Bierwisch's article appeared, treating what is more or less the same material in a generative framework (Manfred Bierwisch, "Some Semantic Universals of German Adjectivals," *Foundations of Language,* III [1967], 1–36). The article is challenging in the way that special rules are found; but as the situational component is not allowed to play any part, I still disagree with such an approach from a more general viewpoint.

111. A. W. de Groot, *Structurele syntaxis* (The Hague: Servire, 1949), p. 78.

ing is differently applied, but because it is not necessarily the *meaning* that is applied. It seems conceivable that sentences with self-reference would somehow suit "implied meaning" in a sense close enough to mine to be identified with it, and for the moment I do not wish to assume that we have some different variety here. My "quotation" involves, interestingly enough, not only the lexicon but also grammar; what I have in mind here is the phenomenon earlier dubbed "echo," as in sentences like *Who told what to whom?*, and the like.[112] I will now confine myself to lexical "quotation." Examples are *Your analogies are not analogous* or *Your evidence is not convincing*. Such sentences cannot be handled by collocational rules involving only conjunctive application, for then there are semantic contrasts for which there is no explanation. However, the words *analogies* and *evidence* are obviously adaptations (perhaps sarcastically so) to the use of these words (or some other way of implying their meaning) by the conversation partner. This is a genuine case, also, of referential crossover, for *analogies* and *evidence* are used for referring to elements not constituting analogies and evidence, though they did so in the case of the conversation partner. To state that we have referential crossover here is to say that the application is not conjunctive. But then, what is it? A certain measure of similarity with the mention-for-use occurrence of lexical items cannot be denied. Problems such as these must be further investigated.

As a second and last problem I take the phenomenon of *Gegensinn*. Thus, Latin *altus* means both "high" and "deep," and *sacer* means both "sacred" and "accursed." But is it correct to say that both constitute the "meaning" of those words? If so, the solution is not to be found in application. The *Gegensinn* phenomenon has been little studied so far.[113] I do not know of any publication apart from Abel and one by Hofstätter (the latter, since it is a psychological study, I am not competent to evaluate).[114] Apparently *Gegensinn* in the lexical sense is much more frequent in Semitic languages than it is in Indo-European lan-

---

112. See Chomsky, *Aspects of the Theory of Syntax*, p. 158; Jerrold J. Katz and Paul M. Postal, *An Integrated Theory of Linguistic Descriptions* (Cambridge, Mass.: M.I.T. Press, 1964), p. 109.

113. The term dates from Carl Abel, *Gegensinn der Urworte* (Leipzig: Wilhelm Friedrich, 1884).

114. Peter R. Hofstätter, *Vom Leben des Wortes: Das Problem an Platons Dialog "Kratylos" dargestellt* (Vienna: Braumüller, 1949).

guages. Almost as a matter of course one thinks in this connection also of sarcastic remarks amounting to a complete opposition between meaning and application (*You are a big help!*), but I mention this only to suggest that a great deal of material from stylistics is yet awaiting a linguistic treatment. Many of them will have to be tackled by a theory dealing with implied meaning in the sentence.

A few closing remarks on lexical collocation are in order. This level, the lowest in our hierarchy, though it has nothing to do with grammar, is yet highly relevant for well-formedness. Well-formedness may be (and is here) understood as including grammaticalness without being confined to it. Thus, lexical collocation rules can be set up to preclude deviance of a kind that grammar is powerless to prevent. Thus, *Colorless green ideas sleep furiously* will be deviant in many speech settings, while it will not be so in others, as Hill's panel once showed.[115] What is more, it must be doubted whether any sentence grammatically well-formed can be shown to be deviant lexically, prescinding from any speech setting whatsoever. On the other hand, some forms of language, or some speech settings giving rise to them, are so exceptional (such as certain forms of poetry or specimens of James Joyce's prose) that any theory of language can afford not to include them. Poetry is, moreover, known to violate even rules of syntax, and this is another reason for such exclusions. But even then the linguist will be left with many sentences that rationalistic theories will not know what to do with, except for relegating them, as I am advised Postal has occasionally recommended doing informally, to the "garbage component."

Linguistics is concerned with natural language, but it is not enough to pay lip service to this principle and then succumb to all kinds of epistemological preconceptions hailing back to culturally limited samples of the history of ideas. Indo-European languages are, to be sure, in certain ways in accord with ideas that have arisen in the history of the West (or perhaps we should reverse this statement and say that Indo-European languages have formed the basis for Indo-European thought); however, the gradual and, lately, rapid accumulation of cultural material outside direct spoken language, in a culture which has thereby grown to be objectifying, and visualizing, has, instead of pre-

115. Archibald A. Hill, "Grammaticality," *Word*, XVII (1961), 1–10.

serving a worthwhile minimum of oral-aural samples of language, profoundly influenced scientific theory formation and philosophy more generally. It has been the objective of this paper to show in reasonably complete detail and argumentation, so far as is possible within such a short compass, that phenomenology has a great deal to offer for the rejuvenation of linguistic theory.

BIBLIOGRAPHY

Aarsleff, Hans. "The History of Linguistics and Professor Chomsky." *Language*, XLVI (1970), 570–85.

Abel, Carl. *Gegensinn der Urworte*. Leipzig: Wilhelm Friedrich, 1884.

Austin, J. L. "A Plea for Excuses." Pp. 123–52 in Urmson and Warnock, 1961.

Bach, Emmon. "Nouns and Noun Phrases." Pp. 90–122 in Bach and Harms, 1968.

———— and Harms, Robert T., eds. *Universals in Linguistic Theory*. New York: Holt, Rinehart & Winston, 1968.

Bar-Hillel, Yehoshua. "Husserl's Conception of a Purely Logical Grammar." *Philosophy and Phenomenological Research*, XVII (1957), 362–69.

————. "On a Misapprehension of the Status of Theories in Linguistics." *Foundations of Language*, II (1966), 394–99.

Berger, H. "Van de Saussure tot Chomsky." *Tijdschrift voor Filosofie*, XXXII (1970), 175–96.

Bierwisch, Manfred. "Some Semantic Universals of German Adjectivals." *Foundations of Language*, III (1967), 1–36.

Bloomfield, Leonard. *An Introduction to the Study of Language*. New York: Holt, 1914.

————. *Language*. New York: Holt, 1933.

Bühler, Karl. *Sprachtheorie: Die Darstellungsfunktion der Sprache*. Jena: Gustav Fischer, 1934.

Caws, Peter. *The Philosophy of Science: A Systematic Account*. Princeton, N.J.: D. Van Nostrand, 1965.

Chomsky, Noam. *Syntactic Structures*. New York: Humanities Press, 1957.

————. Review of B. F. Skinner, *Verbal Behavior*. *Language*, XXXV (1959), 26–58.

————. "Some Methodological Remarks on Generative Grammar." *Word*, XVII (1961), 219–39.

————. *Current Issues in Linguistic Theory*. New York: Humanities Press, 1964.

Chomsky, Noam. *Aspects of the Theory of Syntax.* Cambridge, Mass.: M.I.T. Press, 1965.

———. "Topics in the Theory of Generative Grammar." Pp. 1–60 in Sebeok, 1966.

———. *Cartesian Linguistics.* New York: Harper & Row, 1966.

———. "The Formal Nature of Language." In Lenneberg, 1967.

———. *Language and Mind.* New York: Harcourt, Brace & World, 1968.

Comte, Auguste. *Cours de philosophie positive* (1830–42). 6 vols. Paris: Baillière, 1877.

Cornford, F. M. *From Religion to Philosophy: A Study in the Origins of Western Speculation.* New York: Harper & Row, 1957.

———. *Principium Sapientiae: A Study of the Origins of Greek Philosophical Thought.* New York: Harper & Row, 1965.

Dik, S. C. "Oppervlaktestruktuur en dieptestruktuur." *Forum der Letteren*, X (1969), 19–41.

Dinneen, Francis P. *An Introduction to General Linguistics.* New York: Holt, Rinehart & Winston, 1967.

Dodds, E. R. *The Greeks and the Irrational.* Sather Classical Lectures, no. 25. Berkeley: University of California Press, 1951.

Doroszewski, W. "Quelques remarques sur les rapports de la sociologie et de la linguistique." *Journal de psychologie normale et pathologique* (special number, *Psychologie du langage*), XXX (1933), 82–91.

Durkheim, Emile. *Sociologie et philosophie.* Paris: Alcan, 1924. English translation by D. F. Pocock, *Sociology and Philosophy.* Glencoe, Ill.: Free Press, 1953.

Eliade, Mircea. *The Sacred and the Profane: The Nature of Religion.* Translated by Willard Trask. New York: Harper & Row, 1959.

Esper, Erwin A. *Mentalism and Objectivism in Linguistics: The Sources of Leonard Bloomfield's Psychology of Language.* New York: American Elsevier, 1968.

Farber, Marvin. *The Foundation of Phenomenology: Edmund Husserl and the Quest for a Science of Philosophy.* New York: Paine-Whitman, 1962.

Fillmore, Charles H. "The Case for Case." Pp. 1–88 in Bach and Harms, 1968.

———. "On Generativity." Pp. 1–19 in *Working Papers in Linguistics*, no. 6. Columbus, Ohio: Ohio State University Computer and Information Science Research Center, 1970.

Flugel, J. C., and West, D. J. *A Hundred Years of Psychology.* 2d rev. ed. London: Methuen, 1964.

Fodor, Jerry A., and Katz, Jerrold J., eds. *The Structure of Language: Readings in the Philosophy of Language.* Englewood Cliffs, N.J.: Prentice-Hall, 1964.

Garvin, Paul L., ed. *Method and Theory in Linguistics*. New York: Humanities Press, 1971.

de Groot, A. W. *Structurele syntaxis*. The Hague: Servire, 1949.

Gusdorf, Georges. *Mythe et métaphysique*. Paris: Flammarion, 1953.

Hall, Robert A., Jr. "Fact and Fiction in Grammatical Analysis." *Foundations of Language*, I (1965), 337–45.

Harris, Zellig S. *Methods in Structural Linguistics*. Chicago: University of Chicago Press, 1951.

Havelock, Eric A. *Preface to Plato*. Cambridge, Mass.: Harvard University Press, 1963.

Hill, Archibald A. "Grammaticality." *Word*, XVII (1961), 1–10.

Hofstätter, Peter R. *Vom Leben des Wortes: Das Problem an Platons Dialog "Kratylos" dargestellt*. Vienna: Braumüller, 1949.

van de Hulst, H. C., and van Peursen, C. A. *Phaenomenologie en natuurwetenschap*. Utrecht: Bijleveld, 1953.

Husserl, Edmund. *Logische Untersuchungen; Erster Band, Prolegomena zur reinen Logik; Zweiter Band, Untersuchungen zur Phänomenologie und Theorie der Erkenntnis, I. Teil; Zweiter Band, Elemente einer phänomenologischen Aufklärung der Erkenntnis, II. Teil*. 5th ed. Tübingen: Max Niemeyer Verlag, 1968. 1st ed., 1901; 2d rev. ed., 1913. English translation by J. N. Findlay, *Logical Investigations*. 2 vols. New York: Humanities Press, 1970.

―――. "Philosophie als strenge Wissenschaft." *Logos*, I (1910), 289–314. English translation in Quentin Lauer, ed. and trans., *Phenomenology and the Crisis of Philosophy*. New York: Harper & Row, 1965.

―――. *Ideen zu einer reinen Phänomenologie. Erstes Buch: Allgemeine Einführung in die reine Phänomenologie*. Ed. Walter Biemel. The Hague: Nijhoff, 1950. 1st ed., 1913. English translation by W. R. Boyce Gibson, *Ideas: General Introduction to Pure Phenomenology*. New York: Humanities Press, 1931. Paperback ed., New York: Collier Books, 1962.

―――. *Erste Philosophie. Erster Teil: Kritische Ideengeschichte*. Ed. Rudolf Boehm. The Hague: Nijhoff, 1956. 1st ed., 1923.

Karttunen, Lauri. "Definite Description with Crossing Coreference: A Study of the Bach-Peters Paradox." *Foundations of Language*, VII (1971), 157–82.

Katz, Jerrold J. "Mentalism in Linguistics." *Language*, XL (1964), 124–37.

――― and Fodor, Jerry A. "The Structure of a Semantic Theory." Pp. 479–518 in Fodor and Katz, 1964.

――― and Postal, Paul M. *An Integrated Theory of Linguistic Descriptions*. Cambridge, Mass.: M.I.T. Press, 1964.

Kwant, R. C. *Fenomenologie van de taal.* Utrecht: Het Spectrum, 1963. English translation by Henry J. Koren, *Phenomenology of Language.* Pittsburgh: Duquesne University Press, 1965.

Labov, William. "The Study of Language in Its Social Context." *Studium Generale*, XXIII (1970), 30–87.

Lenneberg, Eric H. *Biological Foundations of Language.* New York: John Wiley & Sons, 1967.

Lyons, John. *Introduction to Theoretical Linguistics.* Cambridge: At the University Press, 1968.

Marchand, Hans. *The Categories and Types of Present-Day English Word-Formation.* 2d rev. ed. Munich: C. H. Beck, 1969.

Merleau-Ponty, Maurice. *Phénoménologie de la perception.* Paris: Gallimard, 1945. English translation by Colin Smith, *Phenomenology of Perception.* New York: Humanities Press, 1962.

———. "Le Langage indirect et les voix du silence." *Les Temps modernes*, LXXX (1952). Reprinted in Maurice Merleau-Ponty, *Signes.* Paris: Gallimard, 1960. English translation by Richard C. McCleary, "Indirect Language and the Voices of Silence," in Maurice Merleau-Ponty, *Signs.* Evanston, Ill.: Northwestern University Press, 1964.

———. *L'Oeil et l'esprit.* Paris: Gallimard, 1964. English translation by Carleton Dallery, "Eye and Mind," in Maurice Merleau-Ponty, *The Primacy of Perception and Other Essays*, ed. James M. Edie. Evanston, Ill.: Northwestern University Press, 1964.

Pap, Leo. "A Note on *Lingual* vs. *Linguistic.*" *General Linguistics*, II (1951), 42.

van Peursen, C. A. "Edmund Husserl and Ludwig Wittgenstein." *Philosophy and Phenomenological Research*, XX (1959), 181–97.

———. *Fenomenologie et analytische filosofie.* Hilversum/Amsterdam: W. de Haan/J. M. Meulenhoff, 1968.

———. *Wetenschappen en werkelijkheid.* Kampen: Kok, 1969.

Postal, Paul M. Review of André Martinet, *Elements of General Linguistics. Foundations of Language*, II (1966), 151–86.

Reichling, A. J. B. N. *Het woord: Een studie omtrent de grondslag van taal en taalgebruik.* 2d ed. Zwolle: W. E. J. Tjeenk Willink, 1967. 1st ed., 1935.

———. "Het handelingskarakter van het woord." *Nieuwe Taalgids*, XXXI (1937), 308–21.

———. "Over het personaal aspect in het taalgebruik." Pp. 283–310 in B. H. Erné, C. C. de Bruin *et al.*, eds., *Bundel . . . de Vooys.* Groningen: Wolters, 1940.

Richardson, William J. *Heidegger: Through Phenomenology to Thought.* New York: Humanities Press, 1963.

Robins, R. H. *Ancient and Mediaeval Grammatical Theory in Europe.* London: G. Bell & Sons, 1951.

Robins, R. H. *General Linguistics: An Introductory Survey.* London: Longmans, 1964.

————. "The Development of the Word Class System of the European Grammatical Tradition." *Foundations of Language,* II (1966), 3–19.

Ryle, Gilbert. *The Concept of Mind.* London: Hutchinson, 1949.

de Santillana, Giorgio. *The Origins of Scientific Thought.* Chicago: University of Chicago Press, 1961.

Sapir, Edward. *Language.* New York: Harcourt, Brace, 1921.

de Saussure, Ferdinand. *Cours de linguistique générale.* Edited by Charles Bally, Albert Sechehaye, and Albert Riedlinger. Paris: Payot, 1949. 1st ed., 1915. English translation by Wade Baskin, *Course in General Linguistics.* New York: Philosophical Library, 1959.

Sebeok, Thomas A., ed. *Current Trends in Linguistics.* Vol. III: *Theoretical Foundations.* New York: Humanities Press, 1966.

Siertsema, B. *A Study of Glossematics: Critical Survey of Its Fundamental Concepts.* 2d ed. The Hague: Nijhoff, 1965.

Spiegelberg, Herbert. *The Phenomenological Movement.* 2 vols. The Hague: Nijhoff, 1960.

————. "A Phenomenological Approach to the Ego." *The Monist,* XLIX (1965), 1–17.

Staal, J. F. *Euclides en Pāṇini.* Amsterdam: Polak & van Gennep, 1963.

————. "Euclid and Pāṇini." *Philosophy East and West,* XV (1965), 99–116.

Urmson, J. O., and Warnock, G. J., eds. *J. L. Austin: Philosophical Papers.* London: Clarendon Press (Oxford University Press), 1961.

Verhaar, J. W. M. *Some Relations between Perception, Speech, and Thought.* Assen: van Gorcum, 1963.

————. "Phenomenology as an Attitude." *Bijdragen,* XXVIII (1967), 399–421.

————. "Dewart and the New Neo-Thomism." *Continuum,* V (1968), 634–42.

————. "Some Notes on Language and Theology." *Bijdragen,* XXX (1969), 39–65. Reprinted, under the title "Language and Theology," in *Continuum,* VII (1969), 3–29.

————. "Method, Theory, and Phenomenology." Pp. 42–91 in Garvin, 1970.

————. "Philosophy and Linguistic Theory." *Language Sciences,* no. 14 (1971), 1–11.

Wann, T. W., ed. *Behaviorism and Phenomenology: Contrasting Bases for Modern Psychology.* Chicago: University of Chicago Press, 1964.